The Chinese Annals of Batavia, the *Kai Ba Lidai Shiji* and Other Stories (1610–1795)

European Expansion and Indigenous Response

Editor-in-Chief

George Bryan Souza (*University of Texas, San Antonio*)

Editorial Board

Cátia Antunes (*Leiden University*)
João Paulo Oliveira e Costa (CHAM, *Universidade Nova de Lisboa*)
Frank Dutra (*University of California, Santa Barbara*)
Kris Lane (*Tulane University*)
Pedro Machado (*Indiana University, Bloomington*)
Malyn Newitt (*King's College, London*)
Michael Pearson (*University of New South Wales*)

VOLUME 28

The titles published in this series are listed at *brill.com/euro*

The Chinese Annals of Batavia, the *Kai Ba Lidai Shiji* and Other Stories (1610–1795)

Translated, edited, and annotated by

Leonard Blussé
Nie Dening

BRILL

LEIDEN | BOSTON

Cover illustration: Silver copy of the golden medallion offered to Governor General Jacques Specx by the grateful Chinese community in 1632. Haarlem, Teylers Museum. Inv. TMNK 00460.

Library of Congress Cataloging-in-Publication Data

Names: Blusse, Leonard, 1946– editor. | Dening, Nie, editor.
Title: The Chinese Annals of Batavia, the Kai Ba Lidai Shiji and Other
   Stories (1610–1795) / translated, edited, and annotated by Leonard Blusse,
   Nie Dening.
Description: Leiden ; Boston : Brill, 2018. | Series: European expansion and
   indigenous response ; Volume 28 | Includes bibliographical references. |
Identifiers: LCCN 2017052798 (print) | LCCN 2018000035 (ebook) | ISBN
   9789004356702 (E-books) | ISBN 9789004355392 (hardback : alk. paper)
Subjects: LCSH: Jakarta (Indonesia)—History—18th century—Sources. |
   Chinese—Indonesia—Jakarta—History—18th century. |
   Massacres—Indonesia—Jakarta—History—18th century.
Classification: LCC DS646.29.D5 (ebook) | LCC DS646.29.D5 C47 2018 (print) |
   DDC 959.8/22004951—dc23
LC record available at https://lccn.loc.gov/2017052798

Typeface for the Latin, Greek, and Cyrillic scripts: "Brill". See and download: brill.com/brill-typeface

ISSN 1873-8974
ISBN 978-90-04-35539-2 (hardback)
ISBN 978-90-04-35670-2 (e-book)

Copyright 2018 by Koninklijke Brill NV, Leiden, The Netherlands.
Koninklijke Brill NV incorporates the imprints Brill, Brill Hes & De Graaf, Brill Nijhoff, Brill Rodopi, Brill Sense and Hotei Publishing.
All rights reserved. No part of this publication may be reproduced, translated, stored in a retrieval system, or transmitted in any form or by any means, electronic, mechanical, photocopying, recording or otherwise, without prior written permission from the publisher.
Authorization to photocopy items for internal or personal use is granted by Koninklijke Brill NV provided that the appropriate fees are paid directly to The Copyright Clearance Center, 222 Rosewood Drive, Suite 910, Danvers, MA 01923, USA. Fees are subject to change.

This book is printed on acid-free paper and produced in a sustainable manner.

Contents

General Series Editor's Foreword VII
Preface X
Acknowledgements XIII
List of Illustrations XVII

PART 1
Introductory Material

1 A Historical Sketch of Batavia in the Seventeenth and Eighteenth Centuries   3

2 A Chinese Urban Society in the Tropics   15

3 Chinese Sources for the History of the Chinese Community in Batavia   25

4 Critical Comments on the *Kai Ba Lidai Shiji* and Its Genesis   30

5 A Diachronic Overview of the Contents of the *Kai Ba Lidai Shiji*   37

6 Editorial Notes on the Sources of the *Kai Ba Lidai Shiji*   42

PART 2
The Chinese Annals of Batavia

A Chinese Chronicle of the Historical Events at Yaolaoba (Galaba)   51

PART 3
Accompanying Texts

1 *Brief Account of Galaba* (噶喇吧紀略), by Cheng Xunwo (程遜我)   205

2 Selections from the *Biography of Cai Xin* (蔡新傳) and from *Historical Materials in the First Historical Archive of China Concerning the Debates about Banning the Overseas Trade to the Nanyang during the Qianlong Period*   219

3 Selections from *The Chinaman Abroad: An Account of the Malayan Archipelago, Particularly of Java*, by Ong-Tae-Hae (王大海, Wang Dahai), translated by W.H. Medhurst   229

4 *Jialaba* (甲喇吧, Galaba), by Gu Sen (顧森)   238

Appendices

Appendix 1: The Appointment of Captain Tsoa Wanjock   243
Appendix 2: Name Lists   246
1 Governors General   246
2 Chinese *Kapiteins* (Captains)   249
3 Chinese *Luitenanten* (Lieutenants)   251
4 Chinese *Boedelmeesters* (Curators)   256
5 Chinese Secretaries   279
6 Chinese *Soldaten* (Soldiers)   281
7 Chinese Undertakers   281
8 Non-Chinese Names   283
Appendix 3: Glossary of Malay and Dutch Terms in *Kai Ba Lidai Shiji*   290

Bibliography   293
Index of Personal and Geographical Names   300
Subject Index   316

General Series Editor's Foreword

Over the past half millennium, from circa 1450 until the last third or so of the twentieth century, much of the world's history has been influenced in great part by one general dynamic and complex historical process known as European expansion. Defined as the opening up, unfolding, or increasing the extent, number, volume, or scope of the space, size, or participants belonging to a certain people or group, location, or geographical region, Europe's expansion initially emerged and emanated physically, intellectually, and politically from southern Europe—specifically from the Iberian peninsula—during the fifteenth century, expanding rapidly from that locus to include, first, all of Europe's maritime and, later, most of its continental states and peoples. Most commonly associated with events described as the discovery of America and of a passage to the East Indies (Asia) by rounding the Cape of Good Hope (Africa) during the early modern and modern periods, European expansion and encounters with the rest of the world multiplied and morphed into several ancillary historical processes, including colonization, imperialism, capitalism, and globalization, encompassing themes, among others, relating to contacts and, to quote the EURO series' original mission statement, "connections and exchanges; peoples, ideas and products, especially through the medium of trading companies; the exchange of religions and traditions; the transfer of technologies; and the development of new forms of political, social and economic policy, as well as identity formation." Because of its intrinsic importance, extensive research has been performed and much has been written about the entire period of European expansion.

With the first volume published in 2009, Brill launched the European Expansion and Indigenous Response book series at the initiative of well-known scholar and respected historian, Glenn J. Ames, who, prior to his untimely passing, was the founding editor and guided the first seven volumes of the series to publication. George Bryan Souza, who was one of the early members of the series' editorial board, was appointed the series' second General Editor. The series' founding objectives are to focus on publications "that understand and deal with the process of European expansion, interchange and connectivity in a global context in the early modern and modern period" and to "provide a forum for a variety of types of scholarly work with a wider disciplinary approach that moves beyond the traditional isolated and nation bound historiographical emphases of this field, encouraging whenever possible non-European perspectives ... that seek to understand this indigenous transformative process and period in autonomous as well as inter-related cultural, economic, social, and ideological terms."

The history of European expansion is a challenging field in which interest is likely to grow, in spite of, or perhaps because of, its polemical nature. Controversy has centered on tropes conceived and written in the past by Europeans, primarily concerning their early reflections and claims regarding the transcendental historical nature of this process and its emergence and importance in the creation of an early modern global economy and society. One of the most persistent objections is that the field has been "Eurocentric." This complaint arises because of the difficulty in introducing and balancing different historical perspectives, when one of the actors in the process is to some degree neither European nor Europeanized—a conundrum alluded to in the African proverb: "Until the lion tells his tale, the hunt will always glorify the hunter." Another, and perhaps even more important and growing historiographical issue, is that with the re-emergence of historical millennial societies (China and India, for example) and the emergence of other non-Western European societies successfully competing politically, economically, and intellectually on the global scene vis-à-vis Europe, the seminal nature of European expansion is being subjected to greater scrutiny, debate, and comparison with other historical alternatives.

Despite, or perhaps because of, these new directions and stimulating sources of existing and emerging lines of dispute regarding the history of European expansion, the editorial board of the series will continue with the original objectives and mission statement of the series and vigorously "... seek out studies that employ diverse forms of analysis from all scholarly disciplines, including anthropology, archaeology, art history, history (including the history of science), linguistics, literature, music, philosophy, and religious studies." In addition, we shall seek to stimulate, locate, incorporate, and publish the most important and exciting scholarship in the field.

Towards that purpose, I am pleased to introduce volume 28 of Brill's EURO series, entitled: *The Chinese Annals of Batavia, the Kai Ba Lidai Shiji and Other Stories (1610–1795)*. In it, two well-known scholars, Leonard Blussé and Nie Dening, have selected several key manuscripts written in Chinese and impressively translated into English and eruditely annotated them to provide an excellent general overview of the history of the city of Batavia, as Jakarta, on the island of Java in the Indonesian Archipelago, was known during the Dutch period, i.e. from the early 17th to mid-20th centuries. Written by Chinese inhabitants of a Dutch-ruled city in a Malay world toward the end of the eighteenth century, they offer a truly indigenous perspective and insight into the history of European expansion from one group of several indigenous peoples who encountered and lived alongside the Dutch over the period.

Blussé and Nie have produced an exemplary volume. In their translation of the *Kai Ba Lidai Shiji*, which is the main text that is presented, they faced significant challenges as translators on account of the various extant versions of it. They deftly engaged, combined, and intertwined each into singular version that provides a fluid, coherent, and enjoyable reading experience. Their handling of the dialectical variances in Chinese and the orthographical challenges in corresponding Dutch text of the numerous toponyms, demonyms, and personal names that are found in the original manuscripts is a major and an important achievement. *The Chinese Annals of Batavia, the Kai Ba Lidai Shiji and Other Stories (1610–1795)*, as a consequence, will be an important addition to multiple audiences in diverse disciplines. In addition to being a major contribution to the field of European Expansion and Indigenous Response, Sinologists, experts in Southeast Asia and historians in multiple subfields, including global history, urban history, and intercultural history to name only a few will want to read and engage this work.

George Bryan Souza

Preface

This study contains the annotated translation of a curious autonomous history of the Chinese community of Batavia in the seventeenth and eighteenth centuries. The *Kai Ba Lidai Shiji* or *Chinese Annals of Batavia* was composed by an anonymous Chinese inhabitant of the town in the late 1790s. During the nineteenth century various manuscript versions of the same text circulated among the Batavian Chinese elite before it was published, first in a local journal in the 1920s and then in a well-edited and annotated Chinese version by Xu Yunqiao in a 1953 issue of the 南洋學報 (*Journal of the South Seas Society*).[1]

In the six introductory chapters of Section A, we aim to provide today's reader with contextual information about this unique historical narrative, which was originally addressed to a Chinese reading public more than two hundred years ago. Chapter one contains a brief introduction to the history of 'Chinese Batavia' in the seventeenth and eighteenth centuries. Chapter two presents a sketch of the urban administration of this colonial city. In chapter three, we introduce pioneering scholars to whom we feel obliged for their ground-breaking research on the Chinese texts that we have translated and annotated here. Chapters four and five introduce the *Kai Ba Lidai Shiji* itself. The sixth chapter consists of editorial notes on the sources and the different manuscript versions that we have used for our translation.

Section B contains the complete annotated translation—the first into English—of *The Chinese Annals of Batavia*.[2] The title of the *Kai Ba Lidai Shiji* (開吧歷代史紀) literally means 'The opening up [or development (開拓, *kai-tuo*)] of the kingdom of Galaba through successive generations'. But for the sake of convenience, we have called it simply *The Chinese Annals of Batavia*.[3]

---

1 Hsu Yun-Tsiao (Xu Yunqiao), ed., '開吧歷代史紀, The Early Accounts of Chinese in Batavia (a revised and annotated edition)' *Nanyang Xuebao* 南洋學報 [Journal of the South Seas Society] 9:1 (1953): 1–63.

2 The existing manuscript versions on which we have based our translation have slightly different titles: *Kai Ba Lidai Shiji* (開吧歷代史紀), or *Kai Yaolaoba Lidaishi Quanlu* (開咬咾吧歷代史全錄).

3 The character *Ba* in the title of the manuscript is not originally an abbreviation of *Batavia*, but it refers to the Malay word *kelapa* (coconut) which gave its name to the former kingdom of Sunda Kelapa (in Chinese, 噶喇吧, Galaba or Gelaba). Nonetheless, after the Dutch takeover in 1619, Bacheng (吧城) came to stand for the city of Batavia. Curiously the Chinese name of Yecheng (椰城, coconut town) is still used to denote Indonesia's capital Jakarta. According to Koos Kuiper, in the name 噶喇吧 the character 噶 *ge* should be read as *ga*, i.e. Galaba. In his monograph about the Dutch interpreters of Chinese in the Indies he notes concerning their

The translated texts about Batavia in this study have been written from distinct perspectives: a Chinese insider of the city composed the *Kai Ba Lidai Shiji*, while the other narratives in the subsequent chapters of Section C were written by Chinese visitors or observers who wrote down their impressions of Batavias outsiders. These chapters contain short essays or reports that have been selected on account of their fine descriptions of Batavia or because they cast light from different perspectives on the discussions at the Chinese court about the massacre of Chinese at Batavia in 1740, the Angke or Hongxi massacre (洪溪惨案 or 紅溪惨案) as it is usually called.[4]

The *Brief Account of Galaba* (噶喇吧紀略, *Galaba Jilüe*), is a detailed description of Batavia written by a former visitor to Batavia, the Fujianese literatus Cheng Xunwo. He composed this essay in the aftermath of the 1740 massacre at the request of Cai Xin, a court official and fellow countryman. Owing to his Fujianese background, Cai Xin had been asked by a superior

---

translations into Chinese: 'The transcription of geographical names was also not consistent, even for the names of main towns. The Chinese continued to designate Batavia by its ancient name Kalapa, which had earlier been transcribed as 咬𠺕吧 or 噶喇吧 *Ka-la-pa*, simplified as 吧城 *Ba*-town, but the Dutch interpreters transcribed it as 加蚋巴 *Ka-la-pa*, 茄剌巴 and 咖留巴. See Koos Kuiper, *The Early Dutch Sinologists (1854–1900): Training in Holland and China, Functions in the Netherlands Indies* (Leiden: Brill 2017), 751. The syllable 噶 in 噶喇吧 is generally used to represent sounds. It is now pronounced in standard Mandarin as *ga*. See 新华字典 *Xinhua zidian* (Beijing: Commercial Press, 2011), 145. This is confirmed as the usual reading when used to represent sounds in *Hanyu da cidian* 漢語大詞典, vol. 3. 503 (Shanghai: *Hanyu da cidian chubanshe* 漢語大詞典出版社, 1986–1993), and in *Hanyu da zidian* 漢語大字典, vol. 1, 681 (Chengdu: Sichuan cishu chubanshe 四川辞书出版社, 1986–1990).

Other Chinese transcriptions of the name Kalapa confirm this reading. For instance, in 噶喇吧紀略, this transcription is followed by 甲喇吧, which would certainly be pronounced Kalapa (compare 甲必丹, Kapitan). The first syllable of Yaoluoba 咬𠺕吧 is pronounced *ka* in Minnanhua/Hokkien. The first syllable of the other names for Kalapa 加蚋巴, 茄剌巴 and 咖留巴 would in Minnanhua be pronounced as *ka*. This character has the literary reading of *ka*, and the colloquial readings of *ke* (Amoy, Xiamen) and *kɛ* (Tsiangtsiu, Zhangzhou). In other geographical names it is always used to represent *ka*, not *ke*. About the readings of *ka*, *ke*, and *kɛ*, see Carstairs Douglas, *Chinese–English Dictionary of the Vernacular or Spoken Language of Amoy, with the Principal Variations of the Chang-chew [Tsiangtsiu] and Chin-chew [Quanzhou] Dialects* (London: Trübner 1873); with *Supplement* by Thomas Barclay (Shanghai: The Commercial Press 1923. Taipei: SMC Publishing Co (reprint)), p. 187.

4 The Angke River runs through Batavia. *Ang* means red in Minnanhua, and local Chinese etymology falsely but poignantly asserts that the river received it name because it was coloured red by the blood of the victims of the massacre. The name, however, predates this terrible event.

at the grand secretariat of the imperial court to give advice on how to assess what had happened in Batavia. Cai Xin in turn asked his old friend Cheng Xunwo, whom he happened to meet in Beijing, to write a short report for him. In Chapter two of Section C we have included various reports about the Batavian massacre to the throne: from the biography of Cai Xin in the local gazetteer of the city of Zhangzhou, we extract the report that Cai Xin sent to the grand secretariat after he had met with Cheng Xunwo. The title of the other reports such as 'Provincial Military Commander Wang Jun of the Fujianese Naval Forces sincerely presents a memorial to report about what he has heard about the situation in the country of Galaba', speak for themselves. They were written at the request of the imperial authorities in Beijing.

In 1850, the British missionary and sinologist W.H. Medhurst published under the title *Ong-Tae-Hae, The Chinaman Abroad*, a translation of Wang Dahai's delightful *Haidao Yizhi* (Anecdotes about the Sea Islands or Island Memories), a book published in 1806.[5] In chapter three of Section C we have extracted from the memoirs of this wandering preceptor his description of Batavia and a few selected portraits he drew of local Chinese individuals whom he had met during his stay in the 1780s.

Chapter four of Section C offers the translation of a short essay by another eighteenth-century literatus, Gu Sen (顧森), entitled *Jialaba* (Batavia), in which he tells what he has heard about Batavia from a merchant who had visited the town.

Chinese accounts about the Chinese presence in Southeast Asia during the early modern period, whether written by Chinese overseas or in the Middle Kingdom itself, are quite rare. That is why we have brought together these connected materials into one monograph. Although we provide these translated texts with an historical introduction and contextual remarks, we stress that our intent is not to write a history of Batavia's Chinese community in the seventeenth and eighteenth centuries, nor a monograph on the so-called Chinese massacre of 1740. That study is in fact in preparation. Here we have aimed to make available to the reader some very interesting eighteenth-century Chinese sources and let them speak largely for themselves. In the copious factual footnotes, we have refrained from commenting excessively about the right or wrong information that the authors give. Had we not, the texts would have been smothered by the annotation and thus lost their freshness and authenticity.

---

5   Ong-Tae-Hae, *The Chinaman Abroad: An Account of the Malayan Archipelago, Particularly of Java*, translated by W.H. Medhurst (London: 1850). The same translation appeared a year earlier in Shanghai as *The Chinaman Abroad: or a Desultory Account* (etc.). A recent Chinese edition: 王大海: 海島逸志, 香港: 學津書店出版 1992.

Acknowledgements

This annotated translation project stems from a rather accidental meeting with the grand old man of Overseas Chinese historical studies, Professor Xu Yunqiao (Hsu Yun-Tsiao, 1905–1981) some forty years ago. I happened to meet Professor Xu on the heels of Michèle Boin, who went to see the already long-retired Professor Xu in downtown Singapore. Michèle hoped to gain new information about the disappearance of the well-known Chinese novelist Yu Dafu in northeast Sumatra in the last months of the Pacific War. Xu Yunqiao and Yu Dafu had been close friends and Michèle cherished the expectation that Professor Xu might be able to tell her a bit more about the writer who was the subject of her *thèse de troisième cycle* at the Sorbonne. Professor Xu, however, knew little more than the rumour that Yu Dafu had been murdered in the last days of the war by the Japanese occupiers.

The conversation then took a ninety-degree turn when I told Professor Xu that I was well-aware of his writings. During my stay at Kyoto University as a research student, I had participated in a study group that, under the leadership of Professor Hibino Takeo, had been translating Wang Dahai's *Haidao Yizhi* into Japanese, and in that context we had frequently looked at Xu Yunqiao's excellent annotated text edition of two manuscript versions of the *Kai Ba Lidai Shiji* (*The Chinese Annals of Batavia*). Professor Xu confessed that the annotation to the *Kai Ba Lidai Shiji* had caused him and his friend Tan Yok Seong, who had assisted him, much headache, because he had found it hard to extrapolate many original Dutch terms that were written down in characters in the Chinese text. Reading them aloud in the Hokkien (Minnanhua) dialect he was able to get close to the sound of the original words or names, but still faced difficulty in explaining their meaning. In addition, Professor Xu bemoaned the fact that he had been unable to solve many historical questions because he could not handle Dutch archival documents and printed sources. When we took leave of Professor Xu, he would not let us go before we had promised that one day we would make an English translation of the *Kai Ba Lidai Shiji* with annotations based on multiple sources, including the Dutch archives he had been unable to consult.

In academic life, promises and priorities do not easily mix. Michèle actually played for some time with the idea of translating the text but soon gave up. In the years that followed, I had to devote myself to other business, first engaged in the improvement of cultural relations between The Netherlands and Indonesia, and later teaching subjects that had little to do with China at the Leiden University history department, thus drifting away from my initial interests.

Quite out of the blue, and thanks to Drs. Myra Sidharta, in 1993 I ran across the totally neglected archival remainders of the former Kong Koan (Gongguan, 公館) or Chinese Council of Batavia, which had been stashed away in an old warehouse in Jakarta. Not long after General Suharto's takeover in 1965, the government had closed all Chinese-language schools, forbade the possession of Chinese books, and admonished Indonesian citizens of Chinese ancestry to give up their Chinese name and adopt an Indonesian one. Fortunately, all these anti-Chinese measures were rescinded by President Abdulrachman Wahid, alias Gus Dur, after he came to power in 1999.

The Kong Koan archives were bestowed upon Leiden University in 1994, on the condition that I should take it upon myself to preserve and restore the papers and make them available for scholarly research. Thus, in a later stage of my academic career, I became something of a sinologist again, or should I say an 'overseas sinologist'. Thanks to close cooperation with a number of colleagues at Xiamen University and Xiamen University Press, the minutes of the meetings of the Chinese Council covering a period of almost 150 years—the main body of the Kong Koan archives—have now been completely edited, annotated, and published in fifteen volumes.[1] It has turned out to be a veritable treasure-trove of information for countless master's theses at Chinese universities and two doctoral theses at Leiden.

In the meantime, all the other documents of the Kong Koan have been made accessible on the internet[2] thanks to the efforts of Dr. Chen Menghong, chair of the Friends of the Kong Koan Foundation, and, in the latest stage, by Dr. Koos Kuiper of the Leiden University Library, who also gave us myriad excellent advices.

Shortly after my retirement from Leiden University in the summer of 2011, after a forty years absence I found myself back at the *Jimbun Kagaku Kenkyujo* (人文科学研究所) of Kyoto University, where I had studied in the early 1970s. Professor Nie Dening of Xiamen University, fellow co-editor of the *Gong'an bu* source publications, and the undersigned had been invited as visiting scholars in the framework of the 'Asian Mega Cities' research project, a collaborative effort between the Universities of Tokyo and Kyoto to engage in research about

---

1 Nie Dening, Wu Fengbin, Hou Zhenping, Chen Menghong, and Leonard Blussé, et al., eds., 聶德寧，吳鳳斌，侯真平，陳萌紅，包樂史，*Gong An Bu* (*Minutes of the Board Meetings of the Chinese Council 1787–1920*), 吧城華人公館(吧國公堂)檔案叢書：公案簿，1787–1920, 廈門：廈門大學出版社 2002–17.

2 www.leidenuniv.nl, library, Chinese Special Collections, Kong Koan archive.

early modern Batavia and its Chinese community. During our stay in Kyoto, Nie Dening and I spent part of our time translating into English the *Kai Ba Lidai Shiji* as well as the related Chinese texts found in the present volume. Without the kind hospitality of Professors Iwai Shigeki and Kagotani Naoto of the Jimbun, the behind-the-scenes organizational capabilities of Dr. Ryuto Shimada of Tokyo University, and the critical remarks and suggestions by our Japanese companions in the project—in particular, Dr. Murakami Ei and Dr. Yamasaki Takeshi—we would never have been able to carry out our task.

Since our stay in Kyoto, both Dr. Nie and I have been involved in various other projects, but we kept cooperating on the final publication of the translation and annotation of the *Kai Ba Lidai Shiji*. Professor Zhuang Guotu, former dean of the Institute for Southeast Asian Studies, *Nanyang Yanjiuyuan*, 南洋研究院 of Xiamen University, Dr. Liu Yong, Dr. Wang Wangbo, and the institute's scholarly librarian, Dr. Zhang Changhong, arranged for annual research meetings of several weeks, which enabled us to concentrate exclusively on the job at hand. Thanks to all these people, we were able to finish not only the editing of the fifteenth and last volume of the *Gong An Bu* series, but also the present rather complicated translation and annotation project in the autumn of 2016.

In addition to the assistance of the aforementioned people and organizations, we also received help from various quarters while translating and revising the text. First, we would like to thank our 'comrade in arms', the erudite Professor Claudine Salmon of CNRS in France. Claudine was always ready to immediately answer our queries either on the spot in Xiamen or by email. Professor Wu Fengbin and Dr. Chen Menghong, who have played such invaluable roles in opening the Kong Koan archive, also provided much useful information. Drs. Tristan Mostert, editor of the *Atlas of Mutual Heritage* kindly assisted with providing maps and illustrations. Mrs. Marijke van Wissen, secretary of the Leiden History department coordinated many administrative arrangements. Many thanks also to Gong Hong (龚虹), Ellen Kramer and the first secretary of the Chinese embassy at The Hague, Mr. Yang Xiaolong, who is something a history buff himself.

We were lucky to still have full entry to the stacks of the library of the now defunct Sinological Institute of Leiden University and the magnificent reading room of the KITLV institute before everything was rearranged and synthesized into the much-heralded Asian Library of Leiden University. I am sorry to say that, whatever may be the luxury of a combined library on Asia and better electronic facilities in a specially-designed and -built floor on top of the central library, the merging of the various libraries into one Asian library has dramatically reduced free access to the printed sources, to the sorrow of both serious researchers and students who like to have the real thing at hand. Digitization and the internet have immensely improved the ability of 'mining' formerly hard to get sources, but librarians are wrong to presume that therefore it is no longer necessary to make use of such hardware as well-designed research guides and indexes or to have access to the stacks. There is no such thing as a *tabula rasa* for the sake of modernisation. As the saying goes: 切勿良莠不分一起抛, Don't throw the baby out with the bathwater!

Professor Nie Dening took upon himself the rather thankless task of completely revising all the Chinese name lists by carefully comparing the Dutch data with the Chinese ones. Dr. Samuel Cha Hsin, who is working on a monograph on the Chinese *boedelmeesters* (inheritance curators) of Batavia, gracefully provided us with the lists that he has been drawing up in recent years and thereby saved us a lot of extra work.

Once again, we wish to express our thanks to the institutional backing of Kyoto University, Xiamen University, and Leiden University, which has enabled us to carry out this project at our own pace. Mr. Lincoln Paine and Dr. Koos Kuiper took the daunting task upon themselves to edit the complete text including the footnotes and hopefully rooted out most of the inconsistencies in the transcriptions of names. Words cannot express how indebted we feel to their efforts. Many thanks also to the general editor of the *European Expansion and Indigenous Response* series, Dr. George Bryan Souza, the unknown referees and Wendel Scholma of Brill for the constructive comments which all have been included.

But without the pioneering work of the late Professor Xu Yunqiao, the crucial role of Drs. Myra Sidharta in saving the Kong Koan archive and its transfer to the library of the Sinological Institute of Leiden University, and finally the late Ir. Liem Ho Soei, who provided us with the manuscript *Kai Yaolaoba Lidaishi Quanlu* (The complete records of the opening of Yaolaoba) on which we have based our translation, we would not have been able to carry out our work.

To Myra and the memory of our friend Liem Ho Soei, who unfortunately passed away before we had finished the job, we dedicate this book in gratitude.

Leonard Blussé and Nie Dening
Research School for Southeast Asian Studies, Xiamen University
Xiamen, March 2017

List of Illustrations

1 Map of Batavia circa 1740, anonymous. Rijksmuseum Amsterdam   4
2 Chinese junk, F. Morel-Fatio. Private collection   9
3 *The Chinese Massacre*. Adolf van der Laan, 1740, print. Private collection   13
4 Anonymous artist, Chinese grave of Lieutenant Kouw Tjanko (probably Xu Cange, who died in 1770). KITLV collection, Leiden University Library   20
5 Wooden tablet of Captain Oey Bian Kong. 1792. Asian Library, Leiden University   35
6 The Leiden manuscript. Asian Library, Leiden University   43
7 The Liem manuscript, Friends of the Kong Koan Foundation. Asian Library, Leiden University   46
8 Silver copy of the golden medallion offered to Governor General Jacques Specx by the grateful Chinese community in 1632. Chinese text is probably: 昭光織白氏高志, 惠政流芳百世強. "For the glory of the lofty spirit of Mr. Specx (Chet Pek Si), whose gracious government will leave its fragrance strongly for a hundred generations". Haarlem, Teylers Museum. Inv. TMNK 00460   63
9 The Chinese hospital of Batavia, Johannes Rach (Danish artist, in Batavia 1762–83). Rijksmuseum Amsterdam   94
10 A Chinese procession to the appropriate place to make offerings [to the gods] and seek expiation whenever high mortality or other sufferings strike that nation, Johannes Rach. Atlas van Stolk   109
11 Governor General Adriaen Valckenier. Rijksmuseum Amsterdam   117
12 Map of Batavia and Ommelanden. J.W. Heydt, surveyor and architect, in Batavia 1737–41. Private collection   121
13 Map of the situation at Batavia during the Chinese siege (1740), print. Private collection   129
14 Governor General Gustaaf Willem van Imhoff. Rijksmuseum Amsterdam   140
15 Chinese *wayang* or street theater. Jan Brandes (Lutheran Minister, 1779–1785 in Batavia). Rijksmuseum Amsterdam   157
16 Dutch wedding. Jan Brandes. Rijksmuseum Amsterdam   162
17 The burning of the image of 'Twabakong' (Dabogong) and Chinese officers paying their respects during the Qingming festival. Jan Brandes. Rijksmuseum Amsterdam   167

18 Drilling the Chinese militia at Batavia. Jan Brandes. Rijksmuseum Amsterdam   183
19 Chinese sailors staying over at the VOC-wharf in Amsterdam, Jacob de Vos, c. 1790. Rijksmuseum Amsterdam   187

PART 1

Introductory Material

∴

CHAPTER 1

A Historical Sketch of Batavia in the Seventeenth and Eighteenth Centuries

The history of Indonesia's capital, Jakarta, is an intriguing one because in many respects it represents the multi-layered history of Indonesia itself. Yet this metropolis also displays unique characteristics that entitle it to a special place in Asian if not global history thanks to its impressive pedigree. It is heir to the ancient port city of Sunda Kalapa of the Hindu kingdom of Pajajaran (923–1579), which was renamed Jayakarta when it was conquered by the Javanese Prince Fatahillah in 1527 and became a vassal of the Islamic sultanate of Banten. In 1619, the city changed hands again when Jan Pietersz Coen, governor general of the Verenigde Oost-Indische Compagnie (VOC), United (Dutch) East India Company, seized its territory and turned the Javanese port principality into the headquarters of the Company in Asia and baptised it Batavia.[1] Under VOC rule, a Dutch-style fortress town with city walls, townhouses, and canals was built, while at the same time the surrounding tropical jungle was cleared and turned into vegetable gardens, rice paddies, and sugarcane plantations. Until its demise in 1799, the Dutch continued to use the Batavian roadstead as the general rendezvous for all their Asian shipping.

During the nineteenth century, the colonial government that replaced the Company regime tore down the walls and filled in the canals of 'Old Batavia', and moved its offices several miles inland. When a western-style colonial 'garden city' interspersed with Indonesian *kampongs* subsequently emerged, Batavia's morphology and its appearance underwent dramatic changes. Finally, in 1949 the city became the capital of the Republic of Indonesia and regained its former name, Jakarta. In other words, over a thousand years this urban settlement has, like a snake, shed its skin under the successive regimes—Hindu, Islamic, colonial, and, finally, republican—that have ruled and enlarged it.

The present-day metropolis of Jakarta sprawls unrestrained in all directions and is quickly devouring what is left of its former countryside. Together with its satellite cities Bogor, Tangerang, and Bekasi it is often called Jabotabek. Owing

---

1 The Verenigde Oost-Indische Compagnie (VOC) was established in 1602 and abolished in 1799. With a charter from the States General of the Dutch Republic it governed over all Dutch establishments east of the Cape of Good Hope and possessed the monopoly of all overseas Dutch trade with Asia.

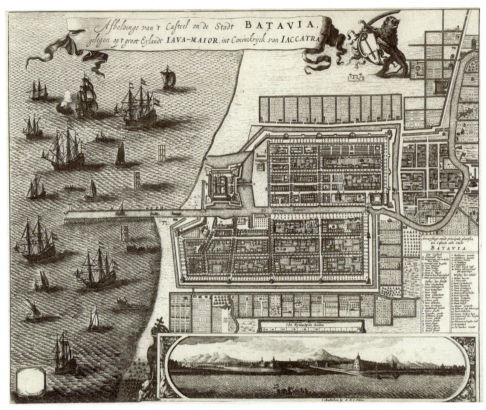

FIGURE 1   *Map of Batavia circa 1740, anonymous*
RIJKSMUSEUM AMSTERDAM

to its unchecked expansion, Greater Jakarta has turned into an urban jungle that must be tamed anew. History is not without paradoxical developments.

Connected Histories

What distinguished VOC-era Batavia from other urban settlements in Southeast Asia was its Janus face, with both Dutch and Chinese features. Built in an era that witnessed the encounter and subsequent entanglement of the overseas networks of Dutch and Chinese entrepreneurship in the Indonesian archipelago, the port city came to serve simultaneously as a Dutch and a Chinese colonial settlement, and as such represented a striking mode of collaboration between the monopolistic Dutch East India Company and the freely operating overseas Chinese entrepreneurs.

In Europe's coastal waters and the Atlantic, the Dutch cherished a long tradition of free maritime enterprise, but when they ventured into financing long-distance voyages to Asian waters, they embraced a new business concept—the monopolistic, chartered joint-stock company—by which they tied all existing Asia-bound companies into the United East India Company in 1602.[2]

Like their Dutch counterparts, the sailors of China's south-eastern coastal province of Fujian could boast of a long history of private entrepreneurs in China's coastal and overseas trade. But with the imposition of maritime prohibitions (海禁, *haijin*) by the Ming government, when the imperial court-sponsored voyages of Admiral Zheng He were halted in 1433, these long-distance merchants saw their trading networks with Southeast Asia curtailed. For more than a century China's overseas trade now came to depend mainly on shipping carried out by foreign tributaries. This unhappy situation, which led to much illegal trade and piracy in Chinese coastal waters, continued until 1567, when the Ming court changed its policy and again allowed its own subjects to sail abroad. Under strict conditions of the so called *Dongyang Xiyang* system, private shipping interests in Fujian province gained permission to sail the Eastern Ocean (東洋, *Dongyang*) and Western Ocean (西洋, *Xiyang*) routes of the South China Sea—that is, eastward to the Philippine islands where the Spaniards had established themselves, and in a south western direction coasting along Vietnam and Cambodia, crossing the Gulf of Siam, and then proceeding along the Malay peninsula and Sumatra as far as the port of Banten on western Java in the Indonesian archipelago.[3] As the immediate result of this new surge overseas by Chinese private traders in the last decades of the sixteenth century, Chinese settlements mushroomed all around the fringes of the South China Sea. No wonder, then, that the first Dutch sailors to reach Banten in 1595 encountered a recently established but prosperous 'China town' there.[4]

---

2 F.S. Gaastra, *The Dutch East India Company: Expansion and Decline* (Zutphen: Walburg Pers, 2003).

3 Zhang Xie 张燮, *Dong xi yang kao* 東西洋考, Account of the Eastern and Western Oceans (Beijing: Zhonghua Shuju, 1981); Leonard Blussé, 'Fuchienese Commercial Expansion into the Nanyang as Mirrored in the *Tung Hsi Yang K'ao*', *Review of Culture* 13–14 (1991): 140–49.

4 Leonard Blussé, 'Western Impact on Chinese Communities in Western Java at the Beginning of the 17th Century', *Nampo Bunka* 2 (1975): 26–57.

The Iberian Example

As is well known, the Portuguese were the first European sailors to enter the Indian Ocean after they rounded the Cape of Good Hope in 1498. Within a hundred years, they created the Estado da India, a veritable thalassocracy with trading settlements widely spread across Monsoon Asia. Centred on Goa, their headquarters on India's west coast, the Estado da India encompassed the Monsoon Seas from East Africa and the Persian Gulf eastward across the Indian Ocean and South China Sea to the mouth of the Pearl River in China, where they founded Macao, and from there onwards via the East China Sea to the port of Nagasaki in Japan.

The Spaniards, who had expanded westwards towards the Americas, did not arrive in Asia until the 1560s, when they founded the colonial city of Manila, on the island of Luzon, and inaugurated the so-called Manila galleon trade between Mexico and the Philippines. Almost immediately, Manila was connected with the Chinese economy by the booming Eastern Ocean trade of Fujianese shipping.

The Spanish colonial city of Manila came to serve as a source of inspiration for the Dutch, who did not fail to notice that this town derived its prosperity from the Chinese settlers who came to the Philippines to trade their commodities for the American silver that was annually brought by Spanish galleons. 'Around the city of Manila', Governor General Jan Pietersz Coen reported to the directorate of the Company, 'live about 20,000 families, most of them from China, but also many Japanese and other nations from who the Castilians living *intramuros* (about 1,000 families) draw tribute, tolls, and other emoluments with which they maintain their state'.[5] Almost as soon as he had established Batavia in 1619, Coen realized that, in the absence of sufficient numbers of Dutch settlers, the new city urgently needed an enterprising middle class of shopkeepers and craftsmen. He felt that there was no people that could serve him better than the Chinese.[6]

But the Spanish model of 'living apart together' with the Chinese, was not adopted lock, stock, and barrel by the Dutch. While the Spanish colonial administration anxiously segregated the large number of Chinese immigrants in the Parian, Manila's Chinatown, Coen integrated the Chinese newcomers *within* Batavia's population and thus laid the foundation for a multicultural

---

5 H.T. Colenbrander, *Jan Pietersz Coen, Bescheiden omtrent zijn verblijf in Indië* (Den Haag: Martinus Nijhoff, 1919), 4.64.

6 'Daer is geen volck die ons beter dan Chinesen dienen en soo licht als Chinesen te becomen sijn'. F. de Haan, *Oud Batavia* (Batavia: Kolff, 1922), 1.76.

urban settlement. This arrangement of attracting Chinese migrants and settling them within the walls was not an early example of the kind of social engineering that the Dutch are so fond of today, but was simply a step taken out of necessity. Because the town lacked sufficient numbers of Dutch settlers, the Chinese who took their place needed to be protected, too, against attacks from outside.

Batavia was built in a hostile environment: The new city and the surrounding gardens and pastures for cattle were easy prey for tigers, crocodiles, and rampaging bands from the nearby Sultanate of Banten. And what is more, within ten years of its foundation in 1619, Batavia was assaulted twice by enormous armies sent by the *susuhunan* of the up-and-coming kingdom of Mataram in Central Java. In the preceding years, this expansive ruler had brought to heel all coastal towns of Java apart from Batavia and Banten. To his dismay, well-defended Batavia turned out to be a bridge too far.[7]

Convivencia

In the past, I have ironically styled the curious entanglement between the commercial networks of the VOC and the Fujianese entrepreneurs in the Indonesian archipelago as *Strange Company*. Yet insofar as Batavia is concerned, this project of collaboration may in hindsight be better described as an attempt at a *convivencia*, a coexistence of culturally different but remarkably comparable urban lifestyles.[8]

---

7 Leonard Blussé, 'Driemaal is scheepsrecht. Batavia 1619, 1627–1629', in Herman Amersfoort, Hans Blom, Dennis Bos, and Gijsbert van Es, eds., *Belaagd en belegerd* (Amsterdam: Balans, 2011), 147–69.
8 I realize that in Spanish historiography the 'coexistence' hypothesis of *la Convivencia*, with its emphasis on religious tolerance, has met with considerable criticism—*vide* David Nirenberg's thesis that 'violence was a central and systematic aspect of it' and Eduardo Manzano Moreno's statement that 'the concept of convivencia [in Spanish history] has no support in the historical record'. The latter was specifically referring to Arab sources. See https://en.wikipedia.org/wiki/La_Convivencia. I do agree that the Dutch-Chinese political relationship in Batavia was based on unequal power relations. (See Leonard Blussé, *Strange Company: Chinese Settlers, Mestizo Women and the Dutch in VOC Batavia* (Dordrecht-Holland: Foris, 1986), introduction). Yet in the present case there exists ample support in the contemporary Dutch and Chinese historical records, including the *Kai Ba Lidai Shiji*, which forms the main theme of the present study. My views on the curious Dutch-Chinese relationship in Southeast Asia were initially met with great skepticism when I proposed them thirty years ago, but by now they seem to have gained acceptance.

Both South China and the Low Countries nurtured urban cultures characterized by brick houses standing closely packed along canals within city walls. Even if Batavia was laid out according to the designs of the famous Dutch city planner Simon Stevin, it was constructed largely with the help of its Chinese contractors, masons, and carpenters. Already in 1625, an astute observer wrote that 'Chinese are here in great numbers, an industrious people, on whom depends all of the prosperity of Batavia, because without them no markets would be held, and no houses and defence works would be built'.[9] In his imposing survey of the Dutch possessions in Asia, *Oud en Nieuw Oost-Indiën*, published in 1726, François Valentijn remarked that the Chinese actually occupied the best parts of the city.[10] Protected by Dutch laws and urban institutions, these Chinese immigrants took root and developed into a capitalistic middle class as tax farmers, artisans, shopkeepers, innkeepers, businessmen, and landowners.

This is exactly what Batavia's founder, Jan Pietersz Coen, had in mind when he lured and forced Chinese from nearby Banten to move to his newly created city. He even tried to blockade all Chinese shipping from Manila and divert it to Batavia. Thus, from the outset, the Chinese community of Batavia came to be served by an umbilical cord of Chinese shipping that connected them with the home region in South Fujian, in the same way that the Dutch were served by the VOC fleets that annually arrived from and departed to the Low Countries.

A big difference between the two shipping routes was that Dutch ships spent on average six months braving storms and hardships on the Atlantic and Indian Oceans while the *va et vient* of the Chinese junks was favoured by the steady monsoon seasons. Setting out for Java around Chinese New Year, the Chinese could return home in June, just before the typhoon season set in. For the Chinese, the average crossing took only one month.

Year in and year out, considerable effort was required to man the VOC ships with thousands of able-bodied sailors, merchants, and soldiers willing to brave the long ocean voyage. More than half of those aboard the VOC ships—especially the soldiers—were recruited from poorer parts of Europe outside the Dutch Republic. In its heyday, the VOC was served by a work force of 20,000 to 30,000 Europeans in Asia.[11]

---

9   The Reverend Justus Heurnius quoted in De Haan, *Oud Batavia*, 1.76.
10 François Valentijn, *Oud en Nieuw Oost-Indiën*, 5 vols. (Dordrecht: Johannes van Braam, 1724–27).
11 Gaastra, *The Dutch East India Company*; Leonard Blussé, 'Northern European Empires in Asia, the VOC', in Hamish Scott, ed., *Early Modern European History, 1350–1750* (Oxford: Oxford University Press, 2015), 2.227–53.

FIGURE 2
Chinese junk, F. Morel-Fatio
PRIVATE COLLECTION

The Chinese case could not have been more different. Whenever a junk was leaving the port of Xiamen in Fujian for Batavia, there were hundreds of people elbowing each other aside to get aboard, either to barter their wares on a business trip or to emigrate and start a new life overseas. Every year around February, Fujianese junks sailed with dozens of pedlars carrying plenty of Chinese export merchandise like paper ware, ironware, crude and fine porcelain, silk, and tea. But the most important 'export item' the junks carried were the hundreds of Chinese migrants looking for work overseas. When in June it was time to catch the south eastern monsoon and sail home from Batavia with return cargoes of tropical products and other goods available in Batavia, like spices, edible birds' nests, silver *rials* of eight, and European cloth, many enterprising Chinese newcomers (*orang baru*), opted to stay behind and put down roots in and around Batavia.[12]

The transportation costs of passengers on a Chinese junk were generally advanced, to be paid back on arrival in Batavia. This put the newcomer at least temporarily in debt to a local moneylender. In addition to this, even the poorest migrant remained obliged to remit money home to support his kin financially. This interactive connection of resources, by which the sojourners

---

12 Leonard Blussé, 'Junks to Java: Chinese Shipping to the Nanyang in the Second Half of the Eighteenth Century', in Eric Tagliacozzo and Chang Wen-Chin, eds., *Chinese Circulations: Capital, Commodities, and Networks in Southeast Asia* (Durham: Duke University Press, 2011), 221–58.

abroad and the people at home in Fujian continued to depend on each other, has been aptly labelled a 'human corridor'.[13]

According to the regulations of the Qing government that ruled the Chinese empire between 1644 and 1911, Chinese traders had to return from overseas in the same year or, if they were unable to so, in the next one. People who ignored this rule risked severe punishment, as did their relatives back home. These regulations in the Chinese home ports and the no less severe restrictions in Batavia were meant to keep a grip on the apparently inexhaustible outflow of emigrants from China into Batavia, but in the long run they proved useless.[14]

The VOC administration allowed the Chinese to rely on their own shipping network from Fujian to Batavia because throughout most of the seventeenth century, VOC ships were barred from Chinese ports. In addition to this, it should be pointed out that the only people able to meet the peculiar consumption needs of Batavia's Chinese community were the experienced Chinese pedlars who came every year with their trading goods.

The Chinese of Batavia not only enjoyed exceptional privileges, but they also basically ran the engine of the urban economy. Intermarrying with Indonesian wives, Chinese sojourners created the largest ethnic group among the free people of Batavia, who comprised Europeans, Mardijkers (free Christian citizens of Asian origin, sometimes former slaves), and various free ethnicities from all over the Indonesian archipelago. For security reasons, Javanese were not allowed to reside in town, but they formed the largest ethnic group in the surrounding countryside, the Ommelanden. Of the estimated 35,000 people living within Batavia's city walls, roughly half were slaves of Indian and non-Islamic Indonesian background. They were owned by free citizens of all the above-named ethnicities and the VOC personnel, or were working as Company slaves in the so called Ambachtskwartier (handicraft quarter).[15] Slaves working in private households often were also hired out as skilled craftsmen. Slavery in Batavia was not necessarily a life sentence, either, because slaves were frequently freed in the wills of their owners, and because they could also purchase

---

13 Philip Kuhn, *Chinese Among Others: Emigration in Modern Times* (Lanham: Rowman & Littlefield, 2008).

14 See 'The VOC and the Junk Trade to Batavia: A Problem in Administrative Control', in Blussé, *Strange Company*, 97–155.

15 Although the so-called *Daghregisters*, or diaries of Batavia, give an annual count of the town population, these censuses are not reliable. De Haan estimates the population during its most prosperous years, between 1700 and 1730, at 20,000 souls within the walls and another 15,000 in the suburbs. When epidemic waves of malaria began to hit the city in 1732, the life-threatening situation resulted in a flight towards the healthier Ommelanden and the in-town population began to recede. De Haan, *Oud Batavia*, 2.348.

their own freedom. In fact, the high rate of manumission was a distinctive feature of Batavian society. In the early years, slaves were imported from the Indian subcontinent, but by the end of the seventeenth century almost half of them came from Sulawesi, one quarter from Bali, and the rest from other Indonesian islands like Buton and Sumbawa.[16] Slavery was a predominant institution almost everywhere in the relatively sparsely populated societies of the Indonesian archipelago, where raiding for manpower had been a common practice from time immemorial.[17] Yet the employment of slaves under legislation derived from the ancient Roman law was of course an innovation of Dutch colonial society.

The same mode of Sino-Dutch collaboration occurred in the wide-scale development of the Ommelanden, which was converted from a dense tropical forest into carefully nurtured sugarcane plantations and rice paddies. In addition to the settlements of native Javanese, Batavia was surrounded by *kampongs* of various Indonesian ethnicities from beyond Java, who provided the Company with auxiliary military forces in times of war.[18] These various ethnicities, including Malays, Ambonese, Balinese, and Bandanese, also owned slaves and employed them in various occupations.[19]

The cash-crop cultivation of sugarcane in the Ommelanden was developed and carried out by a locally recruited workforce and Chinese specialized labour supervised by Chinese overseers. The Chinese also played a dominant role as suppliers of fruit and vegetables to Batavia's markets, to say nothing of the many ships that lay anchored in the roadstead. The labour force on the plantations was provided mainly by privately-owned slaves or workers recruited by the Javanese elite in the surrounding regions, such as the sultan of Cirebon, who sent seasonal corvée workers.

---

16   Hendrik E. Niemeijer, *Batavia. Een koloniale samenleving in de 17de eeuw* (Amsterdam: Balans, 2005), 61.
17   Anthony Reid, ed., *Slavery, Bondage & Dependency in Southeast Asia* (St Lucia: University of Queensland Press, 1983), 1–43.
18   Remco Raben, *Batavia and Colombo: The Ethnic and Spatial Order of Two Colonial Cities, 1600–1800* (PhD diss., Leiden University, 1996).
19   Bondan Kanumoyoso, *Beyond the City Wall: Society and Economic Development in the Ommelanden of Batavia, 1684–1740* (PhD diss., Leiden University, 2011).

Nature Hits Back

The last decade of the seventeenth century witnessed the ruthless destruction of the natural habitat of the Ommelanden. To provide fuel for the cauldrons in which sugar was boiled, the tropical forest was cut down on a grand scale, which led to widespread erosion. This deterioration of the natural environment translated into often obstructed rivers that were reduced to meagre streams during the dry season but turned into veritable torrents that caused extensive flooding in the Ommelanden and Batavia itself during the rainy season.

In hindsight, it is not altogether surprising that this ecological disaster ultimately contributed to outbreaks of all sorts of tropical diseases. In 1733 malaria came to Batavia, never to leave again in the early modern period. Quite suddenly the headquarters of the VOC, which only two decades earlier Valentijn had lauded for its pleasant climate, turned into an unhealthy habitat visited by recurring epidemics that devastated the urban population: Within the space of one generation, the city gained the unpropitious repute of being a death trap for its inhabitants and visiting sailors, alike. No longer celebrated as the Queen of the East, it now became known as the Graveyard of the Orient.

A debate is still smouldering about where to lay the blame for the sudden emergence of malaria in Batavia and environs. There can be no doubt that the first outbreak occurred in 1733 during the digging of an extension of the Mookervaart Canal in the western Ommelanden. Yet it has been proposed that the extensive construction of fishponds around Batavia may have created an ideal breeding ground for the anopheles mosquitoes.[20] The suggestion of the author of the *Kai Ba Lidai Shiji* that the extended salt flats close to the city may have been the real culprits introduces a new argument to the debate.[21]

During the 1730s, the decaying natural environment coupled with a crisis in sugarcane cultivation owing to the loss of export markets in Asia resulted in widespread unemployment in the agricultural sector of Batavia's Ommelanden and gave rise to banditry and a loss of local administrative control, proving once more the adage that 'the abuse of people and the abuse of nature are often interrelated'.[22]

---

20   P.H. van der Brug, *Malaria en Malaise. De VOC in Batavia in de achttiende eeuw* (Amsterdam: Bataafse Leeuw, 1994).
21   See below, *Kai Ba Lidai Shiji*, 1730–31.
22   Judith Shapiro, *Mao's War against Nature* (Cambridge: Cambridge University Press, 2001), xiv.

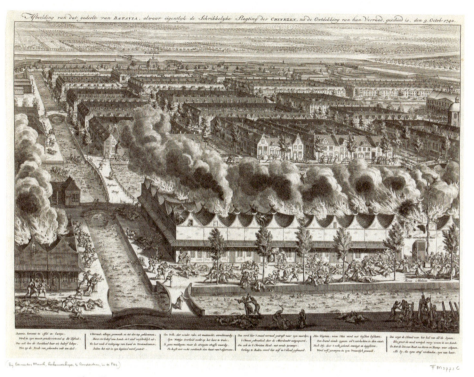

FIGURE 3   The Chinese Massacre. *Adolf van der Laan, 1740, print*
PRIVATE COLLECTION

Evil Dreaders are Evil Doers

In the long run, the Sino-Dutch *convivencia* model could not suppress indefinitely the latent hostility that emerged between the Dutch and the Chinese. In October 1740, after more than a century of peaceful coexistence between the Chinese and their Dutch, Malay, Mardijker, and other fellow-townsmen, a gruesome massacre of Batavia's Chinese community occurred. The precipitating event was an assault on the city in the first week of October by hordes of Chinese malcontents and unemployed coolies from the sugar plantations who, during this period of severe economic downturn, were revolting against the Batavian government's short-sighted and heavy-handed security measures. On the suggestion of the former governor of Ceylon, Gustaaf Willem, Baron van Imhoff, the decision was even taken to send 'undesirable' Chinese agitators to Ceylon. 'Chinese whispers' that those who were shipped on board were thrown overboard once at sea proved the proverbial straw that broke the camel's back.

It is interesting to see that this trope returns repeatedly in the Chinese sources, while it is overlooked in the Dutch ones.

Facing the waves of Chinese rebels assaulting the city walls, the town population of Batavia, reinforced by sailors recruited from the roadstead, ran amok and took on their Chinese fellow citizens for fear that these might join the revolt of their countrymen outside the walls. Within one week, approximately 8,000 Chinese men, women, and children were slaughtered in an orgy of violence.[23]

The massacre had a tremendous impact not only on Batavia itself but also on Javanese society in general. After failing to capture Batavia, the Chinese rebels withdrew and moved their remaining forces towards central Java, where they teamed up with Javanese insurgents against the reigning susuhunan of Mataram, Pakubuwana II (r. 1726–49) and started the so-called *Perang Cina*, or Chinese War (1741–43).[24] The seemingly endless infighting between the different factions at the court of Mataram that followed as a result of this civil war did not come to an end until 1755 when an armistice was finally brokered and the kingdom of Mataram was divided up between the sultan of Yogyakarta and the susuhunan of Solo.

In spite of the terrible massacre, Chinese shipping continued to visit Batavia's roadstead and, almost as if nothing had ever happened, within a decade the Chinese presence in the city regained much of its former stature. The chief difference was this: initially the Chinese were no longer allowed to reside within the city walls but were relocated as in Spanish Manila, *extramuros*, in a separate Chinatown called *Chinese kamp*. Yet within twenty years, many of them were back again living *intramuros*. By the end of the eighteenth century, the city of Batavia gradually lost its former grandeur as the most important harbour city in Southeast Asia, when the Dutch East India Company, irrevocably crippled by the Fourth Anglo-Dutch War (1780–84), went bankrupt in 1799, as a result of which all Dutch possessions in the Indonesian archipelago passed into British hands during the Napoleonic Wars. The final blow came after the restitution of Java to the Dutch government in 1816, when the port of Batavia was overtaken by the newly established British crown colony at Singapore (1819).

---

23 Blussé, *Strange Company*, 73–96; Claudine Salmon, 'The Massacre of 1740 as Reflected in a Contemporary Chinese Narrative', *Archipel* 77 (2009): 149–54; and J.T. Vermeulen, *De Chineezen te Batavia en de troebelen van 1740* (Leiden: Eduard IJdo, 1938).

24 W.G.J. Remmelink, *Emperor Pakubuwana II, Priyayi & Company and the Chinese War* (Leiden: KITLV, 1991).

CHAPTER 2

A Chinese Urban Society in the Tropics

In October 1619, only five months after founding Batavia on the ashes of the Javanese town of Jayakarta, Governor General Coen appointed his close friend and associate, the Chinese merchant Bencon, alias Su Mingguang, So Bing Kong, Souw Beng Kong (蘇鳴崗, 1580–1644), to the position of headman or captain (甲必丹, *kapitein*) of the Chinese citizenry, with responsibility for collecting the monthly poll tax that all male Chinese residents had to pay. He also instructed him to settle all lesser civil affairs among his fellow countrymen.[1] The linguistic and cultural divide between the Dutch and Chinese was so great that the viceroy recognized the benefits of having a Chinese headman resolve social issues amongst the 400 to 500 Chinese households in town. He also allotted Bencon a plot of land named Mangga Dua where he could build his mansion: 'In front of his gate Captain Su Mingguang hung a lantern and a board on which was written 開國元勳, "the pioneer of opening up the country"'.[2]

Bencon's appointment was the first in a long line of Chinese captains who, in later years assisted by other Chinese officers, continued to administer the Chinese community of Batavia for three centuries. As the years went by, this semi-official body of Chinese public officials became known as the Kong Koan (Gongguan 公館) or Kong Tong (Gongtang 公堂), or, in Dutch, the Chinese Raad (Chinese Council). It was essentially a 'self-help' institution that met once or twice a week to discuss and resolve social and economic issues. Matters of great importance, however, were referred by the Chinese officers to the board of aldermen (*schepenbank*) of the city administration on which the Chinese captain also sat. Serious crimes were handed over to the Council of Justice in Batavia's town hall.

As already mentioned, good intentions notwithstanding, the collaborative enterprise between the Dutch and the Chinese ended in a nightmare in 1740. In the aftermath of this terrible pogrom, some people in the administration wishfully floated an idea about how to solve once and for all the problem of the uncontrollable Chinese immigration: the Chinese should no longer be allowed to settle in Batavia. Yet the city could not exist without its industrious Chinese

---

1 B. Hoetink, 'So Bing Kong. Het eerste hoofd der Chineezen te Batavia', BKI (*Bijdragen tot de Taal-, Land- en Volkenkunde van Nederlandsch-Indië*) 73 (1917): 344–415, and BKI 79 (1923): 1–44.
2 *Kai Ba Lidai Shiji*, 1620.

urban middle class, and within a decade the Chinese were back, albeit no longer settling *intramuros* as before, but in the *Chinese kamp*, the 'China town', on the southern perimeter of Batavia.

Embedding the Kong Koan (Chinese Council)

In the aftermath of the massacre, it was realized that the panic and chaos had occurred at a time of extreme tension and when there was a complete disruption of cross-cultural relations and information sharing. Under normal circumstances, the Chinese officers in town would have warned in time the colonial authorities against the trouble brewing among their fellow countrymen in the countryside. Yet when it became known that the revolt had been plotted at a sugar plantation belonging to the Chinese captain without him knowing anything about it, it was clear that even the connections between the Chinese urban elite and Chinese labourers at the sugar mills in the countryside had short-circuited.

Suffice it to say here that, to avoid any further administrative communication problems in the future, in 1742 the High Government (*Hoge Regering*) of Batavia—that is, the governor general and council of the Indies (*Raad van Indië*)—decided henceforth to provide the newly appointed Chinese captain and his officers with an official office, the Kong Tong, where the Kong Koan could hold its weekly meetings. Here the Kong Koan was to store and preserve all its administrative papers, such as the minutes of the meetings as well as all documentation concerning weddings, cemeteries, temples, and hospitals in its own archival depository. These measures may have been akin to locking the door after the horse had bolted, but it cannot be denied that from then onwards the Kong Koan was formally recognized as an administrative organ and it maintained its own archive available for consultation whenever that might be necessary. And thus, under the care of a specially appointed secretary of the Kong Koan, paid for by the government, a Chinese archive was created that eventually would cover all official activities of the community until the Japanese occupation of 1942.

At first sight, the administrative structure of Batavia was similar to that of any Dutch city, with its board of aldermen, sheriff, council of justice, orphans chamber, curators, penitentiaries, hospitals, weigh-houses, tax farm system, and so on. Unlike in the homeland, however, where the management of these civil institutions was in the hands of elected individuals, in Batavia the most important positions were held by appointees drawn from the upper echelons of the Company. In addition to Dutch-Roman law, the authorities also introduced the *Bataviasche statuten*, a compendium of special laws that addressed the unique features of colonial society.

The colonial administration of Batavia during the VOC period functioned in an *ad hoc* manner and ruled the town by decrees and public notices, the so-called *plakaten*, or placards. Every important decision taken by the High Government was promulgated by public decree or placard (*plakaat*). While J.A. Van der Chijs published all extant *plakaten* in the seventeen volumes of the *Nederlandsch-Indisch Plakaatboek, 1602–1811* at the end of the nineteenth century, and two excellent urban histories of early modern Batavia have been written on the basis of research in the local VOC archives now kept in the Arsip Nasional Republik Indonesia (ANRI),[3] an institutional history of Batavia based on the *plakaten* remains to be written.[4] On the basis of the dates of the placards, the debates in the High Government that preceded their publication can be traced back in the resolutions, the 'Resoluties van Gouverneur Generaal en Raden' in the VOC archives at ANRI.[5] Because the promulgation of each placard represents an extemporary measure undertaken in response to an urgent issue, the placards are more a reflection of reality than reality itself.

This leads us to the key question: In what institutional context should we situate the functioning of Batavia's Kong Koan? If the Kong Koan was set up specifically to vouchsafe a Chinese mode of living in the Dutch colonial city of Batavia, the Chinese officers were there to assist their countrymen in making a living in a decidedly foreign institutional context with its own laws and customs. In other words, the captain and his lieutenants were expected to do more than just keep peace and order in a volatile society that was continuously replenished with sojourners and adventurers from China. They also had to 'acclimatize' their kinsmen to social conditions that were often quite different from those in the hometowns back in Fujian. At the same time, they also bore the responsibility of safeguarding the typically Chinese features of their community, such as proper modes of dress and daily customs concerning typical rites of passage such as birth, marriage, and death. A connected question concerns the extent to which Chinese life in Batavia really differed from domestic

---

3   The archivist Frederik de Haan published the much-lauded *Oud Batavia* in 1922: F. de Haan, *Oud Batavia* (Batavia: G. Kolff 1922). Unfortunately, this elegantly written book, intended for a broader public, lacks footnotes. In his 2005 study, *Batavia, een koloniale samenleving in de 17de eeuw*, Henk Niemeijer has thrown new light on social issues like town–hinterland relations, security, and 'naturalisation' (*inburgering*).

4   J.A. van der Chijs, *Nederlandsch-Indisch Plakaatboek, 1602–1811*, 17 vols. (Batavia: Landsdrukkerij, 1885–1900).

5   See https://sejarah-nusantara.anri.go.id/.

life in the home districts (故鄉, *guxiang*) of southern Fujian. Here we can only note in passing a few issues that played out in Chinese Batavian life.

The Problem of Female Partnership

On the crucial issue of how to people a colony, Governor General Coen bluntly posed the question 'Who does not know that the human race cannot exist without women?'[6] Facing a lack of Dutch women in the Indies, he and his successors soon recognized that the only practical way to solve the problem was the 'Romulus approach', named after the founder of Rome who encouraged his followers to abduct and marry the wives of the neighbouring Sabines. The Portuguese followed this expedient by marrying native women wherever they went, and the Dutch followed suit, ultimately creating a mestizo society in the Indonesian archipelago.

The Chinese faced the same problem, although they regarded the prospect of a native wife from a slightly different perspective. Young Chinese men who went abroad were often obliged to marry first in their home village so that they could at least provide their parents with a useful daughter-in-law, possibly a hastily conceived child, and some insurance that he would return home, or at least support his family from abroad by sending them remittances. Upon his arrival in the Indies, the Chinese newcomer would have to repay his passage before he could start thinking of acquiring sufficient funds to buy himself a female slave or propose to the daughter of a locally established Chinese family. In this regard, Wang Dahai remarks, 'Those who come originally from China are preferred as sons-in-law, while those in the country are not esteemed. In the former case, a pair of wax candles may serve for a dowry, which is delightfully cheap'. Gu Sen tells us why a native wife was a great asset to any Chinese sojourner: she gave him access to the marketplace where indigenous women (then as now) played a prominent role.[7] Some preferred Balinese women because they did not object to preparing and eating pork, an essential ingredient

---

6 In an indignant letter to the directors of the VOC, the Gentlemen XVII. See 'The Caryatids of 17th Century Batavia: Reproduction, Religion and Acculturation under the VOC', in Blussé, *Strange Company*, 156–71.

7 W.H. Medhurst ed, *Ong-Tae-Hae, The Chinaman Abroad, or, A Desultory Account of the Malayan Archipelago Particularly of Java* (Shanghai, 1849), 9. See Gu Sen's account in part 3, chapter 4, p. 238.

in Chinese cuisine. Slave girls would first have to be manumitted before they could be legally accepted as Chinese wives. The progeny of these Chinese-Indonesian associations, which gave rise to a rather unique culture of their own, were called *peranakan*. In the Kong Koan records there are examples galore of happy and unhappy alliances between Chinese husbands and native women. One may read the sad story of a Chinese merchant who does not seem to have had much patience with the other sex. Sailing home to Batavia with a female slave whom he had purchased in Bali, he threw the young girl overboard because she would not stop crying and protesting her fate.[8] At the other end of the spectrum, there is the story of Captain Siqua's Balinese wife who, the *Kai Ba Lidai Shiji* tells us with a mix of dismay and admiration, succeeded her husband to the captaincy after his death and ruled the Chinese community 'like a man'.[9]

The Kong Koan registered Chinese marriages and passed on the information to the Dutch authorities for tax purposes.[10] The marriage register of the 1775–91 period shows an average of 206 Chinese weddings per year. Surprisingly 54 percent of the Chinese bridegrooms were older than thirty-one, while 61 percent of the brides were between thirteen and nineteen years old. In 35 percent of all marriages, the age difference between groom and bride was more than fifteen years.[11] Indigenous wives often accompanied their Chinese husbands when they returned to China—witness the unfortunate lieutenant Chen Yilao, who upon his return home was banished with his whole family to the western regions.[12] As Claudine Salmon has pointed out, however, elaborate gravestones

---

8 Nie Dening, Wu Fengbin, Chen Menghong, Hou Zhenping, and Leonard Blussé, et al., eds., 聶德寧，吳鳳斌，陳萌紅，侯真平，包樂史, *Gong An Bu* (Minutes of the Board Meetings of the Chinese Council 1787–1920), 吧城華人公館（吧國公堂）檔案叢書：公案簿, 1787–1920 (廈門：廈門大學出版社 2002–2017), vol. I, 3.

9 See *Kai Ba Lidai Shiji*, 1649.

10 See Myra Sidharta, 'The Role of the Go-Between in Marriages in Batavia', in Leonard Blussé and Chen Menghong, eds., *The Archives of the Kong Koan of Batavia* (Leiden: Brill, 2003), 46–59.

11 Leonard Blussé and Wu Fengbin, *18 Shijimo Badaweiya Tangren shehui*, 18 世紀末吧達維亞唐人社會 [The Chinese community of Batavia at the end of the eighteenth century] (Xiamen: Xiamen University Press, 2002), 321; Leonard Blussé, 'One Hundred Weddings and Many More Funerals a Year: Chinese Civil Society in Batavia at the End of the Eighteenth Century', in Blussé and Chen, *The Archives of the Kong Koan of Batavia*, 8–28.

12 Ng Chin-keong, 'The Case of Ch'en I-lao: Maritime Trade and Overseas Chinese in Ch'ing Policies, 1717–1757', in Roderick Ptak and D. Rothermund, eds., *Emporia, Commodities and Entrepreneurs in Asian Maritime Trade, c. 1400–1750* (Stuttgart: Steiner, 1991), 373–99.

FIGURE 4   *Anonymous artist, Chinese grave of Lieutenant Kouw Tjanko (probably Xu Cange, who died in 1770)*
KITLV COLLECTION, LEIDEN UNIVERSITY LIBRARY

show that native wives were held in great esteem.[13] Wang Dahai relates the story of a virtuous native wife who even went to Fujian to help out her husband's family.[14] No less illustrative of the absence of women from China is the anecdote in the *Kai Ba Lidai Shiji* about a certain Mr. Wang Jie who, defying all Chinese laws, in 1699 arrived by junk in Batavia having brought his Chinese wife all the way from Xiamen. This was unheard of, because Qing law made it a capital crime for Han women to leave China. The appearance of this fashionably dressed Chinese lady—she may even have had bound feet—created such consternation in Batavia that the Dutch governor general was prompted to invite the couple to his office so that he could have a look at this Chinese beauty.[15]

13   Claudine Salmon, 'Ancient Chinese Cemeteries of Indonesia as Vanishing Landmarks of the Past (17th–20th c.)', *Archipel* 92 (2016): 23–62.
14   See Wang Dahai's portrait of the 'The Wife of One Soo' in Ong-Tae-Hae, *The Chinaman Abroad*, part 3, chapter 3, p. 234.
15   *Kai Ba Lidai Shiji*, the year 1699.

Cemeteries and Funeral Practices[16]

In China, the selection of sites for tombs was a family affair in which the *fengshuishi* (風水師, geomancer) played an important role in identifying a favourable site. Not so in the flatlands of Batavia. The raising of the tumulus of a Chinese grave inevitably resulted in the excavation of the surrounding soil, which would create pits that during the rainy season turned into breeding grounds for mosquitoes. This explains why the VOC authorities early on relegated the Chinese dead to specially designated burial grounds away from the city. The first such graveyard was in the vicinity of Mangga Dua, where one can still find the lone grave of the first Chinese captain, Bencon, in the midst of a densely-populated kampong. By 1660, there was already a need to build a new cemetery because the old one was filled up. The taxes impounded on funerals (three *rijksdaalders* and another twelve for a tombstone with a Chinese inscription) went to pay for the Chinese hospital, which was run under Dutch auspices.[17] In 1668, the Company sold a plot of land west of Fort Jacatra to the Chinese and in 1745 the Kong Koan purchased a piece of land for funerary purposes at Gunung Sari, where a mansion was transformed into the Senthiong (新塚, or 'new cemetery') Temple. This graveyard has long since been removed, but the temple is still there and in use.[18] The Kong Koan reserved special plots for the ruling elite in these cemeteries, but also set apart areas for the destitute. The dimensions of graves were all carefully prescribed.[19] On occasion, wealthy Chinese also expressed the wish to be buried in their place of birth in Fujian, but that, too, was subject to a separate tax by the Dutch.[20]

Local Taxes

Throughout the second century of its existence, Batavia's annual balance showed a large deficit. This was hardly surprising because the VOC headquarters were saddled with all kinds of expenses that really concerned the

---

16 For an excellent survey of the Chinese cemeteries of Batavia, their rise and fall, see Claudine Salmon, ed., 'Chinese Deathscapes in Insulindia', *Archipel* 92 (Paris: 2016).
17 28 December 1640, *Plakaatboek* 1.454–55; and 11 June 1660, *Plakaatboek* 2.335.
18 Claudine Salmon and Denys Lombard, *Les Chinois de Jakarta: temples et vie collective* (Paris: Editions de la Maison des Sciences de l'Homme, 1980).
19 Li Minghuan, 'A Portrait of Batavia's Chinese Society Based on the Tandjoeng Cemetery Archives', in Blussé and Chen, *The Archives of the Kong Koan of Batavia*, 80–105.
20 25 August 1755, *Plakaatboek* 7. 116, 28 June 1771, *Plakaatboek* 8.694.

management of the Company but not the city itself. The only way to contain these losses was by raising local taxes, and as a result virtually everything in the city was taxed. The colonial authorities did not collect taxes directly. Every year they auctioned off the right to collect the various levies to tax farmers. Apart from the poll tax (*hoofdgeld*) that every Chinese male adult in town had to pay, and a couple of taxes on Chinese customs such as *wayang* (Chinese opera) performances, gambling, opium smoking, and marriage and funeral rituals, the Batavian tax system was not all that different from its Dutch counterpart. The Chinese poll tax, which was levied monthly, yielded by far the greatest share of all taxes. Because Chinese tax farmers collected the bulk of the city's taxes, they came to play a prominent role in Batavian society. To give an example, fifteen of the twenty-one different taxes farmed out in 1644 were acquired by Chinese bidders, including those that yielded the greatest profits, such as the poll tax and the taxes on the slaughterhouse, the weigh-house, Chinese gambling, the textile *pasar* (market), and so on.[21] The *Kai Ba Lidai Shiji* mentions some of these levies and also the antagonism that arose from the imposition of new taxes: Witness the anecdote about Qiu Zuguan (Khoe Tsouwko), a Chinese officer who, by introducing a surtax on wedding ceremonies, had made himself so unpopular that in 1721 the designated bearers of his coffin refused to carry him to his final resting place.[22]

Social Services

In a colonial society in which Chinese overseas sojourners lived far from their extended families, the handling of inheritances became a concern of utmost importance for the authorities. In the Portuguese Estado da India, this problem was dealt with by the Catholic Church, which established the so-called Casa de Misericórdia. Thanks to the large sums of money that the Casa administered, over the years this charity developed into a loan office from which Christian people could borrow money. Similarly, the authorities in Batavia were compelled to establish a board of curators (*boedelkamer*) after vehement quarrels over the partition of estates, spectacular bankruptcies, and the discovery of insolvent estates of prominent Chinese citizens created an uproar in town.

---

21 Nakamura Takashi (中村孝志), 'バタビィア華僑の徴税請負制度について, The Contract System in Tax Collection by the Chinese Merchants in Batavia', 東洋史研究 *Toyoshi Kenkyu* 28:1 (1969): 62.
22 According to the Dutch sources, this should be 1732. *See also* pp. 101 and 269.

Henceforth, proper measures were taken and Chinese of means, like their Dutch counterparts, had to draw up a will in front of a Dutch notary in town.[23]

The Collegie van Boedelmeesters (board of curators), consisting of two Dutch and two Chinese curators (*boedelmeesters*), was established in 1640; but it was dissolved eight years later at the request of the Chinese, who complained that the 'faithlessness' of those who had recently immigrated made it practically impossible to evaluate their estates.[24] The result was total chaos in the apportionment of the Chinese estates, so in 1655 the board of curators was re-established, ironically enough at the request of the Chinese, who now recognized the useful function of this institution.[25] Henceforth the curators could liquidate estates, set aside money for the rightful heirs both in Batavia and China, and, in some instances, take care of underage heirs and orphans.

Here again, the case of Captain Siqua is illustrative: in his testament of 1666 he declared that he had community property (*gemeenschap van goederen*) with his Balinese wife 'in Dutch fashion', and he divided his inheritance among his five children—four from his Balinese partners in Batavia, and one from his first wife in China—and he included a gift to the poor and destitute Chinese in town.[26] As the Chinese elite developed into a more or less capitalist class, thanks in some measure to the legal protection of property, the curators came to play an increasingly important role in the stabilization of Batavian Chinese society.[27] Those sojourners who decided to return to their country of origin with goods and chattels had to pay a fixed fee on the total value of what they were taking home.[28]

Prominent Chinese who served one or two three-year terms as curators were eligible for the position of lieutenant and, ultimately, captain, and over the years it actually became a *sine qua non* for promotion. The Dutch and Chinese *boedelmeesters* used to hold their meetings in the Chinese hospital, which was under their jurisdiction. This hospital had been founded in 1640 'for the poor

---

23 26 May 1640. 'Aanstelling van Boedelmeesteren voor Chinesche sterfhuizen'; 'Voorlopige instructie van Boedelmeesteren', *Plakaatboek* 1.438–45.
24 *Plakaatboek* 2.123.
25 Ibid., 212. Hence the Chinese estates were managed by a board consisting of both Dutch and Chinese curators. The *Kai Ba Lidai Shiji* mentions the names of only the Chinese boedelmeesters.
26 De Haan, *Oud Batavia*, 1.502.
27 Leonard Blussé, 'Wills, Widows and Witnesses: Executing Financials Dealings with the Nanyang—A Glimpse from the Notebook of the Dutch Vice-Consul at Amoy, Carolus Franciscus Martinus de Grijs', in Ng Chin-keong and Wang Gungwu, eds., *Maritime China in Transition 1750–1850* (Wiesbaden: Harrasowitz, 2004), 317–34.
28 29 April 1749, *Plakaatboek* 5.611.

ill and other impotent and miserable [Chinese] persons who are treated so inhumanly and barbarously'.[29] The archive of the curators, together with that of the Chinese hospital, including a great deal of interesting statistical material about the Chinese population, was unfortunately burned in 1811 during the British invasion, a fact mentioned by Stamford Raffles in *The History of Java*.[30]

---

[29]   13 August 1640, *Plakaatboek* 1.446. See also Iwao Seiichi's article about the Chinese stone slab (nowadays turned upside down in the garden of the De Klerck house) that was engraved on the occasion of the restoration of the hospital in 1799: Iwao Seiichi (岩生成一), ジャカルタの「新建養済列福戸捐金姓氏」の碑, On the Inscription of the *Yang-chi-yuan* 養濟院 (Chinese Hospital) in Jakarta', 南方文化 *Nampo-Bunka, Tenri Bulletin of South Asian Studies* 2 (1975): 13–25.

[30]   De Haan, *Oud Batavia*. 389. According to Raffles, 'On the occasion of the capture of this island, part of the most valuable papers were lost or destroyed, and amongst them the register in which was stated the Chinese population, and the number of their deaths and marriages annually'. See Thomas Stamford Raffles, *The History of Java* (Oxford: Oxford University Press, 1965), vol. 2, app. A, i.

CHAPTER 3

Chinese Sources for the History of the Chinese Community in Batavia

The documents of the Kong Koan archive of the Chinese community in Batavia unquestionably constitute the most extensive archival deposit of any Chinese urban population group of the Qing dynasty (1644–1911) inside or outside China.[1] Why this should be so is easily explained: It is the result of the close relationship that existed for hundreds of years between the Chinese urban elite and the Dutch colonial administration.

Unfortunately, only part of the Kong Koan archive has withstood the onslaught of time. The tropical climate in combination with ink erosion and paper-consuming vermin like silverfish and white ants have taken their toll, to say nothing of the total neglect of the papers after Indonesian independence, when the Suharto regime banned the possession of Chinese written material. Consequently, a sizable part of the archive has turned to dust over the years. These ravages notwithstanding, Leiden University Library is today home to some 600 kilograms of well-preserved archival papers.[2]

All surviving *gong'an bu*, the Chinese minutes of the weekly meetings of the Kong Koan, covering (with lacunae) the period from 1787 to 1920 have been edited, annotated, and published in fifteen volumes by Xiamen University Press.[3] This source publication project, carried out jointly by scholars from Leiden and Xiamen, has over the past decade given rise to extensive academic research in China.[4] Two PhD theses about prominent nineteenth- and twentieth-century Chinese community leaders have been defended in recent years

---

1 For an introduction to the contents of the Kong Koan archives, see Blussé and Chen, *The Archives of the Kong Koan of Batavia*.
2 Thanks to the *Metamorfoze* programme in which the Dutch Royal Library, the Friends of the Kong Koan Foundation, and Leiden University cooperated closely, the surviving part of the Kong Koan archive has been fully restored and inventoried.
3 Nie Dening, Wu Fengbin, Chen Menghong, Hou Zhenping, and Leonard Blussé, et al., eds., 聶德寧，吳鳳斌，陳萌紅，侯真平，包樂史，*Gong An Bu (Minutes of the Board Meetings of the Chinese Council 1787–1920)*, 15 vols., 吧城華人公館（吧國公堂）檔案叢書：公案簿, 1787–1920, 廈門：廈門大學出版社 2002–2017.
4 We are currently awaiting publication by Dr. Monique Erkelens of two volumes of the edited and annotated Malay-language minutes, Malay having replaced Chinese as the official language of the Kong Koan in its last decades.

at Leiden University, and Xiamen University Press has published a monograph about Batavia's Chinese community in the final years of the eighteenth century and a complete survey of all marital records of the Kong Koan.[5]

In addition to the minutes of the meetings of the Kong Koan, records from the following registers have been partly preserved:

a. the registration of Chinese marriages, divorces, and deaths in the city of Batavia until 1919, when municipal reforms were implemented,
b. the management of real estate rented or sold to people for housing or funeral plots,
c. the management of charitable organizations,
d. the management of local Chinese temples, and
e. the supervision and support of Chinese-language education in Batavia.[6]

Older Chinese Sources on the Chinese Community of Batavia

If the nineteenth century and the beginning of the twentieth century are relatively well covered by the preserved Kong Koan records, what about the seventeenth and eighteenth centuries? In addition to the preserved *gong-an bu* minutes of the late 1780s[7] and the *Kai Ba Lidai Shiji*, only two extensive eighteenth-century accounts by Chinese witnesses to life in Batavia have been preserved, as noted in chapter one. The *Haidao Yizhi,* or 'Island memories' by Wang Dahai, was translated by W.H. Medhurst. During the 1780s, Wang Dahai taught the children of the Chinese captain of the Javanese port city of Pekalongan, but he also spent some time in Batavia.[8] Equally interesting is

---

5 Chen Menghong, *De Chinese gemeenschap van Batavia, 1843–1865: Een onderzoek naar het Kong Koan-archief* (Leiden: Leiden University Press, 2011); Monique Erkelens, *The Decline of the Chinese Council of Batavia: The Loss of Prestige and Authority of the Traditional Elites amongst Chinese Community between 1900–42* (PhD diss., Leiden University, 2013); Blussé and Wu, *The Chinese Community of Batavia at the End of the Eighteenth Century*; Wu Fengbin, Nie Dening, and Xie Meihua 吴凤斌，聂得宁，谢美华，*Yajiada huaren hunyin* 雅加达华人婚姻，1772–1919, *The Chinese marriages in Jakarta: Marriage registrations of Chinese in Batavia*, 1772–1919 (Xiamen: Xiamen University Press, 2010).
6 All these data have now been made fully accessible on the internet by Dr Chen Menghong. See www.leidenuniv.nl, library, Chinese Special Collections, Kong Koan archive.
7 Nie, Wu and Blussé, eds., *Gong An Bu*, vol 1, covering 1787-10-31 to 1791-2-8.
8 W.H. Medhurst ed., *Ong-Tae-Hae, The Chinaman Abroad: An Account of the Malayan Archipelago, Particularly of Java* (London: 1850).

the *Brief Account of Galaba* (噶喇吧紀略, *Galaba Jilüe*) by Cheng Xunwo (程遜我), another private teacher who spent several years on Java during the 1730s just before the great massacre.⁹ These and a few other sources will be discussed in more detail in the last chapter.

The Chinese Annals of Batavia

Nowhere does the author of the *Kai Ba Lidai Shiji* explain what compelled him to write his urban memoir or to compose it in the way he did. Nonetheless, it is clear that he had two objectives in mind: to reconstruct the list of people involved in the administrative duties of the Kong Koan during the VOC period, and to tell in detail the terrible events of 1740. He larded the dry data about the tenures of the Chinese captains, lieutenants, and *boedelmeesters* with a mishmash of interesting anecdotes and stories about the ups and downs of Batavia's Chinese population. Obviously with some Dutch help, the author was able to collect the correct dates about the successive Dutch governors general throughout the whole VOC period.¹⁰ We remain in the dark about the identity of the author, but as will be shown below, it seems plausible to suggest that he was the secretary of the Kong Koan.

The original manuscript was copied several times during the course of the nineteenth century for, as far as we know, there are at least five handwritten manuscripts. In 1953, Professor Xu Yunqiao (otherwise spelled Hsu Yun-Tsiao, Hsu Yun-Ts'iao, or Hsü Yün-ch'iao, 1905–1981), the well-known Singapore historian of Chinese life overseas, published an excellent annotated edition in the *Nanyang Xuebao* journal that we have gladly consulted for our translation.¹¹ This was based on two manuscripts at his disposal, but Professor

---

9   We have gladly consulted Claudine Salmon's excellent French translation of this interesting source, 'Un Chinois à Java (1729–1736)'. *Bulletin de l'École française d'Extrême-Orient* 59 (1972): 279–318. See also Claudine Salmon, 'The Massacre of 1740 as Reflected in a Contemporary Chinese Narrative'.
10 He probably collected the data on the governors general from the *Naamboek van den Hoog Edelen Gestrengen Heeren Commissarissen Generaal over geheel Nederlandsch Indië en Cabo de Goede Hoop, item van den Wel-Edelen Heeren der Hoge Indiasche Regeering zo tot, als buiten Batavia* (Batavia: Pieter van Geemen, 1786).
11 Hsu Yun-Tsiao (Xu Yunqiao), ed., '開吧歷代史紀, The early Accounts of Chinese in Batavia (a revised and annotated edition)' *Nanyang Xuebao* 南洋學報 [Journal of the South Seas Society] 9:1 (1953): 1–63.

Xu was unable to refer to the two versions now kept at the East Asian Library of the Leiden University Library.¹²

The English Reverend Walter Henry Medhurst (1796–1857), a prospective missionary in the service of the London Missionary Society, deserves credit for being the first scholar to 'discover' the *Kai Ba Lidai Shiji*. Upon his arrival in Asia in 1816 Medhurst learned to speak, read, and write Chinese at the society's mission station in Malacca, because at the time it was still impossible to study in China itself, which was closed to all Europeans save for a few Roman Catholic priests. After residing more than twenty years in Malacca, Penang, and Batavia, Medhurst was finally able to settle in Shanghai in 1842, when the Treaty of Nanjing opened that port to Western enterprise. During his stay in Batavia, the Reverend Medhurst was not only involved in spreading the gospel, but he also functioned as an informal liaison between the Dutch colonial administration and the local Chinese community leaders of the Kong Koan. It was at this time that he translated the *Kai Ba Lidai Shiji*, which may have been pointed out to him by one of the Chinese officers—or even by the learned Chen Naiyu (陳乃玉), who, in 1832 and 1837, wrote two prefaces and re-edited the manuscript.

After his arrival in Shanghai, Medhurst continued to carry out translation work on all kinds of texts, including the Bible and official documents, and he also composed a Chinese-English and English-Chinese dictionary. In addition, the indefatigable vicar wrote several books about China to enlighten the Western reading public about the recently opened 'Middle Kingdom'. It was here, too, that he published his translation of the *Haidao Yizhi*, the 'Island memories' of Wang Dahai. A few biographies of local eminencies and a description of Batavia from this book have been included in chapter 10.¹³

Although Medhurst's original English translation of the *Kai Ba Lidai Shiji* no longer survives, his efforts have not been completely lost. In 1841, shortly before Medhurst's departure for Shanghai, the editors of the *Tijdschrift voor Neêrland's Indië*, P. Mijer and W.R. van Hoëvell, published a Dutch re-adaptation of his English translation in their journal.¹⁴ That we are dealing with a paraphrased rendering becomes clear once the Dutch text is compared with the published Chinese text edition by Professor Xu Yunqiao and the two versions kept at

---

12   Both manuscripts have been digitized and are online in the Kong Koan archive site of the Leiden University Library.
13   Medhurst, *Ong-Tae-Hae, The Chinaman Abroad*.
14   W.R. van Hoëvell and P. Meijer, eds., 'Chronologische geschiedenis van Batavia, geschreven door een Chinees, uit het Chineesch vertaald door W.H. Medhurst', *Tijdschrift voor Neêrland's Indië* 3:2 (1840): 1–145.

Leiden University. The two Dutch editors seem to have embellished, or should we say 'orientalised', the original tales in the text.

One more scholar to whom we feel heavily indebted is B. Hoetink. A hundred years ago this scholar wrote several excellent articles about the Chinese officers of Batavia. This sinologist, a student of Gustaaf Schlegel, the first Dutch professor of Chinese language at Leiden University, served twenty-eight years as a Chinese interpreter and other functions in the service of the colonial administration of the Netherlands Indies before his retirement in 1906. He played an important role in improving the conditions under which Chinese labour was recruited for the Sumatran tobacco plantations at the end of the nineteenth century, and later served as inspector in Deli, North Sumatra, overseeing improvements to the harsh labour conditions of the Chinese coolies employed on tobacco plantations.[15] After his retirement he devoted considerable effort to the study of the Chinese officers who served during the VOC period and wrote three very informative biographies about them.[16] Thanks to the precise personal data that he collected about the Chinese officers in the (Dutch-language) VOC archives in The Hague and Batavia (he even consulted the rich notarial archives), we can now better discern fact from fiction.

---

15 Koos Kuiper, *The Early Dutch Sinologists (1854–1900), Training in Holland and China, Functions in the Netherlands Indies* (Leiden: Brill 2017), 888–895, 1011–1019.

16 See B. Hoetink, 'Chineesche officieren te Batavia onder de Compagnie', *BKI* 78 (1922): 1–136; idem, 'Ni Hoekong, kapitein der Chineezen te Batavia in 1740', *BKI* 74 (1918): 447–518; idem, 'So Bing Kong. Het eerste hoofd der Chineezen te Batavia', *BKI* 73 (1917): 344–415, and *BKI* 79 (1923): 1–44; and, idem, 'De weduwe van kapitein Siqua', *Chung Hwa Hui Tsa Chih* 2: 1–2 (1918): 16–25.

CHAPTER 4

Critical Comments on the *Kai Ba Lidai Shiji* and Its Genesis

Notwithstanding the excellent Chinese text edition of the *Kai Ba Lidai Shiji* by Xu Yunqiao, no attempt has been made in western sinological literature to look seriously at this historical source. Maybe philologists felt that this vernacular history of an overseas Chinese urban community in a Dutch colonial setting fell outside their field of interest.[1]

The *Kai Ba Lidai Shiji* may be an ugly duckling because it barely corresponds with any of the existing genres of Chinese historiography. The annalistic approach (编年, *biannian*)—literally, 'stringing together the years'—goes back all the way to the Spring and Autumn (春秋) Classic by Confucius, a consecutive chronicle of events, each year having a detailed account of the various occurrences but offering quite a different sort of content. Given the fact that it is an urban history, one might think that there would be some connection with the well-known genre of the local gazetteer (地方志, *difangzhi*), but as far as the composition and content go, it is clear that we are dealing with a completely different type of narrative. The traditional Chinese local gazetteer contains a catalogue of subjects that are dealt with in separate chapters: topographical features, official buildings, water conservancy, academies, successful candidates of imperial examinations, fiscal information, local customs, biographies, inscriptions, and miscellaneous topics.[2] If some of these subjects are touched upon in the *Kai Ba Lidai Shiji*, the approach is seemingly haphazard.

---

1   From the myopic point of view of the sinologist *pur sang*, this may be a logical reaction, as the following brief aside may illustrate. In 2014, one of the authors was invited to give a talk at Cambridge University for an audience of sinologists. To his own surprise, no less than to that of the audience, it turned out that the university library possessed none of the by-then thirteen volumes of the *Gong An Bu* or the other publications on the Kong Koan of Batavia by Xiamen University Press. One of the librarians who was present admitted that this was a typical example of institutional blinders: the employee of the Chinese library does not order books on Southeast Asia, while the employee purchasing books on Southeast Asia does not order books in Chinese. Since then we have verified the same phenomenon in other university libraries.
2   Endymion Wilkinson, *Chinese History: A Manual* (Cambridge: Harvard University Press, 2000), 154–67.

The anonymous author composed his historical narrative with few literary frills, freely using vocabulary from the Minnan dialect spoken in southern Fujian, and sprinkling his text with characters that reproduce the pronunciation of Malay and Dutch names and terms.[3] Presenting a gallery of more or less gripping episodes, the author comes to Batavia's history with his own priorities. It is exactly these syncretic features, so characteristic of the Chinese overseas experience in general, that makes the text interesting, apart from the simple fact that there are almost no other contemporary texts written by Chinese authors describing overseas Chinese urban life.

Another unique characteristic of the *Kai Ba Lidai Shiji* is that, writing in a straightforward style, the author expresses his sympathies and antipathies without reservation or concern about hurting people's reputations. Although copyists later added their own comments to the text, there is no official censor to be seen in the text. For all the colourful anecdotes sprinkled over the dry summing up of the tenures of the various, captains, lieutenants, and boedelmeesters, the *Kai Ba Lidai Shiji* has its kaleidoscopic effects, but it is by no means just a pretty rendering of past events, and here we are not just referring to the horrid tale of the massacre. In the final analysis, it is basically a work of reconstruction, or should we say constructive invention.

By interpreting the past behaviour of prominent Chinese and Dutch individuals alike, the anonymous historian holds a mirror up to his readers in an effort to keep them on the straight and narrow path of proper behaviour. He engages our interest and demands our attention by lauding people for their good deeds and criticizing them for their wayward behaviour. Those who, in his view, have not behaved themselves await punishment. A case in point is the already mentioned tragicomical anecdote about the recalcitrant pallbearers carrying the coffin of the one-time boedelmeester Qiu Zuguan. While on their way to the cemetery, reflecting on the fact that 'he had had a crooked heart, churning out plans to harm people', they suddenly took such an intense dislike to the deceased that they dropped his coffin on the road and refused to carry it any further. Several other Chinese individuals are said to have been punished by heaven for their misconduct with the worst fate that can befall a Chinese male: to die without issue.

The author is equally opinionated about various Indonesians and Dutchmen: the quarrelsome visiting prince from Ternate; the self-aggrandizing Captain Jonker of Manipa; the faithless wife of the sultan of Banten; and the overbearing Malay captain who kidnapped a beautiful girl for his son. All are criticized for their inability to restrain their passions. Nor does he spare VOC

---

3 See the attached Name Lists (pp. 246–89) and Glossary (pp. 290–92).

officials: Governor General Diederik Durven is nicknamed 'the godless King', on account of his lewd behaviour, while the author holds up for special censure the ineffective, fainthearted Governor General Adriaen Valckenier and his nemesis, the unscrupulous and ambitious Gustaaf Willem van Imhoff, as well as the corrupt Chinese Captain Ni Hoekong, all three of whom he holds responsible for the terrible massacre of October 1740.

Notwithstanding the wealth of anecdotes of human interest throughout the narrative, and the factual treatment of the Chinese massacre of 1740, today's reader occasionally feels disappointed that so little is said about daily life in Batavia. Yet considering that the author addressed himself to his own inner circle of the Chinese elite, he must have thought that more detailed information about how daily affairs were organized and administered within the community was familiar and therefore of little interest to his readers. Consequently, he has little to say about the familial ties among the Chinese officers serving in various ports throughout the archipelago, or about their relations with their families back in their hometowns in China, although a few surviving inscriptions in temples around Xiamen testify to the fact that these relations could endure.[4] We learn hardly anything about the various ways in which the Chinese officers themselves were involved in shipping either to China or within the archipelago, and so on. For those activities, one must consult the VOC archives or the *gong'an bu* of the nineteenth century.

As the annotation based on a comparison between the Chinese sources and the VOC documentation shows, the Chinese manuscript is frequently inaccurate when it comes to recording dates. This is rather ironic because by providing a profusion of dates, and even indicating that this or that person held office for so many years, months, and days, the author has tried to impress on the mind of the reader how very precise his annotation is. But given the fact that he did not compose his historical narrative until the last decade of the eighteenth century, it is clear that he must have encountered considerable difficulty in collecting materials for the previous two hundred years. Regarding events of the seventeenth century, the author was groping in the dark and had to depend on

---

4   These inscriptions bear out how close the ongoing religious ties continued to be in the Xiamen-Batavia corridor. The *Chongxing Longchi Beiji* (重興龍池碑記), Inscription for Rebuilding Longchiyan Temple) can be found in the Longchiyan temple in Longchiyan in the district of Tong'an (同安龍池岩). The *Baguo Yuanzhu Beiji* (吧國緣主碑記, Inscription of Donors from Kalapa) has been preserved in the Qingjiao Ciji Donggong temple of Xiamen (廈門青礁慈濟東宮). Both inscriptions record the contributions of overseas Chinese from Galaba (Batavia) for the restoration of the Longchiyan and Ciji Donggong temples, respectively, in Kangxi 35 (1696) and Kangxi 36 (1697).

hearsay for biographical information on the Chinese officers and their terms in office. Had he had access to the Dutch archival sources, this would not have caused any problems, but he clearly did not have them at hand, because, as we shall see, he had it completely wrong when he explained the aftermath of the massacre. Again, it should be remembered that we are dealing with a work of historical reconstruction. As Xu Yunqiao has pointed out, the descriptions of the events after the 1770s are quite reliable, but the further the author harks back to the past, the murkier his portrayal of events becomes. Yet just because much of what he recorded may have been based on pure hearsay and Chinese whispers does not mean it is of less interest, because the stories he tells must have been part of local lore and probably true in their broad outline if not necessarily in their detail.

How then did the author set out to construct and compose his tale? What template did he use? As we have seen, he did not really have a traditional Chinese example to follow. First, he had to create a basic chronological structure for a narrative in which several concerns overlapped. How was he to allot space to the various individuals, institutions, physical objects, important events, and stories of human interest that he planned to deal with in his narrative? He did so by opting for a temporal, annalistic approach and presenting his data in a chronological, year-by-year account. He created, as it were, a family tree of the administration of Chinese Batavia.

The next major problem was deciding on which calendar to use. This problem he solved by applying both the Chinese lunar calendar *and* the western Gregorian calendar. In the Qing dynasty, dates were generally given in the form of the reign-year of the current emperor, followed by the lunar month and day. The same applies for the present text: Chinese dates give the year of dynastic rule and the cyclical characters of the calendar of the ten Heavenly Stems and the twelve Earthly Branches, the *tiangan dizhi* (天干地支), but in addition to this, the dates are given according to the Dutch calendar, which are preceded by He (和), short for the Ming dynasty name commonly used in the Indies: Helan (和蘭). To give an example, the opening lines of the *Kai Ba Lidai Shiji* run as follows: 'In the twelfth moon of the 38th year of the Wanli [萬曆] emperor of the Great Ming [大明] dynasty, *gengxu* [庚戌, the cyclic year of the Chinese lunar calendar], the first month of the Dutch year 1610'.

This same triple calendar is applied from beginning to end. The imperial calendar legitimized the rule of the reigning emperor over 'all under heaven' (天下, *tianxia*), while the Gregorian calendar legitimized Dutch rule over Batavia. Even today, events of the imperial past are dated in China according to the dynastic calendar rather than by the western calendar. The transition from the Ming to the Qing dynasty, the 'change of the mandate of Heaven'

(革命, *geming*) in 1644 was, therefore, a serious matter. It was not just a change of political regime, but a succession of events in which everything was in upheaval and out of balance. As one of the Chinese annotators of the text remarks:

> In China at the time, dust storms and terrible rains raged. At night, tens of thousands of horses and wild animals fought with each other, their shrieks spread everywhere, snow and ice were almost one foot thick. It is said that footprints of giants and elephants were observed.[5]

It is well known that Chinese living overseas for a considerable time continued to defy the legitimacy of the Manchu government by refusing to change their hair style (that is, by adopting the pigtail, or queue) or by steadfastly maintaining for several decades a calendar according to the reign periods of the Nan Ming (Southern Ming period). The Chinese captains of Malacca, for instance, are known to have refused to write down the name of the reign period off the current Qing emperor but preferred to use the imaginary Longfei 龍飛 period instead. The same applies to the example given in the entry for the year 1775 of the *Kai Ba Lidai Shiji*, when the events of 1739–40 are dated Longfei 4 instead of Qianlong 4. (See note 277, p. 176)

If the calendars provide the chronological backbone, or rather the trunk, of the *Kai Ba Lidai Shiji*, the successive tenures of the Dutch governors general, combined with short characterisations of each of these princes or kings (王, *wang*) or viceroys, as the author calls them, form the branches to which the tenures of the Chinese officers are conveniently attached. According to the author, the appointments of the governors general were confirmed by the 'sovereign in the mother country'. To show the importance of the Chinese captaincy, he asserts that the appointments of the Chinese officers were also ratified in the same way. He obviously had no clear idea how the Dutch East India Company was run, namely, by the joint directorship of the Gentlemen XVII who, by a special charter, were authorized to rule the overseas territories in the name of the States General of the Seven United Provinces of the Netherlands.[6] When, however, in 1748, after a long period without stadtholders, Prince William IV of Orange-Nassau was re-installed, he was also awarded the title of *opperbewindhebber* (supreme director) of the VOC. From that moment on, the 'sovereign in the mother country' was personified by the Prince of Orange.

---

5 *Kai Ba Lidai Shiji*, 1644.
6 By the second half of the eighteenth century, the appointments of the governors general were indeed confirmed by the Stadtholders Willem IV and Willem V of Orange-Nassau in their position of *opperbewindhebber* (supreme director).

FIGURE 5   *Wooden tablet of Captain Oey Bian Kong. 1792*
ASIAN LIBRARY, LEIDEN UNIVERSITY

Genesis of the Text

This brings up the question of the genesis of the *Kai Ba Lidai Shiji*. How did the author hit upon the idea to write this history? This we will probably never be able to ascertain, but it is not impossible that he was inspired by some events or a particular request to take up the job of recording the history of Chinese Batavia. This leads us to the following observation, which may also help us uncover the identity of the author himself.

When Oey Bian Kong (黃綿光, Huang Mianguang, *aka* 黃綿公) was appointed captain in 1791, he commissioned the secretary of the Kong Koan, Wu Zuanshou (吳纘綬), to provide a text for a large wooden panel that he wished to hang on the wall of the office on the occasion of his accession.[7] Out of deference to his predecessors, Captain Oey wished to show the full pedigree of the captains who had held office before him. This wooden panel and four others

---

7 Wu Zuanshou was the son of the former Lieutenant Wu Panshui (吳泮水). The full texts of the wooden panels have been published by Xu Yunqiao, 'Baguo Gongtang yu Huaqiao Shiliao' 吧國公堂與華僑史料 (The Chinese Council of Batavia and Overseas Chinese sources), *Journal of the South Seas Society* 南洋學報 12 (1955): 17–22.

ordered by Captain Oey's successors still exist and adorn the walls of the Asian Library of Leiden University.

The text of the oldest tablet begins with extolling the first captain, Bencon, alias Su Mingguang, because he brought prosperity to the city by sailing to his home province of Fujian to invite his fellow countrymen to come and engage in trade at the newly founded port of Batavia. Successfully so, for the following year he returned with several junks in his wake, and this was the beginning of the lasting link with the homeland. Or, to put it in Philip Kuhn's terminology, Bencon created the corridor that was to serve the folks back home and the sojourners in Batavia. Making a big jump in time, the panel then mentions that in 1742, after the 'great uproar', Lin Mingge (Lim Bing Kong) was appointed captain, and that the Kong Koan began its official work at that time. Finally, Oey Bian Kong declares that 'following the examples set by his illustrious predecessors, he will devote himself to the well-being of his people'. This promise of proper behaviour is followed by the list with the names of all the Chinese captains until then.

As noted, the wooden panel describes the massacre of 1740 simply as the 'great uproar' without further elaboration. It seems only natural that Wu Zuanshou, the Chinese secretary who researched the names of all the Chinese captains so far, felt obliged to do the same thing for all the other Chinese officers and employees (lieutenants, boedelmeesters, undertakers, and so on) as well as to record in full the whole miserable tale of the Chinese rebellion and the massacre that followed. And thus the *Kai Ba Lidai Shiji* may well have been conceived.

CHAPTER 5

A Diachronic Overview of the Contents of the *Kai Ba Lidai Shiji*

The initial half-century period covered by the *Kai Ba Lidai Shiji*, 1619–70, begins with the appointment of Su Mingguang (Bencon), as the first Chinese captain immediately after the foundation of the city. Curiously the second Chinese Captain, Lin Liuge (林六哥, Lim Lacco), a Muslim Chinese who had previously served as leader of the Chinese community in Banten and later was instrumental in mediating between Batavia and Banten in troubled times, is completely ignored. Nor does his name figure on the wooden board listing the names of all Chinese captains. Whether this was intentional is unclear, but given the fact that in the eighteenth century a distinction was made between the *peranakan* Chinese Muslims and other Chinese, this suggestion seems not unreasonable.

The first part of the *Kai Ba Lidai Shiji* mentions the frenzied building activities and rural infrastructure projects that marked the first decades of Batavia's existence. The introduction of the physical outlay of the city is followed by an account of the establishment of the various tax farms, almost all of which eventually wound up in Chinese hands. The hilarious story of an improperly dressed and barefoot, but rich, Chinese who showed up at the warehouse where the annual auction of the tax farms occurred and outbid his countrymen is told with great relish, though not without the moralistic last word that this behaviour set the tone for the subsequent moral decline of the Chinese.

Upon the death of Captain Yan Erguan, alias Siqua (顏二觀) in 1668, Governor General Joan Maetsuycker decided to provisionally designate Siqua's Balinese widow as the new leader of the Chinese community instead of selecting a new Chinese community leader for the captaincy. Dismayed, the author of the *Chinese Annals* concludes that this 'hen cackling like a rooster in the morning' foretold the overturning of the *yin* (陰) and *yang* (陽) principles, and even the ultimate disaster between the Chinese and the Dutch.[1]

On 14 June 1678 Governor General Rijcklof van Goens and the Council of the Indies decided—'because the captaincy of the Chinese inhabitants of this city of Batavia has remained vacant since the passing away of Siqua in 1665 and has been partly been taken over by his widow, and because now again for some time various requests have been made'—to formally reappoint a Chinese

---

1 *Kai Ba Lidai Shiji*, 1648.

captain.² With the investiture of Captain Tsoa Wanjock (蔡煥玉 Cai Huanyu) a pattern was set for the subsequent rituals surrounding the appointments of Chinese captains. In the eighteenth century this ceremonial developed into a triumphant parade involving hundreds of participants.³

The Qing government's repeal of a several decades old ban on overseas trade in 1684 caused a rapid increase in the number of Chinese immigrants reaching Batavia and ushered in a new era in the port city's history. The Chinese author draws attention to two new and very important institutions that, according to him, were inaugurated around that time at the instigation of a member of the Chinese elite: the *weeskamer* (orphans chamber) for the well-being of Chinese immigrants and their families, and the appointment of the Chinese boedelmeester, or inheritance curator. As already pointed out, these institutions had been established several decades earlier on the initiative of the VOC administration and originally against the will of the Chinese themselves.

The author does stress that both the hospital and the board of curators became important pillars of Chinese society in Batavia. The introduction of new tax farms, the extensive enlargement of cemeteries, and the establishment of schools and temples show that the community grew substantially in the 1680–1720 period. If various anecdotes sprinkled throughout the tale already point to a moral decline among the Chinese inhabitants, the author sees the 1710s as the start of a period of natural disasters and social unrest such as conspiracies, robberies, and murders by bandits in the surrounding countryside, all of which were a prelude to the Chinese rebellion and subsequent massacre in 1740.

We will not venture to give a summary of the events leading up to that calamity here. What is important to mention at this juncture is that the Chinese account of the rebellion and the massacre that occurred in the first week of October 1740 is corroborated in most of its details by the Dutch sources in the VOC archive.⁴ Three culprits behind the drama are singled out: the pleasure-loving Chinese Captain Ni Hoekong (連富光 Lian Fuguang), who lacked compassion for his fellow Chinese and neglected his duties, the irresolute Governor General Adriaen Valckenier, and his arch-enemy, the overambitious second in

---

2 See Appendix 1, *The Appointment of Captain Tsoa Wanjock*.

3 See for instance the description in the *Kai Ba Lidai Shiji* of the investiture of Captain Tang Enge on 15 February 1775.

4 Vermeulen, *De Chineezen te Batavia en de troebelen van 1740*. For a partial English translation see, Tan Yeok Seong, 'The Chinese in Batavia and the Troubles of 1740', *Journal of the South Seas Society* 9:1 (1953): 1–68. A new monograph on the Chinese rebellion and the subsequent massacre of Batavia's Chinese citizenry in 1740 based on recently discovered sources is under way.

command, Gustaaf Willem, Baron Van Imhoff. That these two gentlemen profoundly hated each other and thereby impaired unity of command when it was most needed does not escape the attention of the Chinese author.

There follows a detailed, day-by-day description of the uprising by the Chinese rebels in the Batavian hinterland, the siege and the fighting around the city walls, and finally the massacre of the Chinese in town. Many were slaughtered without offering any resistance, but some who saw their lives in peril were prepared to defend themselves, including a boedelmeester who was caught red-handed with a carriage full of hidden arms.

The account of this disaster is followed by moral comments by the Chinese commentators who added their own views. Interestingly, they put the onus on Van Imhoff while the Dutch accounts tend to point to Valckenier. Here the author runs astray because he completely misunderstands the true course of events in the colonial administration immediately after the massacre. His account has it that Van Imhoff assumed power after the rebellion was suppressed and then sent Valckenier to the Netherlands to be punished. In reality, it was the other way around. On 6 December 1740, Governor General Valckenier arrested Van Imhoff and two fellow councilors of the Indies for insubordination and put the three under house arrest pending the departure of the first homeward-bound ships. Van Imhoff and his comrades left on 10 January 1741 for Holland, where they had to defend themselves against Valckenier's charges that they had committed 'insubordination'. Upon their arrival, however, they quickly cleared themselves of Valckenier's accusations and then in turn accused the governor general of having given the signal to start the mass killing, and initiated a civil lawsuit against him for defamation.

Van Imhoff returned to Batavia on 26 May 1743, because ironically, unbeknownst to either himself or Valckenier, the Gentlemen XVII had appointed him governor general before news of the massacre became known in Holland. In the meantime, Valckenier had left Batavia after receiving notice of his dismissal on 6 November 1741. He was arrested upon his arrival at Cape Town and sent back to Batavia to face a lawsuit on account of his conduct during the Chinese massacre. Awaiting a final verdict, he remained under arrest in Batavia Castle for almost ten years before his death on 20 June 1751, even having outlived his great antagonist Van Imhoff by a few months.

The period after the 1740s is by far the best documented in the *Kai Ba Lidai Shiji*, most likely because it was only then that the Kong Koan was officially established and provided with its own secretary who, among other tasks, managed the Chinese Council's archives, which meant that ample Chinese archival material must have been at the author's disposal. In the 1750s, an account is given showing how two Chinese lieutenants saved the Company by deploying their private troops to beat the army of the sultan of Banten. This served to prove that manly Chinese could also fight and be brave. One of the Chinese commentators even insinuates that if the Chinese had been as brave in 1740, events might have taken a very different turn.

Many insights into social life are presented in the following pages, such as Chinese financial scandals surrounding the handing out of false permits and counterfeiting money, and religious events such as a purifying *jiao* (醮) ritual to collect and send to heaven all those wandering ghosts still roaming Batavia and the Ommelanden thirty years after the massacre. The author also comments with nostalgia about the pomp and circumstance surrounding the installation of Captain Tang Enge in 1775, an event he must have witnessed himself, because he laments that by the time of his writing, none of the heroes of that magnificent spectacle were still alive.[5] Captain Tang Engguan himself died within a year of his investiture, which leads one of the Chinese commentators of the text to add scathingly that this 'grand ceremony fit for the imperial court' provoked the wrath of heaven 'which should teach a lesson to the later generations'.

The last twenty years of the *Chinese Annals of Batavia* include many references to social and political unrest, such as the growing agitation and insecurity in the Ommelanden and the outbreak of the Fourth Anglo-Dutch War (1780–84). The author also becomes increasingly moralistic in tone. People who misbehave are punished either within their lifetime or after. Sly schemers who betrayed Chinese refugees after the 1740 massacre or unreliable recruiters of Chinese sailors for the VOC reap short-term financial profits, but in the end the punishment from heaven awaits them because they remain without offspring. The economic impact on Batavia society of the Fourth Anglo-Dutch War can be easily discerned from the measures that the VOC administration takes in terms of financial measures to stay afloat. No less remarkable are the frequent entries about recruitment of native soldiers including even the Chinese themselves.

The oldest (Liem) manuscript terminates in 1793, but the other versions continue two more years and provide some extra information such as the visit to Batavia of the tight-lipped British envoy to the Chinese court, George Macartney, 1st Earl Macartney. The final story about Zheng Chunguan, a swindler who, together with his family, is taught a lesson and meets his doom, has all the traits of a moralist's tale. The most remarkable entries are, however, the curious comments about the confusing events taking place in Europe in the

---

5 This remark makes sense if the anonymous author wrote his account in the late 1790s, but makes Chen Naiyu's claims to authorship quite absurd.

aftermath of the French Revolution. Peace on earth is predicted within five years: 'In 1800, the peoples of all kinds in the world will return in the fold of one government, and will all get along like brothers, be in accord with customs and laws, and hold in awe and veneration Heaven's will'. Alas! That expectation was not fulfilled.

In Conclusion

Summing up the above, what does the *Kai Ba Lidai Shiji* amount to as an historical text? Although parts of the *Chinese Annals of Batavia* consist of bare enumerations without any plot, the author has tried to enliven his narrative with entertaining stories. If there is an underlying motive to be found in these annals, it is that the author did not necessarily mean to give every Chinese officer of the Kong Koan his place in history, but attempted to interpret the present by providing exemplary tales of yore. His tale suggests that doom awaits a society that does not follow properly the tenets of the ancients.

Whatever its defects as an historical source, thanks to its characterisations of various Chinese, Indonesian, and Dutch individuals, the *Kai Ba Lidai Shiji* provides us with an insight into the mind of an educated Chinese observer of Batavia at the end of the eighteenth century, and shows his thoughts about the curious Sino-Dutch *convivencia* that existed during the era of the VOC.

CHAPTER 6

Editorial Notes on the Sources of the *Kai Ba Lidai Shiji*

According to Chen Yusong (陳育崧, Tan Yeok Seong), who collaborated with Professor Xu Yunqiao (許雲樵) in the publication of the special issue of the *Nanyang Xuebao* (南洋學報) dedicated to the annotated edition of *Kai Ba Lidai Shiji*, there must have circulated among Batavia's elite several manuscript versions which slightly differed from each other.[1] First of all, there was the text that Medhurst translated into English, and this version was later published re-adapted in Dutch as the *Chronologische Geschiedenis van Batavia, Geschreven door een Chinees*, in the 1840 issue of the *Tijdschrift voor Neêrland's Indië*. This Chinese manuscript most likely was in the possession of the Kong Koan of Batavia (吧國公堂). Before this copy was destroyed or taken away during the war, it was fortunately transcribed by Chen Yusong in 1940. It is one of the manuscripts that Xu Yunqiao used for his annotated combined text edition of the *Kai Ba Lidai Shiji*.

The other version that Xu Yunqiao used was the text that was published by Zhang Zitian (張子田) as *Huaqiao Kai Ba Lidai Shilüe* (華僑開吧歷代史略) in the *Qiaowu Xunkan* journal (僑務旬刊) 130 (21 July 1924) and later again by He Haiming (何海鳴) in the *Huaqiao Congshu* (華僑叢書) (issue of 21 July 1941).[2] These nowadays difficult to access publications were based on a manuscript version made by Yang Bodong (楊伯東) in 1896, which Zhang Zitian had recovered in the town of Sukabumi in 1921. Like the Kong Koan version transcribed by Chen Yusong, the Yang Bodong version included before the main text an *Ode of Galaba* (噶喇吧賦) as well two short prefaces (小序, 又序) written in 1832 and 1837 by the learned Batavia-based literatus Chen Naiyu.[3] In addition, the *Brief Account of Galaba* (*Galaba Jilüe*, 噶喇吧紀略), written by Cheng Rijie (程日炌), alias Cheng Xunwo (程遜我), was appended to it. The Kong Koan manuscript also contained lists, drawn up by a certain Mr. Yang Ying (楊應), of the names of, respectively, (a) the Dutch governors general, (b) the Chinese

---

1 Chen Yusong, 'Preface', in Hsu Yun-Tsiao, 'The Early Accounts of Chinese in Batavia, A Revised and Annotated Edition' 開吧歷代史紀校注, *Nanyang Xuebao* 南洋學報 9:1 (1953): 6.
2 Their prefaces can both be found in *ibid.*, 5.
3 We have decided not to include an English version of the *Ode* because the contents of this hard-to-translate *tour de force* of flowery literary allusions add little to the main text.

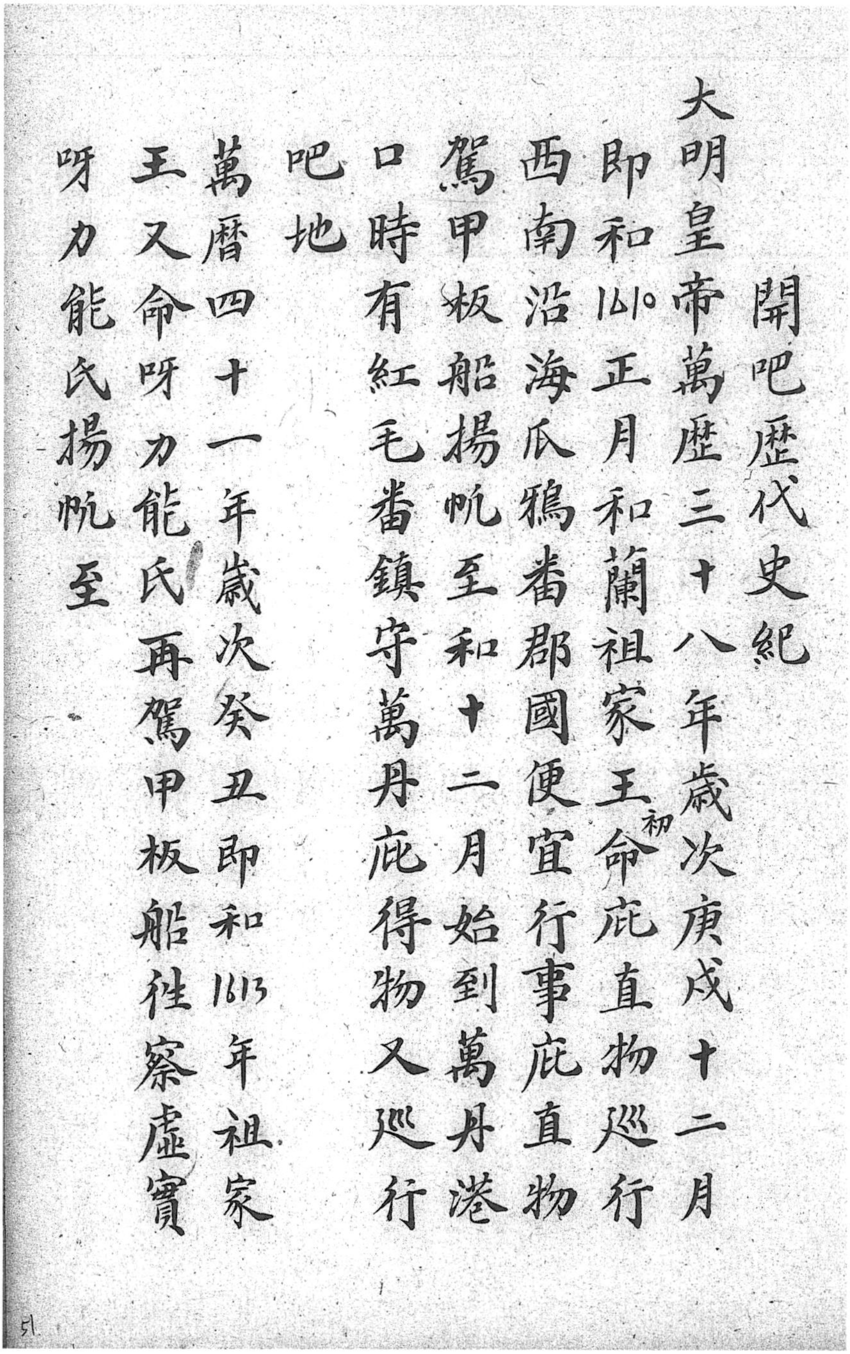

開吧歷代史紀

大明皇帝萬歷三十八年歲次庚戌十二月
即和 1610 正月和蘭祖家王命庇直物巡行
西南沿海瓜鴉峇郡國便宜行事庇直物
駕甲板船揚帆至和十二月始到萬丹港
口時有紅毛峇鎮守萬丹庇得物又巡行
吧地
萬歷四十一年歲次癸丑即和 1613 年祖家
王又命呀力能氏再駕甲板船往察虛實
呀力能氏揚帆至

FIGURE 6 *The Leiden manuscript*
ASIAN LIBRARY, LEIDEN UNIVERSITY

captains, (c) the Chinese lieutenants, and (d) the Chinese boedelmeesters. As Xu Yunqiao has pointed out, Yang Bodong also added lists with the names of (e) the Chinese secretaries, (f) the Chinese *soldaten* (soldiers, the lowest-ranked employees at the Kong Tong), and (g) the undertakers (土公, *tugong*), or supervisors of the Chinese cemeteries.

For his annotated text edition in the *Nanyang Xuebao* of 1953, Xu Yunqiao merged and edited both the Kong Koan and Yang Bodong versions into a single text, carefully pointing out the differences between the texts and including the comments that had been added by various readers, such as the anonymous 'John Chinaman' or Tangren shi (唐人氏), Lin Cuipu (林萃璞), and Lin Jiuru (林九如), all of them probably Batavia literati. From Yang Bodong's manuscript he added two comments by Chen Xuelan (陳雪瀾) in 1894, and two comments written by Yang Bodong himself. We have included all these comments in our translation.

According to Chen Naiyu's two prefaces, the history of the first twenty-five Dutch governors in Batavia from 1619 to 1740 had been recorded by an anonymous predecessor, but he then somewhat conspiratorially asserts that he felt compelled to record the history after 1740 because he thought it was helpful for the world 'to write down the truth rather than express feelings'. He goes on to say that it took him five years to finish the subsequent history. Why he did not extend the history to his own lifetime but stopped in the 1790s he does not explain. Whatever the case may be, on the basis of Chen Naiyu's assertions Xu Yunqiao quite wrongly decided that he should be recognised as the author of at least the second part of the history. However, for reasons that will be introduced below, we believe however Chen Naiyu certainly was not the author, even if he played an important role in editing the versions of the *Kai Ba Lidai Shiji* that Xu Yunqiao used for his edition.

In addition to the two versions perused by Xu Yunqiao mentioned above, there exist two more manuscript versions. Leiden University Library possesses a copy of the *Kai Ba Lidai Shiji* that contains Chen Naiyu's (陳乃玉) *Ode of Galaba*, as well the two prefaces that he wrote in 1832 and 1837. It also includes the aforementioned lists of Dutch governors general and Chinese captains, lieutenants, boedelmeesters, secretaries, soldiers, and Chinese undertakers. All these lists end by the year 1840.

The Leiden manuscript, a gift by B. Hoetink to the University Library, was transcribed from a manuscript version that was acquired by the Bataviaasch Genootschap in 1909. According to the *Notulen van de algemeene en directievergaderingen van het Bataviaasch Genootschap van Kunsten en Wetenschappen*, XLVII-1909, 160-161 the secretary B.A.J. van Wettum presented to the manuscript department a copy of the *Kai Ba Lidai Shiji* which had been acquired from the Goan Sing firm. We have not been able to trace that manuscript back in the National Library of Indonesia, which now keeps all the books of the former Bataviaasch Genootschap.

The Leiden copy bears exactly the same title as the copy of the Kong Koan manuscript, *Kai Ba Lidai Shiji* (開吧歷代史紀), and also covers the period from 1610 to 1795, and it contains the same comments as the Kong Koan manuscript that was copied by Chen Yusong. Based on the dating of Chen Naiyu's prefaces, it is quite possible that he may have brought the text to Medhurst's attention.

Finally, in 2005 Leiden University library acquired yet another copy donated to the Friends of the Kong Koan Foundation by Ir. Liem Ho Soei (林和瑞, Lin Herui) who in turn had received it as a personal present from an old friend of his, Drs. Oey Giok Po, the first curator of the Echols Collection on Southeast Asia of Cornell University. For obvious reasons, we have chosen to name this version the 'Liem manuscript', after this benefactor, who played such an important role in the rescue operations of the Kong Koan archive.

The Liem manuscript differs in several respects from the manuscripts discussed above. First of all, its title, *Kai Yaolaoba Lidaishi Quanlu*, 'The complete records of the opening up of Yaolaoba' (開咬𠺢吧歷代史全錄) is different. Furthermore, it contains neither Chen Naiyu's *Ode of Galaba* (噶喇吧賦) nor his prefaces. The appended lists of the Dutch governors general and those of the Chinese captains, lieutenants, boedelmeesters, and secretaries end before 1800, and those of the soldiers and undertakers are lacking. Obviously, the Liem manuscript therefore antedates the other manuscripts. There are also numerous discrepancies in the text between this manuscript and the others.[4]

Like the Leiden and both Batavia manuscripts, the Liem manuscript starts in January 1610, but it ends in February 1793, two years earlier than any of the other manuscripts. In the same way, the Liem manuscript contains the comments by Tangren shi ('John Chinaman'), Lin Cuipu, and Lin Jiuru, but it is striking that they are written in a briefer and more natural style. In addition to this, the Liem manuscript contains many spontaneous exclamations and comments throughout the text, in the translation often indicated by ~ and italics, by round brackets or placed in indented text. These sharp and straightforward notes are nowhere to be seen in the other versions.

In summary, in our opinion the Liem manuscript is the earliest and most original version of all the manuscripts presently known. It preserves straightforward remarks that have been omitted or polished in the thoroughly revised later versions by Chen Naiyu. For these reasons, we have chosen the Liem manuscript as the point of departure for our English translation and annotation. This does not mean that we have disregarded Chen Naiyu's additions or

---

4 咬𠺢吧—Yaolaoba—reads in Minnanhua *Kalapa*.

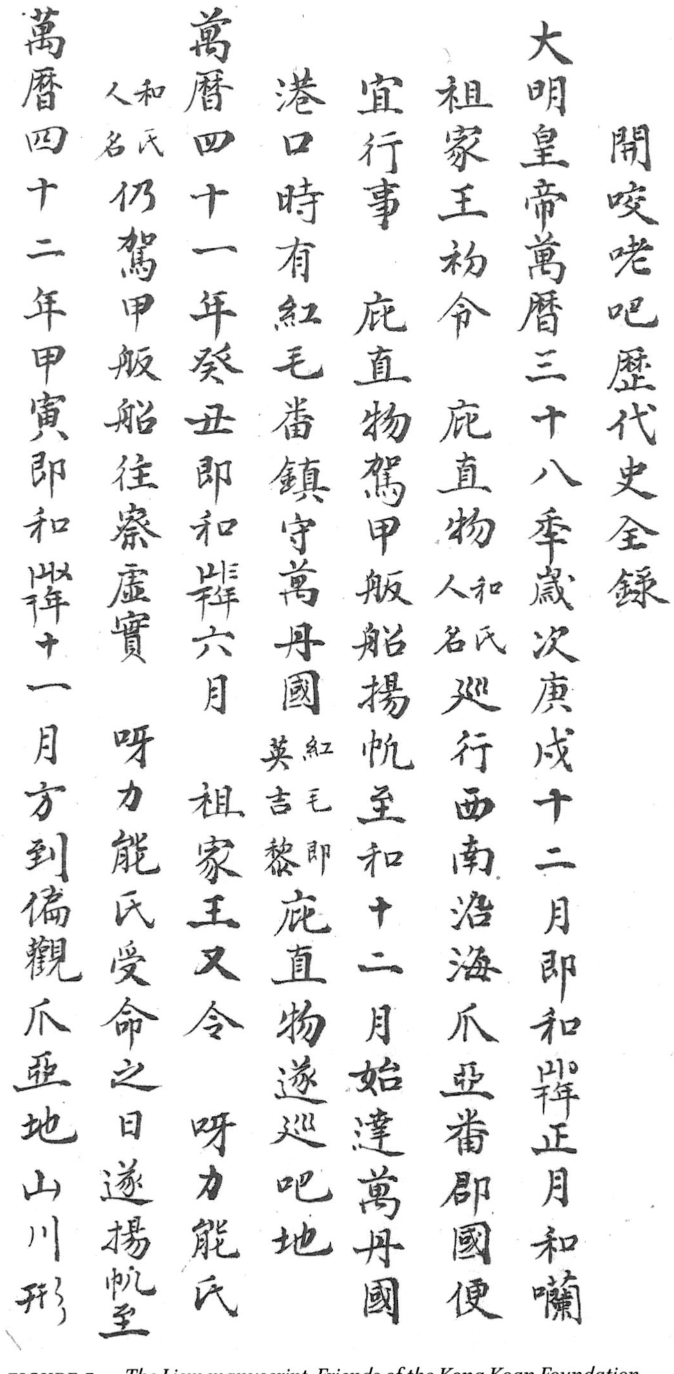

開咬咾吧歷代史全錄

大明皇帝萬曆三十八季歲次庚戌十二月即和蘭紀正月和蘭

祖家王初令 庇直物和氏人名 巡行西南沿海爪亞番卽國便

宜行事 庇直物駕甲舨船揚帆至和十二月始達萬丹國

港口時有紅毛番鎮守萬丹國 紅毛卽黎 庇直物遂巡吧地

英吉黎

萬曆四十一年癸丑即和蘭六月 祖家王又令 呀力能氏

和氏 仍駕甲舨船往察虛實 呀力能氏受命之日遂揚帆至

人名

萬曆四十二年甲寅即和蘭十一月方到偏觀爪亞地山川形

FIGURE 7　*The Liem manuscript, Friends of the Kong Koan Foundation*
ASIAN LIBRARY, LEIDEN UNIVERSITY

Xu Yunqiao's revised and annotated edition, including all the comments from the two texts that he used. Wherever we found in Medhurst's Dutch translation of 1840 occasional stories not found anywhere else—they may have been inserted by his Dutch editors—we have duly noted this. In short, every time Xu Yunqiao's annotated edition has any content to add to the Liem version we have made sure to include it in our translation.

Finally, some further remarks about the additional accounts that we have added in separate chapters to the main text.

Cheng Xunwo, the author of the *Brief account of Galaba*, was a Chinese literatus from Zhangpu County in Fujian Province (福建漳浦), who served as a private teacher in Java from 1729 to 1736. He was lucky enough to return home before the massacre occurred in Batavia. In 1741 he happened to be in Beijing, where he met his Fujianese compatriot Cai Xin (蔡新), a compiler at the Hanlin (翰林) Academy. At the latter's insistence, he wrote an account of Batavia with the modest title *A Brief Account of Galaba*.

Following the example of Chen Naiyu, we have included this piece because of its clear and informative description of the topography and 'unusual features' of Batavia. In fact, Cheng's report sheds light on various issues that the author of the *Kai Ba Lidai Shiji* takes for granted. There are various versions of this essay, but we were able to use the copy of the *Galaba Jilüe* contained in the extremely rare *Xunmintang Congshu* (遜敏堂叢書) edition, preface 1851, in the possession of the Institute for Research in Humanities (Jimbun Kagaku Kenkyujo) of Kyoto University.

To gain some understanding of the attitude and opinion of Chinese high officialdom toward the massacre in Batavia and the possible consequences for Chinese overseas shipping to the Nanyang (南洋) at that time, we have also translated Cai Xin's reply to the Great Secretariat's Fang Bao (方苞), a celebrated scholar official who had asked for advice on these issues.[5] His report is contained in the 'Biography of Cai Xin' in the *Guangxu Zhangzhou Fu Zhi* (光緒漳州府志·卷之三十三，人物六，蔡新傳). Cai Xin, also named Cai Geshan, 蔡葛山 (1707–1799) was born in Zhangpu county of Zhangzhou prefecture in Fujian province. He obtained the *jinshi* (advanced scholar) degree ranking fourth in the imperial examinations of 1736.[6] In addition to Cai Xin's report, we have added several reports from local officials who briefed the emperor on

---

5   For his biography, see 'Fang Pao (1668–1749)' in Arthur W. Hummel, *Eminent Chinese of the Ch'ing Period (1644–1912)* (Washington: United States Printing Office, 1943), vol. 1, 235–37. In 1739 Fang Pao is said to have fallen in disgrace and to have been deprived of all rank, but he clearly remained an influential figure at the court.

6   For his biography see 'Ts'ai Hsin (1700–1799)' in *Ibid.* 2. 734.

the news from Batavia that had reached the coastal provinces. Based on all these reports, the Qianlong Emperor decided that, however tragic the fate of the Chinese inhabitants of Batavia may have been, these were all people who had forsaken the mother country by disobeying the imperial commands and settling down abroad.[7]

In addition, we have included the essay *Jialaba* (甲喇巴) written by Gu Sen (顧森), which was inserted into Chen Yusong's preface to Xu Yunqiao's revised and annotated edition. The author of *Jialaba* recorded what a neighbour called Yin (殷) had told him about his adventures as a sea merchant and his visit to Batavia in the early years of Qianlong period.

Wang Dahai (王大海, Ong-Tae-Hae), a scholar who hailed from the city of Zhangzhou, in south Fujian (福建漳州), resided in Batavia, Semarang, and Pekalongan between 1783 and 1793. He is the author of a charming and colourful little book about his life on Java with the title *Haidao Yizhi* (海島逸志, Anecdotes about the Sea Islands). Completed in 1791, the book was first published in 1806. W.H. Medhurst published an English translation in 1849, with the title *The Chinaman Abroad: or a Desultory Account of the Malayan Archipelago, Particularly of Java*. We have, with proper gratitude, borrowed a few very informative excerpts from Medhurst's original translation of this extremely rare book.[8]

Finally, we have added various appendices. Appendix 1 contains the translation of a Dutch contemporary report in the 'Daghregister' (diary) of Batavia describing in detail how the Chinese captain of Batavia was installed in his office.

As mentioned above, the various versions of the *Kai Ba Lidai Shiji* contain lists of the Dutch governors general and the Chinese officers and employees of the Kong Koan. Having ascertained that many of the dates in these lists are wrong, imprecise, or incomplete, we have completely revised them on the basis of the very precise archival data of the VOC archives.

---

7 Jennifer Cushman, 'Duke Ch'ing-fu Deliberates: A Mid-Century Reassessment of Sino-Nanyang Commercial Relations', *Papers on Far Eastern History* 17 (Canberra: Australian National University, 1978).

8 See also Claudine Salmon, 'Wang Dahai et sa vision des 'Contrées insulaires' (1791)', in *Mélanges de sinologie offerts à Monsieur Jacques Gernet*, *Études chinoises* 13: 1–2 (1992): 21–257, and idem, 'Wang Dahai and his View of the 'Insular Countries (1791)', in *Chinese Studies of the Malay World, A Comparative Approach*, Ding Choo Ming and Ooi Kee Beng, eds. (Singapore, Eastern University Press, 2003), 31–67.

PART 2

The Chinese Annals of Batavia

∴

A Chinese Chronicle of the Historical Events at Yaolaoba (Galaba)

In the twelfth moon of the 38th year of the Wanli [萬曆] Emperor of the Great Ming [大明皇帝], *gengxu* [庚戌],[1] the first month of 1610 the sovereign of the mother country, Holland,[2] for the first time ordered Pieter Both[3] to go on a tour of inspection to Java and the vassal countries in the southwestern

---

1   *Gengxu* (庚戌): the cyclic year of the Chinese lunar calendar.
2   The Republic of the Seven Provinces of the Netherlands (1597–1795) did not have a king but a *stadhouder*, or sovereign with limited power. The United Dutch East India Company (*Verenigde Oost-Indische Compagnie*, or VOC) was established in 1602 and the States General issued an *octroy* (charter) giving it a monopoly on all Dutch trade east of Africa and west of the Americas. Its management was made up by seventeen directors, the so-called Gentlemen XVII, who represented the various port cities that participated in the Company: Amsterdam (eight members), Hoorn and Enkhuizen (two members), Rotterdam and Delft (two members), Middelburg and Vlissingen (four members). To avoid equally divided votes, a seventeenth member was nominated in rotation by another city in Holland or Zeeland. All orders concerning the affairs of the Company in Asia emanated from the Gentlemen XVII. The charter on the Asian trade was formally abolished on 31 December 1799.

   The anonymous Chinese author mistakenly thought that the orders from Holland were personally given by the Dutch *stadhouder*, the Prince of Orange Nassau.

   This misunderstanding can be easily understood because starting from 1748, Prince Willem IV and after him Prince Willem V both served as *opperbewindhebber* (supreme director) of the VOC.
3   Pieter Both, governor general from 19 December 1610 until 6 November 1614, was born in Amersfoort in 1568. He first sailed to the East Indies as commander of a fleet of four ships of the Nieuwe or Brabantsche Compagnie (one of the many companies united in the VOC) in December 1599. In November 1609, the directors of the VOC decided to install a central management in Asia consisting of a governor general assisted by the Council of the Indies (*Raad van Indië*). After the founding of Batavia in 1619, this administrative organ was generally called the High Government (*Hoge Regering*) of Batavia. Pieter Both departed with a fleet of eight ships and arrived in Banten on 19 December 1609 of the same year. His instructions called for him to select a suitable location for the headquarters or *rendez-vous* for the VOC in Asia. On 6 November 1614, he handed over his powers to his successor Gerard Reijnst. On 27 December 1614, Both set sail on board of the *Banda* in the company of three other ships to return home. On the night of 5/6 March 1615, the *Banda* and two other ships went down with all hands in a heavy storm while at anchor in the roadstead of Mauritius. P.J.A.N. Rietbergen, *De eerste landvoogd Pieter Both (1568–1615)* (Zutphen: De Walburg Pers 1987). (Most information on the lives of the governors general is based on M.A. van Rhede van der Kloot, *De Gouverneurs-Generaal en Commissarissen-Generaal van Nederlandsch-Indië 1610–1888*,

coastal regions, and to act as circumstances might require. Pieter Both set sail on a square-rigged sailing ship.[4] By the twelfth month of the same year, he first arrived at the port of Banten.[5] Because the Englishmen (Hongmao fan, 紅毛番, that is, Red-haired Barbarians)[6] guarded Banten then, Pieter Both went on to inspect Galaba (噶喇吧, or 咬咾吧).[7]

In Wanli 41, *guichou* [癸丑], June 1613, the sovereign of the mother country ordered Gerrit Reijnst,[8] in turn, to set sail and examine the actual conditions overseas. Gerrit Reijnst hoisted the sails and reached his destination.

In Wanli 42, *jiayin* [甲寅], November 1614, he surveyed all Java, the outline of its hills and streams, fathoming the depth and width of the water routes, and he mapped these out in a book. [Having done so], he ordered Pieter Both to take home the gathered data and present them to the sovereign of the mother country. Meeting with the Dutch sovereign, he clearly reported in detail what he had seen and knew, whereupon the sovereign joyfully said, 'It can be swiftly captured'.[9] Pieter Both performed his duties [over the course of] five years and five months abroad. Yet Gerrit Reijnst still remained at the bay of Galaba making friends with the ruler of Galaba.

> The ruler of Galaba appointed by the native king *susuhunan* [*shunlan*] is called *pangeran* [*panjilan*], that is a prince who has not yet the position of a king. Not only princes but also royal appointees are called *pangeran*.[10]

---

    historisch-genealogisch beschreven ('s Gravenhage, 1871); and F.W. Stapel, *De Gouverneurs-Generaal van Nederlandsch-Indië in beeld en woord* (Den Haag: Van Stockum, 1941).

4   The term *jiaban chuan* (甲板船, probably derived from the Malay word *kapal*) was used exclusively for square-rigged European sailing ships.

5   The sultanate of Banten (Bantam) was situated on Java's northwest coast.

6   Throughout the text, the English and British are called Red-haired Barbarians, or simply Red Hairs, a sobriquet originally used only for the Dutch.

7   Galaba was the Chinese name for Sunda Kalapa, the old name for the port of the local Kingdom of Jayakarta. After the Dutch occupied Jakarta in 1619 they baptized it Batavia but the Chinese continued to call it the Kingdom of Galaba. The place name Jakatra, (Rujijiao 如吉礁) is only sporadically used in the present Chinese manuscript.

8   Gerrit Reijnst, governor general from 6 November 1614 until 7 December 1615, was born in Amsterdam. His date of birth is not known. He served originally at the board of directors of the Nieuwe of Brabantsche Compagnie but became a board member of the VOC after 1602. He was appointed governor general on 20 February 1613 and departed on 2 June 1613 with a fleet of nine ships under the command of Admiral Steven van der Hagen. He died of dysentery in the VOC factory at Jakatra on 7 December 1615.

9   Pieter Both never reached Holland, but went down with his ship near the island of Mauritius on the way home. See note 3.

10   The ruler of the central Javanese kingdom of Mataram was called the susuhunan of Mataram. *Pangeran* is the Javanese title of a local ruler or prince.

In **Wanli 43**, *yimao* [乙卯], 4 May 1615, Gerrit Reijnst presented silks, satins, and cotton piece goods that he carried in his ship, to the king of Galaba, called the pangeran, and beseeched him to allow him to repair the broken parts of his ship, and to provide him with a place to stay, so that he could carry out all [his] duties. The pangeran was very pleased and allowed him to do so. In the twelfth month of the same year, Gerrit Reijnst fell ill and passed away, and was interred at Rujijiao (如吉礁, Jakatra). He served in total three years and seven months.

Now the story goes that in the south there was then a country called the Moluccas,[11] a territory of the Portuguese. These people were extraordinarily cunning. Because the Tang (Chinese) people[12] came to trade at this place, they were very well acquainted with them. Using silver as a bait, the Portuguese asked the Chinese to point out a good place for building a castle. When the construction was finished, they then schemed to betray the Chinese. Pieter Both found out about this situation and when he arrived in the mother country, he presented the map of Galaba to the sovereign, and at the same time reported that the wealth of the Moluccas could be taken. The sovereign of the mother country immediately ordered Laurens Reael[13] to fit out the ships and to make a plan and go and seize the Moluccas.

On the nineteenth day of the seventh month of 1615, Reael arrived inside the port of the Moluccas, and daily traded his merchandise with the Portuguese and other barbarians. He appeased them with sweet words and eloquence and made them harbor no misgivings. After softening them up for one month, one

---

11 Maliujia (麻六甲, Ma-lak-ka in the Minnan dialect) normally denotes Portuguese Malacca, but this town was not occupied by the Dutch until 1641. No doubt here the reference is to the Moluccas (Maluku) or Spice Islands. In 1603, Admiral Steven van der Hagen established Fortress Victoria on the island of Ambon, the first Dutch fortress in the Spice Islands.

12 Throughout the Chinese text, the traditional term *Tang* (唐) or *Tangren* (唐人) denotes China or the Chinese. 'People of the Tang [dynasty]' is how the Chinese of China's southeast coast used to address themselves. Only once—in 1643—does the author use the usual term, *Zhongguo* (中國) or Middle Kingdom, referring to the Chinese government.

13 Laurens Reael, governor general from 19 June 1616 until 21 March 1619, was born in Amsterdam on 22 October 1583. He had an excellent educational background and received a doctorate in law at Leiden University in 1608. He departed as commander of a fleet of four ships in May 1611 and soon after his arrival joined the Council of the Indies. In 1615, he was appointed governor of the Moluccas, and on 19 June 1616 he was elected governor general to succeed Gerrit Reijnst, who had died. The Gentlemen XVII accepted his request to step down on 31 October 1617, but he was unable to hand over his powers to Jan Pietersz Coen until 21 March 1619. After his return to the Dutch Republic he served in various diplomatic missions. On June 1625, he was appointed *bewindhebber* (director) of the Amsterdam chamber of the VOC, and he continued in that position until his death of the plague on 21 October 1637.

Sunday Reael secretly gave the order to prepare all the cannons of the ships for firing, and then suddenly stuck them out [of the gun-ports]. In one rush his troops forced their way into the Portuguese fortress. The incessant firing of the great ship cannons made the mountains crumble and shook the earth. The Portuguese were immediately terrified and at a loss about what to do. Frightened out of their wits, they all ran into the mountains to save their skins.

This proves that cheaters are yet cheated by others; robbers just rob their own countries! Fearsome is the revenge of Heaven!

Reael then secured [Dutch rule] and put things in order in the Moluccas, and ordered the ships to return home to report to the sovereign of the mother country.

In the fourth month of Wanli 44, *bingchen* [丙辰], 5 May 1616, the sovereign of the mother country sent a letter to the Moluccas and ordered Laurens Reael to make a plan and capture Kalapa (咖嘮吧). But Reael's plans did not succeed.

In the sixth month of Wanli 45, *dingsi* [丁巳], 20 July 1617, he subsequently returned home by ship.[14]

There was then in the mother country a man from Hoorn with the name of Jan Pieterszoon Coen.[15] This man was wise and full of stratagems. The sovereign of the mother country treated him with respect and secretly ordered him

---

14   Reael did not return until 6 August 1619. The Liem manuscript mistakenly says *dingyou* (丁酉), that is, 1625.

15   Jan Pieterszoon Coen (8 January 1587–21 September 1629) was born in Hoorn. Between 1601 and 1607 he apprenticed as a merchant with Justus Pescatore (Visscher) in Rome. In 1607, he left for the Indies as junior merchant in the service of the VOC. In 1612, on his second voyage to the Indies, he had risen to the position of *opperkoopman* (senior merchant). After a stint as president of the Bantam and Jakatra factories, in 1613 he was appointed director general of all trade in the Indies. He was appointed governor general on 25 October 1617, but did not succeed Laurens Reael until March 1619. In 1618, he fortified the Jakatra factory, which was promptly besieged by English troops and armies of the sultan of Banten and the pangeran of Jakarta. After securing help from the Dutch fleet in the Moluccas, he rescued the Jakatra garrison on 30 May 1619, and established the town of Batavia on the ashes of the *kraton* of Jakarta. In 1621, Coen conquered the Banda Islands, and in 1622 he sent an ill-fated expedition in search of free trade with China. On 23 February 1623, Coen stepped down and returned to the Netherlands to explain his policies. On 3 October 1624, he was reappointed governor general against the opposition of the English East India Company, which deemed him responsible for the so-called 'Amboyna Massacre'. To avoid any trouble, he left Holland in 1627 disguised as a common sailor and arrived in Batavia on 30 September 1627. During Coen's second term as governor general, Batavia was twice unsuccessfully besieged by the troops of the Kingdom of Mataram. He died of an illness during the second siege on 20 September 1629.

to seize Galaba. On the day he received the order, Coen dressed up as a sailor, and in the ninth month he left the mother country. Just before he reached Batavia at the end of the December, Coen asked the captain of the ship to summon a meeting. The ship captain disregarded him. He thereupon asked him two, three more times to convene, and secretly told the captain the orders of the sovereign of the mother country. Only then did the captain recognize him and pay him due respect.[16]

Upon arriving in the port of Galaba, Jan Pietersz Coen took the precious merchandise carried in the ship and presented silks and cotton piece goods to the pangeran named Shilao'erlanzhao (Selalilada).[17] When the pangeran was very pleased, Coen asked him for a piece of land the size of a cowhide,[18] to use as a temporary base. The pangeran allowed him a spot at Xinchi (新池, New Pond)[19] to set up a camp to settle down. ~ *To raise a tiger is to court calamity!* ~ Jan Pietersz Coen then soaked the cow skin, and sliced it as thin as a silk thread, pulled it straight in a circle and ordered his people to purchase bamboo and build a fence with it. He made space in all four corners, and covered these with canvas, but built inside them four bulwarks. When the construction was ready, his men brought forwards the ship cargo of piece goods and intentionally put these outside the walls in broad daylight. But at night

---

16 Coen did not sail in disguise in 1617. He was actually staying in Banten. But in 1627, when Coen set out from Holland for his second term as governor general, he boarded the fleet incognito to avoid British opposition and only made himself known to the captain after the ships were at sea.

17 His name was Wijaya Krama.

18 This refers to the well-known story of the founding of Carthage in North Africa by Queen Dido. This trope can be found throughout popular literature in Asia. In Taiwanese folktales, the Dutch are said to have used the same ruse to acquire a plot of land to build Zeelandia Castle. Even the purchase of a plot of land on the island of Manhattan to found Nieuw Amsterdam (New York), is said to have been based on the same trick. See Jason Baird Jackson, 'The Story of Colonialism, or Rethinking the Ox-Hide Purchase in Native North America and Beyond'. *Journal of American Folklore* 126:499 (2013): 31–54, and Andrew Newman, 'The Dido Story in Accounts of Early Modern European Imperialism—An Anthology'. *Itinerario* 41:1 (2017): 129–50.

On 10 November 1610, an agreement was reached between Pangeran Wijaya Krama and the Dutch whereby the latter were authorized to purchase a plot of land of 50 square fathoms (94 square meters) and construct an edifice upon payment of 1,200 *rials* (2,700 guilders). They had to pay tolls on all export merchandise that had been purchased in Jayakarta with the exception of Chinese merchandise and foodstuffs. Portuguese and Spaniards would not be allowed in the city. See W. Fruin-Mees, *Geschiedenis van Java* (Weltevreden: Commissie voor de Volkslectuur, 1920), 2.69.

19 The first factory building in Jayakarta was constructed in 1610.

they secretly carried big casks with gunpowder and big cannons hidden inside and brought them within the walls.

The Javanese were all amazed. When they saw the abundance of Dutch goods and realized that the bamboo fence was not strong, their covetous desires were raised. Thereupon they gathered in groups to steal the [Dutch] merchandise and the piece goods. Jan Pietersz Coen daily ordered his people to fire the guns and beat the drums, to confuse the heart of the pangeran. The next day the pangeran sent a man to ask: 'Why are you firing guns and beating the drums day and night?' Jan Pietersz Coen then went to see the pangeran and said: 'This place is teeming with robbers—countless goods are stolen all the time; therefore, I order my men to beat the drums day and night and stand guard, keeping them from having a peaceful slumber. Those that fire the guns make the robbers feel terrified, so that they do not dare to steal; that is all there is to be said about it'. The pangeran believed him, and this was exactly what Jan Pietersz Coen had reckoned.

> At this time, the English, the French, and the Swedes all desired to occupy this place, but when they heard about Jan Pietersz Coen's exceeding craftiness, the English sent ships to await a chance to rob and murder him. Yet their wish was not fulfilled, so they gave up and left.[20]

In the fourth moon of Wanli 46, *wuwu* [戊午], of 1618, the sovereign of the mother country ordered ships to go to Galaba and obey Jan Pietersz Coen's orders. Coen ordered all the recently arrived ship captains to attach their men to his own soldiers. He issued the order to divide the soldiers into four detachments. One of these he instructed to guard the four corners of the castle, and he hurried forth with three-fourths of his troops 'with their mouths gagged' to assail the palace of the pangeran. After he had issued the orders, every officer led men and horses to carry out their tasks. In this way, they turned this kind person [the pangeran] into their enemy, and turned his land into a battlefield.

---

20   The Swedes were not yet present in Asia. The French ship *l'Espérance*, from the port of Dieppe, had indeed reached Java's shores, but it was promptly seized on Coen's orders; H.T. Colenbrander, *Jan Pietersz Coen, Bescheiden omtrent zijn verblijf in Indië* ('s-Gravenhage: Martinus Nijhoff, 1919–34) 1.608. In the winter of 1618, the English formed an alliance with the sultan of Banten and the pangeran of Jakarta and tried to dislodge the Dutch from their stronghold in Jakatra, but they failed to do so.

This shows that the pangeran ran into trouble because he acted without foresight. In the end, he ran away; what a pity!

Now it so happened that the pangeran on that day was leisurely engaged in conversation and not expecting anything when he suddenly saw the Dutch soldiers penetrate like the incoming tide. The pangeran was at loss what to do. He urgently ordered his soldiers to hurry and resist the enemy. Who could have known that every Dutch soldier fought so bravely? Everyone trying to be first, their force could not be checked. The Javanese natives awoke as from a dream; there was no way they could resist! When they resisted, they were mowed down in scattered confusion by the Dutch soldiers. Now even more the Dutch chiefs led their troops and within a short time they killed large numbers of their enemies. The Javanese hurried away like homeless dogs in all directions to save their skins. In the end, no one wanted to return to take care of his affairs.

It really hurts to think of this!

In the fourth moon of Wanli 47, *jiwei* [己未], 30 May 1619,[21] the pangeran, filled with hatred because of the Dutch deceit, certainly wished to take revenge. Therefore, he gathered a great number of men and horses to wage a decisive battle against the Dutch to recoup his land. The latter then lacked men and horses. They fired their guns continuously, but the soldiers of the pangeran were numerous, like ants; they stormed forwards like fearsome wolves. The Hollanders were not able to fire their guns in time, and in an instant they were ruthlessly killed by the Javanese soldiers. Just at this dangerous moment, they [the Dutch] suddenly hatched a plan.

It is said that man is resourceful in emergencies. It is truly like that.

They [the Dutch soldiers] quickly threw smelly dung all around.

The stink was terrible!

Those who were hit just had to cover their noses and run away.

This is because the native barbarians abhor stench.

---

21 The following tale, including the comments, is a collation of the Leiden and Liem manuscripts.

In short, they withdrew more than a mile!

> Today's place name, Xinchi [New Pond], is also called Kota Shi [高踏屎, Shit Town] because of this event.[22]

Just then the French and Swedish ships arrived together. Jan Pietersz Coen sent a messenger to ask them to join forces and help, promising them that on the day of victory he would reward them.[23] Those officers gladly agreed to do so, and led their ships and men forward and readied their guns. Together with the Hollanders their divisions advanced against the Javanese soldiers. They fired continually, one after the other. The Javanese soldiers were killed and mauled in heaps. Their bones were pulverised and their bodies flew in all directions. The remaining soldiers were sick with fear and fled away in all directions. The pangeran was routed and did not dare to return to his palace. Herding his forces and chasing the enemy away, Jan Pietersz Coen advanced towards the pangeran's *kraton*[24] and found it empty of people. Only one piece of the king's garments had been left behind. Jan Pietersz Coen took it as a memento and thereupon he took possession of the land of the pangeran. He then erected a fortress tower at Jakatra[25] and very quickly constructed a town and a moat and houses for the Hollanders so they could settle down and live in peace. He asked the local natives to return to their occupations. Moreover, he gave silver in compensation to the commanders of all the ships for their meritorious service in assisting him during the war. Thereupon, the world was at peace. Jan Pieter Coen thus became the king of Galaba.[26]

---

22 The Kota Shi episode is based on facts, but it is told here out of context. In reality, the event occurred during the siege of Batavia by the troops of Mataram several years later. The story was first narrated by Governor General Camphuijs in his history of Batavia. See Leonard Blussé, 'Driemaal is scheepsrecht. Batavia 1619, 1627–1629', in Herman Amersfoort, Hans Blom, Dennis Bos, Gijsbert van Es, eds., *Belaagd en belegerd* (Amsterdam: Balans, 2011) 147–69.

23 The support from French and Swedish ships is pure fantasy.

24 *Kraton*, the living quarters of the pangeran.

25 如吉礁, Rujijiao, in Minnanhua Na-kiet-ta.

26 The actual sequence of events is as follows: a combined siege of the Dutch fortified trading lodge by British, Jakartan, and Bantenese troops in December 1618; the withdrawal of Coen to seek reinforcements in the Moluccas; the protracted encirclement of the Dutch lodge; and, finally, the return of Coen in May 1619 followed up by the total destruction of the Javanese town and the *kraton* of Jayakarta, and the founding of the city of Batavia on its ashes. For a succinct account in English, see George Masselman, *The Cradle of Colonialism* (New Haven: Yale University Press, 1963). 377–89.

Afterwards the pangeran who had been routed withdrew into the interior of Java. He was ashamed and angry beyond words. He ordered all his headmen to assemble for deliberation. He raised all his soldiers and sent them along the sea and land routes to recapture the places occupied by the Hollanders. When Jan Pietersz Coen heard about this, he immediately ordered a native interpreter to meet the pangeran halfway and to address him politely and kindly, saying: 'Why would you lose soldiers and bring harm to your people by taking up arms again? This is just a small place. Only lease it to me for a temporary residence, to turn it into a place where we can trade. If we Hollanders obtain some profits, we are willing to pay the land rent every year, as much as is necessary, to be used for the necessities in your *kraton*. If you need expenditures for your royal affairs, we Hollanders can supply them if you ask for them. Is this not excellent'?

> He proposed this plan to calm him down. When the pangeran heard that the Hollanders would bring money and pay rent, he agreed. He then ordered his troops to return inland and established a kingdom in Mataram.[27] And he no longer brought up what had happened.

At the time, [Chinese] junks only visited Banten. In the fifth month of the same year [Wanli 44], the sixth month of the Dutch calendar, Jan Pietersz Coen let it be known to all junks and Chinese [that they should] come to Batavia to trade. He forbade the junks to go to Banten and engage in trade with that city's people any longer. Coen also built town walls, dug a harbour, [and] built bridges and roads. When he had just started to make laws and regulations and had almost finished, he sent a memorial to the sovereign of the mother country.

Then Chinese came in droves to Batavia to trade and made manifold profits. When Batavia was established, everybody used Chinese coins for export and import purposes.[28] As a result, more and more people came. There were just a few hundred Chinese people then.

In the ninth moon of Wanli 48, *gengshen* [庚申], 13 September 1620, the sovereign of the mother country ordered a ship to deliver a letter to Batavia for Jan Pietersz Coen ordering him to appoint a Chinese to serve as *kapitein*

---

27   Lannei (覽內) is the Chinese name for the Kingdom of Mataram. Under its leader, Sultan Agung, the powerful Kingdom of Mataram took shape around this time, but this had no connection whatsoever with the expelled pangeran of Jayakarta in central Java.

28   Leonard Blussé, 'Trojan Horse of Lead: the *Picis* in Early 17th-Century Java', in F. van Anrooy ed., *Between People and Statistics. Essays on Modern Indonesian History* (The Hague: Martinus Nijhoff, 1979) 33–48.

[captain][29] of the Chinese people and to immediately appoint Su Mingguang (蘇明光, Bencon) to the position of Chinese captain.[30] The Company gave a golden seal and credentials as well as a platoon of Dutch soldiers ~ *twelve men* ~ to stand watch in front of the gate of the captain. Su Mingguang discussed administrative affairs in the official hall. All this was put in proper order. All Chinese people who came to Batavia to engage in trade came to report to the captain, who provided them with a Dutch permit. There were then already 400 to 500 Chinese households. These merchants earned a living in trade, all of them making abundant profits. From then on, they reaped quite plentiful proceeds. Su Mingguang, who served as captain but had no territory, entreated the Company to issue him a plot of land to live on.

Because he was of high standing he wanted to move to a bigger house.

Jan Pietersz Coen gave Mangga Dua to serve as the captain's main dwelling. In front of the gate he hung a lantern and a board on which was written 'the founding father of the country'.

How imposing! How eminent!

That year no [Chinese] ships came to Batavia, therefore Su Mingguang asked permission to return to the mountains of Tang (唐山, China), to proclaim the invitation to Chinese ships to come to Batavia, to trade and help Batavia flourish. The king of Batavia agreed. At the end of the year, Su Mingguang came

---

29 *Jiada* (甲大) or *Ka* (*pi-tan*) *toa* (甲必丹大).

30 Su Mingguang—his tombstone reads Su Minggang (蘇鳴崗), in Minnanhua So Bing Kong or Souw Beng Kong—a native of Tong'an (同安) in Fujian province, was called Bencon by the Dutch. According to the resolution of the Governor General and Council of 11 October 1619, Bencon was appointed 'to keep order and police' the roughly 400 Chinese living in town. Bencon is said to have been a personal friend of Jan Pietersz Coen, who often consulted him on Chinese matters. Bencon stepped down in 1636 and left for China, but decided to remain on the island of Formosa (Taiwan). He returned to Batavia on 14 March 1639 and passed away there on 8 April 1644. His tomb has survived the ages and has been recently restored. See Hendra Lukito, *Riwayat Kapitan Tionghoa Pertama di Batavia Souw Beng Kong (1580–1644) Konservasi, Pelestarian dan Pengakuan Makamnya sebagai situs vaga budaya* Jakarta: Yayasan Kapitan Souw Beng Kong 2013. B. Hoetink has devoted two detailed biographical articles to Su Mingguang: 'So Bing Kong, het eerste hoofd der Chineezen te Batavia (1619–1636)', *Bijdragen tot de Taal-, Land- en Volkenkunde van Nederlandsch-Indië* (1917) 73: 344–415 and (1923) 79: 1–44. Contrary to what the Chinese author suggests, the Chinese captains were not appointed by the authorities in Holland but by the governor general.

back to Batavia with a Chinese junk and again served as [Chinese] captain. How great were his merits and contributions!

In the twelfth moon of Tianqi [天啟] 3, *guihai* [癸亥], 1 February 1623, Great King Jan Pietersz Coen invited all the headmen to a banquet and told them he wished to return to the mother country and transfer his position to a native from Amsterdam, Pieter de Carpentier.[31] All the headmen gladly applauded the proposal and elected the latter to act as king of Batavia. All matters, great and small, were executed according to the laws and edicts of the former king. He [Carpentier] did not dare to change anything, so peace prevailed. Then Jan Pietersz Coen took leave of the headmen and sailed on a ship home to the mother country.

In the eighth moon of Tianqi 7, *dingmao* [丁卯], September 1627, the former King Jan Pietersz Coen arrived by ship in Batavia. Pieter de Carpentier then restored to him the throne and in the eleventh month he returned by ship to the mother country. His glory was very significant.

> Pieter Coen was a native from Hoorn, and in this year he came back from Holland to continue his reign until his death in Batavia.

In the ninth month of the first year of Chongzhen [崇禎], *wuchen* [戊辰], the twentieth day of the tenth month of 1628, in an edict sent to Batavia the sovereign of the mother country again confirmed the appointment of Jan Pietersz Coen to the position of great king of Batavia and in the rank of *gouverneur generaal* promoted him one rank higher to the real kingship of Batavia.[32] After he received his appointment, Jan Pietersz Coen very diligently took care of the affairs of the country and put all his efforts into rendering the country prosperous. The construction of the town, the port, bridges, and roads, the management of the community, all this he personally supervised and inspected. For days and months on end he did not dare take a rest or idle.

> He inspired both respect and admiration.

---

31 Pieter de Carpentier, governor general from 1 February 1623 until October 1627, was born in Antwerp on 19 February 1586. After studying in Leiden, he joined the VOC and arrived in Batavia on 19 October 1616 in the capacity of *opperkoopman* (senior merchant). On 23 March 1619, he joined the Council of the Indies and one year later he was appointed director general, that is, second in command to Jan Pietersz Coen. After his return to Holland in 1628 he was appointed *bewindhebber* of the Amsterdam chamber of the VOC. He passed away on 5 September 1659.

32 This is one of the few times that the Dutch term for governor general is spelled out in Chinese.

At that time, the whole territory from the head stream of the Angke River all the way to the garden of the king consisted of jungle and grassland, bare and swampy, but from then on people began to cultivate sugarcane and vegetable gardens. They cleared off the wild grasses and the trees. The Hollanders then built garden houses and water pavilions ~ *a beautiful spectacle to behold!* ~ in order to enjoy themselves at leisure along the higher reaches of the Angke River. From Pasar Senen, Kampung Melayu, to Banten and Lembang and Tanjung, the land extending in all these four directions was originally wilderness but was then developed into [cane fields with] sixty sugar mills. The men of the sugar mills cut the forest day and night until the firewood ran out. The sugar mills moved further inland, closer to the forests. Starting out from near the city, the millers expanded [their plots] farther and farther away.

The Hollanders gradually started to build gardens and houses locally, and to cultivate the fields. They planted trees and rice and established markets, and increasingly the Chinese began to live in Mangga Dua and Jalan Panjang. After the walls and moats were ready, they moved into and outside of the walls. Therefore, Mangga Dua and Jalan Panjang declined.[33]

In the eighth moon of the second year of the Chongzhen year period, the year *jisi* **[己巳], 20 September 1629,** Jan Pietersz Coen fell critically ill, so seriously that he could not work anymore. He summoned all the councilors and headmen to come and discuss the temporary transfer of the government to Jacques Specx[34] and instructed him 'If you become the lord of Galaba, you must carry on all unfinished projects according to my intentions. Abiding by these instructions, carry them out, and establish the fundamental principles for administering the country'. On 24 September, Specx was promoted to great king; Jan Pietersz Coen died in the castle. He was buried within the church of the castle.

---

33 The last two paragraphs are drawn from the Leiden manuscript.
34 Jacques Specx was born in the city of Dordrecht in 1589. He served as chief of the VOC factory in Hirado, Japan, from 1609 to 1613 and from 1614 to 1621. In Batavia, he joined the Council of the Indies and served in various functions such as president of the city council and the church council. He left for Holland in 1627 but returned in Batavia on 22 September 1629, one day after Jan Pietersz Coen had died. He therefore could not possibly have met him. On 25 September, he was elected governor general by the Council of the Indies, but the Gentlemen XVII did not confirm this appointment. On 17 March 1632, they appointed Hendrick Brouwer, who assumed office on 7 September of the same year. Upon Specx's departure, the Chinese citizens of Batavia bestowed on him a golden commemorative medal to express their gratitude for all he had done for them during his tenure. A silver copy of this medal is now kept in Teylers Museum in Haarlem. Specx served as a director of the VOC from 1647 to 1651. He passed away in July 1652.

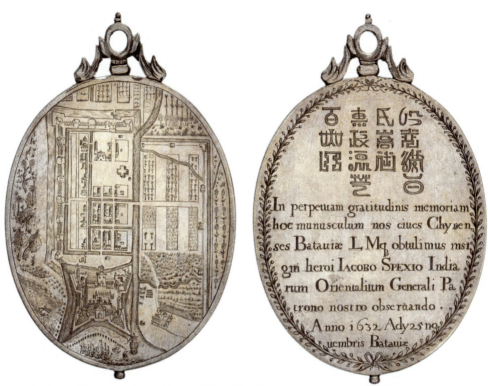

FIGURE 8   *Silver copy of the golden medallion offered to Governor General Jacques Specx by the grateful Chinese community in 1632. Chinese text is probably:* 昭光織白氏高志, 惠政流芳百世强. *"For the glory of the lofty spirit of Mr. Specx (Chet Pek Si), whose gracious government will leave its fragrance strongly for a hundred generations"*
HAARLEM, TEYLERS MUSEUM. INV. TMNK 00460

On that day, the headmen then acknowledged that Jacques Specx (a native of Dordrecht) was to act as king of Batavia and take charge of the affairs of the country. From the moment Jacques Specx took charge, he worked hard night and day. He abided by the instructions of his predecessor. He oversaw all things personally and he supervised and inspected the public works. If all people who act in high positions can act according to the instructions of the earlier great king, wouldn't that be doubtlessly highly auspicious?

In the fourth year of Chongzhen, *xinwei* **[辛未], September 1631,** when the Large South Gate was built and the city walls were completed, the date *1631* was inscribed above the gate.[35] That year, in the fourth moon of the Chinese

---

35   The year 1631 is written here in western numbers as it was on the gate itself.

calendar, the founder of [Chinese] Batavia, Captain Su Mingguang,³⁶ died of an illness and was buried at Mangga Dua in his own garden.

The great king of Batavia, Jacques Specx, then appointed Pan Mingyan [潘明岩, Bingam] to the position of great captain and at the same time reported this to the sovereign in the mother country so that he would know.³⁷

The construction of the town of Batavia had not yet been completed. Therefore, all goods and money were stored at Pulau Onrust (King's Island). He built walls and houses and constructed a wall and placed big cannons on top and installed soldiers to guard them. He appointed officials to administer this place and constructed ships at yards in its midst.

In addition, the Company built water-supply ships, sailing with the [sea] wind every afternoon to moor at the town and transport water for the use of those on the island. In the evening, they came to town and the next morning they returned [with the land wind] to the island. On another small island, a windmill was set up to saw timber for use. This was very convenient. The great king [that is, the governor general] and the second king [director general], the major, the public prosecutor, the *fiscaal*, [and] the inland *temenggong*, all lived inside the castle then; only the outer *temenggong* (*landdrost*) and the *commissaris der inlanders* (commissioner for native affairs), who managed the 'countryside affairs', guarded the land outside the town.³⁸

At the time, the company initiated the opening of a big pawnshop *kantoor* (office) in the 'Second King (*Directeur Generaal*) Street' to collect and pawn

---

36   This is incorrect. He died in 1644. See biographical note 30. The dates of the terms of office in the *Kai Ba Lidai Shiji* are almost always wrong or imprecise. Henceforth, the correct dates, drawn from the VOC archives, will be provided in the footnotes.

37   How ill-informed the author is about the early period becomes clear from this statement. He has completely omitted the second Chinese captain, Lim Lacco (林六哥, Lin Liuguan), who succeeded Bencon upon his departure in 1636. According to the resolution of the Governor General and Council of 28 July 1636, he was appointed on that date on the strength of his having served previously as a diplomatic courier between Batavia and Banten. The appointment was publicly declaimed in front of the city hall by two members of the Council of the Indies and various other high officials. Before he moved to Batavia in 1623, Lim Lacco, who was a convert to Islam, had resided for many years in Banten, where he had acted as confidant and councilor to the sultan. His son Boycko served as an interpreter in Formosa. Lim Lacco passed away in February 1645. B. Hoetink, 'Chineesche Officieren te Batavia onder de Compagnie', *Bijdragen tot de Taal-, Land- en Volkenkunde van Nederlandsch-Indië* 78 (1922): 11–14.

38   *Temenggong* is a Malay title. The official Dutch term for inner *temenggong* was *baljuw*, or police officer. The police officer serving outside the city, the outer *temenggong*, was called the *landdrost*, or bailiff.

goods and every kind of precious metal and diamonds. The monthly interest was eight *fanams* for every hundred guilders.[39] Every half year, one could collect one's goods or return the interest, in order to benefit the merchants when they urgently needed cash. This strengthened the fundamentals of carrying on trade. The Company placed soldiers in front of the gate and guarded it day and night, to prevent the risk of robbery and fire.[40]

In the eighth moon of Chongzhen 5, *renshen* [壬申], September 1632, an edict was received from the sovereign in the mother country, to approve the appointment of Pan Mingyan to the position of captain.[41] Pan Mingyan observed the government edicts and regulations of his predecessor. He did not dare to break the laws or go astray.

> Pan Mingyan opened the 'watermill port' for the sovereign. He built houses and a watermill to saw the wood and timbers for the use of the Company. The sovereign was very satisfied and pleased and praised Pan Mingyan for his extraordinary abilities and gave him the land of Glodok for himself and his posterity. From then on, the Pans were exceedingly rich.

In the eighth moon of Chongzhen 6, *guiyou* [癸酉]**, 13 September 1633,** the king summoned the councilors and told them he wished to return to the mother country and asked: 'Who can take charge of the state's affairs?' The headmen deliberated and agreed that Hendrick Brouwer could tackle the job.[42] By the

---

39   One *fanam*, or *dubbeltje*, is equal to two *stuivers*. Consequently, the monthly interest was a little less than 1 percent.
40   The last three paragraphs are taken from the Leiden manuscript.
41   On 8 February 1645 the Council of the Indies decided to delay the appointment of the successor of Lim Lacco until the arrival of the junks from China so that the *nakhodas* and great merchants could also be participate in the selection of the right candidate. The resolution of 4 March 1645 states that 24 prominent Chinese were consulted. Twelve of them gave preference to Pan Mingyan alias Bingam who was already residing 23 years in Batavia. (For the list see Hoetink, 'Chineesche officieren', 17.) On 6 March 1645 Bingam was provisionally appointed for one year but he continued to serve until his death on 25 March 1663. His testament shows that he passed away owing a large sum of money to the Company. His wealth was melted down in large areas of sugarcane fields and other possessions.
42   Hendrick Brouwer was appointed by the Gentlemen XVII in the Low Countries and sent to Batavia to replace Jacques Specx, He was born in 1581 and made his first trip to the East in 1606. On his second voyage in December 1610 he commanded three ships to the Orient. In 1612, he sailed to Hirado, Japan where he replaced Jacques Specx who succeeded him again in 1614. In October 1615, he returned to Holland and served the Company 15 years as director. He served as governor general from 5 September 1632 until 1 January 1636. After

third day of the twelfth month of this year, he [Specx] took leave of the councilors and returned by ship to the mother country. The high officials immediately acknowledged Hendrick Brouwer as acting king. Captain Pan Mingyan went to see the king and asked him to install a lieutenant (*luitenant*, 雷珍蘭, *leizhenlan*) to take part in serving the Company affairs.[43] Occupying the position of the head of the Chinese, he asked to position a flagpole outside his gate as the Dutch do. On the first day of every month he raised a flag. All house rents and interest payments could be received when the flag was raised. The king, upon hearing this, nodded and agreed. After he had consulted with the councilors, he agreed to appoint Guo Xunge (郭訓哥, Que Hoenko)[44] to the rank of lieutenant and Lin Lianguan (林蓮觀) to the rank of *soldaat* (*dashi*, 達氏, soldier).[45] He also allowed the captain to position a flagpole in front of his gate, just like the Dutch, and raise the flag on the first day of the month. The *soldaat* was paid by the Company.[46] The installation of lieutenants and soldiers started from the tenure of Captain Pan. Because this was a good plan therefore it succeeded. Is this not beautiful!

On the eighth moon of Chongzhen 8, *yihai* [乙亥], September 1635, the sovereign in the motherland ordered a ship to bring an edict to Batavia to raise Antonio van Diemen to the position of king of Batavia. Hendrick Brouwer thereupon retired. Some high officials of the Company went to see the captain

---

his return to the Netherlands he was elected as one of the Gentlemen XXI, the directors of the West India Company (WIC). He died during an expedition to Chile in 1643.

43 According to the Dutch sources the first *luitenant* (lieutenant) and *vaandrig* (ensign) were not appointed until 29 June 1678. See Appendix 1. The names of these two officers were, respectively, Lin Shishi (Lim Si Say) and Litsoecko. Guo Xunguan was appointed in 1705.

44 *Guan* (觀, or 官) was a popular honorific added to names of South Fujianese men during the Ming and Qing periods. According to contemporary sources, 'It is the custom in Fujian to call people *lang* (郎), to call the son and grandson of officials *she* (舍), and to call respectable men *guan* (官)'. *Guan* (官) and *guan* (觀) are homophones, and most people used *guan* (觀) as their name. 'Friends call one another *lao* (老). This custom is also the same in Xiamen.' Zhou Kai (周凱), *Xiamen Zhi* (廈門誌, Xiamen Gazetteer), chap. 15, '*Records of Local Customs*' (風俗記).

45 The Chinese Lieutenant is first referred to in Dutch sources in 1678, at the occasion of the appointment of Captain Tjoa Wanjok (蔡煥玉). J.A. van der Chijs, *Nederlandsch-Indisch Plakaatboek 1602–1816* (Batavia: Landsdrukkerij, 1885–1900), 3.6 and *Daghregister* 1678, 327–29. See Appendix 1.

46 Dutch sources mention the captain, lieutenant and ensign (*vaandrig*), a rank that cannot be found anywhere in the Chinese sources. On the other hand, instead of the term soldier (*soldaat*), the Dutch sources often refer to a Chinese *bode* (messenger).

of the Chinese and discussed with him their desire to set up a system of Chinese domestic administration, and make every effort [to ensure] that the wardens [*wijkmeesters*] patrolled at night. Afterwards this proposal did not result in anything. Thereupon they discussed requiring a residence permit. Every month after the raising of the flag, the Chinese people had to pay nineteen *fanams*. Everyone who purchased a permit and engaged in trade had to carry one; whoever did not possess one could be arrested and punished. Those with a permit could avoid corvée or militia service and peacefully engage in business. All the Chinese happily observed this regulation.[47]

In the first moon of the ninth year of Chongzhen, *bingzi* [丙子]**, February 1636,** the former king, Hendrick Brouwer, returned by ship to the mother country. The various headmen then paid their allegiance to Antonio van Diemen as king of Batavia.[48] After he had taken charge, Van Diemen realized that Jan Pietersz Coen's construction plans had not yet been completed when he died. Therefore he followed up the instructions left behind. He built the East Gate of Batavia. Above the gate, he placed a medallion with the portrait of a lion and an engraved name and date [under it].

The sultan of Banten and his son were then quarrelling over the throne. Sultan Haji asked the English for assistance, but the English did not dare to assist. Thereupon Sultan Haji was at loss. He was besieged in his castle. When he was in great danger, he ordered a tunnel dug from within the castle to the

---

47   The poll tax (*hoofdgeld*) had already been introduced by Governor General Coen on 9 October 1620. A payment of one and a half *rials* a month exempted Chinese citizens from the obligation to serve in the local militia or contribute money for the fortification of the city; *Plakaatboek*, 1.76–77. As of 14 November 1620, the Chinese were obliged to produce the license proving that they had paid the poll tax on a monthly basis. *Plakaatboek*, 1.88–89. On 27 April 1648, this payment was reduced to half a *rial*.

48   Antonio van Diemen was born in 1593 in Culemborg. Bankrupt after losing his fortune as a merchant, he enlisted as soldier under a false name and left for the Orient in 1618. Upon his arrival in Batavia, he was appointed clerk (*klerk*) and within four years he rose to the rank of senior merchant. Joining the Council of the Indies in 1626, he became director general in April 1629. Between 1631 and 1633 he stayed in the Netherlands. After his return in Batavia he served three more years as director general before he succeeded Hendrick Brouwer in 1636.

   His governor generalship lasted until his death on 19 April 1645. The Batavian law code (*Bataviasche Statuten*) was introduced under Van Diemen's rule, and it continued to be used as the law book for the VOC until the early nineteenth century.

outside, and told someone to take a letter out of the palace and take a ship to Batavia to seek help.[49]

In the second spring moon of the tenth year of Chongzhen, *dingchou* [丁丑], **April 1637**, Captain Pan Mingyan died in Glodok.[50] Yan Erguan (顏二觀, Siqua) thereupon sent a petition to the great king asking for the position of captain.[51] The king thereupon immediately appointed Yan Erguan to act as captain and reported this to the sovereign in the mother country.

In Chongzhen eleven, *wuyin* [戊寅], **1638**, disorder erupted in Tangshan (唐山, i.e. China) and [the government] closed the ports. Consequently, the Chinese ocean junks could not come to Batavia. At that time, the sovereign in the mother country sent an edict approving the installation of Yan Erguan as captain. The king of Batavia, Van Diemen, constructed the Small South Gate (Kleine Zuiderpoort), and attached above it the date of construction, 1638.

In Chongzhen twelve, *jimao* [己卯], **1639**, China was in great upheaval. Chinese junks could not engage in trade. The Chinese captain submitted a petition with the proposal to establish a weigh-house and a gambling house and to add one more lieutenant. After deliberation with the councilors, the king

---

49   This story seems to refer to the quarrel between the old Sultan Agung and his successor, Sultan Haji, in 1682.

50   Bingam actually died on 25 March 1663—*twenty-six years* later!

51   *Zan* or *Gan Siqua* probably arrived from China as early as 1626. The Governor General and Council decided to appoint Siqua, 'a pious and honest citizen, well beloved by his nation', on 10 April 1663. On 23 April, Governor General Joan Maetsuijcker issued a proclamation in which he appointed Siqua captain of the Chinese citizenry and authorizing him, like his predecessor, Bingam, to deal with and resolve all small matters among the Chinese population. Large or more ambiguous cases he was to pass on to the proper authorities. The Batavia Castle *Daghregister* of the same date describes how Siqua was welcomed by various high officials at the castle square in the company of several eminent local Chinese and surrounded by a great mass of silk flags and banners. His commission was proclaimed in both Dutch and Chinese. Chinese visitors were invited inside, where Siqua was saluted and congratulated by the governor general. After this ceremony, the gentlemen rode on horseback to the town hall where the proclamation was again issued in both languages to the common people. At the culmination of the festivities, Siqua entertained the officials to a lavish dinner at his house on the eastern side of the river. All this shows how highly the position of Chinese captain was regarded.

Siqua's testament was drawn up on 28 April 1666. He turned out to have five children by three Balinese wives and one Chinese wife in China and was married in the Chinese manner. However, under Dutch law he had community property with Niai d'Siko of Bali, with whom he had no children. Siqua's imposing tomb has been described by various visitors to Batavia. Hoetink, 'Chineesche officieren', 22–27.

agreed and allowed it.[52] The tax of the weigh-house was granted every year to the captain. The profits from the gambling house were given to the wife of the captain for her daily needs of *sirih*.[53]

He Liange (何蓮哥, Ho Lienko) was appointed lieutenant; therefore from Captain Yan onwards there were two lieutenants.[54]

> *John Chinaman* (唐人氏) *comments*:[55] the installation of the gambling house was to enrich himself at the expense of others. This was the fault of Captain Yan. Yan Erguan not only could not inspire the people to follow good behaviour, but he also submitted a petition to install a gambling house. Consequently, his conduct was improper, and he enriched himself at the expense of others. He stands condemned through the ages. He should be without posterity!

In the sixteenth year of Chongzhen, *guiwei* **[癸未], 1643,** our Chinese government (Zhongguo) had not yet pacified the troubles in the mainland (Tangshan).[56] That was because the Dashing Robber illegally took up arms, the rebels responded to his call, and masses of criminals ran amok.[57] Therefore, the capital met with upheaval; the emperor committed suicide. Manchu troops invaded and plundered. The king of Qing established a new dynasty. Alas! May the late emperor benefit us and relieve us. With the Chongzhen period the great Ming came to an end in the spring of this year.

---

52 To prevent tampering with the weights, Coen had installed the *waag* (weigh-house) on 1 November 1620; *Plakaatboek*, 1.79. The tax on the weigh-house was farmed to a freeburgher and Captain Bencon on 6 November 1626; *Plakaatboek*, 1.204.

53 Coen had already introduced the tax on gambling on 1 November 1620, and Bencon and Jancon were appointed to supervise its collection; *Plakaatboek*, 1.78. Betel-nut chewing was (and is) a common practice throughout Southeast Asia. It requires three different ingredients: the areca nut wrapped in betel leaf (*paan*), and slaked lime paste to bind the leaves.

54 This is incorrect. Until 1683 no second lieutenant was appointed.

55 The anonymous commentator who throughout the text seems to represent '*die gesunde Volksempfindung*'. With a wink to Medhurst's title of Wang Dahai's book and the contemporary term 'John Company' we have chosen to baptize this commentator 'John Chinaman'.

56 In this sentence Zhongguo refers to the Chinese government, and Tangshan refers to the country, mainland China.

57 The Dashing Robber (闖賊) refers to the rebel Li Zicheng (李自成), who styled himself Chuangwang (闖王), the Dashing King. He occupied the capital.

The first moon of the seventeenth year of the Chongzhen Huaizong Duan Emperor [崇禎懷宗端皇帝] is the same as the first year of the Shizu Zhang Emperor of the Great Qing dynasty [大清世祖章皇帝], *jiashen* [甲申], 1644.

In Fengyang prefecture (鳳陽府), the birthplace of Ming Taizu [the founding emperor of the Ming dynasty] in the year seventeen of Chongzhen, an earthquake suddenly occurred. This proves that good and evil were foreboded, and could not be avoided.

The first year of the Shizu Zhang Emperor, the first year of the Shunzhi [順治] period, *jiashen* [甲申], 1644.

The Shunzhi emperor was the son of the Mude (木德) deity, therefore he was vigorous in spring and obtained the world. Dust storms and terrible rains were then raging in China. At night tens of thousands of horses and wild animals fought with each other, their shrieks spread everywhere, snow and ice were almost one foot thick. It is said that the footprints of giants and elephants were observed. On that day, Fengyang suffered an earthquake.[58]

In the second spring moon of Shunzhi 2, *yiyou* [乙酉], March 1645, the Great King Van Diemen fell critically ill and summoned the headmen to confer in order to charge Cornelis van der Lijn[59] to provisionally act as king and take care of the affairs of state. On the nineteenth day of the fourth month of 1645, the great king died and on the twentieth he was buried in the great church of the castle.[60] The authorities then acknowledged Cornelis van der Lijn as their king, and sent a missive to inform the sovereign in the mother country.

---

58 Liem manuscript.
59 Cornelis van der Lijn, a native of the city of Alkmaar, arrived in 1627 in Batavia with the rank of assistant. In 1632 he was appointed senior merchant and five years later, he joined the Council of the Indies as extraordinary councilor. He was appointed director general in 1640 and succeeded Van Diemen as provisional governor general on 19 April 1645. He was officially appointed by the Gentlemen XVII on 10 October 1646. Van der Lijn reduced the Chinese poll tax to half a *rial*. He resigned on 7 October 1650 and returned to the Dutch Republic. At his departure from Batavia the Chinese citizens of the town presented him with a 'jewel' that was valued at 1989 guilders. (Van Rhede van de Kloot, *Gouverneurs-generaal*, 50) After having served in various official functions in his native town Van der Lijn passed away on 27 July 1679.
60 The exact date is 19 April 1645.

In the third year of Shunzhi, *bingxu* [丙戌], 1646, the sovereign of the mother country ordered a ship to bring a letter to Batavia to confer the title of King on Cornelis van der Lijn.

At that time, the weights and measures of the weigh-house were inaccurate. The people protested daily. The king discussed this with the headmen of the people.[61] He standardized measures and weights and stipulated that everybody high and low should use the Company's measures and weights. They were not allowed to make them themselves. The mark of the Company had to be applied twice a year. The costs of applying the mark on every balance cost one *fanam* and two cents. Those who were caught [weighing] without having received a mark had to pay a fine of twenty-five *rials*. He ordered the soldaat to go to every street to proclaim these regulations that should be observed by all the Chinese and the natives. This is truly a fine method of ruling the world.

At the time, the king of the Bugis fought with the king of Makassar. The war went on without interruption, but because the Bugis were weaker, their king ordered someone to go quickly by ship to Batavia to ask the Company to raise soldiers and assist him in the war.[62]

In the first moon of the fourth year of Shunzhi, *dinghai* [丁亥], February 1647, the Great King Cornelis van der Lijn summoned the headmen for deliberations and it was decided to recruit soldiers. He immediately ordered 500 Dutch soldiers to gather under the Amboynese Captain Jonker and the Balinese Captain Djisin. They divided the troops over three ships and went to Makassar and attacked.[63]

---

61 The weigh-house was introduced on 1 November 1620 and Captain Bencon and his influential friend Jancon were appointed to fix the weights (*dacing*) at Bencon's house. In the *Statutes of Batavia*, which were introduced on 5 July 1642, during the reign of Antonio van Diemen, it was ordered that all merchandise heavier than 50 pounds should be weighed at the public weigh-house. *Plakaatboek*, 1: 79, 568. On 29 December 1661, it was decided that henceforth only the Dutch balance and the Dutch weights should be used in the weigh-house because of the 'great frauds and forgeries' that had been committed with the weights that had been used in the past. *Plakaatboek*, 2.357.

62 Makassar (Kingdom of Gowa) indeed subjugated the neighbouring kingdoms of Wajo, Boni and Sopeng. The emissary referred to in the text is most likely Prince Aru Palaka of Sopeng, in alliance with whom Cornelis Speelman was to conquer Makassar in 1667.

63 Captain Jonker was born around 1630 on the island of Manipa in the Moluccas. He accompanied his father when the latter was sent to Ambon as hostage. In 1656, he began serving as ensign under the governor of Ambon, Willem de Vlamingh van Oudshoorn, and later followed Rijckloff van Goens on his army campaigns in India, where he distinguished himself by his great valour and was severely wounded in his left hand. Raised to the rank of captain, he served in Ambon between 1660 and 1665, but was appointed head of the

In the eighth moon of Shunzhi 5, *wuzi* [戊子], September 1648, Captain Yan Erguan passed away and he was buried in the Company cemetery at Mangga Dua. The Great King Cornelis van der Lijn met with the councilors and installed as captain the widow of Yan Erguan, Yan Erya (顏二雙, Gan Dji Nyai), a Balinese native, to succeed in the position of her late husband, and at the same time drew up a missive and reported to the sovereign in the motherland.[64]

> *John Chinaman comments*: This Balinese lady had no wisdom and no agenda. Her customs were different from those of the Chinese. Is it not strange that she suddenly was put in charge of the Chinese? One can imagine the moral standing of the people then. Most curious is that Guo Xunge (郭訓哥, Que Hoenko) who served as lieutenant more than ten years, acknowledged her as captain.[65] Given that Erguan's wife served as captain, there are examples of women who ruled the country during the Han and Tang dynasties. Why then would it be special for barbarian countries! But from these examples we can see that these countries were doomed to fall apart. The *Shangshu* (尚書) says: When the hen rules the morning (牝雞司晨), what does that portend? It leaves us with foreboding. The turning upside down of the yin (陰) and yang (陽) principles dates from Van der Lijn. Afterwards this was confirmed by the fighting and disasters between the Tang people and the Dutch.[66]

Amboynese in Batavia on 1 January 1665. He participated again in several expeditions to Sumatra, Makassar, Ternate, and Ambon. In recognition of his outstanding contributions, in 1672 he was awarded 'an act of a raise in income' on parchment with seals in a golden box. During the expedition to East Java in 1679 he was temporarily assigned as bodyguard to the susuhunan of Mataram and succeeded in capturing Trunajaya, the head of the rebels, for which he was awarded a golden chain with medal. Finally, he distinguished himself during the campaign against Sultan Abu'l Fatah of Banten in 1682–83. After his protector and friend Governor General Speelman passed away, Captain Jonker gradually faded away in his dwelling along the Marunda River close to Tanjung Priok. Suspected of a conspiracy, he was killed while being arrested in 1689.

64 This happened eighteen years later. After the death of her husband on 26 April 1666, the widow of Captain Siqua, Niai d'Siko of Bali, acted as head of the Chinese for twelve years before she died in December 1678. B. Hoetink, 'De weduwe van Kapitein Siqua-Djanda Kapitein Siqua', *Chung Hwa Hui Tsa Chih* (1918) 2-1:16–25 and 98–107. For an interesting contribution on the social status of Chinese women in Southeast Asia see Claudine Salmon, 'Women's Social Status as Reflected in Chinese Epigraphs from Insulinde (16th–20th Centuries)', *Archipel* 72:1 (2006): 157–94.

65 This is incorrect. Guo Xunge (郭訓哥, Que Hoenko) was appointed lieutenant fifty-five years later, on 5 May 1705!

66 The *Shangshu*, or *Classic of History*, is one of the five classics of ancient Chinese literature.

In the ninth moon of Shunzhi 6, *jichou* [己丑], October 1649, the sovereign of the mother country sent a letter to Batavia, allowing the wife of Yan Erguan to be officially appointed captain and to receive the position of her husband Yan Erguan. The lieutenants were Guo Xunge and He Liange, and Lin Lianguan served as soldaat.[67] When Lady Yan Erguan, this Balinese lady, served as captain, every time she went to the *bicara* [assembly] hall she behaved like a man. She solved problems in the official hall clearly and quickly. It can be said that she was a strong man among the native women. But the Company administered men's affairs with a woman. She outmatched the two lieutenants, yin and yang collapsed. This had great consequences for the majesty of the government as it ran counter to destiny and fortune. Every time her monthly period arrived, she made an excuse that she was sick and did not go out. And the *bicara* affairs [the issues to be discussed] she left to a black [native] clerk to act upon, therefore this was more and more inconvenient.

Now, the three Company warships that had taken soldiers to Makassar almost three years before still had not achieved anything. The provisions were running out. Just when the situation became desperate, there happened to arrive Huang Juguan (黃舉觀) and Wang Faguan (王法觀), who together had fitted out a junk with a cargo of more than three hundred *che* (車)[68] of rice for sale in Makassar. Unexpectedly, they were spotted by the Dutch commanders, who sent people to purchase this rice. Considering the situation in which they found themselves, the two feared that if they did not allow the Dutch to purchase the rice, the latter would seize it by force anyway. But if they did sell it to them, they were afraid that payment would not be forthcoming. Therefore, selling was not as good as doing them a favour by presenting all the rice to the Company to serve as victuals for the soldiers. That being the case, they expected to be highly rewarded. When the Dutch headmen heard that they were willing to help them out with the army provisions, they were very happy. These two men can be said to have laid the foundation of the later glory at Makassar.

In the ninth moon of Shunzhi 7, *gengyin* [庚寅], October 1650, the Great King Van der Lijn wished to retire and discussed this with his councilors and recommended Carel Reiniersz, a native from Amsterdam.[69] On the seventh

---

67   Guo Xunge and He Liange were appointed lieutenant on 5 May 1705 and 10 June 1707, respectively.

68   1 *che* (車) equals 1000 *jin* (斤), that is, 500 kilograms.

69   Van der Lijn and his second in command, Director General François Caron, were actually recalled on suspicion of malpractice, but subsequently cleared. Carel Reiniersz was born in Amsterdam in 1602. He served as senior merchant and local director on the Coromandel coast before he returned to Batavia, where he was appointed councilor of

day of this month, he stepped down and assigned Reiniersz with the temporary powers of the king and let him manage the affairs of the country. The Great King Reiniersz ordered the outer *temenggong* also to take care of the affairs of the Chinese captain.[70]

> This sufficiently shows the inappropriateness of the appointment by the former king of the widow of Yan Erguan to the position of captain.

He also ordered the outer *temenggong* to take care of the *bicara* [in this case, discussions about Chinese matters] and furthermore installed a new official to specially supervise inland affairs, named *commissaris* [*der inlanders*], one official to supervise the coastal affairs, named the *zee fiscaal*, another official (the inner *temenggong*) called the *baljuw*, and yet another, the outer *temenggong*, called a *landdrost*; and this he thereupon memorialized to the sovereign in the mother country asking for approval.

At the time the Lieutenant Guo Xunge and his elder brother Guo Qiaoge (郭喬哥, Que Kiauko) discussed the establishment of a Chinese public cemetery, because the authorities did not allow our people to be buried in the Company's cemetery.[71]

Every time a Chinese died there were always worries about where to inter him. Thereupon Guo Qiaoguan took the lead recruiting our people to subscribe and donate, depending on their wealth, to the building of the cemetery. The people gladly followed this up, and he thereupon bought a plot of land named Dongzhong (東塚) and appointed one person to be the undertaker (土公, *tugong*). So from then on, our Chinese people no longer faced the

---

the Indies in 1638. After a short stint in Holland during the 1640s, he returned to Batavia in 1645, when he was appointed president of the city council. His appointment to the position of governor general by the Council of the Indies upon the departure of Cornelis van der Lijn was not ratified by the Gentlemen XVII, who summoned him home in 1653. He passed away, however, in Batavia on 18 May 1653.

70 The first *landdrost* was appointed on 8 February 1651 'to stop the large-scale vagabondage by the native inhabitants'; *Realia* 2.133.

71 According to the Dutch sources the two benefactors, Guo Qiaoge and Guo Xunge, were not appointed lieutenant until 10 June 1695 and 5 May 1705, respectively! The *Plakaatboek*, 1.454–55 (28 December 1640) mentions that a tax should be levied on Chinese funerals (excluding poor people) to help support the Chinese hospital. On 11 June 1660, the tax was raised from two *rials* to three rixdollars. Inscriptions on the Chinese tombs were taxed 12 rixdollars, also to benefit the Chinese hospital. This decision was taken 'because the Chinese asked to be allowed to open a new cemetery because the old one was filled up with tombs'. See *Plakaatboek*, 2.335–36. Permission was given on 11 June 1660. See *Realia* 1.279.

problems of acting counter to prohibitions. This is truly a wonderful example of unostentatious benevolence. At that time Huang Shigong (黃石公) was appointed undertaker.

> *John Chinaman comments*: The establishment of the public cemetery enables the dead to rest in peace in the underworld. Reason in principles and knowledge of righteousness in the hearts of the two Guos showed that these two worldly-wise men could rule the nation. They were able to extend their glory to their descendants.

In the twelfth moon of Shunzhi 8, *xinmao* **[辛卯], 12 January 1651,** the former king, Cornelis van der Lijn, returned by ship to the mother country. In the same month, a letter came from Makassar reporting peace. The Company from that time on held the land of Makassar.

> From the year *dinghai* [丁亥], when it sent out soldiers to attack Makassar, until the year *xinmao* [辛卯], it took the Company altogether four years to defeat Makassar.[72]

In the seventh moon of the lunar calendar, Lieutenant Guo Xunguan passed away and was buried at Tanjung. If in the world there are such men who are good then the management of the country's affairs will also be prosperous and honourable. The Great King Reiniersz then appointed Guo Junge (郭郡哥, Queeconko) lieutenant.[73]

> At this moment, the English, who had lived in Batavia before, observed its situation. They also meant to occupy Batavia, so they built a castle and a moat pending future plans. But when they saw that the Company had obtained such a large plot of land, the situation of a coiling dragon and a crouching tiger, a terrain of great strategic importance, awe-inspiring and for the moment prosperous, they gave up their plans. There still is an empty fortress at Bomian (泊面, the *Boom*).[74]

---

72 After many failed attempts to conclude a lasting treaty with the king of Makassar, the latter was finally subjugated by Cornelis Speelman and Arung Palaka on 1 January 1667. See C. Feddersen, *Principled Pragmatism, VOC Interaction with Makassar 1637–68 and the Nature of Company Diplomacy* (PhD diss., Leiden University, 2016).

73 As already pointed out, these events did not occur until forty years later.

74 The *boom* was a wooden pole barring the entrance of the inner harbour where the customs duties were levied. The text probably refers to the still extant *Uitkijk* (watchtower), which commanded the roadstead. Already in 1624, the English withdrew from Batavia to

In the ninth year of Shunzhi, *renchen* [壬辰], 1652, the Great King Reiniersz followed up the intention of the former King Jan Pietersz Coen and completed the citadel (Jincheng, 金城, Batavia castle). He also constructed the North Gate, and it was hereby completed. Above the gate, he put a picture of a sailing ship. He also built the West Gate, and on the gate attached a plate. Within this medallion was a stone with the depiction of a sword standing up.[75]

> *John Chinaman comments*: This was the portent of struggle from then on. It all sprouted out of this.

In the fourth month of Shunzhi 10, *guisi* [癸巳], May 1653, when the great king fell seriously ill, he convened the councilors for deliberations and transferred his position to Joan Maetsuijcker to take charge as acting king of the country's affairs. On the eighteenth the great king passed away and he was buried on the twentieth in the church of Batavia castle. The councilors then sent a memorial to the sovereign in the mother country.

In the ninth month of Shunzhi 11, *jiawu* [甲午], October 1654, the sovereign of the mother country ordered a ship to take to Batavia an edict that authorized Joan Maetsuijcker to serve as king of Batavia.[76]

> Joan Maetsuijcker was from Amsterdam. When this man served as king he was cajoled. The general state of affairs was disordered. Captain Cai Huanyu [蔡煥玉, Tsoa Wanjock] taking advantage of the king's favours,

---

the island of Lagundi, near the Sunda Strait, but the following year they had to be evacuated from this settlement by the Dutch because the garrison had fallen gravely ill. Shortly afterwards they settled down in the port of Banten.

75 The coat of arms of Batavia consists of a laurel wreath with sword pointing upwards. This was looked upon by the author as a bad omen.

76 Joan Maetsuijcker was born in Amsterdam on 14 October 1606. He studied law at Leuven in the Spanish Netherlands and departed for Batavia in 1635 with the rank of Pensionary of the Council of Justice. He served between 1636 and 1641 as president of the Orphans Chamber, the chairman of the Board of Aldermen, and bailiff and president of the Council of Justice. In the meantime, he composed the local law code, the *Bataviasche Statuten*, in 1641. He was consecutively appointed extraordinary and ordinary Councilor of the Indies in 1641 and 1644. In 1645, he became governor of Ceylon and in 1650 director general. He provisionally succeeded Carel Reiniersz as governor general on 18 May 1653, and was in 1654 officially appointed by the Gentlemen XVII. He passed away in Batavia on 4 January 1678.

engaged in merrymaking. He made the king prosperous and was improperly assigned by him seven tax farms [*pachten*]. If you do not discern between high and low, how can there be a general state of affairs? Those who originate bad precedents, aren't they detestable?[77]

In the fifth moon of Shunzhi 12, *yiwei* [乙未], June 1655, an envoy of the king of Ternate came on a Dutch ship with two decks to Batavia to congratulate the Company. The great king ordered him lodged in a house near the East Gate. The temper of this man was very irascible.[78] He did not like that the common people often passed in front of his gate. He ordered his men to capture people who passed the gate unaware and had them beaten up. There was no way the Company's officers could stop him.

> How is it possible that one could not stop this violent behaviour? If we afterwards must confront such violent ruffians, what to do?[79]

In the eighth moon of this year, Yan Erguan's wife, who had received the title of captain, passed away. Following the native style, she was buried at their own [Balinese] cemetery at Jakatra. The widow of Yan Erguan received the captaincy of her husband in the year *wuzi* [1648] and served in this position seven years and one month.[80] The state of affairs at Batavia crumbled and from that

---

77 These remarks are way off the point as in reality Captain Cai Huanyu was not appointed until 29 June 1678, twenty-four years later, while Governor General Maetsuijcker died on 4 January of the same year.

78 This was 'Prince Rotterdam', who had already stayed in Batavia in 1681. See *Realia* 3.274. François Valentijn met Prince Rotterdam in Batavia in 1686 but gives a totally different description of his character. 'He was very polite, at least superficially, and did not need to travel to Italy to acquire the pretences of the court. He spoke Dutch reasonably well, although he was better at understanding than at speaking'. See Valentijn, *Oud en Nieuw Oost-Indiën*, 1.350. He was the younger brother of Sultan Sibori, *aka* 'koning Amsterdam', who after he had planned an insurrection was captured and banished to Batavia in August 1681. In July 1683, he was allowed to return to Ternate after he had formally acknowledged that Ambon and Buru belonged to VOC territory. See Gerrit Knaap, *Kruidnagelen en Christenen. De VOC en de bevolking van Ambon 1656–1696* (Leiden: KITLV, 2004), 56–57.

79 This scene has been misinterpreted in the Dutch version based on Medhurst, 'Chronologische geschiedenis', 25. The editors thought that Governor General Maetsuijcker's temperament was described.

80 She actually served no less than twelve years.

day went wrong. The Great King Maetsuijcker then immediately appointed Cai Huanyu (蔡煥玉) captain and informed the sovereign of the mother country.[81]

On the fourteenth day of the twelfth moon of 1665 there was a large earthquake. On the next day three more shocks were felt.[82]

In the eighth moon of Shunzhi 13, *bingshen* [丙申], **September 1656**, the sovereign of the mother country ordered a sailing ship to take a missive to Batavia in which he authorized the appointment of Cai Huanyu to the position of captain. The great king was very enamoured of this man at the time. Everything Huanyu suggested to him, the king would carry out as he suggested. He asked for an office building for the captain where he could hold his *bicara* meetings with the lieutenants. He also implored him to do away with the Dutch guards at his gate, and, in addition, bought a flower garden at Bazhilan (八芝蘭, Pecinan). The captain was day and night in his garden drinking, carousing, and merrymaking at leisure.

> *John Chinaman comments*: The prevalence of prostitutes in later days originated here. The misbehaviour of the captain was all too clear.

In Shunzhi 17, *gengzi* [庚子], **1660**, the great king decided with the *shuangbing* (雙柄, *schepenen*, board of aldermen or city council), to have seven tax farms auctioned off on the twenty-ninth of the twelfth month in the warehouse of

---

81   Please note that Cai Huanyu was not appointed until 23 years later, i.e. on 14 June 1678! For a contemporary description of the investiture, see Appendix 1. He was one of the oldest Chinese inhabitants and had already lived forty years in Batavia when he was elected captain, because he was *'de recktlykste, beminste ende voornaamste'* (the most flexible, amiable and prominent) of them all. This old gentleman had already served as boedelmeester in 1661–62, 1664–65, and 1669–1676.

Because of his advanced age, but also because the Chinese had asked for more representatives, in addition to the captain, a lieutenant (*luitenant*), Lin Shishi (林時使, Lim Si Say) and an ensign (*vaandrig*), Li Zuge (李祖哥, Li Tsoeko) were also appointed for the first time; *Plakaatboek*,3.6. Captain Cai Huanyu (Tsoa Wanjock) was interred on 5 October 1684. Conducted with much pomp and circumstance, his funeral procession was preceded by a company of soldiers in mourning mode; Hoetink, 'Chineesche officieren', 31–35.

Lin Shishi (Lim Si Say) also served as boedelmeester in 1674, 1676, and 1677. He passed away in 1678.

Li Zuge (Li Tsoeko/Soeko) was appointed lieutenant on 16 May 1679. He had served as boedelmeester in 1665, 1668–69, 1673–74, 1677, and 1678. He served as guardian of Captain Bencon's son, who later married his daughter. He passed away between 1680 and 1682. His grave was situated next that of Captain Bencon. His wife, Tan Hiamtse, died in 1722 and was buried alongside Captain Bencon's widow; Hoetink, 'Chineesche officieren', 96–97).

82   Medhurst, 'Chronologische geschiedenis', 28.

the citadel and invited tenders.[83] The officials sat down according to their rank and looked on. When people made competitive tenders, they immediately wrote down their names.

> 1, poll tax [*hoofdgeld*]; 2, gambling tax [*pacht op de spelen*]; 3, *shaban* sales tax [*vergunning voor straatventen,* that is, tax on street peddlars]; 4, slaughter of pigs and sheep tax [*slagtpacht*]; 5, tax on fish ponds [*vispacht*]; 6, tax on paddy [*rijst*]; 7, tax on sale of liquor [*sterke drank*].

Those who had made the highest bid received these farms. No matter whether they were Chinese, Dutch, or native, all the people who wanted to be present and watch or wished to bid had to be properly dressed and wear shoes and stockings. Only then were they permitted to enter the warehouse. If they did not, they were denied entrance.

There was then a man named Wang Wangguan (王旺觀) who recently had struck it rich, from rags to riches. Improperly dressed and without socks and shoes he barged into the warehouse. The Dutch soldiers at the gate could not stop him. He did not care, but pushed himself in and shouted that he wanted to obtain the poll tax.

> How did he obtain this so quickly? I think this kind of vulgar person behaves brusquely like this, and intentionally does not care about being accepted. So, if the officers and established people do not bid for the farms, this is shameful. Then one must certainly bid again. Instead of this he achieved success. Therefore, in later times people could not despise and ridicule others.

When the high officials asked him for collateral, Wang Wangguan answered, 'I don't need a guarantee; it should suffice if I can give a down payment'. Thereupon he handed over the total sum of the tax farm for the whole year to clear the situation. From then on, at all tax farm auctions anybody with or without shoes and stockings could enter the warehouse and tender a bid.

> *John Chinaman comments*: That the Chinese do not behave properly began with this Wang Wang[guan]. Those with dishevelled hair who wear their clothes in the wrong way, began with this bellwether. Had he no descendants? That is just because rich people misbehave like that!

---

83 *Plakaatboek*, 2.312–21, 20 December 1658: 'Voorwaarden, waarop de volgende imposten ende incompsten den 1en januari 1659 aan de meestbiedende zouden worden opgeveijlt ende verpacht'.

THE STORY OF ONG ONGKO [WANG WANGGE]:[84]

A very rich Dutchman who was residing in the countryside, was robbed by his own slaves, who took away a box containing a lot of money and let it sink in a river to avoid discovery. Thereupon they left to murder their master. Ong Ongko was then still a poor fellow, who made a living collecting coconuts.

When the slaves arrived at the river, he was sitting high in one of the coconut trees at the side of the river, and saw, without being perceived by them, the place where they had sunk the box.

As soon as they had left, he slipped down and dived into the river. He towed the box upriver against the current and left it there. When it suited them, the slaves returned to pick up the box. But when they could not find it they searched for it downstream, not imagining that it could have been moved upstream.

After much seeking they gave up. Thereupon Ong Ongko showed up again and secured the booty. This enabled him to pay for all the tax farms together, without offering any collateral.

In Kangxi 8, *jiyou* [己酉], June 1669, Captain Cai Huanyu passed away and was buried in the Longyan garden of Bazhilan.[85]

At that time, Lieutenant Guo Junguan addressed a petition to the great king and asked to be appointed to the captaincy, and Lin Jingguan (林敬官, Limkeenqua) asked to be allowed to occupy the position of lieutenant. The Great King Maetsuijcker installed Guo Junge (郭郡哥, Queeconko) as captain,[86]

---

84   The suffixes *ge* 哥 and *guan* 觀 are often interchanged. This story is noted down in Medhurst, 'Chronologische geschiedenis', 27–28. It was probably added by the Dutch editors because it cannot be found in the existing Chinese texts.

85   This is incorrect. Cai Huanyu, served as captain from 14 June 1678 until his death on 5 October 1684.

86   The dates and connections are also incorrect. On 3 August 1685, Governor General and Council discussed who should succeed Captain Cai Huanyu and Lieutenant Huang Jiuge, (黃舅哥 Oeij Koeko), both of whom had died. Lieutenant Huang Jiuge, who was appointed on 16 January 1682, is not mentioned in the Chinese text. He had been the captain of the Chinese in Makassar and had also served as boedelmeester in Batavia from 1679 to 1681; Hoetink, 'Chineesche officieren', 97–98.

On 3 August 1685, it was decided to appoint Guo Junge captain, because he had functioned for a considerable time as chief of the Chinese before the 'troubles in Banten'. Quepauko, who had recently been chosen as boedelmeester was appointed lieutenant. The next day Guo Junge asked to be excused from the captaincy owing to

and Lin Jingguan and He Liange as lieutenants and Lin Lianguan as soldaat and Huang Shigong as undertaker.

> The Guanyinting (觀音亭, Guanyin temple, in Malay *klenteng*) was established in Shunzhi 7, *gengyin* [庚寅], 1650.[87] Lieutenant Guo Xunge and his elder brother Guo Qiaoguan proposed to collect donations and build the temple, but they were unable to accomplish this then; it was finally finished when Guo Junge served as captain.[88]
>
> Here we can see that this was not achieved because several people were truly sincere, but owing to the power of the captain. They worshipped the Buddha and various deities, and they invited monks to live inside and carry out the rites for the gods and chant the sacred sutras and keep the statues of the gods pure and clean. In the rear of the temple they worshiped the statue of their forefather, Guo Liuguan (郭六觀). In the case of the Shangdi (玄天上帝, Xuantian Shangdi) temple at Tanjung,

---

his 'incompetence and incapacity'. It turned out that in reality he had been accused of bringing about the 'unexpected and suspect death of the Chinese Lieutenant Couko and Boedelmeester Bousiqua, who both had clearly been ready to serve as captain'. After some pressure, he accepted the appointment; Hoetink. 'Chineesche officieren', 31–47.

Lieutenant Lin Jingguan, alias Jacob Lim Keenko, was appointed second lieutenant on 4 August 1685 (together with Guo Baoge (郭包哥, Que Pauko/Quepauqua), 'to be able to maintain the affairs of the Chinese who are already many in number'. He had been elected boedelmeester in 1683 and 1684. In 1699, he was allowed to establish two sugar mills on his estate Camiri, six miles inland along the Grote Rivier; Hoetink, 'Chineesche officieren', 98–99.

Lieutenant Guo Baoge is not mentioned in the Chinese text. He was committed to prison for debt on 1 April 1692, but the following June he fled to Semarang, where he joined rebellious Chinese who wanted to surrender the city to the susuhunan. After he had been extradited by the ruler of Mataram, he was sentenced to be broken on the wheel in Japara; Hoetink, 'Chineesche officieren', 98.

Lieutenant He Liange was appointed many years later, on 10 June 1707, having served as boedelmeester in 1705 and 1706. He had been given permission to establish two sugar mills and a lumber mill at Pamanukan and Cassem in 1707, but he had to give them up because of the 'intrusions and obstinacy of the [local] Javanese'; Hoetink, 'Chineesche officieren', 103.

87 This temple was baptized Jinde Yuan (金德院, Temple of Golden Virtue) in 1750 and still exists. See Claudine Salmon and Denys Lombard, *Les Chinois de Jakarta, temples et vie collective* (Paris: Editions de la Maison des Sciences de l'Homme 1980), 72–86.

88 Here again the author is confusing facts: Guo Junge was appointed captain on 3 August 1685. Guo Qiaoge and Guo Xunge were not appointed lieutenants until 10 June 1695 and 5 May 1705.

the sugar mill operator Dai Shangxun (戴上勳), who was running a sugar mill at Tanjung, was responsible. Because his prayers for sunny and rainy weather were very effective, he proposed discussing the effort to collect donations and build the temple.[89]

It is said that to this today whatever is prayed for at this temple is granted by the deity.

In the sixth moon of Kangxi 9, *gengxu* [庚戌], July 1670, the sovereign of the mother country sent an edict to Batavia authorizing the official appointment of Guo Junguan to the captaincy, and of Lin Jingguan and He Lianguan to the position of lieutenant and of Lin Lianguan to the position of soldaat.

The king of Mataram in Semarang (called the pangeran, sultan, or susuhunan) and his brothers were then contending for control of the country. He raised soldiers and fought big battles at Zhibayu (芝吧嶼; Cibayu) and Lihan (例漢). They fought incessantly, causing such turmoil that not even chickens and dogs were left in peace! The susuhunan sent a missive to Batavia and asked the Company to raise soldiers and come to his aid.

The Great King Maetsuijcker summoned all the councilors for consultation and reached a proper decision. He ordered a commissioner to lead 1,000 Dutch soldiers together with Bugis, Balinese, and Ambonese soldiers, distributed them over three ships, and sent them via Semarang to Mataram to assist in the war.[90]

---

89   Commentary taken from the Xu Yunqiao edition. On the Xuantian Shangdi temple, see Salmon and Lombard, *Les Chinois de Jakarta*, 99–100.

90   Cornelis Speelman, a member of the Council of the Indies, left for Japara with 1,200 soldiers in December 1676. He first concluded a treaty with Susuhunan Amangkurat I in February 1677 in exchange for important concessions for the VOC. He then tried to do the same with a pretender to the throne, Trunajaya, a Madurese prince who had beaten the susuhunan's forces in October 1676, and who was by then occupying all of east and central Java. When the negotiations did not bear fruit, Speelman attacked Trunajaya's forces at Ampel (near Surabaya), but Trunajaya escaped to Kediri. While Speelman first headed for Madura to conquer the island, Trunajaya seized and plundered the capital of Mataram, Karta. The susuhunan and his eldest son, Pangeran Anom, fled to seek protection from Speelman, but Amangkurat I died on the way in Cirebon and was interred at Tegal-wangi. Anom succeeded his father as Amangkurat II (r. 1677–1703). After Governor General Maetsuycker passed away in January 1678, and Speelman was recalled to Batavia to serve as director general, several commanders succeeded the latter as field commanders. With the assistance of Aru Palaka and his Buginese troops, Commander Jacob Couper and Captain François Tack were finally able to corner Trunajaya in December 1679 and captured him together with the crown jewels. Upon meeting face to face with Trunajaya, Susuhunan Amangkurat II personally ran his kris through his prisoner. Once Pangeran

After the commissioner arrived in Mataram, he led his troops and encircled the enemies, so that these ran out of victuals and plans; afterwards he attacked with stratagems when the enemies were unprepared. He beleaguered them from *gengxu* [庚戌, 1670] until *yimao* [乙卯, 1675]—altogether five years. Only then was the enemy convinced that they should not dare to start a war again and [only then] was peace secured. From then on, the susuhunan did not face the trouble of war again. The commissioner divided his soldiers to assist the king to protect this place.

> The origin of the war sprang from the rebellion of Trunajaya who took up arms against the king of Lannei (覽內, Mataram). After the vanquished king died on the road, his sons battled each other for the succession. Thus, disaster was brought on the poor people, from outside by the rebels and from inside by this fraternal feud. The eldest son then asked the Dutch for assistance. After they had put the assumed successor on the throne, the Dutch joined forces with the troops of the king and began their attack against the rebels. After some skirmishes and perpetual quarrels, they hatched a secret plan to surprise the enemy, who, devoid of resources, surrendered.
>
> When the headman of the rebels was brought before the king, he promised him obedience and asked for forgiveness. With his own hands the king loosened his shackles and said, 'My brother, I am greatly rejoiced to see you here, and would gladly forgive you, but unfortunately I swore some time ago that this sword would not return into its sheath before it had first pierced your heart'. Saying so he ran his kris though the rebel, and then exclaimed, 'May this heart be devoured'. Thereupon his servants jumped on the corpse, tore out the heart and devoured it together. How dismal! How terrible!
>
> Seeing that the rebellion had been defeated, and his brother slain so that peace had returned to his country, the king thanked the Dutch for their assistance, and offered to accompany them to their own territory. The Dutch, however, fearing that new rebellions might occur in the same way, thought it preferable to leave behind several hundred soldiers to guard the country. The king accepted this gratefully, not thinking that the Dutch might take advantage of this to promote their own ends.[91]

Puger, a brother of the susuhunan, had also been pacified, the Mataram court was able to settle down at a new location, Kartasura near Wonokerto.

91 Medhurst, 'Chronologische geschiedenis', 29–30.

Thereupon the commissioner sailed back victoriously with the remaining soldiers to Batavia to report his accomplishments. The Great King Maetsuijcker immediately appointed Guo Qiaoguan as captain of the Tang people in Semarang. In this year, he ordered him to go to Semarang to manage his affairs.[92]

In Kangxi 11, *renzi* [壬子], 1672, the Great King Maetsuijcker supervised the public works and built a port and a ditch within the town. Everywhere he constructed stone bridges, big and small, fourteen altogether. Only inside the East Gate did he build a three-cornered [draw]bridge. On the bridge, he put up a sign reading 1675, and he also installed a *pasar* [market] for the Chinese people and native people to engage in business and gain profits. We continued to use our Chinese coins as currency.

In Kangxi 14, *yimao* [乙卯], 1675, construction of the bridges and the market was completed.

In the fourth moon of Kangxi 17, *wuwu* [戊午], fifth month of 1678, the king fell critically ill. He summoned all the members of the council and aldermen for deliberation and they elected Rijcklof van Goens to act as king, to manage the affairs of state. The Great King Maetsuijcker passed away on the fourth and was buried inside the great church. Maetsuijcker served twenty-five years as king. The officials acknowledged Rijcklof van Goens as their acting king.[93]

In the fifth moon of Kangxi 18, *yiwei* [乙未], the sixth month of 1679, the sovereign of the mother country ordered a ship to take an edict to Batavia and formally confirmed Rijcklof van Goens as king. In his meeting with the members of the Council, the king said, 'I hear that the susuhunan, the king of Semarang in Mataram, has several big cannons in his possession. This is quite

---

92 See also Liem Thian Joe, *Riwajat Semarang 1416–1931* (Semarang: Boekhandel Ho Kim Yoe, 1933), 9–10.

93 Rycklof van Goens was born on 24 June 1619 in Rees, a town in the Duchy of Cleve in present day Germany. In 1628, he left for the Indies together with his father, an officer in the service of the VOC. On 9 May 1631, he was sent (at the age of only twelve!) to serve the governor of Coromandel. He climbed the ladder from assistant in 1634 to merchant in 1642. Between 1648 and 1654 he was sent as an emissary to the court of Mataram five times. After having served on various other missions and important positions in Batavia he was elected to the Council of the Indies in 1653. In the same year, he led an expedition to Ceylon and Goa. After a visit to the Dutch Republic in 1655, he was appointed admiral and supreme commander and commissioner of Ceylon, Malabar, and Coromandel, where he conquered various Portuguese settlements. As governor of Ceylon, from 1660 onwards he conquered the remaining Portuguese settlements on the island. In 1675, he was appointed director general and on 4 January 1678 he succeeded Maetsuycker as governor general. Van Goens asked for an honourable discharge and resigned on 25 November 1681. He passed away in Amsterdam one year later, on 14 November 1682.

serious. If there is any disaster, what to do about it? Therefore, we should plan to put them out of order'. He thereupon ordered a Dutch officer to prepare abundant presents and to go by ship to Semarang in Mataram and present the presents to the susuhunan saying: 'Our great king of Batavia admires your great virtue. He has dispatched me to visit you, to offer these insignificant presents, to express our neighbourly relations, and our friendship'.

When the susuhunan heard this, he was very pleased. He accepted all the presents, gave a banquet and entertained the Hollanders. While they were talking, he engaged in bluffing. The susuhunan sent an officer to invite the Dutch headman to come to his palace. When they met, the king said, 'I hear that your chief had something very precious that you are willing to show us'. The Dutch chief answered, 'I don't have any precious things, but if you pour silver into the cannons outside the gate and make their colours more bright and glossy, then that is really an incomparable treasure'.

The susuhunan trusted him and ordered his underlings to bring the big guns out. The Dutch chief secretly told his men to quickly melt white copper and pour it into the cannon, so that the touch hole of its barrel was sealed off. After half a day of work the plan was carried out. He then reported to the susuhunan.

When the susuhunan saw the result he was mightily pleased. The Dutch chief said, 'Because I have already run out of silver, I am returning to my ship to take a rest. On another day, I will come again to consult with you and have a drink'. He then immediately took his leave. The Dutch chief secretly thought by himself: 'If this ploy is found out by the susuhunan, that will be harmful indeed'. The next day he went to see the susuhunan and excused himself saying that because of an emergency he had to return and that he specially came to take leave of him.

Thereupon he boarded his ship, hoisted the sails and returned to Batavia to report on the completion of his task. The great king and the councilors were all mightily pleased and said, 'Now that the touch holes of the big cannons of Mataram are already plugged, there will never be any trouble. We should honour his great achievements'. Immediately the chief was promoted to the position of commandant. This chief's name I don't know. So, without proper information I do not dare to leave his details to posterity.

> *John Chinaman comments*: The plan of the chief was not wonderful at all. If you say that you pour silver into cannons to render it shining and bright in the eyes, then this is just bluffing little children. After all, if the silver is in the gun and the shining is outside the cannon, then silver is silver and colour is colour, there is no connection between the two. There is nothing else to it. The susuhunan lacked intelligence, and so did everybody in his

royal household. As a result this made the Dutch chief's plan succeed. To seal off the touch hole of a cannon, is not that a distressing thing? This happened in Kangxi 19, *gengshen* [庚申], 1680. That is all.

In the third moon of Kangxi 20, *xinyou* [辛酉], April 1681, the Great King Rijcklof van Goens fell ill and abdicated. He consulted the councilors and *schepenen* (aldermen). Together they all decided to appoint Cornelis Speelman to the position of acting ruler to take care of the country's affairs.[94] He drew up a report to inform the sovereign of the mother country.

There was at the time a doctor among us Chinese named Zhou Meidie (周美爹, Thebitsia). The Great King Van Goens was always a very close friend of his and trusted his medical skills. At the time, he said to the high officials, 'I would like to take Zhou Meidie with me to the mother country, so that he can also cure my own illness'. The high officials agreed with this.[95]

On the twenty-fifth [day] of the eleventh month of this year they embarked together and returned to the mother country. When Zhou Meidie arrived in Holland, Van Goens provided him with a house. He placed Hollanders outside the gate to guard him. Food and clothing and articles for daily use were all supplied without fail. Yet he was not allowed to roam around as he liked. After he had lived there less than a year he wished to go back to Batavia.

In the fifth moon of Kangxi 21, *renxu* [壬戌], June 1682, the sovereign of the mother country ordered a ship to take an edict to Batavia granting the elevation of Cornelis Speelman to position of great king of Batavia. Zhou Meidie also returned on the same ship to Batavia to congratulate the great king. The

---

94   Cornelis Speelman was born in Rotterdam on 3 March 1628. He arrived in Batavia as an assistant in 1645 and quickly rose to the rank of general accountant (*boekhoudergeneraal*) of the VOC in 1657. From 1663 until 1665 he served as governor of the Coromandel Coast. In 1666, he served as admiral on a military expedition to Makassar with his ally the Boni prince Aru Palaka. After their victory in 1667 he concluded the *Bongaaisch contract*, a treaty that regulated further relations in South Sulawesi (Celebes). In 1669, he sailed again to Makassar to completely subjugate the kingdom. In 1671, he joined the Council of the Indies as an ordinary member. In 1678, he was appointed director general and on 25 November 1681 he succeeded Rijckloff van Goens, having been appointed by the Gentlemen XVII one year earlier on 29 October 1680. Speelman passed away on 11 January 1684.

95   This story is only partly true. Thebitsia did visit the Dutch Republic, but in the accompany of Governor General Joan van Hoorn, whose personal friend and doctor he was, some thirty years later. See Leonard Blussé, 'Doctor at Sea: Chou Mei-yeh's voyage to the West (1710–1711)', in *As the Twig is bent ... Essays in Honour of Frits Vos*, edited by Erica de Poorter (Amsterdam: J.C. Gieben, 1990), 7–30.

king and his councilors convened and decided to grant Zhou Meidie the honour of opening a large *payung* (開大傘) wherever he went. He did not have to concern himself with attending meetings. Whenever high officials fell ill, they all asked him to cure them. Therefore, he was then called the number one miraculous doctor in Batavia.

> Good luck and good fortune, therefore his medicine was very efficacious. When Zhou Meidie arrived in Batavia, the Dutch inhabitants did not know that the government of Holland had given him a hat and a cane. When, on a certain occasion, he came to words with a Dutchman, Zhou Meidie pulled the cane that he had been given and beat the opponent, who finding out that this cane was a royal gift, did not dare to offend him again.[96]
>
> *John Chinaman comments*: This doctor was not famous in China; he was only famous in Holland. Is this not allotted to him by Heaven?

In the first moon of Kangxi 23, *jiazi* [甲子], March 1684, the Great King Speelman fell ill and the councilors convened for deliberation and suggested appointing Johannes Camphuijs to manage the affairs of the country.[97] On the thirteenth [day] of the first moon of the Chinese calendar, the Great King Cornelis Speelman passed away and on the fifteenth he was interred in the great church.

The councilors together acknowledged Johannes Camphuijs as acting king and respectfully sent a memorial to the sovereign of the mother country. In the fourth moon of the same year, Soldaat Lin Lianguan died and was buried in the Chinese cemetery. He had served fifty-one years and ten months as soldaat.

Captain Guo Junguan sent a petition to the great king and asked him to appoint again a soldaat to ensure that affairs could be carried out. The great

---

96 Medhurst, 'Chronologische geschiedenis', 33–34.
97 Johannes Camphuijs was born in Haarlem on 18 July 1634. Trained as a silversmith, he sailed in 1654 in the rank of assistant to Java, and by 1670 he was *opperkoopman* (senior merchant). In 1671, 1673, and 1675, he served as head of the Deshima factory in Nagasaki, Japan. On the island of Edam in the Bay of Batavia he built himself a Japanese house where he spent his leisure time. Camphuijs sent Engelbert Kaempher, the author of *The History of Japan* (1727) to Japan. Having been appointed extraordinary councilor he was appointed ordinary Councilor of the Indies in 1681. On 11 January 1684, after Cornelis Speelman had passed away, this modest man was elected by his fellow council members as acting Governor General. On his repeated requests, Camphuijs was honourably discharged by the Gentlemen XVII on 17 December 1690. He was finally succeeded on 24 September 1691. He passed away at Batavia on 18 July 1695.

king approved and then appointed Hong Shiguang [洪石光] to the position of soldaat.

The envoy of the king of Ternate who had come to Batavia in the summer of *yiwei* [乙未, 1655], was still there. The former king, Joan Maetsuijcker, had ordered him to reside in a house within the East Gate. Until *jiazi* [甲子, 1684], he lived in Batavia altogether thirty-three years! In Galaba, the people disliked his irascible character and his savage behaviour. He thought highly of himself. Because he was so coarse, the king personally quickly ordered him to go home. At that time, the Great King Camphuijs hosted a banquet and invited the councilors and the envoy of Ternate—do not say his name, his atrociousness is known well enough.[98] When they were having dinner, he ordered him to quickly return to his country and in the eleventh month of the same year he took leave of the great king and embarked on a ship and was honourably returned to his native country.

In the summer of the 24th year of Kangxi, *yichou* **[乙丑], August 1685,** the sovereign of the mother country sent an edict by ship to Batavia formally investing Johannes Camphuijs with the kingship. At this time, Undertaker Huang Shigong passed away and was buried in the Chinese cemetery. He served as undertaker thirty-nine years and six months. The Chinese captain immediately appointed Yan Jingguan (顏經觀) as undertaker. At the same time, Lieutenant He Lianguan asked the king to be allowed to retire because he wanted to return to the Mountains of Tang (Tangshan, China). The great king allowed him [to do so], so that in the sixth month of the same year he took leave of the king and returned by junk to his hometown.[99]

There was a captain of Cirebon [named] Chen Muge (陳穆哥, Tambocco), who had served there as captain for more than three years. Because he wanted to go to Batavia, he resigned and gave the position of captain to Chen Canlang (陳燦郎, Tansjauko), to fill the vacancy.

---

98   Prince Rotterdam of Ternate. See note 78, p. 77.

99   Nowhere in the Dutch sources is mentioned that Lieutenant He Lianguan returned home to China.

       The lieutenant who asked for permission to return to China was Wang Wuge (王五哥, Ong Gouko), not mentioned in the Chinese text, who on 31 March 1694 had succeeded Guo Baoge (Que Pauko) after his flight to Semarang. He was selected on the recommendation of 'several well off Chinese textile dealers, shopkeepers, and other merchants in town, as well by the *nakhodas* of the junks from China'; Hoetink, 'Chineesche officieren', 99–100.

Whether the captain of Cirebon came to Batavia to ask for the position of captain is not clear, therefore I do not dare say more about this.

Chen Muge petitioned the king to give him the position of former Lieutenant He Lianguan. The great king thereupon appointed him lieutenant.[100]

In the sixth moon of Kangxi 25, *bingyin* **[丙寅], July 1686,** Guo Junguan went to see the king and asked him to be allowed to retire. The great king permitted it. Junguan then in the same month bid goodbye to the king and he returned to his native country with honour on a junk.

He served for thirty-seven years and then returned home. One can see that his behaviour deserved recognition on this account.

Lin Jingguan originally served as lieutenant; he thereupon petitioned the king to be given the position of captain.[101] Li Rongge (李容哥, Lie Joncko) then asked to be appointed lieutenant. The great king of Batavia sent a memorial to the sovereign in the mother country to inform him. That year in the eight month, in the autumn, Zhou Meidie passed away and was buried in the cemetery.[102]

In Kangxi 26, *dingmao* **[丁卯], October 1687,** the sovereign of the mother country sent an edict to Batavia appointing Lin Jingguan to the captaincy. The great king conferred with the councilors to add another four tax farms. The first one was a tax on Chinese tobacco, the second on in- and outgoing water

---

100   Like his predecessors, Chen Muge (Tambocco) was recommended both by local merchants and the *nakhodas* (resolution of 16 June 1702). On 26 February 1692, he had succeeded in Cirebon the local 'shaven' (Muslim) Chinese, Kiay Aria Martinata in his functions as *shahbandar* and captain of the local Chinese community; Hoetink, 'Chineesche officieren', 100–101.

101   This is a total mix up, because it was Guo Junguan who served ten years, from 3 August 1685 to June 1695. On 10 June 1695, the Council of the Indies discussed his request to be relieved from his position because of 'high age and increasing infirmity' and decided to replace Guo with Lin Jingguan (Limkeenqua). Guo Junguan can hardly have been as infirm as he asserted, because on 20 July 1696 he was allowed to go with seven of his compatriots to Timor, and he was still alive in 1703; Hoetink, 'Chineesche officieren', 47.

Consequently, Lin Jingguan became captain on 10 June 1695 and served until 1707. Under the name Jacob Limkeenko, he had served as boedelmeester in 1683 and 1684, and as lieutenant from 4 August 1683 until he was formally installed on 29 June 1695. To avoid 'a too large confluence of people', this time the ceremony was not held in the castle but in front of the town hall. On the first of December 1699 he received permission to erect two sugar mills on his estate, Comiry, along the Grote Rivier; Hoetink, 'Chineesche officieren', 48–50.

102   The precise date is unknown, but the Chinese doctor returned to Batavia in 1711.

traffic [at the *pabean* or *boom*], the third on lanterns and candles, the fourth on the sale of rice.[103] This [last] tax is called the *midui* (米堆). Including the seven earlier farms there were now altogether eleven [tax] farms. Every year on the thirtieth [day] of the twelfth month after there was a competitive bidding in the warehouse, the possessor of the new mandate (*mandaat*) could assume his occupation on the first day of the first month of the Dutch calendar.

In Kangxi 28, *jisi* [己巳], May 1689, the Company again appointed two lieutenants. Because the wife of Lin Senguan (林森觀, Lim Somko) was able to heal Dutch people, she often visited the great king and said to him, 'There are already many Chinese people; you should add another two lieutenants to regulate everything'. As the great king willingly approved of this idea, Lin Senguan and Cai Weiguan (蔡威觀) sent a petition to the great king, who convened with his councilors and took the decision to appoint these two people to the lieutenancy. From then on there were four lieutenants.

> So at the time there were Captain Lin Jingguan, Lieutenants Chen Muge, Li Rongge, and the two newly appointed, Lin Senguan and Cai Weiguan, the soldier Hong Shiguang, and the undertaker Yan Jingguan.[104]

That year on the twenty-third [day] of the twelfth month of the Chinese calendar, a junk came to Batavia. The former Captain Guo Junguan returned to Batavia aboard this junk, and bringing presents he gave these to the great king. Guo Junguan then had no title or position to speak out; he was just like the common people.

> Guo Junguan spent three years in China, and after 1691 he was appointed *boedelmeester* and retired in Kangxi 33, *jiaxu* [甲戌], 1694, and then passed away.[105]

In the fifth moon of Kangxi 29, *gengwu* [庚午], June 1690, the captain of Makassar, Huang Juguan came to Batavia to pay his respects to the king and

---

103 Medhurst adds a fifth tax levied on cock fighting.
104 Cai Weiguan does not figure in the Dutch materials. Li Rongge (Lie Joncko) was appointed third lieutenant on 5 May 1705, the same day as Guo Xunge (Que Hoenko). He was still alive but 'aged and almost finished' in 1726; Hoetink, 'Chineesche officieren', 102.
105 Here is another mix up, this time between Guo Junguan (Queeconko) and Guo Qiaoge (Que Kiauko). Guo Qiaoge made a trip to China in 1702. At his request, he had been permitted to purchase 150 piculs of tin by the VOC administration; Hoetink, 'Chineesche officieren', 100.

present gifts. He reported on the situation in Makassar and announced that he had handed over the captaincy to Wang Faguan, who was now replacing him. These people had earlier meritoriously helped the Company by supplying rice to the Company, and together they had obtained the position of captain in Makassar.[106]

In addition, the following: When Guo Junguan had not yet retired, he went to an audience with the great king and reported, 'If our Tang people fall ill or become insane and go crazy, they have nothing to fall back on. We should build a hospital building to accommodate them.[107] No matter whether they are Chinese or natives, captains, or normal people, if they die without having made a testament, the authorities should take their money, their slaves, and household items and auction all of them off to the highest bidder, and then turn the proceeds into the coffers of the *weeskamer* and the hospital to supply the sick with their daily food. We should install a manager (*mandor*) to run the hospital, and appoint a Dutchman secretary of the *weeskamer* to manage the ongoing financial affairs.

In case there are young [orphaned] boys and girls whose parents shortly before their death have drawn up a testament in which they express their wish to transfer their possessions to the *weeskamer* as interest-bearing capital, then every month the proceeds from this capital can be used for raising the boys and girls. Once they are grown up and ready to get married, they can apply for the capital that their late parents have turned into the *weeskamer*. The secretary of the *weeskamer* then will check the cash account and return it. It cannot be embezzled. A free school should be built and a Chinese teacher should be invited to teach the children whose parents have passed away and whom nobody is teaching, and [also] the poor children. If it is like this, then sick people can live out their lives. Poor children will not meet difficulty going to school.

The great king immediately discussed this with his councilors and approved of this proposal. That year a workforce was recruited and the construction of the *weeskamer*, the hospital, the school and the meeting hall of the *weeskamer* was started. After these buildings were completed, Guo Junguan was appointed boedelmeester or lieutenant of the *weeskamer*. The king bestowed a

---

106 See references to this in the year 1649.

107 *Meisegancuo* means the Chinese hospital. *Meisegan*, or *weeskamer* reads in Minnanhua as *Bi-sek-kam*, 美色甘. The Dutch *weeskamer* was established by a resolution of the High Government on 1 October 1624. See *Plakaatboek*, 1.173, 187, and 2,522. The Chinese boedelmeesters were installed by no later than 5 November 1655. They were to administer the inheritances of Chinese citizens and fund the Chinese hospital and orphanage (*weeshuis*) from the proceeds; *Plakaatboek*, 2.212, and Blussé, *Strange Company*, 82–83.

golden seal, and ordered the boedelmeester together with the secretary of the *weeskamer* to check the accounts and supervise the hospital.[108] It was decided to restrict the tenure of the curator to three years and then appoint somebody else. The first estate manager then was Boedelmeester Guo Junguan.

> *John Chinaman comments*: It seems the Dutch erected this school for Chinese children because they knew that the flowery nation exceeded the surrounding countries in literature. Since China surpasses other peoples because it possesses poetical discourses, literary compositions, civilised ceremonies and exalted music, on which the responsibilities of humans are founded, and from which the five cardinal virtues sprout. But the Dutch books differ from Chinese works; and by giving up their own doctrines and teaching those of China, the Western people showed that they were willing to conform to the wishes of the people, and showed tolerance and cordiality towards strangers.[109] The establishment of the free school, the orphanage and the hospital, all were very beneficial for our Tang people [in Batavia].

In the eighth moon of Kangxi 30, *xinwei* [辛未], 4 September 1691, the Great King Camphuijs summoned his councilors and discussed with them that he wished to retire at Batavia. The councilors respectfully elevated Meester Willem van Outhoorn to manage the state affairs as acting king.[110] Thereupon

---

108 The decision to found a Chinese hospital was already taken on 13 August 1640 'in regard to the poor, sick and other impotent and miserable people who are treated unmercifully and barbarously [by their own kin]'. The government set aside a plot on the western side of the Rhinocerosgracht. A collection was held among the well-to-do Chinese, and proceeds from the taxes on Chinese funerals and *wayang* performances were reserved for financing the daily expenses of the hospital; *Plakaatboek*, 1.446,454–55. In 1666–67, the hospital was renovated and put under direction of a Dutch 'regent' who received a payment of eight rixdollars a month; *Plakaatboek*, 2.420–21, 539.

109 This paragraph can only be found in Medhurst, 'Chronologische geschiedenis', 37–38.

110 Born at Lariki on the island of Ambon (4 May 1635), Willem van Outhoorn was the first Indies-born Governor General. After acquiring his master's degree in law (*Meester in de rechten*) at Leiden University (27 November 1657), he returned to the Indies in 1659 and was appointed member of the Council of Justice in 1662. In 1679, he was appointed councilor of India. He served in various other important functions before he was elected acting governor general on 17 December 1690 and was formally installed on 24 September 1691. At his own request, he was honourably discharged on 20 September 1701. He handed over his position to his son-in-law, Joan van Hoorn, on 15 August 1704. He passed away on 27 November 1720. For his charming letters to his granddaughter, Pieternel van Hoorn,

Camphuijs resigned and lived a life of leisure to his own liking until the end of his life. Camphuijs served as king for eight years and eight months. The captain of Makassar, Huang Juguan, died and was buried at the Pumao Shan (朴昂山) cemetery. He died within one year after his arrival in Batavia. The acting king, Meester van Outhoorn, and the councilors memorialized the sovereign in the mother country.

In the ninth moon of Kangxi 31, *renshen* [壬申], October 1692, the sovereign of the mother country ordered a ship to bring an edict to Batavia and formally installed Meester van Outhoorn as king.

In Kangxi 32, *guiyou* [癸酉], 1693, Boedelmeester Guo Junguan's mandatory period term [of office] had expired and the great king appointed Lin Jingguan in his place.[111]

In Kangxi 33, *jiaxu* [甲戌], 1694, Guo Junguan died and he was buried at the Gaolaoqu [高勞屈園, Krokot] garden.

> Guo Junguan served eighteen years as captain, nineteen years and four months as lieutenant, and three years as boedelmeester, altogether forty years and four months. He made a name for himself in all three positions. In addition, he returned to China for three years; when he again came to Batavia he petitioned for the establishment of the *weeskamer*, and for the building of a hospital[112] and a free school with the name of Mingcheng Shuyuan (明誠書院) to benefit posterity. A great enough merit for ten thousand generations!
>
> He returned to China to visit and worship his ancestors' tombs. He did not forget about his origins. When he came to Batavia he served as boedelmeester. He did not care whether he was serving in a high or low position. He set a standard; his life was fully devoted to charity. He lived peacefully into advanced old age. This is truly an example of a virtuous man who is worthy of heavenly care! This is precisely so![113]

---

see Bea Brommer's opulently illustrated work, *To My Dear Pieternelletje, Grandfather and Granddaughter in VOC time, 1710–1720* (Leiden: Brill, 2015).

111 Captain Guo resigned and lived at least until 1703; see also note 101, p. 89. This time the order of succession is correct, but Lin Jingguan (Limkeenqua) was not formally appointed until 29 June 1695.

112 This is incorrect; both institutions had been established decades earlier.

113 These two paragraphs are taken from the Leiden manuscript. As a matter of fact lieutenant Gao Genguan (Ko Kinko) founded this school in 1775. See note 283, p. 179.

FIGURE 9   *The Chinese hospital of Batavia, Johannes Rach (Danish artist, in Batavia 1762–83)*
RIJKSMUSEUM AMSTERDAM

In the sixth moon of Kangxi 34, *yihai* [乙亥], 18 July 1695, the former great king died and was buried on the twentieth in the great church. Camphuijs passed away within five years after his retirement.

The Ambonese Captain Jonker was personally engaged in the service of the Company in the expeditions to Makassar, Banten, and Mataram. Everywhere he obtained laurels for already fifty years until now! But on account of the praise heaped on him, this man became very arrogant. He always had a wayward behaviour. He secretly plotted to foment a rebellion, attacking from within and without. At this moment, his dark plans were unmasked, the councilors found out and secretly informed the great king. The king ordered his men to go to Jonker and invite him for a meeting. Jonker feared disaster and did not come.

> Bad guys also get scared!

The great king then summoned the councilors to make a plan to catch him. Thereupon he ordered the Dutch chiefs to send people to summon Jonker. But the latter refused to come even more firmly.

> Stupid guy, if you disobey you are finished!

The Dutch commanders issued an order to the soldiers to destroy his house with their guns. Although Jonker was not hurt, he sat on his chair panicked out of his senses. Under these circumstances, the soldiers shot Jonker while he was sitting on the chair.

This is really overdone!

Actually, he was already unconscious; he could have been taken alive! And then, after close examination into whether he had really committed a crime, he could be meted out a death punishment. Would that not also have been possible?[114]

All this occurred **in the twelfth moon of Kangxi 35, *bingzi* [丙子], February 1696.**

When in the fourth moon of the same year the three-year term of Boedelmeester Li Junguan (李俊觀, Litsoenqua) expired, the king appointed Wei Huiguan (魏惠官, i.e. 魏惠公, Goey Hoey Kong) and Wang Wuguan (王悟觀) as boedelmeesters. Starting from then there were two boedelmeesters.[115]

In Kangxi 37, *wuyin* [戊寅], September 1698, Lieutenant Cai Weiguan passed away. The great king appointed Lin Chunge (林春哥, Lim Tsoenko) lieutenant.[116] (He had earlier served as captain in Banten; afterwards he came to Batavia, where he settled down.)

---

114 Valentijn gives an interesting insight into the final years of Captain Jonker. He describes how Jonker, a courageous but hot-headed person, became caught up in a feud with a member of the Council of the Indies, Major Isaac de St. Martin, by whom he was so humiliated that he became increasingly alienated from the Dutch elite. He tells in detail how Captain Jonker was killed in 1689; Valentijn, *Oud en Nieuw Oost-Indiën*, 4.319–20.

115 In the VOC sources these gentlemen are respectively mentioned in the years 1708, 1705 and 1685!

116 This is incorrect. He was appointed in 1718. On 28 June 1720, the Council of the Indies decided to nominate to the position of lieutenant Lin Chunge (Lim Tsoenko) and Lin Shenge (Limsonko), because Que Hoenqua had recently died and Li Joncko was infirm. Lim Tsoenko was the father-in-law of the future Captain Lian Fuguang (Nihoekong). He had served as boedelmeester in 1718–19. He passed away before March 1734. Lim Sonko, who served as boedelmeester in 1710–11, is mentioned various times in the resolutions of the Council of the Indies. On 22 August 1727, he was given permission to pursue and round up fully armed with guns—even on the properties of his neighbours—'villains and vagabonds who have recently come to molest his garden and home along the Krokot River during the night.' This shows that the Ommelanden were increasingly becoming unsafe in the second half of the 1720s. Hoetink, 'Chineesche officieren', 104.

In Kangxi 38, *jimao* [己卯], January 1699, a junk came to Batavia with Wang Jie [王界] and his wife on board. When they came ashore the Chinese and the natives all came to have a look. This news spread all over Batavia, until it reached the ears of the great king. Wang Jie's wife, with the surname of Zheng (鄭氏), was graceful and dignified. Her clothing was different from that of the people of Batavia. After the great king had acquired precise information, he decided he wanted to see what a woman from China looked like. He sent people to invite her for a visit, and Wang Jie and his wife came to the office of the king to meet. When the same junk returned to China, all this was reported [to the authorities]. The people who had taken the woman out of the country were arrested, and several of them were sentenced to death.

> It was these two people who were guilty, but they got other people into trouble. This is really lamentable!

When in the same year Wei Huiguan and Wang Wuguan had served their full tenure as boedelmeesters, the great king appointed Lian Luguan (連祿觀) and Chen Caiguan (陳才觀) as their successors.

In the fifth moon of Kangxi 39, *gengchen* [庚辰], June 1700, Boedelmeester Li Junguan passed away. The Great King Van Outhoorn and his councilors deliberated [about the fact] that the company was operating a trade factory in Banten but that it neither had built fortifications nor possessed a long-term policy. Thereupon a letter was sent to Banten ordering the local factor of the VOC to ask the sultan permission for construction. The sultan consented; the Company thereupon recruited workers to start the construction. After eight years, the building was completed.[117]

In Kangxi 41, *renwu* [壬午], 1702, Boedelmeesters Lian Luguan and Chen Caiguan had served their full tenure, the great king appointed Kang Jingguan (康敬觀, Kungkeengko) and Huang Yingguan (黃應觀) as their successors.

In the seventh moon of Kangxi 43, *jiashen* [甲申], August 1704, the Great King *Meester* [Master of Law] Van Outhoorn met the councilors and said he wished to retire. The officers respectfully acknowledged Joan van Hoorn to act as great king. On the fifteenth of the same month Van Outhoorn stepped down and started a life of leisure. The councilors sent a memorial to the sovereign in the mother country to inform him. In this year, the Company minted *dubbeltjes* and *fanams*. Placards ordering the people to use *dubbeltjes* and *fanams*

---

117 Fort Speelwijk, the ruins of which are still extant at Banten Lama (Old Banten). See Valentijn, *Oud en Nieuw Oost-Indiën*, 4.214.

and forbidding the use of Chinese copper money were hung on the four gates of the town.[118]

In the eighth moon of Kangxi 44, *yiyou* [乙酉], September 1705, the sovereign of the mother country sent an edict to Batavia formally investing Joan van Hoorn as great king of Batavia.[119] The terms of tenure of the Boedelmeesters Kang Jingguan and Huang Yingguan were completed and in their place the great king appointed Qiu Zuguan (邱祖觀, Khoe Tsouwko) and Xu Chunguan (許純觀, Khouw Soenko). Qiu Zuguan imposed a new law ordering everybody—Chinese, Dutch, and so on—to purchase from the secretary of the *weeskamer* a burial certificate when a slave passed away. In the event that anyone covered up the death and failed to report it, the arrested person had to pay twenty-five *rials*. Today's purchase of burial certificates for slaves dates from this Qiu Zuguan. He originally served at Zhaoyalan (爪鴉藍) as captain of Banda [Island]. After his return to Batavia he served as boedelmeester.

In the tenth moon of Kangxi 45, *bingxu* [丙戌], February 1706, Captain Lin Jingguan died and was buried in his own garden at Jakatra. He served twenty-one years as captain.[120] The great king promoted Lieutenant Chen Muge to the captaincy, and Boedelmeester Lian Luguan (連祿觀, Nilocko) to the position of lieutenant and reported this to the sovereign in the mother country.[121]

In the third moon of Kangxi 46, *dinghai* [丁亥], April, 1707, the sovereign in the mother country sent a ship with an edict to Batavia investing Chen Muge with the captaincy and Lian Luguan with the position of lieutenant. Moreover,

---

118 There is no such placard on Chinese coinage in the *Plakaatboeken*. The placard of 8 April 1707 prescribing the use of coins comes closest to this. *Plakaatboek*, 3.579. On 24 May 1703, it was decided to order copper *pitjis* (coins) from Japan. *Realia* 2.243.

119 Joan van Hoorn, scion of a prominent Amsterdam family, was born in Amsterdam on 16 November 1653 and at the age of ten accompanied his father Pieter van Hoorn to the Indies. In 1666–68 he joined his father (who had risen to the rank of Councilor of the Indies) on an embassy to the Kangxi emperor of China. Starting from the humble commission of under assistant he rose to the position of merchant and first secretary of the High Government in 1678. Appointed extraordinary member of the Council of the Indies in 1682, and full member in 1685, he carried out a number of diplomatic missions to Banten. He was appointed director general in 1691 and governor general on 20 September 1701. He stepped down on 30 October 1709 after having been honorarily discharged on 2 March 1708. His Chinese friend and personal doctor, Thebitsia (see note 95, p. 86), travelled in his company. Van Hoorn died on 21 February 1711, shortly after his return home to Amsterdam.

120 He served as captain twelve years and passed away on 4 April 1707 in Batavia.

121 Chen Muge (Tambocco) was appointed on 11 April 1707 and publicly installed on 3 June 1707; Hoetink, 'Chineesche officieren', 50–53. In reality, Lian Luguan (Nilocko) was not appointed until 28 June 1729.

the factory chief at Banten sent a missive to Batavia reporting to the great king that some time ago the Company had started building a castle and digging a moat in Banten. Now the work was already completed. When the great king heard the report, he was very pleased and appointed a Dutchman to reside in Banten as commander.

At that time Chen Ronggong (陳榮公, Tan Eengkong) and Wang Yingshi (王應使, Ong Eengsaij) memorialized the great king imploring him to appoint two additional lieutenants. Together with the captain, there were now seven official positions.[122] The great king immediately discussed this with his councilors and decided to appoint Chen Rongguang and Wang Yingshi as lieutenants.[123] Every time the Chinese sent a petition to the great king, he agreed with pleasure. Only rarely he would refuse.[124]

In the seventh moon of this year, Lieutenant Li Rongge passed away. He served altogether for twenty-two years and eleven months.[125]

The great king then appointed the eldest son of Li Yuguan (李裕觀]) Li Hege (李和哥, Li Hoko), to the position of lieutenant.[126] At the time, the councilors of the Company went to see the great king and asked him to retrieve the golden seal that the former great king had given to the captain. The great king then immediately asked Chen Muge to return it, who thereupon gave it back.[127]

---

122   The real situation was as follows: After Lim Tsoenko and Limsoko had been appointed on 28 June 1720, Captain Guo Maoguan (郭昂觀, Que Bauqua) complained that he actually received little aid from either lieutenant because of their 'long and still continuing [declining?] physical disposition'. On 28 December 1725, it was decided to add two more lieutenants to the existing three. The former lieutenant of Cirebon Chen Ronggong (Tan Eengkong) and Boedelmeester Chen Zhongshe (Tan Tionqua, son of the late Captain Tanboqua) joined the corps of lieutenants. Tan Tionqua was boedelmeester in 1717–18, 1725–27. He died in prison on 19 December 1741; Hoetink, 'Chineesche officieren', 104–105.

123   Again, some amendments: On 8 July 1729, it was decided to add two more lieutenants because Captain Guo Maoguan (Que Bauqua) reported that, owing to their bad health, all four lieutenants were generally incapable of assisting him. This meant that the Great King had assented to increasing the number of lieutenants to six. Appointed were Lian Luge (Ni Locko) and Wang Yingshi (王應使, Ong Eengsaij), both men of 'knowledge and experience'. Nilocko had served as boedelmeester in 1716 and 1726–27. He was succeeded as lieutenant by his son Lian Fuguang (Nihoekong) in 1733.

124   Joan van Hoorn was very popular with the Chinese elite in town. When it became known that Van Hoorn would leave, thirty Chinese sent him a petition imploring him to stay. 'Request supplianten Goudjienko e.s., Batavia1709', KITLV manuscript collection, H 316.

125   He actually served twenty-nine years because he passed away in 1734.

126   Li Hege was appointed to succeed Lieutenant Wang Yinshi (Ongeengsai) on 23 June 1733.

127   This is probably the golden seal that was presented in 1690.

In the ninth moon of Kangxi 48, *jichou* [己丑], October 1709, the sovereign of the mother country sent an edict to Batavia calling the Great King Van Hoorn to return home. The king then ordered *Meester* Abraham van Riebeeck to act as his successor and manage the government of the country.[128] On the twentieth of October, the former king Van Hoorn returned home.

The Boedelmeesters Qiu Zuguan and Xu Chunguan together served two terms, altogether six years. After these two had retired, the Great King Van Riebeeck replaced them with Guo Maoguan (郭昂觀, Que Bauqua) and Li Yuanguan (李援觀, Liwanko).

In the seventh moon of Kangxi 49, *gengyin* [庚寅], August 1710, the sovereign of the mother country sent an edict to Batavia investing Meester Van Riebeeck as great king of Batavia. He was a native of the Cape of Good Hope.

In the fifth moon of Kangxi 50, *xinmao* [辛卯], July 1711, Boedelmeesters Guo Maoguan and Li Yuanguan had served out their mandatory terms and retired. The great king then appointed Li Yuguan (李裕觀, Li Tsoeko) and Wang Anguan (王鞍觀, Ongwako) as boedelmeesters.

In the ninth moon of Kangxi 51, *renchen* [壬辰], October 1712, Lieutenant Lin Senguan passed away and was interred in the Longyan garden at Bazhilan. He served altogether twenty-three years and one month as captain. Thereupon the Great King Van Riebeeck appointed Guo Weige (郭威哥, Que Oeijko) lieutenant.[129]

In the tenth moon of Kangxi 52, *guisi* [癸巳], November 1713, the great king fell terminally ill and summoned the councilors for deliberation and they decided to entrust the position of great king to Christoffel van Swoll so that he could act in that position and manage the country's administration.[130] On the eleventh, Van Riebeeck passed away and on the twentieth he was buried in

---

128 The son of Jan van Riebeeck, founder of the settlement at the Cape of Good Hope, Abraham van Riebeeck was born at the Cape on 18 October 1653. After receiving his doctor's degree in law at Leiden University (25 March 1673) he left for Java with the rank of junior merchant and arrived in May 1677. He served as envoy and fulfilled various other important functions before he was appointed Councilor of the Indies on 24 September 1691. He served as director general under his son-in-law, Joan van Hoorn, and succeeded him on 2 March 1708. An adventurous traveller, he died of exhaustion after exploring Java's south coast on 17 November 1713.

129 Resolution of the Governor General and Council, 12 March 1734, in which is mentioned that Guo Weige actually succeeded Lin Chunge (Lim Tsoenko) and not Lin Senge (林森哥, Lim Somko). Hoetink, 'Chineesche officieren', 107.

130 Christoffel van Swoll was born in Amsterdam in 1663. He arrived on 19 June 1684 with the rank of assistant and climbed via the general secretariat to the rank of merchant in 1691. In 1696 he was appointed secretary of the Council of the Indies and became an ordinary

the great church. The councilors then sent a memorial to the sovereign in the mother country to inform him.

By the fourth moon of Kangxi 53, *jiawu* [甲午], May 1714, the sovereign of the mother country sent an edict to Batavia formally investing Christoffel van Swoll with the position of great king. Boedelmeesters Li Yuguan and Wang Anguan had served out their mandatory terms and retired. The great king thereupon installed Chen Zhongshe (陳忠舍) and Wang Chenggong (王成功, Ongseenko) as their successors.

Zhongshe was the eldest son of Captain Chen Muge.

In the tenth moon of Kangxi 54, *yiwei* [乙未], November 1715, Boedelmeester Xu Chunguan passed away and was buried.

In the second moon of Kangxi 55, *bingshen* [丙申], March 1716, there was a heavy downpour. A flood suddenly rushed into the city and the feet of the ramparts were flooded for six days and nights until it receded.

In the fifth moon of Kangxi 56, *dingyou* [丁酉], June 1717, the mandatory term of Boedelmeester Chen Zhongshe was completed and he asked to be reappointed. The great king approved and thereupon he continued to carry out his duties.

In Kangxi 57, *wuxu* [戊戌], November 1718, Great King Christoffel van Swoll fell critically ill and summoned the councilors and decided to hand over his position to Hendrick Swaardecroon so that he could act as great king and take care of the affairs of the country. The councilors memorialized the sovereign of the mother country to inform him. On the fourteenth of that month, Christoffel van Swoll passed away and was buried in the great church. Swaardecroon accepted the throne and took charge of the country's affairs.[131]

---

member on 26 September 1701. After succeeding Van Riebeeck in November 1713, he was officially installed by the Gentlemen XVII in 1715. He passed away on 12 November 1718.

131 Henricus Swaardecroon (Zwaardecroon) was born in Rotterdam on 26 January 1667. He arrived 1685 as secretary to Commissaris-generaal Van Reede tot Drakestein in 1685. After ten years he was promoted to senior merchant. Between 1694 and 1702 he served in various capacities in India and Ceylon. Appointed secretary of the Council of the Indies in 1703, he became an extraordinary member the following year and an ordinary member in 1715. He succeeded Van Swoll on 13 November 1718 and was formally installed by the Gentlemen XVII on 10 September 1720. At his own request, he was honourably discharged on 16 October 1725 and stepped down on 8 July 1725. He passed away on his estate, Kaduang, on 12 August 1728.

At that time, there occurred one catastrophe after another: fire clouds appeared, enormous floods reached to the feet of the walls, mountains collapsed and the earth split, sulfur flooded down. In the bay, dead fishes and clams floated around everywhere; all water creatures were poisoned. The earth tremors of Batavia continued for three days before peace was restored. When the mandatory period of Boedelmeester Wang Chenggong was completed, he stepped down and the great king appointed Ye Jingguan (葉敬觀, Jap Keengko) as his successor.

In the seventh moon of Kangxi 58, *jihai* [己亥], **July 1719**, the sovereign of the mother country formally invested Hendrick Swaardecroon with the title of great king. This man liked to ride horses, and to dress up in military apparel, drill the troops, and parade the horses, but he also leisurely roamed around the countryside. He was a native of Rotterdam.

In the fourth moon of Kangxi 59, *gengzi* [庚子], **May 1720**, Boedelmeester Chen Zhongshe had served out two mandatory terms. In his place the great king appointed Chen Tiansheng (陳天生, Tan Tien Seeng).

In the sixth moon of Kangxi 60, *xinchou* [辛丑], **July 1721**, Boedelmeester Qiu Zuguan died. Originally he was to be buried at Krokot, but when the bearers of the coffin arrived and they were asked to bring the coffin to Ganwang Shan (甘望山, or 甘夢山) cemetery to bury him there, they were unhappy. In addition, they contemplated that when he was alive he had a crooked heart, churning out plans to harm people, so the bearers increasingly took an intense dislike to him and thereupon put the coffin down on the road. Nobody was willing to carry his coffin any further. The Chinese officers who were sending him off, mourned at the death of their own kind. They did their best, asking the people to help, speaking sweet words like: 'Why should you be so angry as to put the coffin on the road. If the natives see this it will make us Chinese lose face!'

The bearers were forced to take the coffin to Danlan Wang (丹藍望, Tanah Abang), but there they halted again. In whatever way they were implored, they were no longer willing to carry the coffin one more step. Natives therefore had to be hired to carry the coffin to Ganwang Shan cemetery.

> *John Chinaman comments*: If you are in a superior position, the people harbour expectations towards you, but if so much hate is heaped up on somebody after his death, then we may know how this person behaved himself during his lifetime. We should learn from this.

In the fifth moon of Kangxi 61, *renyin* [壬寅], **June 1722**, a *Serani* (a mestizo or mixed-blood person], Pieter Erberfeld, and a Javanese, Kuilaozhen

(奎勝陣), teamed up secretly planning a rebellion.[132] They fabricated weapons and hid them in a cave at a secret location. When their plot was exposed there was a man who took the initiative to inform against them. Great King Hendrick Swaardecroon summoned the councilors to decide on how to deal with this. Thereupon he ordered a Dutch officer to lead the Company's soldiers to encircle the [culprit's] house and bind him up and keep him under arrest. He ordered his men to enter the secret underground cave and they searched out the weapons, which proved that their plans were for real. Thereupon they were drawn apart and quartered in the sixth moon. Their limbs were exposed on the four city gates, while their two robbers' heads were displayed at a street crossing to expose them to the weather and display them to the public.

By the third moon of the first year of Yongzheng [雍正], *guimao* [癸卯], April 1723, the Company had seized the house of the rebel Pieter Erberfeld at Xinchi and built a big church on the precincts, and when the church was ready[133] the Company also erected a large stone slab with inscription with a sculpture of Peter Erberfeld's skull on top for public display.[134] In the fourth moon of that year, Ye Jingguan completed his term as boedelmeester and retired. In his place the councilors appointed Lian Fuguang (連富光, Nihoekong).

> Lian Fuguang was a lieutenant. He was the eldest son of Lieutenant Lian Luguan (Nilocko). Later, when in the seventh moon of third year of Qianlong [乾隆], *wuwu* [戊午], 1738, Captain Guo Chunguan (郭春官, Que Tjoenqua) passed away, Lian Fuguang served as boedelmeester. His household was exceedingly wealthy; his family occupied five positions at the same time. He presented a wagonload of silver to the great king and at the same time turned in a petition asking for the position of captain. The great king greedily accepted the bribe and agreed to raise him to the captaincy and memorialized the sovereign in the mother country. In *jiwei* [己未], 1739, and *gengshen* [庚申], 1740, he [Lian Fuguang] suffered the

---

132 For the whole story, see Leonard Blussé, 'Jakarta: Erberveld-monument, de nieuwe kleren van de koningin van het oosten', in Maarten Prak ed., *Plaatsen van herinnering, Nederland in de zeventiende en achttiende eeuw* (Amsterdam: Bert Bakker, 2006), 390–99. According to some slanderers, Swaardecroon charged his neighbor Pieter Erberfeld with treason in order to seize his land.

133 This is the still extant Portugese Buitenkerk.

134 The text reads as follows: *Uijt een verfoejelijcke gedagtenisse teegen den gestraften landverraader Pieter Erberveld sal niemant vermoogen te deeser plaatse te bouwen, timmeren, metselen of planten nu ofte ten eenigen daagen. Batavia den 14 april 1722.*

'In abominable memory of the punished traitor Pieter Erberveld nobody will be allowed to build, put up, lay bricks, or plant now or ever on this spot'.

malice of the evil great king, resulting in the calamity of all Batavia. The great wealth of Fuguang went up in smoke afterwards as he became an outcast banished to Ambon. This certainly is to be deplored.[135]

In the eighth moon of Yongzheng 2, *jiachen* [甲辰], 1724, Boedelmeester Wang Anguan passed away and was buried in the new cemetery at Hongqiao (紅橋, Jambatan Merah) in his own garden. Boedelmeester Chen Tiansheng completed his term and the great king appointed Wang Taiguan (王泰觀, Ongthayko) in his place.

In the sixth moon of Yongzheng 3, *yisi* [乙巳], July 1725, Great King Hendrick Swaardecroon announced that he wished to retire on account of his old age and summoned the councilors for deliberation and decided to transfer the throne to Mattheus de Haan to manage the country's affairs.[136] He memorialized the sovereign in the mother country to inform him of this. After his retirement, Great King Hendrick Swaardecroon lived a life of leisure in the town of Batavia. Sometimes he rode his horse-drawn coach on the road. Seizing the reins, he went sightseeing [through] nature, or roved among flowers and willows (that is, enjoyed himself with ladies of pleasure) freely and easily enjoying the last years of his life. In the tenth moon of the same year Lieutenant Lin Chunguan (林春官, Lim Tsoenko) passed away and was buried at Danlan Wang. The new great king appointed Lian Zhongguan (連鍾觀, Ni Tonqua) in his place.[137]

In the seventh moon of Yongzheng 4, *bingwu* [丙午], August 1726, an edict from the sovereign of the mother country arrived in Batavia investing Mattheus de Haan with the great kingship of Galaba and also ordered him to recruit soldiers and pacify the rebellion in the country of Cochin [on the Malabar coast of southwest India]. The great king and the councilors deliberated and ordered a Dutch commander to lead his soldiers and Bugis and Balinese soldiers, and

---

135 For a full biography of Lian Fuguang (Nihoekong), see B. Hoetink, 'Ni Hoekong. Kapitein der Chineezen te Batavia in 1740', *Bijdragen tot de Taal-, Land- en Volkenkunde van Nederlandsch-Indië* 74 (1918): 447–518. See also note 170.

136 Mattheus de Haan was born in Dordrecht in 1663. At the age of eight he accompanied his father who was a junior merchant in the service of the VOC to the Indies. By 1698, De Haan had climbed to the rank of first merchant of Batavia Castle. In 1700, he was appointed first secretary of the Council of the Indies. He became a full member in 1710 and rose to the position of director general in 1722. He succeeded Swaardecroon on 16 October 1724 and was formally appointed by the Gentlemen XVII on 8 July 1725. He passed away on 1 June 1729.

137 Here again the dates are completely wrong. The decision to appoint Lian Zhongguan (Ni Tonqua) was taken on 13 June 1738; Hoetink, 'Chineesche officieren', 109.

dividing them among the sailing ships he set course for the land of Cochin.[138] In the eighth moon of this year, the term of Boedelmeester Lian Fuguang was completed; the great king appointed Lian Yuanguang (連元光, Nigoangkong) in his place. (Lian Yuanguang was the second son of Lian Luguan. Fuguang's eminent family was basking in glory like this). In the ninth month Captain Chen Muge passed away and was buried in the Longyan garden of Bazhilan (Pecinan). His administration was unremarkable. He just lived into high age. At the time, Guo Maoguan (郭昴官, Quebauqua) very much enjoyed the favours of the great king, who thereupon promoted Guo Maoguan to the captaincy and memorialized the sovereign in the mother country.[139]

> When Guo Maoguan (郭昴觀) was captain, the lieutenants were Lian Luguan (連祿觀), Chen Ronguan (陳榮光), Wang Yingshi, Li Heguang (李和光), Guo Weige, [and] Lian Zhongguan. Hong Shiguang served as soldaat, Yan Jingguan as undertaker, and Chen Caiguan (陳才觀) as boedelmeester.

In the eleventh moon, Boedelmeester Chen Caiguan passed away and was buried at the cemetery of Pumao Shan. In the twelfth moon, junks came to Batavia reporting great starvation in Tangshan [China]. The people were starving in countless numbers.

In the eighth moon of Yongzheng 5, *dingwei* [丁未], September 1727, the sovereign of the mother country sent an edict formally elevating Guo Anguang to the captaincy. In the ninth moon, Lieutenant Lian Luguan passed away and was interred at his own garden at Glodok.[140] The Great King Mattheus de Haan

---

138 The High Government states in its missive of 22 October 1725 that Commander Jacob de Jong of Malabar had warned about threatening moves by the *zamorin* (lord of the sea) of Calicut and wished to deter this 'by force of arms'. The Batavia government did not agree with this but dispatched a detachment of 100 soldiers anyway. *Generale Missiven* 8.8.

139 Tamboco or Tanboqua passed away on 23 February 1719. On 3 March 1719, the Council of the Indies decided to appoint as his successor Guo Maoguan (Que Bauqua), who had served as boedelmeester in 1707–1708, 1711–12, and 1714–15. He was appointed on 11 July 1719. Guo Maoguan was interred on 2 June 1733 on a plot of land on the Westerveld, the eleventh part of *blok* P, which had been donated to him and which by a resolution of 4 January 1726 was allowed to be used by him and his descendants; Hoetink, 'Chineesche officieren', 53–54.

140 He actually died after four years of service on 22 January 1733. Notarial act of 18 August 1733, Notary Wichelhuijsen, no. 4977.

promoted Boedelmeester Chen Zhongguan (Tan Tionqua) to the position of lieutenant.[141]

In the eleventh moon of the same year, Boedelmeester Wang Taiguan passed away and was interred in the rear of the cemetery. The great king then appointed Lin Yangsheng (林養生, Limjanko) to the position of boedelmeester. Lin Yangsheng was the eldest son of Lieutenant Lin Senguan.

In the seventh moon of Yongzheng 6, *wushen* **[戊申], 8 August 1728**, the retired Great King Hendrick Swaardecroon was interred with the ritual befitting the great king in the great church at Xinchi.[142] He had lived for another four years and seven months, after his retirement.

At the time, Captain Guo Maoguan conferred and decided with the six lieutenants to build a [new] cemetery. He ordered people to encourage all the Chinese people to donate money with pleasure according to their ability, and purchased a big vegetable garden at Bomao Shan (勃昂山) to turn it into a cemetery. The captain appointed the eldest son of Yan Jingguan, Yan Luanguan (顔鑾觀), as undertaker. The father as well as the son served as undertakers. In the seventh moon, Boedelmeester Kang Jingguan passed away and was buried at the cemetery. In the ninth moon, Soldaat Hong Shiguang passed away and was interred at the new cemetery.[143] He served as soldaat for forty-four years. The great captain then went to report to the great king and asked him to appoint another soldaat. The great king gave his permission and the captain then appointed Guo Fuguan (郭扶觀) as soldaat. In the eleventh moon of this year, Boedelmeester Li Yuanguan passed away and was interred at Galaba Dua (咖嘮吧賴, or 咬嘮吧賴).

In the fifth moon of Yongzheng 7, *jiyou* **[己酉], June 1729**, the Great King Mattheus de Haan fell critically ill and summoned his councilors for consultation and they decided to appoint *Meester* Diederik Durven as acting king to manage the affairs of the country.[144] They memorialized the sovereign in

---

141   Tan Tionqua had served as boedelmeester in 1717–18 and 1725–27. He passed away on 19 December 1741.

142   The Portugese Buitenkerk, which was situated close to his own manor outside the city gate.

143   The *Plakaatboek* of 21 November 1729 mentions that the Chinese cemeteries and the roads leading to them should be surrounded by mulberry trees to promote sericulture. Plakaatboek 4.234.

144   Diederik Durven was baptized in Delft on 13 September 1676. He graduated at Leiden University on 19 July 1702. He arrived in Batavia to join the Council of Justice in 1706 and was appointed extraordinary Councilor of India in 1720. In 1722–23 he was sent to the Parang Mountains to direct the works at the silver and gold mines there. After a short stint as president of the Council of Justice, in 1724 he joined the Council of the Indies

the mother country and on the second of the sixth month Mattheus de Haan passed away and was interred in the church on the fourth. In the seventh moon of that year, Boedelmeester Lian Yuanguang had served his full term and stepped down and the new great king appointed thereupon Lian Lianguang to the position of boedelmeester.

> Lian Lianguang was the son of Lian Luguan, and the younger brother of Lian Fuguang, so one family had produced four officers.

In the eighth moon, Lieutenant Chen Ronggong passed away and was buried in his own garden. He served as lieutenant for twenty-three years.[145] At the time, a certain Yang Chengguang (楊成光, Io Seenkong) received the favours of the new great king. Subsequently he asked the great king for the position of lieutenant and he immediately appointed him.[146]

In the eleventh moon of Yongzheng 8, *gengxu* [庚戌], December 1730, the sovereign of the mother country sent an edict officially investing Diederik Durven with the position of great king. Not long afterwards the king summoned the councilors for deliberation and they decided to impose an official system for the Company, creating a set of rules indicating the difference in clothing and means of transport between the high and low, so that affairs would not be

---

as an ordinary member. In June 1729, he was elected acting governor general, but the Gentlemen XVII did not agree with this choice and sacked him on 9 October 1731. He was recalled with three members of the Council. After trying in vain for years on end to sue the Gentlemen XVII for his unfair dismissal, he passed away on 26 February 1740.

145 Here are the facts: Chen Ronggong had been appointed lieutenant of the Chinese in Cirebon (Resolution of the Governor General and Council, 3 June 1707) before he was appointed lieutenant in Batavia on 28 December 1725. By resolution of the Governor General and Council of 18 October 1729, he was appointed Chinese captain in Cirebon. He passed away in early 1734 and may have been interred in Batavia afterwards. Hoetink, 'Chineesche officieren', 104–105.

146 Yang Chengguang (Io Seenkong) was indeed appointed to succeed Chen Ronggong (Tan Enkong), who had left for Cirebon. On 21 October 1729, Yang Chengguang was chosen 'because none of the boedelmeesters here' had presented himself for the position. Yang turned out to be a difficult person. During the weekly meetings of the Chinese officers, 'he so much perturbed the meetings with his turbulent character that decisions could not be taken without a headache'. Consequently, Captain Lian Fuguang (Nihoekong) and his lieutenants asked Yang to be dismissed from his position 'to prevent more affronts and abuses'. As a result, the Governor General and Council decided on 10 June 1738 to dismiss him, but allowed him to retain his rank and honors as ex-lieutenant. Hoetink, 'Chineesche officieren', 106–07.

mixed up. And thereupon a placard was hung on each of the four gates of the town in view of everybody.¹⁴⁷

1. The councilors are to wear velvet cloth and can ride a gilded coach with a *payung* on top (蓋大傘), with two runners in front and two lamps on the coach.
2. The chairman of the aldermen shall not wear velvet but is allowed to ride in a wagon with gold rims, with a *payung*, with one runner in front of the wagon, and one lamp on the wagon.

    In the event that a Dutchman using his wealth breaks the law, he will be punished 250 *rials*. By no means will he be pardoned.
3. The Chinese captain, the lieutenants, and boedelmeesters as well as those who have served their terms in office are allowed to carry a great *payung* (准開大傘). Common people shall not abuse the carrying of the *payung*. Trespassers who have the nerve to open their *payung* and misbehave towards high and low officials of the Company and do not honour these edicts will be arrested and sent into exile to Ceylon for twenty-five years.

Great King Diederik Durven also ordered the recruiting of workers to clear the Jiaoning Gang [腳寧港, Mookervaart] and make it flow to the territory of Banten. But before the digging was completed, many workers died of illness. Perhaps there were black devils who wrought disaster. This project was then stopped.¹⁴⁸

The behaviour of the great king was however unreasonable: he liked to engage in lewd behaviour. At the time, people called him *the godless king*. If the king was godless, how could he behave as an upright person?

> LIN CUIPU (林萃璞) COMMENTS: The great king loved to seduce the wives and daughters of others, and Yang Chenggong, making use of his affectionate relations, could obtain the position of lieutenant. So, can't we see what his behaviour was from this?

---

147 This is undoubtedly the placard of 28 December 1729, which circumscribes in an almost comical way, and in much greater detail than offered here, how the ostentatious Batavian citizenry should behave and dress up. *Plakaatboek* 4.239–44.

148 It is indeed generally stated that the first outbreak of malaria occurred during the excavation of the Mookervaart at quite a distance from Batavia. De Haan, *Oud Batavia*, 697, and Blussé, *Strange Company*, 28–29.

In the eleventh moon, Boedelmeester Xu Chunguan passed away and was interred in the cemetery. On the twelfth day, Boedelmeester Huang Yingguan passed away and was buried in the back of the cemetery.

In the fourth moon of Yongzheng 9, *xinhai* [辛亥]**, June 1731,** an epidemic of pestilence broke out at the salt pans outside the West Gate. Innumerable Chinese and indigenous people caught the 'chills and fevers illness' (malaria). There was not enough time to bury people who died in their own houses or along the road.[149] That year robbers emerged from all quarters. At night, they forced doors and robbed houses. Prodding sticks, they dug holes and crawled inside and rampaged around. The people had no means to make a living.

Some people came forward and reported to Great Captain Guo Maoguan: 'Jin Chaomei (金朝梅) has collected a sworn band of brothers around him, several hundred in all. Wherever they go robbing, they behave without any scruples'. The captain then immediately went to see the great king and together they hatched a plan. The great king ordered the captain to lead the Dutch sheriff (*dagou*, 大狗, *schout*) taking fifty men with him at night to patrol everywhere and secretly investigate the situation at Jin Chaomei's house.[150] If they were getting together to rob [people], he should arrest them at once. That night the captain went to his house. Jin Chaomei was just preparing a banquet for his followers. The captain immediately ordered the sheriff and his helpers to encircle the house and arrest Jin Chaomei and his robbers, nine people in all. The others crawled over the wall and the roof and got away without a trace. The captain thereupon bound them up and declared them guilty.

The following day the captain went to see the king saying: 'Jin Chaomei and his robbers have hurt many people. We can make use of the candle (插燭, that is, the Judas chair) and let them die slowly, to discourage people from engaging in evil pursuits in the future'.[151]

The great king and his councilors deliberated and reached the decision to put Jin Chaomei and his men all together on the candle. Among them there

---

149 This entry is of great interest. In 1994, Peter van der Brug published an interesting study on the outbreak of malaria in Batavia, deeming it to be the result of the fishponds (*rawa*) in the immediate vicinity of the city. Given that fishponds are not necessarily ideal breeding spots for the anopheles mosquito, because fish tend to swallow their larvae, the present reference to the salt pans as the villain makes more sense.

150 *Dagou* (大狗), literally 'big dog', is a conflation of the Minnanhua pronunciation *toa* (big) or *tuan* (Mr.) *sekaut* (*schout*). *Schout* (English, 'scout') means head police officer. Kuiper, *The Early Dutch Sinologists*, 670 n. 348.

151 The Judas chair was a form of punishment by which victims were set afire and burned to death from the top down.

FIGURE 10   *A Chinese procession to the appropriate place to make offerings [to the gods] and seek expiation whenever high mortality or other sufferings strike that nation*, Johannes Rach
ATLAS VAN STOLK

was one man who only two days earlier had joined the band to learn the martial arts, and now he was arrested and punished.

Really, too regrettable!

In the fifth moon of that year, Boedelmeester Lin Yangsheng stepped down after he had served his full term and the king appointed in his place Chen Jinguang (陳進光, Tan Tsinkong, alias Gouw Tsing Kong, Gouw Sinkong), who was Lieutenant Rongguang's cousin. Thus, both the elder and younger brothers served as officers. In the ninth moon, Boedelmeester Wang Chengguang (王成光) passed away and was buried at Ganwang Shan cemetery.

In the second moon of Yongzheng 10, *renzi* **[壬子], April 1732,** the Great King *Meester* Diederik Durven harboured a grudge and exiled the Malay captain to Ceylon. Originally, Wandoellah, the captain of the Malays, was exceedingly prosperous.[152] Durven often went to his house to gamble. Once he lost

---

152   The Kapitan Melayu was a very influential figure in Batavian society. He was the intermediary between the High Government and the native rulers of the Indonesian archipelago

and had no money to pay up. Wandoellah then seized Durven's horse carriage and his slaves to use them as collateral and told him to return to his house on foot to fetch the money.

How hateful [to be] without feelings.

Durven was at that moment the secretary of the warehouse [actually, director general, second in command]. He asked Wandoellah whether he could pay him back on another day, but his request was rebuffed.

Shameful, and no place to stand!

He swallowed his pride and had to go back that night [on foot] to collect the money, which he brought to the captain's house and thus redeemed his carriage and servants. He harboured hatred in his heart but kept his countenance; he just drank to dampen his anxiety.

Three days later, the sovereign of the mother country's investiture of Meester Diederik Durven to the kingship of Galaba arrived.

Wandoellah was wealthy and cared nothing for him. In his own houses he placed torture instruments, and punished people as he liked. He only did not dare to sentence them to death. His arrogance was really bad. There were three people who happened to come to his house. The indigenous people called them *xiandali* (仙達裡, holy men). Their behaviour was as follows: They were pure-hearted and did not eat pork meat. They were most revered by the indigenous, but Wandoellah ordered them to take pork ham, the so-called *babi ham* (貓味蚶), and ordered them to eat it. The *xiandali* vehemently refused to eat it.

---

and also acted as master of ceremonies when Malay rulers visited Batavia. The first *kapitan Melayu* was Enci Amat, from Patani, who amongst other positions served four times as interpreter for VOC embassies to the court of Mataram. He returned home in 1652. His successor, Enci Bagoes, also from Patani, died during the war with Banten in 1656. His son Wan Abdoel Bagoes, who lived to the ripe old age of ninety, served in various functions as interpreter, master of ceremonies, and even ambassador. After his death in 1716, he was succeeded by his son Wandoellah, who exercised his duties for sixteen years until he was sacked by Governor General Durven. He was condemned to the rack before being banished. His belongings, estimated at more than 100,000 rixdollars, were confiscated. His private estate, Kampong Melayu, was sold. See De Haan, *Oud Batavia*, 1.374. No successor was appointed for some time, but the Malays living on the east and west sides of Batavia were provided with lieutenants who were subject to the sergeant major of Batavia Castle. Placard of 4 July 1732, *Plakaatboek* 4.321.

He grabbed them by their hair, drenched them with hot water and immersed them in cold water. Afterwards he washed them with wine and humiliated them with all sorts of manners, [all this] just to vent his desires.

At the time, there was a man who lived in his town quarter, who had just married a wife. She was of incomparable beauty 'making the moon close its eyes and flowers blush, causing the fishes to sink, and geese to fall out of the sky'. According to the customs of the indigenous people, the bridegroom should bring his bride to his headman. Because he was presently serving as captain of the indigenous people, he should even more respect him.

When Wandoellah saw the exceedingly beautiful countenance of the girl, he suddenly lusted for her; his desires shot up to the sky and he ordered people to make her stay at his house and did not allow her to go back. He ordered a fake invitation for the groom to come to Xinwuli [欣勿力] to divert himself. Secretly he ordered the groom killed.

The mother of the bridegroom, a widow, waited for five days but did not see her son and daughter-in-law return home. She then went everywhere asking her family where they were, but they all told they had not seen them, but surmised that they might still be at the house of Wandoellah. His mother went there to look for them but did not find any trace [of them]. Very anxious, she ran to the sheriff to report. The sheriff then told the mother to go to the great king and tell him [what had happened]. The road is narrow for enemies! They come face to face with each other. Look out! No matter whether you have wings, you will not be able fly away!

The old hatred of the king suddenly cropped up; seizing this opportunity he flew into a rage. He immediately ordered a Dutch commander to gather his Dutch soldiers and lead them together with the sheriff and his men, advancing both by land [routes] and waterways, reaching the house of Wandoellah and encircling it on four sides.

At that moment, Wandoellah wanted his son to marry. He was just choosing a big diamond on a table. Suddenly everything was in confusion as men and horses arrived. Wandoellah was forthwith arrested. Moreover, all his money, diamonds, and treasure was seized and several hundred slaves were arrested by the Company. The great king and his councilors deliberated and declared him guilty and decreed that on the fourth moon Wandoellah should be brought to the tribunal and given a thrashing.

Afterwards he was branded and sent to Ceylon. The auctioning of his furniture and slaves took altogether half a month before it was finished. How much indeed! Because Wandoellah's crimes mounted up to the sky, he deserved this disaster; it was not just because he had demanded the gambling money from the great king.

John Chinaman comments: Because Wandoellah's monstrous crimes were of his own making, he could of course not escape them. If you say that the king harboured hatred towards him, it is certainly so, but if there had not been this opportunity how could he have burst out in anger? If Wandoellah had known himself that he had committed offences, then he would have been scared and would have observed all the rules and regulations. What could the king have done about it? Unexpectedly Wandoellah's cup of his crimes was full. With so many bad things the king could use his power and redress his grievances.

In May of that year the great king established a flour mill on the left side in front of the castle. With water power one could quickly save the manpower of many people. This was wonderful! All the bakers liked the convenience of the flour mill, they all paid taxes.[153] On May, 28 an edict from the sovereign in the mother country arrived at Batavia ordering Great King Durven to return home. Durven deliberated with the councilors to give the throne to *Meester* Diederik van Cloon. On the twenty fifth of October, Great King Durven returned by ship to the mother country. He had served four years.[154]

In the fifth moon of that year, Boedelmeester Li Yuguan passed away and was buried in the Longyan garden. Boedelmeester Lian Lianguang (連蓮光, Nilienkong) had fully served his term and stepped down. The new acting king immediately appointed Lian Jieguang (連捷光, Ni Tsietkong) in his place. (Lian Jieguang was the fourth son of Lian Luguan). So the father and the brothers altogether served as five officers. On 24 December, an edict arrived from

---

153   For the tax farm conditions of the corn mill, see *Plakaatboek* 4.472–77.
154   Diederik Durven actually served only two years. In a letter of 9 December 1731, the Gentlemen XVII recalled him together with Director General Cornelis Hasselaar and Councilors Hendrick van Baarle and Wouter Hendrickz. They were ordered to repatriate immediately, together with their families and a number of other high officials, 'without salary or any command [over the ships]'. This harsh decision stemmed from 'the "large decay everywhere in India, but especially in Batavia and Ceylon", the "manifold excesses" of higher and lower personnel, neglect of administration, commerce and justice, "from which, if continued in this way, may be expected nothing else but the total ruin of all the business of the Company in India"'. Stapel, *Gouverneurs-Generaal*, 49. Upon his arrival in the Netherlands, Durven started a lawsuit against the Company claiming restitution. When this yielded no results, he approached the States General asking them to interfere. The company kept the case hanging until Durven passed away on 26 February 1740.

the sovereign in the mother country elevating Meester Dirck van Cloon to the position of great king of Galaba. He was a native of Batavia.[155]

In the fifth moon of Yongzheng 11, *guichou* [癸丑], 21 July 1733, a big Company ship arrived in Batavia reporting to the Council of the Indies that the king of the Bugis in Makassar, Alang Chengjiang, (阿郎成江, Aru Sinkang) had rebelled. Popular sentiments were uneasy. He used a commander named Dashe (大舍, Toassa) as the headman of the pirates who engaged in serious robbing of the merchant vessels at sea.[156] The great king met with his councilors and decided to order a commissioner to lead Dutch soldiers together with black devils from Bali—altogether 500 men divided between two ships— to Makassar to suppress the uprising. Also, it was heard that in Bengal and in Ceylon rebellions had occurred and, therefore, orders were also given to another commissioner to recruit Dutch soldiers as well as Balinese, Bugis, and Ambonese—altogether 600 men—and divide them between two vessels and mount an expedition to these two places. In the second moon, the Boedelmeester Chen Tiansheng passed away and was buried at the Damujiao garden (大木腳, the Great Mauk, Tangerang). The Company gathered workers to repair the great church in the town. In the fourth moon, Boedelmeester Ye Jingguan passed away and was buried, and again, in the six month, Chen Jinguan passed away and was buried at the cemetery. The great king thereupon appointed Huang Yanguan (黃燕觀, Oey Inko) boedelmeester. In the tenth moon, Great Captain Guo Maoguan also died and was buried in the Eluowu (鵝羅兀) garden. Guo Maoguan served eight years as captain. His son Guo Chunguan went to see the great king and asked to be allowed to succeed his father.[157] The great king approved and appointed him to the position of great

---

155 Dirck van Cloon was born in Batavia in 1688. He finished his studies in Leiden on 1 April 1707 and left in November 1719 for Batavia with the very high rank of *opperkoopman* (senior merchant). He was appointed head of the Negapatnam factory in 1720 and governor of Coromandel in 1724. In 1730, he joined the Council of the Indies as ordinary member and on 9 December 1731 he was appointed Governor General by the Gentlemen XVII. He acceded to this position on 28 May 1732, but asked to be discharged on 20 December 1733. He passed away on 10 March 1735 on his estate outside Batavia.

156 'Aru Sinkang has re-emerged from his hiding place at Pasir and Kutai and has sown unrest together with the Buginese Toassa and the Mandarese in the bight of Tjenrana'. Missive of 31 October 1733, in *Generale Missiven* 9. 489.

157 On 6 January 1733, the Council of the Indies convened and discussed the death of Captain Que Bauqua, who had been installed on 3 March 1719 and who had until his death 'as is well known functioned in that position with candor'. At the suggestion of Governor General Van Cloon it was decided to not look for a successor among the lieutenants but to observe the son of the deceased captain, Que Tsoenqua, who had assisted his father

captain and sent a memorial to the sovereign of the mother country to report on this. Father and son served as great captains.

In the eighth moon of Yongzheng 12, *jiayin* [甲寅]**, September 1734,** Lieutenant Wang Yingshi passed away and was buried at the big vegetable garden cemetery. He served altogether twenty-eight years and seven months. The accountant of Wang Yingshi, Huang Zhenge (黃箴哥, Oeij Tsomko), submitted a petition to the king asking to be awarded the position of lieutenant. The great king immediately appointed Huang Tiguan (黃提哥, Oeij Theeko) lieutenant. In the ninth moon of that year an edict arrived from the sovereign in the mother country formally elevating Guo Chunguan to the position of great captain.

In the year that Guo Chunguan became great captain, Li Heguang, Guo Weiguan, Lian Zhongguan, Chen Zhongshe, Yang Chengguang, Huang Tiguan—six in all—were lieutenants. Guo Fuguan served as soldaat, Yan Jingguan and Yan Luanguan, father and son, served as undertakers.[158]

In the third moon of Yongzheng 13, *yimao* [乙卯]**, March 1735,** the king fell critically ill and summoned his councilors to deliberate. On 11 March, Abraham Patras was appointed as acting king to take charge of the country's administration and a memorial was drawn up to the sovereign in the mother country to inform him.[159] On the thirtieth of that month the Great King *Meester* Dirk van Cloon passed away and was buried in the great church. He served on the

---

and had served as boedelmeester in 1724–25, and was well-liked by both the Europeans and his own nation. It was decided to organize the public instalment ceremony according to that of his father as described in the *Daghregister* on 11 July 1719. The request by Que Tjoenko to have his father interred with military honour, which had last been done at the funeral of Captain Wanjok, was not granted 'because it has since then passed into disuse apart from the fact that the captain of the Chinese should not be considered as a military [leader] but as a political chief of his nation who also during his life time does not enjoy any honours from the militia'.

158   This is incorrect! According to the resolution of 27 July 1733, the following lieutenants were in office: Lin Chunge (Lim Tsoenko), Lin Senge (Lim Somko), Chen Zhongge (Tan Tionko, 陳忠哥), Yang Chengguang (Io Seenkong), Lian Fuguang (Nihoekong), and Li Hege. This paragraph is taken from the Leiden manuscript.

159   Abraham Patras was born in Grenoble on 22 May 1671. His family moved to the Netherlands after the revocation of the Edict of Nantes in 1685. In 1690, he signed on as a soldier with the VOC but on his arrival in 1691 he was appointed a provisional agent. Via some minor positions (secretary to the Chinese boedelmeester in Ambon, among others), he ascended through the ranks to become a merchant and head of the factory at Jambi (Sumatra) in 1707, Palembang in 1711, and chief of Sumatra's West Coast in 1717. Having served as second merchant of Batavia Castle he became director of Bengal in 1724 and extraordinary councilor of the Indies in 1731. When at the election for the position of Governor General the votes between him and Adriaan Valckenier were equally divided, he was appointed

throne four years and nine months. In the fourth moon, Boedelmeester Lian Jieguang had served his full term and the new king appointed Wu Yuanguang (吳元光) in his place.¹⁶⁰ Wu Yuanguang was the adopted son of Chen Caiguan. He was so lucky! In the same month, on the twenty-eighth, Lieutenant Li Heguang passed away and was buried in the Longyan garden of Pecinan. He served twenty-five years as lieutenant. Huang Zhenge (黃箴哥, Oeij Tsomko) submitted a request asking to be awarded the position of lieutenant. The great king approved and appointed him to that position.

In the seventh moon of Qianlong [乾隆] 1, *bingchen* **[丙辰], August, 1736,** there arrived an edict from the sovereign in the mother country formally elevating Abraham Patras to the kingship of Batavia.

He was a native of Grenoble.

In the same month, news from the front reported that Makassar had been pacified.

After four years of disorder, from 1733 to 1737, peace returned.

In the eighth moon of that year, Boedelmeester Huang Yanguan had served his full term and stepped down. The great king immediately appointed Chen Shangguang (陳賞光, Tan Tsiangko) in his place. Lieutenant Huang Tiguan passed away and was buried in the great vegetable garden cemetery. He served three years as lieutenant. Xu Jinsheng (許進生, Khouw Tsinqua) petitioned for the vacancy of the lieutenant.¹⁶¹ The great king approved and thereupon appointed him lieutenant.

In the fourth moon of Qianlong 2, *dingsi* **[丁巳], May 1737,** Great King Patras fell gravely ill and summoned the councilors and decided to bestow the kingship on Adriaan Valckenier to manage the affairs of the country. On the fourth day of that month, the great king passed away and was interred on the eighth in the great church.

Patras served altogether two years and two months.

---

by lot. He assumed his position on 11 March 1735 but passed away on 3 May 1737 before the Gentlemen XVII had even been able to appoint him.

160   In reality he served between 1729 and 1730.
161   In reality Xu Jinsheng (許進生, Khouw Tsinqua alias Gou Sinseeng) was appointed to succeed Li Hege by a Resolution of 27 May 1738 and served until 1740.

In that season, the construction of the great church in town was completed.[162]

> The building process lasted from 1733 until 1737, altogether five years until completion.

On 28 September, an edict arrived in Batavia from the sovereign in the mother country formally elevating Valckenier to the kingship of Batavia. He was a native of Amsterdam.[163] In this month, a ship of the Company reported from afar that the rebellion in Bengal had been pacified.

> The rebellion occurred from 1733 until 1737, it took in all five years before peace was restored.

In the tenth moon, Boedelmeester Wu Yuanguan passed away and was buried at the cemetery. There was a man, Kang Zhengshe (康政舍, Kung Tsiangko), who sent in a petition asking for the position of Wu Yuanguan. The great king approved of this and installed Kang Zhengshe as boedelmeester. Kang Zhengshe was the eldest son of Kang Jingguan.
During the reign of the Great King Valckenier, the weather was very hot, the sun burning like fire.

> If the weather is like this, you can understand the situation of the people.

Robbers arose from all quarters. At night they would force the doors and rob the households; during the day they robbed and murdered people. Among those arrested there were Chinese. Business was down then; the people could not make any profits. Therefore, it became like this.

---

162 This new church, a building with a large cupola on top, had cost no less than 128,500 rix-dollars and was consecrated on 8 May 1736.
163 Adriaen Valckenier was born in Amsterdam on 6 June 1695, the scion of a very influential patrician family. At the age of nineteen he sailed with the rank of *onderkoopman* and arrived in Batavia on 21 June 1715. He was not promoted to *koopman* until 1725, but from that moment he rose quickly through the ranks as *boekhouder-generaal* (chief bookkeeper), extraordinary councilor (1730), ordinary councilor (1733), and director general 1736. He was elected to succeed Patras the following year. He asked to be relieved of his function as early as 1739. The massacre of the Chinese population of Batavia occurred during his administration. He left on 6 November 1741 as admiral of the return fleet, but was arrested at the Cape of Good Hope. Sent back to Batavia to be tried, he was incarcerated in Batavia Castle, he wasted away in prison and died nine years later, on 20 June 1751, with the trial still pending.

FIGURE 11   *Governor General Adriaen Valckenier*
RIJKSMUSEUM AMSTERDAM

If a cruel king reigns, how can peace be achieved?

In the eleventh moon of that year, Lieutenant Guo Weiguan passed away and was buried at the back of the new cemetery. He served twenty-five years and one month as lieutenant.

The great king then immediately appointed Yang Jiange (楊簡哥, Nio Kanko) lieutenant.[164]

---

164   Yang Jiange was appointed on 31 December 1734. He had submitted a request to be appointed to replace lieutenant Lin Senge, not Guo Weiguan.

In the third moon of Qianlong 3, *wuwu* [戊午], April 1738, the governor of Ceylon, Gustaaf Willem, Baron van Imhoff, arrived in Batavia.[165] His wolf's heart behaved like a dog; he was exceedingly cruel towards the people. If an evil person has an animal's name we can know his character.[166] He came aboard a ship from Ceylon to Batavia and arrived on the fifteenth. When he intended to enter the town, all the councilors of the Company lined up with flying colours and a salute of drums and trumpets. The soldiers stood at attention. The Chinese also lined up with red flags and musical instruments and welcomed him to enter the castle.[167]

They invited the devil into the house!

---

165 Gustaaf Willem, Baron van Imhoff, son of Willem Hendrik von Imhoff and Isabella Sophia Boreel of Amsterdam, was born in Leer, a town in East Frisia. At the age of eighteen he moved to Amsterdam, where the Boreel family was very influential. Via his mother's family, Van Imhoff was related to his predecessor Valckenier, who over the years became his archenemy. On 19 January 1725, he left for the Indies with the rank of *onderkoopman* and arrived in Batavia eleven months later, on 29 November. Thanks to his personal capabilities and patronage by his superiors he rapidly moved upwards in the Company hierarchy: *koopman* in 1726, *opperkoopman* in 1729, *water fiskaal* in 1730, extraordinary councilor of the Indies in 1732. He was appointed governor of Ceylon in 1736 to restore order 'and save that administration from the unusual chaos in which it had suddenly ended up'. He was appointed ordinary councilor in 1737. Unaware of the events of October 1740, the Gentlemen XVII appointed him governor general on 2 December 1740, after they had honourably discharged Valckenier at his own request. Banished by Valckenier to the Dutch Republic due to his obstreperous behaviour, he was soon reinstated and sent back to Batavia in the capacity of governor general, with instructions to restore the Company's affairs. After his return to Batavia on 26 May 1743, the newly appointed Van Imhoff instituted wide-scale reforms, taking many initiatives that in the end did not yield the expected results.

Owing to his often tactless and impatient behaviour, Van Imhoff made several political *faux pas* that had to be fixed by his successor, Jacob Mossel. His brusque treatment of Mangku Bumi, the brother of the susuhunan at the court of Mataram, provoked a civil war in central Java that would eventually split the kingdom into three parts. His banishment of the pretender to the throne in Banten also caused a large-scale rebellion. He died at Batavia on 1 November 1750. Having returned to the Indies as the *hersteller* (the restorer) on a ship of the same name, this ambitious man was eventually nicknamed the *versteller* (the patcher).

166 The central character of his name, 伴熊木, means 'bear'.

167 When Valckenier heard about all the pomp and circumstance surrounding the arrival of his rival, Van Imhoff, he noted that the latter 'was putting himself on the same level, if not above me'. De Jonge, *Opkomst*, 9.314, and Krom, *Van Imhoff*, 56.

Some people said, 'He is a resourceful man, a man of competence and courage'. ~ *If he was really like that, why should he come to Batavia to ask for assistance when his country [Ceylon] was in an uproar?* ~ Therefore, the Chinese and the natives lined up to welcome him with so much ceremony!

> LIN CUIPU COMMENTS: Governor of Ceylon Van Imhoff had never served in Batavia in any capacity or managed state affairs. How come as soon he arrived in Batavia he received a warm welcome from the people with so much ceremony? Moreover, when the rebellion broke out in Ceylon in 1733, the local authorities had sent a letter asking for soldiers to come to their help. How come Van Imhoff could arrive at Batavia, while peace had not yet been reported?[168]
>
> If he had really been such a resolute and resourceful person in his own country, then he could have achieved the victory by himself. And why did he ask the Company to send soldiers to assist in the struggle? Not one of the councilors in Batavia or of the Chinese people could even think about this. Moreover, they were so eager to welcome him. Why? Because of all this, innumerable lives were later killed by his poisonous hand. Heaven let him come to Batavia to confuse the hearts of the great king and the councilors and the resulting disorder was an act of destiny!

In the seventh moon, the Great Captain Guo Chunguan passed away and was buried in the Eluowu garden.[169] He served five years as captain. Boedelmeester Lian Fuguang himself rejoiced in the favours of the great king.[170] He presented the great king with a carriage loaded with silver and sent a petition asking for the captaincy. When the king saw the carriage full of silver, he was eager to

---

168 This is an unfair statement. Van Imhoff had successfully pacified Ceylon.
169 He actually died two years earlier, in July 1736.
170 Lian Fuguang (Nihoekong) was the eldest son of Lieutenant Lian Luge (連祿哥, Nilocko) and one of the many members of that family who served in official capacities. He served as boedelmeester in 1730–31. He succeeded his father as lieutenant in 1733 and was appointed captain on 11 September 1736, at the very young age of twenty-six. He was married to Lim Oatnio (林沃娘), daughter of Lieutenant Lim Tsoenko (林春哥). During the Chinese revolt he was taken into custody at Batavia Castle on 10 October 1740 and incarcerated on the eighteenth. On 21 January 1741, he was submitted to a serious interrogation, but no connection with the rebels could be proven. He was sentenced to be banished for twenty-five years on 6 August 1743 and sent to Ambon, where he passed away on 25 December 1746. For a detailed biography see, Hoetink, 'Ni Hoekong. Kapitein der Chineezen te Batavia in 1740', *Bijdragen tot de Taal-, Land- en Volkenkunde van Nederlandsch-Indië* 74 (1918): 447–518.

receive the bribe and immediately elevated him to the position of captain and sent a memorial to the sovereign in the mother country. At the time, the family of Lian Fuguang was called exceedingly rich.

> Because his name was Fu (富, *wealth*), his family also was rich!

Moreover, father and sons, elder and younger brothers—the family had not less than five officers. Thus he dared to use so much money!

> The saying goes, 'Richness can converse with the gods and sets the ghosts to work. It truly is that way!'

On the tenth of September of this year a ship brought a report that the disturbances in Ceylon had been pacified. The sultan of Banten also sent his headman Panembahan II (Bananmaohan, 巴南貓罕) into exile to Batavia.[171] The great king ordered him taken into custody in the Company's Jakatra garden. In the ninth moon, Boedelmeester Kang Zhengshe passed away. The great king immediately appointed Xu Shuguan (許屬觀, Khou Tsiocko) in his place. Great Captain Lian Fuguang sought an audience with the king and asked him to add one more soldaat. The great king approved and immediately appointed You Tianguan (遊添觀).

Business in Batavia was down then; it was a year of crop failure and the price of rice was high. The people lacked ways to make a living; they loafed about and wandered around doing nothing, and made daily consumption of opium their work. It got so bad that swarms of robbers sprang up everywhere. In the countryside, raiders grouped together and robbed and hurt people's lives. All the robbers that were caught were Chinese who had not paid the Dutch poll tax. Bailiff Xinnao Ming (新蟯明)[172] went to see the king and asked him to thoroughly investigate whether Chinese had paid the poll tax, and to arrest all those without permits, all of whom were brigands.

This Xinnao Ming was a malicious person. Great King Valckenier then convened the councilors and decisions were made following a proposal by Van Imhoff that agreed with that of Bailiff Xinnao Ming. The great king immediately ordered the poll tax permits strictly checked. If Chinese did not have permits, they were arrested and without being released [even to put their affairs in

---

171 This was the cousin of Sultan Zain al-Abidin, Pangeran Putra, also known as the Panembahan. He actually fled to Batavia to seek protection. Johan Talens, *Een feodale samenleving in koloniaal vaarwater. Staatsvorming, koloniale expansie en economische onderontwikkeling in Banten, West-Java (1600–1750)* (Hilversum: Verloren 1999), 198.

172 *Drossaart* (bailiff) Justinus Vinck.

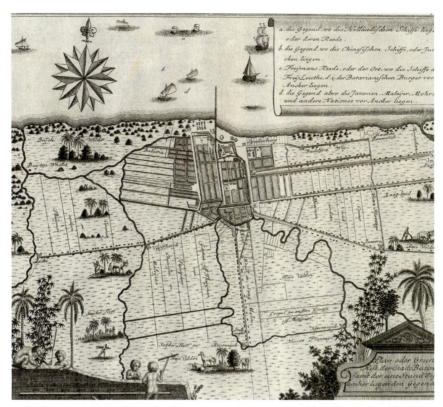

FIGURE 12   *Map of Batavia and Ommelanden. J.W. Heydt, surveyor and architect, in Batavia 1737–41*
PRIVATE COLLECTION

order] exiled to Ceylon for twenty-five years to work on the plantations and establish sugar mills. Great King Valckenier followed up this advice. He ordered Great Captain Lian Fuguang to proclaim this everywhere to the Chinese people. The latter ordered Soldaat You Tianguan to beat the gongs and go everywhere in the streets and markets and inform everybody. By the end of this year, the superior officers ordered the bailiff and his officers to strictly check everywhere for Chinese people without permits. When the Chinese heard about this [order], they ran away in droves. Some of those who could not escape were arrested and locked up in the town gaol.

When Boedelmeester Chen Shangguan had served his full term and stepped down, the great king appointed in his place Li Yiguan (李驛觀, Li Jaco). In the twelfth moon of that year, Boedelmeester Xu Shuguan passed away and was buried in the Galaba garden. The great king appointed in his place Huang Gongguan (黃恭觀).

In the first moon of Qianlong 4, *jiwei* [己未], February 1739, an edict arrived from the sovereign in the mother country officially promoting Boedelmeester Lian Fuguang to the captaincy. On the first day of this month he raised a red flagpole and hung on it a flag with a golden dragon on it. Below, he flew a flag with a golden tiger. ~ *This means that when dragons and tigers fight, the Chinese people will be hurt.* ~ The captain and his wife came out of the gate of his house to salute the flags. After that they laid on a banquet and invited guests and entertained them with a theatre play, flutes, and drums, proudly showing off for three days on end.

At the time, Lian Fuguang was captain, the first lieutenant was Lian Zhongguan, the second Chen Zhongshe (陳忠舍), the third Yang Chengguang, the fourth Huang Zhenge, the fifth Xu Jinsheng (許進生), the sixth Yang Jiange. The first Boedelmeester was Li Yiguan, the second Huang Gongshi (黃恭使, that is, 黃恭觀), Oey Kionko. There were two soldaten: Guo Fuguan and You Tianguan. The two undertakers were Yan Jingguan and Yan Luanguan.

> *John Chinaman comments*: In hard times the Chinese captain should be the shepherd of the people. But he showed no empathy for the people's sorrow; in fact, he enjoyed himself, laying on banquets and pitching tents to show off his glory, feasting for two days on end. On the one hand singing was heard, while on the other hand people were crying. This is not how superiors should behave.

In the fourth moon, Lieutenant Lian Zhongguan passed away and was buried in the public cemetery. He had served fourteen years as lieutenant. When Boedelmeester Li Yiguan and Huang Gongshi served their full term and stepped down, the great king immediately appointed in their place Chen Zhenguang (陳振光, Tan Tsinko) and Lian Fuguang (連福光, Ni Hocko).

I now leave the turn of events temporarily aside.

Coming to the end of this year, the circumstances were absolutely miserable. Robbery flared up from all corners. The people who were caught by the bailiff and his men were Chinese people clothed in black. The bailiff reported this to the great king, who thereupon convened the councilors to deliberate on what measures to take. Van Imhoff thought that these Chinese people in black were good people by day but robbers at night. He said, 'We should immediately give orders that if the bailiff sees people dressed in black clothes, they should all be arrested'. So, every time the bailiff saw people who were wearing these clothes, he arrested them and locked them up. He thus caused alarm among the people and brought about disaster.

The disaster of Batavia all stemmed from the evil plans of this cruel Governor Van Imhoff. From the beginning, he thought that people dressed in black were bad people and thereby made the people suffer disaster. That is really deplorable!

I believe that to advance the government, officials should make love for the people their principle. If one says that people in black are bad people, then half the people are bad. When some people said about this cunning governor, when he had just arrived, that he was a resourceful and virtuous person, weren't they mistaken?

LIN CUIPU SAYS: The Great Captain was the head of the Tang people. He should have had the power sufficient for overcoming difficulties. When the people were in distress, and the officials perverted the laws, he should have remonstrated and clarified to the officials that good and bad do not depend on black and white clothing. He should have tactfully intervened and opened a compassionate heart to move the authorities to listen. Then it could have been done. I think that it could have helped. Moreover, the family of the Great Captain was the wealthiest in all Batavia.

Given that the officials were strictly checking the permits, you should have explained how weal and woe alternate, and you should have warned the Chinese. In that case, would not many people have purchased the permits then? If they really did not have the money to buy the permits, then you, Captain, you could have exercised compassion and paid for them! The amount of money spent would have been limited, but those who would have received compassion were not a few. And many people would sing your praises! Why did you not think of this idea?

If you let the Hollanders arrest and lock up [innocent people] and make the Chinese destitute and homeless, then you just looked on without giving any help. Chinese were jailed because of the colour of their clothes. Whether good or bad, they were put in jail and at night drowned in the sea, burying them in the belly of the river fish. Shrieks of terror sounded everywhere, unbearable to hear and see! You led the country into disaster, you plunged the people into the deepest suffering, and moreover forced them to flee to faraway places, hiding their tracks! Where is your wealth? Where is your conscience? Although the Dutch use their might owing to their destiny, you, Lian Fuguang, the headman of the people bearing a heavy responsibility, how could you stand by or ignore this?

You stupid captain! You administered as if you could not wield your sword and cut. The losses were very big.

> If you had opened your mouth to save the people, and if the Dutch officials stubbornly did not listen, then you could have diminished your responsibility for what happened. How could you, with a closed mouth, be too scared to speak out? Why sit still like a dead body? This so-called life was unfortunate, because an ignorant figure was the leader of the people. How tragic! How lamentable!
>   Every time I see this, I have to stop writing and lament! I say that the foreigners, although they sit in an elevated position, behaved like wolves and dogs. If it is like this: The Dutch officials committed self-indulgent crimes, but you, Lian Fuguang, have also committed a great crime by ingratiating and submitting yourself [to them].

At the time, Great Captain Lian Fuguang fell out with Lieutenant Yang Chengguang during a discussion, because Yang Chengguang was talking nonsense in favour of a relative. During the meeting, the captain reproached Yang Chengguang, but the latter immodestly did not give in. Thereupon they began to quarrel until they started to fight. Fuguang immediately went to see the great king, saying, 'Chengguang is harbouring a grudge for no reason; how can I function as head of the Tang people? I beg to be allowed to give up the position of captain'. With sweet words the great king consoled Fuguang, who then returned home. But when Chengguang also went to see the king, he was scolded by the great king, who ordered him to resign immediately. Chengguang's face turned pale; he was panic-stricken and could not answer anything. He slowly left and returned home, but then said, 'Although I have resigned from my position I can keep my big *payung*! Today's wine I drink today, tomorrow's sorrow I shall deal with tomorrow!'[173]

> Yang Chengguang served as lieutenant nine years, ten months, and seven days. I say Chengguang was really a redoubtable old gentleman when he dared to quarrel and wrestle with the captain!

In the fourth moon of Qianlong 5, *gengshen* [庚申], May 1740, Boedelmeester Chen Zhenguang had served his full term and stepped down. The great king immediately appointed Wang Kuanshi (王寬使, Ong Khoangsay) in his place. Coming to the eighteenth [day] of the eighth moon, that is 9 October, the 'Great Disturbance' (吧國大乱) of Batavia occurred. ~ *the evil king* ~ Van Imhoff issued an order to send to the sea and drown at night all the Chinese people

---

173   About this quarrel see note 146, p. 106.

who had been rounded up outside the town on the sugar plantations and inside the town. He falsely said that he wanted to embark them on the ships.

When the Chinese heard this news, there were increasingly aggrieved and did not know what to do. Secretly, there were some Chinese who were scheming: 'If we sit down and wait for the disaster to happen, what use is that? We had better revolt so that we can escape from death'. The viewpoints were contradictory and confused. Thereupon there were panic-stricken people who ran away to the sugar mills of Babok, Tjien-sit, and Lapacang, which they turned into their temporary stronghold—altogether as many as several hundred people! When ~ *the evil king* ~ Van Imhoff tracked their whereabouts, he commanded Dutch and native soldiers to march to the two sugar plantations to seize them. As soon as the Chinese saw them coming, they panicked and ran away. Some of them who did not know, and those who were not able to get away, had no choice but fight. Only a few native people were wounded; many Chinese were killed. The several hundred that were captured were all escorted into town. All were wearing black clothing.

Van Imhoff ordered them locked up in prison. ~ *How pitiful! Those clothed in black all had to suffer harm from this vile person!* ~

Thereupon, inside the city the people's tempers were everywhere boiling like a cauldron. Rumours rendered the people scared; day and night were without peace. When two men, ~ *the excellent* ~ Lian Huaiguan (連懷觀) and ~ *the vile thug* ~ Lin Chuguan (林楚觀), saw how Van Imhoff was cruelly torturing [his prisoners] and the people's hearts were practically boiling, they discussed the great affair together and decided to take action and strike first to avoid being struck by others. Thereupon they distributed black, red, and white tablets and they agreed on the day of action, hoping to save the situation and to calm the public's feelings.

Who could have imagined that ~ *the vile thug* ~ Lin Chuguan secretly reported the big plan to the Dutch, and continued to falsely slander ~ *the excellent* ~ Lian Huaiguan. Then the strategy of ~ *the evil king* ~ Van Imhoff was already decided.

The empire of Chu (楚) was a barbarian empire and Xiong (熊) was the founder of Chu. Huai (懷) was the first king of Chu. Why then had Chu to revolt against Huai and collaborate with Xiong? This was because Chu knew that Xiong had power, and Huai was powerless. But even if he knew that Huai was without power, Chu should not have collaborated with Xiong. Now while he had allied with Chu why did he turn his back on him? And if he had to turn his back on him, why did not he go elsewhere? Why did he go away and reveal the secret? Xiong was cruel, and it was certain that as soon as he was informed, he would show his brutality and embitter people's lives and envenom them. How could the allies of Huai be preserved any longer under those circumstance? If we judge the true story of the events, then we must confess that Chu's crime was biggest; because even if Chu would have had to die a thousand deaths, this still would not make up for the lives of the supporters of Huai.[174]

He ordered the Chinese soldaten to go throughout the town and beat the gong everywhere, and to convey the following order at the door of every Chinese homestead: 'The Company (公班衙, the government) issues the following order:

> This was not a pardon for life, but it meant to eradicate all families!

'If you Chinese are good people,

> This is cheating. How abominable!

then you should close the doors and stay indoors.'

> Just like sitting ducks awaiting death!

'At night don't go outside, otherwise the soldiers that patrol at night may mistakenly kill people without blame'.

> These were treacherous words! Why say that he feared to hurt those who had not committed crimes. If those without crimes cannot live, how could those with crimes hope for survival. The soldaten sent the Chinese people astray. This was really not a shallow matter!

The Chinese did not see it was a trick! Everybody abided by the order.

> All their lives were finished. Was it not predestined?

Although those who kept the doors closed sat still, their hearts were in turmoil. They worried endlessly in their hearts. They could only relieve their grief by drinking.

---

174 Commentary by Go Tai-hok (吳太福) in Medhurst's Dutch version. This fragment refers to the names of those involved: Lin **Chu**guan (林楚觀), Lian **Huai**guan (連懷觀), and Van **Imh**off (伴熊木). The text is not always clear.

> I am afraid that they could not eat their belly full, but still they ate, because then they still could turn into well-fed ghosts!

To pick up my story again: When Lian Huaiguan handed out his orders, he did not know that Lin Chuguan had already leaked his plans. He continued to confer with the Chinese people about his plans to attack strategic places in the hinterland, and planned for the people of Tangerang [west of Batavia] to attack the gun turret [called] Benteng [175] and those from Bekasi [east of Batavia] to attack the Dutch army camp. And if they obtained victory, they should then attack the city of Batavia. They agreed to collect at the foot of Batavia's walls on the eighteenth of August, and then stage a joint attack.

> Considering the dispatch of his troops, this would seem right, but it did not help that his plans were leaked; on the contrary it wrought harm. Oh, Heavens!

When the three hundred men of Bekasi attacked the Dutch camp, more than two hundred were unexpectedly killed by gunfire, and only some seventy escaped to the stockade of Huang Banguan (黃班觀). The latter had originally agreed to lead his men to attack the East Gate of the town. But his soldiers had not yet arrived! The men from Tangerang attacked the redoubt at Benteng but failed. Fearing that they might miss out on the planned attack, they gathered all their men and went down the Angke River with a large force. When the barbarians of Pakojan saw them, they were all afraid. At the West Gate the barbarians secretly donned Chinese clothes so that they could get away.

When the Chinese force arrived at Jilakien, the natives hauled up the [draw]bridge and set it on fire. Under these conditions, they [the Chinese] took the port and crossed over. Trampling on each other, innumerable people died. The plans of the men from Ironsmith Street (打鐵街, IJzersmids-straat) were doomed, and beating gongs and drums they massively attacked the Pintu Kecil (Small South Gate, Kleine Zuiderpoort) of the town. Because the Dutch soldiers were defending on top of the walls, the attackers could not climb over the wall and get into the city. Then, many native soldiers came to the assistance of the beleaguered town. The Chinese did not gain the upper hand, but they lost people during the clash on the battlefield.

In the afternoon of the eighteenth, ~ *the evil* ~ King Van Imhoff immediately ordered a courageous and able person to rush out of the West Gate on his horse and run to the kampongs of the native people to summon them: 'For good or

---

175   The Malay word *benteng* means stockade or fortress.

ill, extirpate the Chinese people and achieve great merit. The Company will certainly reward you!'

When the various natives heard this order, they called up their people in droves, mastered their courage, and fought in the vanguard and attacked the Chinese.

Just now, when it was not yet decided who was winning or losing, ~ *evil* ~ Van Imhoff climbed on the city wall to see how the Chinese and the natives were confronting each other. The Chinese were armed only with spears, swords, knives, [and] bamboo spears with knives used for killing pigs attached to the end; but they had no muskets or cannons. With bamboo trunks bound with rattan they fashioned cannons. After one shot these fell apart and the bamboo trunk split open.

This was childishlike play! How could these be weapons for fighting?

Moreover, the army of the Chinese was scattered in a disorderly fashion. As a result, Van Imhoff knew that they could not pose a danger anymore. It was all too clear to him. At that point, he ordered the Dutch officers to lead their soldiers within the walls to open the doors of the houses one by one and seize the Chinese inside. No matter whether they were men or women, old or young, they were pulled outside and killed. The cries of the voices were unbearable to the ear. Those who were courageous and understood that they could not avoid death quickly took their swords and jumped outside and called the people together to defend themselves against the enemy. They retaliated by giving vent to their fury, and quite a few Dutch soldiers were also killed; but later, because those [who resisted] were only a small group, they were finally killed off to the last man. All Chinese in the prison and those in the hospital met their doom. Dead bodies blocked the doors; their blood flowed into the ditches and canals.

When Boedelmeester Huang Gongshi (黃恭使) wanted to leave town in his carriage, in which he had hidden arms, these were discovered by the searching soldiers. Thereupon he was immediately cut to death in town. ~ *How sad the fate of this righteous man!* ~

When Captain Lian Fuguang saw that this massacre was so horrendous, he hurriedly steered his carriage to the castle to go and see the great king and ask him for protection.

How shameful and what a disgrace!

The great king did not make any decision.

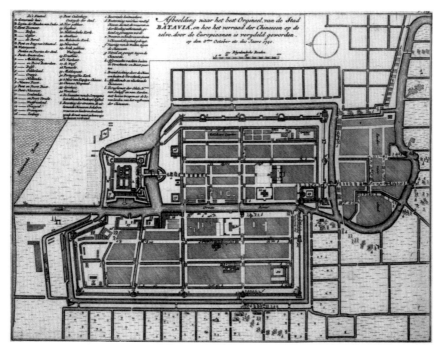

FIGURE 13   *Map of the situation at Batavia during the Chinese siege (1740), print*
PRIVATE COLLECTION

Lian Fuguang really was a disgrace to the captaincy. Originally, he was not a common person. He did not rise with his people, but he brought disgrace on his own head. Really, what use did this man have? This is really shameful!

When Fuguang saw that the situation was going awry, he quickly ran away.

He should have learned from Cao Mo (曹沫).[176] How tragic!

When the Dutch soldiers noticed him, they fired their guns at him; fortunately, they did not hit him.

---

176   Cao Mo, the general of Lu Guo (魯國, Lu State) during the Spring and Autumn period (770–476 BC), was distinguished for his great courage. Cao Mo kidnapped Duke Huan of the Qi State (曹沫劫齊桓公). See Sima Qian (司馬遷), *Historical Records* (史記), 'Biographies of assassins' (刺客列傳).

> You did not start to confront the Dutch soldiers; they took action! He ran back to his house and called together all his family, old and young. Why did you not call the righteous people and with one heart move to the house of the righteous? Together they went to the house of a close Dutch friend of his. You had better turn yourself with your whole family into the slaves of the Dutch! Although he could not bear to hurt them, the Dutchman nonetheless bound up all the family of Lian Fuguang and handed them over to the authorities. You, simpleton, had no foresight; that is why you now are in trouble.

The authorities ordered to put him in jail waiting to declare him guilty once the uprising had been quelled.

> Fuguang served three years as captain.

Almost all the Chinese within the city walls were wiped out. On the nineteenth, the soldiers of the Chinese and the natives outside the town were still fighting one another without coming to a rest. Then Van Imhoff ordered the big guns fired. He first bombarded the small houses outside the Small South Gate and smashed them all to the ground. In town, the row of houses on Porcelain Street also collapsed because of the roaring of the cannons. Moreover, they were set afire and the fire spread to the sky, turning the city red inside and out. ~ *The evil* ~ King Van Imhoff mounted the city wall again and shouted with a loud voice, 'You native soldiers, if you can exterminate the Chinese, the Company will amply reward you!'

So the native soldiers confronted the enemy even more bravely and fought in the vanguard. The Dutch first fired blank shots to deceive their opponents.

> This was a trick of the evil great king.

When the Chinese saw that the cannons fired into their direction but did not kill anybody, they slowly approached the city walls.

> How stupid! How could they not die in this way?

Then the Dutch soldiers put real balls into the barrels and fired. At the same time, the Dutch also fired continuously with their guns from the small gun turret across the bridge at the Small South Gate. The Chinese received hostile fire from left and right. How pitiable! Countless people were killed.

From the eighteenth day, they continued to fight for three days, until the twentieth. The corpses of the Chinese army were littered all over the plain. The stream of blood turned into a river. The survivors ran for their lives scattering in four directions towards the mountains. Some of them ran towards the mountain cliffs, and others hid in the innermost [parts] of empty houses; they were murdered by the native soldiers. Jade and stone [people high and low] were burned together! Heartbreaking and pitiful to the eye this was!

Truly, this was [an example of the saying], 'There is no road to heaven and no door to the earth'.

The Chinese were in dire straits. At that time, the wife of Guo Shou (婓郭壽) led a group of men and women and passed safe and sound to Songsisai on the plain of Salemba (Jiananmo Dapu Songyashi, 茄楠抹大埔松婓屎).

> This is a place name. If, reader, you know where this location is, you should tell me.

A second group, led by Boedelmeester Lian Jieguang, also passed by this place, actually in the territory of Banten, and were safe again. A rearguard of people who then showed up ran into the native headman ~ *crooked traitor* ~ Radin (勝陣), who had received the order from the authorities to cut off and kill them on the road.[177]

At the whim of the moment, all the Chinese were murdered by him.

> How utterly vicious.

He was a Chinese by birth, but he went native. How can one disobey the ancestors and become a Banten headman?

> You cursed talent, you wicked heart!

The corpses and bones lay scattered between the mountains and the streams.

> This cursed slave betrayed his ancestors! How can Heaven and Earth tolerate him?

There were some people who had escaped safely, but in their hearts they felt frightened, worried that they had no place to stay. Thereupon, grouping

---

177 An unknown *peranakan* Chinese turned Muslim.

together they reached a sugar mill. There was a miller (廍爹) ~ *the last character sounds like pig*[178] ~ named Guo Chunguan (郭春觀) ~ *with the heart of a wolf and behaviour of a dog!* ~ who, thinking 'all these people are refugees; they certainly must be carrying precious goods', hatched a scheme to murder them for their money. He addressed the refugees as follows: 'Good brothers, if you are carrying gold and silver, you had better hand it over to me so that I can keep it for you' ~ *You should not lay your murderous hands on them!* ~ 'to prevent the native soldiers from coming to the sugar mill to rob you.'

> It isn't so that the native soldiers would come to rob the sugar mill. They were all invited by you to rob, you pig of a miller! You robbed them yourself!

'You are suffering a lot. Please go and hide yourselves in the sugarcane fields tonight'. When the people heard him speak like this they thought he was right. They all very happily gave up all the gold and silver that they had brought along to Guo Chunguan, who took it. They did not know that Guo Chunguan secretly told Radin to lead his soldiers at night to the cane fields and encircle them. The corpses filled the riverside. All the silver and gold these refugees had put in his care was divided between the two of them.

If someone so heartlessly behaves against reason, then Heaven and Earth will not tolerate it. Later on, within three days, this sugar miller was caught by ghosts of these injured people haunting at large and driving him to death. Thus he ran mad and got lost, disappearing to I don't know where. The heavenly principles are clear and transparent! To commit crimes, what use is that?

> The money that he preyed upon three days earlier had not yet been used. How could the interest be collected so quickly? But the gods did not want interest; they wanted his life. How could it be otherwise?

Coming back to Huang Banguan: Just when he wanted to lead his soldiers to attack the East Gate, he suddenly heard that a large part of the Chinese army had been defeated. Thereupon he led his troops to the sugar mill at Bekasi. He hesitated to move ahead. Some of the soldiers who had been defeated in the town and come to Bekasi all ran to this sugar mill and regarded him as their leader.

> This was the cause of misfortune.

---

178 In Minnanhua the last character (*tia*) of miller has almost the same sound as piglet (ti-a).

The Company found out. It immediately ordered the native headmen to lead their soldiers to challenge them in front of their lair. When this was reported to Huang Banguan, he sent his soldiers to confront the enemy. There were three or four clashes. Who won or lost was undecided. On the following days they fought again. The native soldiers lost several dozens of people; the Chinese army suffered several wounded. When the native army saw that this was a situation in which they could not win, they retreated to town. Huang Banguan determined that his isolated force could not hold out long, so he emptied the camp and simulated a lot of bravado, but took himself and his men into the inner lands of Java. After Huang Banguan left, Van Imhoff led his troops here, but when he arrived in turn he saw that it was just an empty army camp. In the camp remained only a few wounded and ill soldiers. The native army then killed them off with bayonets. ~ *How pitiful!* ~ Thereupon Van Imhoff returned to town with his army and again ordered all the Chinese remaining in Batavia killed, to the last man. Well, then, if one was not killed off, how would one dare to live in this country of tigers and wolves?

Still remaining in prison were Captain Lian Fuguang and Lieutenants Huang Zhenge and Chen Zhongshe; and of the boedelmeesters only Lian Lianguang remained. The others had all dispersed in fright.

> I ask you, captain, lieutenants, and boedelmeester, even if there were these officers, who could they control?

Then there was Huang Yanguan, who, after his defeat, had fled to Semarang on Java. Afterwards he came back to Batavia to create turmoil in the mountains. This I shall speak of later.

On the first [day] of the twelfth month of this year, the sovereign in the mother country sent an edict to Batavia appointing Gustaaf Willem, Baron van Imhoff, to act as king of Batavia to manage the great king's affairs. On the second day, Van Imhoff arbitrarily arrested the old King Valckenier, bound him up ~ *for what crime?* ~ and put him aboard a ship the next day. The ship set sail and returned to the home country with Valckenier to be declared guilty. Valckenier occupied the throne three years and six months.[179]

---

179 This is a mix up of what really happened. The author has completely misunderstood the true course of events. On 6 December 1740, Governor General Valckenier arrested Van Imhoff and the councilors Isaak van Schinne and Elias de Haase on charges of insubordination and put them under house arrest to await the departure of the first homeward-bound ships. Van Imhoff and his comrades left on 10 January 1741 for Holland, where they had to account for their 'crimes'. Upon arrival, they quickly cleared themselves of

The first moon of Qianlong 6, *xinyou* [辛酉], February 1741. Because in Tangshan [China] nothing was known about the uprising in Batavia, junks were sent to Batavia. When they arrived at the roadstead, ~the evil king~ Van Imhoff did not allow the Chinese to enter town and reside there. He ordered them to set up temporary warehouses at Tong'ankou (桶岸口) at the mouth of the river to engage in trade. Although he provided all these Chinese with Dutch permits, he still dispatched a Dutch officer to supervise the comings and goings of the Chinese people and oversee their trading.[180] The Chinese felt afraid within their hearts, and outside they received the disgrace of insults. Moreover, Tong'ankou was filthy and humid. Very many people fell ill and died. In addition, taking advantage of this situation the native policemen intimidated them. Favoured by the dark night they set fire to the warehouses and stole their trade goods. Those who heard about this all felt aggrieved. On the other hand, the cunning King Van Imhoff, who had already put the old King Valckenier aboard ship and sent him back to the mother country, feared that the latter might impeach him with the sovereign in the mother country because of his failures.

Although he had already arrested him, he still feared that he might throw a spanner in the works.

Valckenier's charges and in turn accused him of having staged the massacre. Moreover, they started a lawsuit against him on account of the suffered defamation. What is more, it turned out that, without knowing about the tragic events in Batavia, the Gentlemen XVII had already appointed Van Imhoff as Valckenier's successor.

Governor General Valckenier did not leave Batavia until he had received his dismissal on 6 November 1741. Upon his arrival at Cape Town he was arrested on order of the Gentlemen XVII and sent back to Batavia to face a lawsuit on account of his conduct during the Chinese massacre. Awaiting a final verdict, he remained under arrest in Batavia Castle for almost ten years before he passed away on 20 June 1751, several months after his tormentor, Van Imhoff.

It is surprising that the Chinese author, who gives such a detailed description of the Chinese rebellion and the massacre that ensued, should misinterpret the turn of events on the Dutch side.

180 This was Henry Abbis, an English merchant with long experience in the China trade. He established himself in Batavia in 1735 when he entered the service of the VOC (resolution of the Governor General and Council, 11 February 1735) as supercargo in the China trade. Because there was no Chinese officer left after the massacre of October 1740, he was appointed delegate (*gecommiteerde*) for the Chinese nation and was given a house near the *boom*, the toll beam at the entrance of the port. By a resolution of 23 August 1743, he was appointed *shahbandar*. He passed away in 1744. See Hoetink, 'Chineesche officieren', 134–36.

He quickly summoned the councilors of the Indies and thereupon reached the decision to transfer the position of acting king to Johan Thedens to manage the state affairs.[181] He falsely said he wanted to return to the mother country to discuss affairs.

On 12 February, he went aboard a ship and ordered the crew to set out in great haste at night and sail to the mother country. He thereupon went to see the sovereign and offered an account of all that had happened, one thing after the other: that in fact he had protected the Chinese in Batavia and had brought order out of chaos.

> Yet he did not protect them, but hurt them!

The sovereign of the mother country was very pleased and believed that his appearance and his words could be trusted, because nobody contested his statements. Therefore, he deeply appreciated his abilities and on the spot conferred on him the kingship of Batavia. He gave him a blank letter, and put his stamp on it. He ordered him to return quickly in his own ship to Batavia to take his position and put the country in order. This was exactly the plan of this cunning bandit! That same day he took leave from the sovereign of the mother country and departed. When he arrived at the Cape of Good Hope he happened to meet with the ship of Valckenier, who had just arrived. Van Imhoff ordered him arrested and taken back to Batavia to have him summoned [for trial].

> He suffered a wrongful treatment!

Valckenier was imprisoned in the top of the castle, where he received the punishment of the wooden horse. He was not allowed to go in and out without

---

181 Johannes Thedens was born at Friederichstadt (Germany) in 1680. Recruited as a common soldier he arrived in Batavia on 31 July 1698, but soon transferred to the civil service of the company and gradually climbed the ladder from the lowest to the highest rank: assistant, 1702; bookkeeper, 1709; junior merchant, 1711; merchant, 1717; and senior merchant, 1723. In 1724–25, he served as head of the Deshima factory in Japan and joined the council of justice after his return. In 1729, he was allowed to establish himself as freeburgher in town, but the Gentlemen XVII nevertheless appointed him extraordinary councilor in 1732. Four years later he was appointed ordinary councilor and in 1740 director general. When Valckenier left on 6 November 1741, Thedens was appointed acting Governor General. He resigned his position to Van Imhoff on 28 May 1743, but continued living in Batavia, where he died on 19 March 1748.

authorization. So, finally, he was wronged and died. In the end, he was killed by the poisonous hand of this cunning bandit.[182]

Now the story goes that after Johan Thedens had been appointed acting great king, he summoned the councilors to discuss the uprising of the Chinese and they reached the following decision: to convict and send into exile the captain of the Tang people, Lian Fuguang. The High Government judged that he, as the Chinese captain, had been unable to nip the uprising in the bud and stop it before it had broken out. If he had cleared up the problems and solved the dispute, he could have brought peace and stability to the country. But he had made the country run into a very dangerous situation, and plunged the people into an abyss of misery. ~ *There is no greater crime than this!* ~

Therefore, he should be sent in exile to Ambon and remain there. It was decided that Lieutenant Huang Zhenge[183] and Boedelmeester Lian Lianguang (連蓮觀), because the disaster had not occurred because of them, ought to be released from prison. They were both bound up by the rebels; their situation could be excused; their crimes could be forgiven. So they were both released. The captain was exiled to Ambon. Only Lieutenant Chen Zhongshe (Tan Tionqua),[184] because he was so scared and worried, fell ill and died in prison.

To serve as an official in this way, what a pity!

In the fourth moon of the same year, a sloop arrived in Batavia from Semarang reporting to the Company: Semarang and Mataram both had risen, but were

---

182   Pending his lawsuit, ex-Governor General Adriaen Valckenier remained incarcerated in a watch house of the Robijn redoubt of Batavia Castle, where he died on 20 June 1751 without having been sentenced. The Chinese wooden horse punishment involved placing female victims on top of a wooden saddle with an enormous penis. In reality Valckenier had freedom of movement in the watch house where he was kept under surveillance.

183   Former Boedelmeester Huang Zhenge had been appointed lieutenant on 28 September 1736 to replace Lian Fuguang (Nie Hoekong). He was elected captain by a resolution of Governor General and Council of 21 April 1747.

184   Former Boedelmeester Tan Tionqua, son of Captain Tanboqua, a man of 'proper behavior', passed away in prison on 19 December 1741. While being interrogated on 15 October 1740, Tan Tionqua made an interesting comment on the possible involvement of Captain Lian Fuguang (Nihoekong) in the Chinese rebellion. He said that Lian Fuguang was not implicated in the rebellion, but 'he presumed that he was notoriously guilty, because he possessed very many sugar mills that he was leasing out, and therefore had the occasion to know, and should have known, what was going on'.

pacified by Banlong (班壠).[185] ~ *Banlong is the name of a Dutch official.* ~ This had happened because the year before, Huang Daban (黃大班) had taken his band from Bekasi and marched to Cirebon and Mataram. Along the way, he had collected runaway Chinese and they robbed and killed everywhere. The king of Mataram, unable to recruit soldiers in time, panicked and ran away to an unknown place. Huang Daban then grabbed the crown prince and put him in the vanguard as a [human] shield. When the natives saw the crown prince, they were afraid to risk his life; they did not dare to face the enemy and ran away. Huang Daban ran wild, and plundered innumerable riches. When he arrived somewhere and set up his camp, he daily delighted in gambling. Just then, Banlong received Van Imhoff's order to take command and sent his soldiers on patrol in the town and countryside. When he arrived at that place, he heard the information [about Huang Daban and his band]. He readied his soldiers for the attack. When he had already neared the camp of Huang Daban, the Chinese just happened to be having fun and were gambling. Not one person was on watch to see the enemy approach. Banlong quickly hastened to the front of the camp, and with a loud voice he shouted, 'Kill!' The Chinese panicked and in confusion ran for their lives in all directions.

These good-for-nothings could be of no use.

Banlong pressed forward and chased them to death. At that moment, countless men were cut down or shot down and one by one fell into the water. Huang Daban himself ran away to Bali.

Why did he not tell his gambling companions to run away with him?

The band of the robbers was dispersed. Banlong followed the preference of the local people and installed the crown prince as king of Mataram to manage the state's affairs. Thereby, order was restored at Cirebon, Mataram, and Weichen [Buitenzorg]. In the fifth moon, Boedelmeesters Huang Yanguan and Chen Yilao (陳依老), and Su Junsheng (蘇俊生, Souw Tsoen Seeng), who had run away from the upheaval, returned home to Batavia.

---

185 This is most likely Captain Johan Andreas van Hohendorf. See de Jonge, *Opkomst*, 9.lxxxiv. On 25 November 1741, a day of prayer and thanksgiving was called on account of the victory at Semarang. See *Plakaatboek*, 4.536.

LIN CUIPU SAYS: The uprising of Batavia was caused by Van Imhoff's arbitrary behaviour as a tyrant. He violently rounded up the Chinese and massacred innocent people, and thereby caused the great disaster. If one observes his administration in later days, he set the foundations for ruling the country; one can say that he was a fine minister bringing peace and prosperity. But he had a bad conscience, and was ruthless by nature. Even if he had many stratagems, he still was the robber chief of troubled times and moreover he was unpredictable. Why? Because when the uprising in Batavia had not yet occurred, he declared all people wearing black clothing to be bandits. He captured them everywhere and in the dark night he put the Chinese on board and drowned them in the sea, and he plunged the innocent Chinese into death.[186]

This is how the uprising was brought about. He was brutal and ruthless in this way. Just after the uprising had occurred, the edict of the sovereign in the mother country arrived ordering him to assume the kingship. While it was not yet said that Valckenier had committed a crime, this fierce and ambitious person Imhoff decided to arrest and tie up Valckenier. He put him on board a ship and sent him home to the mother country with a report.[187] But he also concealed the truth from the Chinese to obtain for himself a blameless position and achievement in the future.

But, in hindsight, he feared that Valckenier upon his arrival home would reveal the real violent changes that led to the uprising, and then he would be saddled with [accusations of] terrible crimes. He only served for forty-one days. He planned to return quickly to the mother country, to report to the sovereign how he had put down the rebellion and protected the Chinese. He thought that the sovereign would certainly listen to him and appoint him again as king of Batavia. Already carrying out his plans, on his way back to Holland, Van Imhoff happened to run into Valckenier's ship at the Cape of Good Hope. Seizing the opportunity, he arrested him to put him in prison and torture him, so that Valckenier could not reach the mother country to divulge his cunning plans and the causes of the rebellion.[188]

---

186 Here the commentator refers to the unfounded rumor that the arrested Chinese were thrown overboard under way to Ceylon.
187 This is a complete misunderstanding of what really happened. Valckenier had sent home Van Imhoff and two other councilors De Haze and Van Schinne.
188 Valckenier had been arrested at the Cape and sent back to Batavia to await legal proceedings against him long before Van Imhoff arrived at the Cape.

> He made the people believe that he had received secret instructions to make him do so. So, he succeeded in deceiving the country. The schemes of this ambitious man, strange to say, all worked out! Such a fellow is a so-called robber chief of troubled times. That is how it is!
>
> If only the councilors then could have seen through his dark schemes and gotten angry about his brutality and together made Valckenier king [again], and had sent a memorial to the sovereign in the mother country voicing their grievances and unveiling Van Imhoff's schemes—would that not have been felicitous?
>
> If only Valckenier would have arrived earlier in the mother country to report about Van Imhoff's amoral cruelty and the beginning and the end of the rebellion, then the sovereign of the mother country certainly would have been able to figure out who should win or loose. But Valckenier unfortunately did not reach the mother country. The councilors remained deaf mutes, and all were duped by his tricks. Did not Heaven make Imhoff succeed?

In the third moon of Qianlong 7, *renxu* [壬戌], April 1742, an edict from the sovereign of the mother country reached Batavia conferring the title of great king of Batavia on Gustaaf Willem, Baron van Imhoff.

> After the uprising he was appointed again!

Besides, he was also ordered to select a new captain who had both talent and virtue. The Great King Johan Thedens on that day relinquished his position and retired. He continued to live in retirement at Krokot to enjoy a good time.

> Johan Thedens was in office for a bit longer than one year before he returned his position to the cunning thug.

Van Imhoff hereupon ascended the throne. He issued a proclamation to everybody within and outside the city, including the company servants, the Chinese, the black devils [Mardijkers][189] the Kotjias,[190] and all native people, that they should decorate the front of the gate of each house with lanterns and stream-

---

189 The Mardijkers (from the Malay *Orang Merdeka*, 'free people') constituted a middle class of free native and Indian people of Christian belief. Most of them possessed flowery Portuguese names.

190 *Kotjias*, merchants from Gujarat. The Pekodjaan (Pekojan) quarter of Batavia derives its name from them.

FIGURE 14   *Governor General Gustaaf Willem van Imhoff*
RIJKSMUSEUM AMSTERDAM

ers. Offenders of the order would be fined twenty-five *rials*. Completely surprised and full of fear the people followed the commands. Van Imhoff himself ordered the erection of a decorated archway in Porcelain Street, and he lay on a feast of eating and drinking. When the banquet was over he paraded through the streets with the councilors. For three days and one night the city gates were not closed, enabling people to come in and out to have a look.

A man called Lin Mingguang (林明光, Lim Beenko), who originally served as *shahbandar* (harbour master) at the *boom* (*pabean*) in Banten, came to

Batavia after the uprising and sent a petition to be appointed captain.[191] Van Imhoff consented and elevated Lin Mingguang to the position of captain and sent a memorial to the sovereign in the mother country, and Chen Yilao, Huang Zhenge, and Su Junsheng all petitioned to be appointed to the lieutenancy.[192]

---

191   On 25 June 1743, Governor General Van Imhoff stated in the Council of the Indies that he daily felt embarrassed issuing orders to the 'large number of locally permitted Chinese who still were without any headmen or supervisors'. This made it difficult to force those who were clandestinely residing in town to leave home with the junks. He therefore felt that the Chinese 'should remain under their own headmen so that the administration of these people may be carried out in a regulated and for them convenient way'. Consequently, it was decided to provisionally appoint a new captain and two lieutenants. During the meetings of 28 June 1743, the council discussed the fact that unfortunately Lin Guoshi (Lim Kocko), the most honest and most beloved among his countrymen, had asked to be released from the obligation to serve as captain. It was therefore decided to appoint Lin Mingguang (Lim Beengko) as captain and Huang Zhenge (Oeij Tsomko) and Chen Yilao (Tan Iko) as lieutenants. Notwithstanding the decision of 11 November 1740, by which Chinese were prohibited from living within the walls, it was decided on 6 August 1743 to allow the Chinese captain and the two lieutenants to live in town because it was necessary to revive and pursue the business in town. See *Plakaatboek*, 5.75–76.

By a resolution of 11 September 1742, Lin Mingguang (Lim Beengko), *shahbandar* at Banten, was allowed to rent a house in the southern precincts (*zuider voorstad*) to continue his commerce. On 20 November 1742, he was allowed to settle down.

On 19 August 1743, the *Diary of Batavia* mentions that at 9:00 A.M., in the company of committee members of the council of justice and the advocate fiscal, the sheriff, and bailiff, the 'readmitted' Chinese Lin Mingguang (Lim Beengko) 'without any ceremony' was publicly proposed as new captain at the façade of the town hall, and adds 'For the seclusion of this ceremony see Diary of Batavia of 7 June 1707'. Lin Mingguang (Lim Beengko) received the tax farm enabling him to cook and sell opium on 18 December 1746 (*Plakaatboek*, 5.430–32), but this decision was withdrawn on 19 April 1747 (*Plakaatboek*, 5.462). He passed away around 17 March 1747. His house was purchased to serve as official residence for his successors. His son Lin Chunshe (Lim Thoenko) served as boedelmeester in 1747–48. Hoetink, 'Chineesche officieren', 58–60.

192   Huang Tige (黃提哥, Oeij Theeko) was already appointed by resolution of 26 January 1740. He was to succeed Lieutenant Ni Tionko, who had passed away. Chen Yilao (陳依老, Tan Iko) came to Batavia from Semarang at the end of November 1740. For details, see appendices 3a and 3b in Hoetink, 'Chineesche officieren', 131–32.) He was appointed by resolution of 28 June 1743. On 14 January 1749, it was decided to grant the request of Lieutenant Chen Yilao, who wished to return home with his family. By resolution of 2 May 1749, ex-Lieutenant Chen Yilao was allowed to purchase from the Company 1500 piculs of pepper and 1000 piculs tin at the normal price. By resolution of 23 May 1749, he was allowed to sell his land next to the Krokot River, including the lime kiln and the privilege to burn lime. Upon returning to China he and his family were banished to the western regions.

Su Junsheng became boedelmeester, and besides him a Gujarati and a native were also appointed boedelmeesters to join the management of the *weeskamer*.

In the fifth moon, Boedelmeester Lian Lianguang returned by ship to China. At the time, Van Imhoff also bought a big house from Huang Luanguang (黃鑾光) and made it into the meeting hall of the Chinese captain.[193] A red flagpole was erected in front of the gate and on the first of every month a flag was raised as a sign [to pay the poll tax].[194] Thereupon the great captain asked to appoint a soldaat to manage these affairs. Van Imhoff allowed this and appointed He Cunguan (何忖觀) as soldaat.

In the fourth moon of Qianlong 8, *guihai* [癸亥], May 1743, Van Imhoff moved out of the city into his own garden [estate]. Often at night he would visit the Chinese quarter in disguise.[195] At the time, the councilors decided to auction off sixteen tax farms:[196]

1. The toll of the import and export customs at the *boom*
2. The toll on the traffic by river
3. The *shahbandar*
4. The poll tax
5. The tax on slaughter
6. The taxes on the purchase and sale of rice
7. The tax on cockfighting
8. The tax on gambling
9. The tax on the fish market
10. The tax on selling arack in and outside the city
11. The tax on wholesale sales of rice
12. The tax on tobacco

For details, see Ng Chin-Keong, 'The Case of Ch'en I-lao: Maritime Trade and Overseas Chinese in Ch'ing Policies, 1717–1754', in Roderich Ptak and Dietmar Rothermund, eds., *Emporia, Commodities and Entrepreneurs in Asian Maritime Trade, c.1400–1750* (Stuttgart: Franz Steiner 1991) 373–400.

193 This is incorrect; it happened a few years later. Because of the 'incapacity and lack of resources' of Lin Mingguan's successor, Huang Zhenge (Oeij Tsomko), the Governor General and Council decided to purchase the house of his predecessor, Lin Mingguan, to serve as official residence for him and his successors (25 April 1747).

194 22 November 1743. See *Plakaatboek*, 5.110.

195 After the massacre it was decided that contrary to past customs, the Chinese now should settle in a *Chinese kamp* (Chinese kampong) in *blok* O in the southern suburb (*zuider voorstad*) of Batavia.

196 The new 'general conditions' of the tax farms were implemented on 17 December 1743. See *Plakaatboek* 5.120 and De Jonge, *Opkomst*, 10.xv. For the 25 December 1745 auction of the tax farms for 1746, see *Plakaatboek*, 5.316.

13. The tax on lanterns and candles
14. The tax on flour milling
15. The tax on the *waag* (weigh-house) and opium
16. The tax on the export and import of sugar

The above sixteen farms were auctioned off every year on the thirtieth [day] of the twelfth month in the warehouse of the company. The auction of the tolls paid by the ships at the *boom* of the ports of the Pasisir (the coastal region on the north coast of Java extending eastwards from Cirebon to Surabaya) was held once every three years. As soon as the proclamation had been issued, the Chinese went to see the great captain to discuss the fifteenth tax farm, for opium, [saying] before the uprising, the opium dens were full of people, making it so they could not make a living. Those who consumed it did nothing, and this gradually led to disaster, profoundly harming the people. The captain therefore refused the tax farm on the weigh-house and opium.[197] Thereupon all the councilors attended the auction.

In Qianlong 9, *jiazi* [甲子], **1744,** the Great King demolished the houses of the low and crowded places and refashioned an enlarged space to give the town a better aspect. Outside the Small South Gate, he again built a low fortification and put cannons on top. He built a redoubt facing the seaside. On the island in the sea he built a small fort. In the outer harbor near the Small South Gate and the eastern port next to the fish market he constructed a watergate.[198] He built another castle at Xinwuli (欣勿力) at the seaside, and another one at Tong'ankou.[199] He properly connected and enlarged the circumference [of the city]. At the head of the bridge at Tanah Abang he built a sluice to direct the water and irrigate the rice paddies. In the plain of Buitenzorg, he surrounded a plot of land with a wall and built houses for the people to live in. He established a market to enable the Chinese and native people to trade. And he also built the Company garden and one large mansion with seventy-eight doors at Buitenzorg.[200] In addition, he built a big road that led from there all the way to Cirebon, Semarang and Surabaya.

---

197 Traditionally, the tax farm of the weigh-house remained in the hands of the Chinese captain.
198 See De Haan, *Oud Batavia*, 185. De Jonge, *Opkomst*, 10.xv.
199 See De Haan, *Oud Batavia*, 115, 186. The Liem and the Leiden manuscripts have two different characters similar to 欣 Xin used elsewhere. In 1744 the small fort 't Loo and probably also Dieren were built.
200 Part of the Kampong Baru, 'a plot to the west of the Great River, at the foot of the Salak Mountain, reaching all the way to the Tangerang River' was ceded to Van Imhoff in August 1745. He renamed it Buitenzorg and built a manor where he resided for long periods. The building was handed on to the succeeding governors general—with the stipulation that

In Qianlong 10, *yichou* [乙丑], 1745, Captain Lin Mingguang and the lieutenants planned to build a cemetery. He issued a proclamation to the Chinese population and the *nakhodas* of the junks to donate according to their ability. He used their donations to buy a councilor's garden and the land of the Japanese pavilion at Kemayoran to serve as cemeteries. He appointed three undertakers, each of whom managed his own cemetery: Huang Lianguan (黃聯觀) managed the eastern cemetery, He Cunguan managed the western cemetery, and Su Quanguan (蘇全觀) managed the land of the Japanese pavilion.

In the fourth month of this year, Boedelmeester Su Junsheng had served his full term, so the king ordered him to serve one more term; he also appointed Shi Biaoguan (施標觀, Sie Piauwko) to serve as boedelmeester.

In Qianlong 11, *bingyin* [丙寅], 1746, the Kali Borong was filled up and leveled, and on it a Dutch (*Hongmao*, 紅毛, Red Hairs) church was built. On top of the church there were four geese, and behind it houses were built in the street named Prinsenstraat (爵仔街).[201]

In the tenth moon, the great Captain Lin Mingguang passed away and was buried in the cemetery of the Japanese pavilion. He served four and half years. The great king promoted Lieutenant Huang Zhenge to the captaincy, and he wrote a memorial to the sovereign in the mother country to inform him about this.[202]

---

they could not transfer the property to anyone else (*pactum de non aliendo*)—who continued to enlarge, remodel, and embellish it over time. Nowadays it is the official residence of the president of Indonesia. De Jonge, *Opkomst*, 10.xxxi, and *Plakaatboek*, 5.253–65, on 10 August 1745.

201 Kali Borong was another name for the Groene Gracht (Green Canal). The Lutheran church was situated at the northwestern side of the Heerenstraat. The cornerstone was laid on 26 July 1747 and the church was consecrated on 28 September 1749. See De Haan, *Oud Batavia*, 239.

202 Huang Zhenge (Oeij Tsiomko) survived but was much affected by the massacre of 1740 and its aftermath. He was appointed boedelmeester on 23 June 1734 and on 28 September 1736, he was appointed lieutenant. On 26 September 1740, he was one of the first to inform Governor General Valckenier about the Chinese revolt in the Batavian hinterland. Yet because he was not completely trusted, he was detained and interrogated on 14 October 1740. On the twentieth he appeared together with clerk (*schrijver*) Oeij Djiko before the commissioners of the council of justice to translate a Chinese letter. On 16 November, he was released. The resolution of 29 November 1740 mentions, 'Lieutenant Oeij Tsiomko and Lim Tsouko, who, because of the revolt of their nation have fallen into a deplorable state, request that they may round up and bring again under their servitude their respectively forty and fifty [run away] slaves whenever they chance upon them, so that they may restore their former enterprises in the service of the Company and the commonwealth. On 25 July 1741, Huang Zhenge complained that 'because of the burning down

In the eleventh moon of the same year, the Chinese captain of Banjarmasin, Lin Guoshi (林國使, Lim Kocko, 林國哥), arrived in Batavia to report.[203]

and destruction of his houses and cabins, the plundering of his goods, and the loss of his slaves during the massacre and destruction of his nation, he had now fallen into extreme misery', and that he was not at all able to satisfy his creditors. So, he asked for protection against legal persecution. On 17 December 1743, he warned about a plot by 'Muslims against the Christians and Chinese'. When Chinese officers were again appointed, Huang Zhenge returned to the position of lieutenant.

On 21 April 1747, it was decided to appoint him captain as successor to the recently deceased Lin Mingguang (Lim Beengko) and to promote Boedelmeester Tsou Tsoenseengh (蘇俊生) to the rank of lieutenant. It was furthermore agreed that the person who was elected to the position of captain (this also would apply to his successors in the future) should first make an oath of purge (*eed van purge*) before the Board of Aldermen, as decided on 4 June 1743, i.e. to clear himself from all legal action. Because of the proposed candidate's 'incapacity and lack of resources', it was decided on 25 April to purchase the house of his predecessor Lin Mingguang (Lim Beengko) to serve as official residence.

On 5 May 1747, it was decided that Huang Zhenge should be 'proposed as captain to his nation' following the past examples as noted down in the Diary of Batavia for 1707 and 1719, respectively, in connection with the introduction ceremonies of Tamboqua and Guo Maoguan.

On 6 June 1747, Governor General Van Imhoff issued an edict declaring that, at the suggestion of the Chinese community, the Council of the Indies had resolved to appoint Oeij Somko, 'another able and enterprising person', to the position of captain. Together with the remaining Lieutenants Tan Iko, Lim Koko, and Souw Tsoenseeng, he was to take in hand the affairs of the Chinese citizens. On 9 June 1747, it was decided that contrary to the resolution of 21 April 1747, decisions about the ceremonies surrounding the public presentation of Oeij Tjomko should be deferred to Governor General Van Imhoff himself.

On 25 August 1747, Huang Zhenge was allowed until the end of November a prolongation of the '*surcheance* (delay) of payment on his tax farm obligations', which had been allowed to him on 6 April because of his 'incapacity'.

A resolution of 17 November 1747 shows that he was already ten years in Batavia. On 16 September, the poor Chinese captain was allowed the remission of the tax farm payments that he had asked for. On 26 September 1749, he was allowed to bury his wife, Khoe Etnio, with the same ceremony formerly practised by the Chinese elite ('*lieden van conditie onder hare natie*') before 1740, because the 'present governor general' tried in all kinds of ways to restore the Chinese community to its former condition. On 30 April 1750, Captain Huang Zhenge appointed Oeij Tsilauw (his successor) executor of his will. On 16 June 1750, the latter was allowed to ship the corpse of Huang Zhenge to China so it could be interred there according to the wishes of the deceased. See Hoetink, 'Chineesche officieren', 60–64.

203 At the suggestion of Governor General Van Imhoff, it was agreed to appoint Lin Guoshi (Lim Kocko) to the position of third lieutenant as a reward for his recent service as emissary to the king of Johor. (See resolution of 10 July 1744). He had previously served as captain of the Chinese of Banjarmasin. By a resolution of 16 December 1746, he and

The king praised his abilities, and ordered him to return to Banjarmasin to act as negotiator.

In Qianlong 12, *dingmao* [丁卯], 1747, Lin Guoshi again came to Batavia and presented a report. He moreover asked for the position of lieutenant at Batavia. The king immediately appointed him to that position.

On 10 May, there arrived an edict from the sovereign in the mother country investing Huang Zhenge with the captaincy. Boedelmeester Shi Biaoguan had served his full term and stepped down. The king immediately appointed in his place Huang Yanguan.

> Huang Yanguan had served before the uprising as boedelmeester. Now he reappeared.

In the first moon of Qianlong 13, *wuchen* [戊辰], 21 March 1748, the former King Joan Thedens passed away and was buried on the twenty-third in the great church with a ceremony fit for a great king. A big ship arrived in Batavia then, reporting that the uprising in Ceylon had been quelled.[204]

> The disturbances had continued for sixteen years.

At the same time, it reported that the people in the motherland had been involved in civil strife. Boleshi Putaoya (勃樂氏葡萄衙)[205] gained the day and was now in command of the country. He was respectfully addressed as the *real* sovereign. He had sent an edict to Batavia to appoint Van Imhoff to act

---

four company servants were assigned to welcome in full sea north of Batavia the incoming Chinese junks and make known to them the (good) intentions of the Batavian administration.

204 The Missive of Governor General and Council of 31 December 1748 mentions that 'the attitude of the Candian court had made a big turn in the right direction'. *Generale Missiven*, 11.686.

205 This must refer to 2 May 1747, when, after the long 'stadtholderless period' of 1702–1747, Willem IV of Orange Nassau was installed as hereditary stadtholder (*Prins erfstadhouder*) and captain general of all Dutch provinces. The appointment of the Prince of Orange as stadtholder was proclaimed in Batavia on 7 March 1748. *Plakaatboek*, 5.552. On 22 November 1749, the governor general and Council received a letter of 17 April 1749 that the prince had also accepted the supreme authority of the VOC. See *Generale Missiven* 11.769; and *Plakaatboek*, 5.600. Why the name Putaoya (葡萄衙), "Portugal, Portuguese," is attached to Prince (Boleshi) William IV remains unclear.

as great king of Batavia, that is *Gouverneur Generaal*.²⁰⁶ After Van Imhoff was appointed, he immediately issued an edict to the Company servants and people of every kind inside and outside the city ordering them to place lanterns with streamers as decoration in front of their gate on the twenty-fifth [day] of the same month. At Rejidou (嘧吉斗, i.e. Jakatra) he treated all the headmen to a great banquet and entertained them with drinks, and set off thirty pieces of fireworks ~ *noise and excitement every where*! ~ to congratulate Boleshi Putaoya on his triumph and his elevation to the royal throne.²⁰⁷

At the same time, he ordered his people to seek closer ties with the sultan of Banten and to invite him to come to Batavia. But the sultan was short-sighted and did not see through the profound scheming [of Van Imhoff]. He came together with his wife to Batavia.

> The title of sultan was finished hereby. How pitiful!

Now the title of the wife of the sultan is *ratu*.

> That is the name of the wife of a Malay sultan.

Her character was not amiable. She did not get along with the sultan.

> When husband and wife fall out with each other, this is ominous.

So, she first went to see Great King Van Imhoff and implored him to correct the wrongdoings of her husband and to send him into exile.

> This bitch was really disgusting!

Van Imhoff immediately ordered an examination of his crimes and exiled him to Ambon. Moreover he also imprisoned Ratu Sharifa, the wife of the sultan, on top of the castle wall because she failed to behave as a proper wife.²⁰⁸

---

206 On the recommendation of the Prince of Orange, Governor General van Imhoff was appointed general of the infantry of the United Provinces. See *Plakaatboek*, 5.553, 22 March 1748.
207 This paragraph does not appear in Medhurst's version.
208 The weak Sultan Zain Al-Arifin ruled Banten from 1733, but his powerful and sly wife, Ratu Sharifa Fatima, the daughter of an Arab imam, schemed against Crown Prince Panembahan Pangeran Gusti, who fled to Batavia. Before she married the sultan, Sharifa had been living in Batavia, where she was seen 'to frequent almost daily the houses of

This sentence was right, because when an impudent wife speaks nonsense, Heaven cannot embrace such behaviour. She who harms her husband thereby brings harm on herself.

When the family members of the sultan and his officers heard these tidings, none could bear this and they became very angry.

> The barbarians also cherish the hierarchical order of princes and headmen. That is to be respected.

One of the relatives of the sultan, called Maowushi Wang (貓兀氏望, Ratu Bagus Buang),[209] withdrew into the mountains and, making plans to raise soldiers to take revenge, bided his time.

In the sixth moon, Lieutenant Lin Guoshi died and was buried in the cemetery of the Japanese pavilion. Van Imhoff immediately appointed Lin Jiguang (林緝光, Lim Tjipko) as his successor.[210] Boedelmeester Su Junsheng stepped down when his term was completed, and Van Imhoff forthwith replaced him with Lin Chunshe (林椿舍, Lim Thoenko). ~ *Lin Chunshe was the eldest son of Captain Lin Mingguang!* ~

In Qianlong 14, *jisi* [己巳] **1749,** Van Imhoff took the councilors on a pleasure trip to Pulau Onrust. He also took Ratu Sharifa, the wife of the sultan, and ordered her to live there until her death, and forbade her to move elsewhere. That the wife of the sultan ended up here was retribution for her behaviour.

In the sixth moon, Lieutenant Chen Yilao stepped down from his position and returned home with his wife and children.[211] He served seven years and

---

the most prominent gentlemen'. See M.L. van Deventer, *Geschiedenis van de Nederlanders op Java* (Haarlem: Tjeenk Willink, 1887), 2.155. Conniving with Ratu Sharifa, Van Imhoff banished Pangeran Gusti to Ceylon. In 1748, when Sultan Zain Al-Arifing went mad, he was in turn banished to Ambon. Henceforth, Ratu Sharifa was to rule Banten under the supervision of the VOC, but soon a rebellion broke out under the leadership of a holy man with the name Kiai Tapa, who was joined by Ratu Bagus Buang, the son of Panembahan Pangeran Gusti. (Ratu Bagus was a title given to the child of the sultan and a concubine.) Ratu Sharifa Fatima was dethroned and banished to Ambon but fell ill and passed away on the island Edam in the Bay of Batavia on 10 March 1751. See De Jonge, *Opkomst*, 10.178–79, 181 and Van Deventer, *Geschiedenis*, 2.156–69.

209   Ratus Bagus Buang, the son of the Pangeran Gusti.
210   The name is here Lin Jiguang, but it is usually written Lin Jige 林緝哥.
211   It is interesting to note that on 15 September 1730, it was decreed in Batavia that the Gentlemen XVII had decided that married Chinese returning to China had to be accompanied by their wives and children. *Plakaatboek*, 4.272. Upon arrival in China, Chen Yilao was banished with his family to China's western provinces. For details on this

five months as lieutenant. Van Imhoff immediately appointed Chen Yuansheng (陳遠生, Tan Wang Seeng) in his place.[212]

In the ninth moon of Qianlong 15, *gengwu* [庚午], 3 November 1750, Gustaaf Willem, Baron van Imhoff died of an illness.

> I don't say passed away but say he died, because thus you can gauge how little sorry I feel. (不曰薨而曰死者，人心之戚戚可知)

He was buried in the great church. In his testament ~ *this evil king* ~ ordered Jacob Mossel to act as king and manage the affairs of the country.

> LIN CHENGJIU (林程九) COMMENTS: Because Ceylon was in an uproar, Van Imhoff lost control and ran away. Originally his character was cruel. When he arrived in Batavia he crafted plans that preceded days of unrest. The people feared for their lives day and night. If only Valckenier had possessed a strong and decisive character and the talent to bring peace and stability to the country! If only in unison with all the councilors he could have crafted a memorial to the sovereign in the mother country, they would have made it impossible for Van Imhoff to have his sly plans accepted, and could have peacefully kept him down! Would not that have been the best plan?

---

sad but interesting story see Ng Chin-Keong, 'The Case of Ch'en I-lao: Maritime Trade and Overseas Chinese in Ch'ing Policies, 1717–1754' in Roderich Ptak and Dietmar Rothermund, eds. *Emporia, Commodities and Entrepreneurs in Asian Maritime Trade, c. 1400–1750* (Stuttgart: Franz Steiner, 1991), 373–400.

212 Chen Yuansheng (Tan Wang Seeng) was appointed on 10 December 1748 to succeed Lin Guoge (Lim Kocko). And, 'because the number of Chinese inhabitants was increasing year by year and three lieutenants were not sufficient', it was decided to appoint as fourth lieutenant the secretary of the Chinese council, Oeij Tsielauw (who in later days would become captain), to make it possible to carry out the necessary duties in two pairs. That is to say that, two lieutenants ran the administration in turn with the other two, alternating every month. This enabled these officers to also take care of their own affairs. Chen Yuansheng also ran two arak distilleries that yielded nothing under the present unfavourable circumstances. See resolution of 17 July 1750. On 7 July 1752, Chen Yuansheng requested to be relieved from his office because he could no longer afford to carry out his duties, but this was not accepted. On 13 December 1757, he was issued 'a stone building outside the Diestgate on the Westerveld (part 6 of *blok O*), which could serve as a storeroom for the ashes of the Chinese with the surname Tan (陳, Chen); see Hoetink, 'Chineesche officieren', 113–14.

'Even if this had not happened until after the uprising, they still should have refused his methods of slaughtering people; they should have let it be known inside and outside the town that they would allow the people lead a normal life. In the aftermath, the councilors all together should not only have drawn up a memorial to the sovereign, but to open his ears they also should have sent it quickly to the mother country, to show the pattern of behaviour that had led to the rebellion, and how he committed the same mistakes as in Ceylon. Crimes should redound on him who has committed them. This could in extremis still have been done. But! It was because Valckenier was angry in his heart and procrastinative and indecisive that he let the slander first reach Holland, so that Van Imhoff could spin his evil plans into achievements. That Valckenier was sitting on the wooden horse on the top of the wall, how could it be without a cause?

After Van Imhoff had usurped the throne, he created new tax farms, he built a fortress on Pulau Onrust, he repaired the bridge gates, and constructed watergates. His management and his construction projects benefitted the country and the people. All this is enough to prove he was an able minister in peaceful times, but he was an unscrupulous schemer in times of trouble.

[HERE FOLLOWS ANOTHER COMMENT BY CHEN XUELAN (陳雪瀾), ADDED TO THE YANG BODONG (楊伯東) MANUSCRIPT ON 26 SEPTEMBER 1891.]

Regarding this issue, the author must be mistaken. While reading in the *Daghregister van Batavia* (*Diary of Batavia Castle*) about the massacre of our Chinese during the administration of Valckenier, one sees that he [Valckenier] gave way to his own resentments against the Chinese and feathered his own nest, because when he returned home he carried millions in wealth with him. So, he never discussed this massacre of the Chinese with Van Imhoff and the councilors at meetings. Therefore, the councilors did not approve of his behaviour and secretly plotted to send him back to the mother country. But because Valckenier anticipated this, he put them in jail together with Van Imhoff, and later he packed them on board a ship and sent them back home. When Van Imhoff and the two councilors returned home they reported the affairs to the sovereign. The sovereign was fully convinced of the truth of their memorial, and ordered Van Imhoff to return to Batavia to investigate the crimes. But before he had arrived in Batavia, Van Imhoff happened to meet at The Cape the ship in which Valckenier was returning home. Van Imhoff transmitted the order of the sovereign of the home country and sent Valckenier back to Batavia to be tried. The councilors had already sentenced him, and preparations had been made to punish him by means of the wooden cow and wooden horse, but when the sentence had not yet been carried out, Valckenier, abashed by these developments, died in jail, and was buried in the clothes of a prisoner.[213]

Jacob Mossel assumed the position of acting king and sent a memorial to the sovereign in the mother country.[214] When a member of the sultan's family named Maowushi Wang (Ratu Bagus Buang) heard that Van Imhoff had already died then, he promptly raised soldiers and started a rebellion. There was a native immortal with the name Kiai Tapa. ~ *He was a breatharian, that is he could live without rice. The name Tapa was his holy title.* ~ He joined forces with Ratu Bagus Buang, recruited native soldiers on a large scale, and embarked on a war. The power of the robbers was enormous! Every corner of Banten was in a continuous uproar. All this happened because Van Imhoff during his life harmed the Chinese people, and after death he also harmed the people of Banten. In this year, Captain Huang Zhenge went to see the great king, and asked him to establish the position of secretary (*secretaris*). The king approved of this, and thereupon he appointed Huang Shinao (黃市鬧, Oeij Tsjilauw) secretary, with the privilege of going about with a large *payung* (大傘).[215]

---

213 Thanks to the intervention of his friends and family, this was not the case.
214 Jacob Mossel was born on 28 November 1704 at Enkhuizen. He sailed at the age of 15 as a mariner to Batavia where he arrived on 24 September 1720. Climbing from the position of assistant to governor he served for twenty-one years in almost all possible ranks on the Coromandel Coast. In 1740, he was appointed extraordinary councilor and on 1742 he moved to Batavia, where he was promoted to ordinary councilor In 1745, he became the director of the Opium Societeit and was sent as emissary to the court of Banten one year later. His appointment as director general followed in 1747. When Van Imhoff died on 1 November 1750, Mossel was unanimously elected governor general. During his reign, he solved the political problems with Banten and Mataram that had been created by his predecessor. Mossel sent in 1759 an expeditionary force sent to the Dutch settlement at Chinsura with the intention of challenging the rising power of the English in Bengal, but this motley band of soldiers was badly beaten by Robert Clive. Mossel cancelled many of the measures introduced by Van Imhoff, and installed a *Reglement ter beteugeling van pracht en praal* (measures to restrain display of pomp and circumstance). He passed away on 15 May 1761.
215 Huang Shinao had already been appointed by Van Imhoff in 1747. On 26 May of that year, it was decided to formally appoint as secretary for the meetings of the Chinese Council Oeij Tjie (Tsi) Lauw with the same income—150 rixdollars a year—as the heretofore 'unqualified' secretaries, but 'with the allowance to carry a large *payung*' (umbrella). See the resolution of 4 October 1695. He was sworn in on 11 July 1747. Like the boedelmeesters, the

[HERE FOLLOWS THE ADDITIONAL COMMENT OF YANG BODONG, WRITTEN ON 9 SEPTEMBER 1896, WHEN HE MADE A COPY OF THE ORIGINAL MANUSCRIPT.]

I have the following opinion about this affair. The Chinese people did not match the aspirations of the native sultan and his family, who withdrew into the mountains to ally with Bagus Buang and his men and await the right moment to take revenge. They swore that they would not come to terms with the Dutch but had to take revenge. When they heard that Van Imhoff had passed away, they immediately embarked on war and Banten was razed to the ground by them. The new king [Mossel] was not a resourceful person. He just let them run amok and stood by looking with folded arms. Not a single plan was put into action. He just sat there awaiting death. At that particular moment not a single Chinese with guts helped the sultan, joining forces to destroy Cao Cao (曹操), in this case, the Dutch to avenge the drowned Chinese. This is very lamentable! And, regarding Captain Huang Chengguan at the time, why did he need to make the effort to propose Huang Shinao for secretary? If we look at it from the present perspective, the Chinese people had had no courage already for a long time!

In the third moon of Qianlong 16, *xinwei* [辛未], April 1751, Boedelmeester Lin Chunshe had served his full term and stepped down. The great king (Mossel) appointed Chen Shuguan (陳疏觀) in his place. In the fourth moon, Boedelmeester Su Junsheng passed away and was buried at the cemetery of the Japanese pavilion. In the tenth moon, Captain Huang Chengguan passed away. Secretary Huang Shinao thereupon submitted a petition to be appointed captain. The king approved of this and appointed him to the captaincy.[216]

---

secretary of the Chinese Council was provided with the special privilege that he would not have to pay the poll tax for five Chinese in his retinue. Oeij Tsilauw was appointed lieutenant on 10 December 1748.

216 After Huang Shinao (黃市鬧, Oeij Tsjilauw) made his oath of purge, Governor General Van Imhoff issued an edict on 12 July 1750 declaring that on 7 July the Governor General and Council had decided to appoint Huang Shinao (Oeij Tsjilauw) as successor to Huang Zhenge (Oeij Tsomko) on the basis of the former's proven ability and integrity. In cooperation with Lieutenants Lin Guoshi (Lin Kocko), Souw Tsoenseeng (蘇俊生), Chen Yuansheng (Tan Wang Seeng), and Lim Tjipko (林缉光), he was to deal with and decide on 'all small occurring cases among the Chinese' in the name of Governor General and Council. But 'all large or otherwise dubious cases should be handed over to the relevant offices'. Captain Huang was the author of the *Compendium of Chinese Laws*, a very useful survey of Chinese customary laws for the benefit of the Batavian administration. See Van der Chijs, *Plakaatboek*, 8.476. Although an eminent scholar, Huang Shinao was a total

The following people were then in office: Captain Huang Zhenge, Lieutenants Lin Jiguang (林緝光) and Chen Yuansheng, Secretary Huang Shinao, Soldaat He Cunguan, [and] Undertakers Huang Lianguan, He Cunguan [also soldaat], and Su Quanguan. Huang Shinao served as secretary only for a short time before he was appointed captain. His star as an official can be said to have been sparkling!

He [Mossel] then proposed to appoint Huang Liangquan (黃良全) to serve as secretary.[217] At the time, Wang Rongshi (王榮使, Ong Eng Saaij) and Lin Jiange (林健哥, Lim Kienko) submitted a petition saying: 'In the past there were positions for six lieutenants but now there are only two. Therefore, we implore [you] to add four lieutenants according to the precedent'. The king immediately appointed the two of them to the lieutenancy.[218]

Let me now continue my story of the pacification of Banten. The story developed as follows: In connection with the report of the Banten uprising, the great king convened the councilors to discuss the situation and decided to send an expeditionary army. He ordered Commissioner Djoesit (Yushi, 宇實), together with the native headman Djitlane (Rilaonian, 日嘮唪), to command a force of Balinese, Bugis, Javanese, and Dutch soldiers and cavalry, several thousand men in all, to advance on Banten to face the enemy. Commissioner Djoesit and the native Malay Captain Djitlane both led their own troops into battle. Ratu Bagus Buan and Kiai Tapa, also commanding their soldiers, faced the enemy. A big battle with countless confrontations occurred. Kiai Tapa was

---

failure as headman of his community. He received financial assistance for the upkeep of his home. At his request, on 23 January 1756 he was granted a monthly allowance of 370 rixdollars, but following complaints by his lieutenants he was dismissed because of 'his *méchante* [appalling] way of life, having lost all credit' on 27 August 1756. He was given some respite in paying off his debts on 11 August 1761. See Hoetink, 'Chineesche officieren' 64–69.

217 Quite suddenly, the secretary became an important member of the Chinese Council. See *Plakaatboek*, 5.469. He was formally appointed for the first time on 26 May 1747 and was allowed to carry a large *payung*.

218 On 29 December 1750, Boedelmeester Wang Rongshi (Ong Eng Saaij) was appointed lieutenant, succeeding Huang Shinao (Oeij Tsilauw), who had been made captain. Lin Jiange (Lim Kienko) was appointed boedelmeester in his place. Huang Liangquan (黃良全) was appointed secretary of the Chinese Council with the same privileges as his predecessor. Lieutenant Ong Eng Saaij rented a plot of land named Pondok Jagon (resolution of 21 November 1755). His widow, Louw Sinnio (劉成娘), is mentioned in the resolution of 30 July 1756. See Hoetink, 'Chineesche officieren', 114–15.

On 15 June 1751, Boedelmeester Lin Jianlao (Lim Kienko) was appointed lieutenant to succeed Su Junsheng (Tsou Tsoen Seeng). The Chinese merchant Guo Heguan was appointed boedelmeester and the Chinese interpreter Huang Ranguang (Oeij Tjamko) was appointed secretary of the Chinese Council to replace Huang Liangquan (黃良全).

too courageous to withstand. The Dutch Commissioner Djoesit and the native headman Djitlane were beaten and killed. Thus the two [Dutch] forces were both exterminated.[219] Kiai Tapa led his victorious soldiers to invade and occupy the border territory and marched on to the Suanganzai Yuan (酸柑仔園, Orange Garden) and set up camp.

Lieutenants Wang Rongshi and Lin Jianlao went to see the king and proposed to him that they would lead the troops and fight the enemy. The king approved and the two each lead several hundred Chinese. Wang Rongshi pitched his camp at Kramat. Lin Jianlao and his followers pitched camp at Tanjung Kait in Banten. They agreed that the two armies should pull together shoulder to shoulder and assist each other.

The story goes as follows: when Kiai Tapa saw that there was nothing stirring around, he continued to encroach and rob everywhere, inordinately proud of his courage. When he arrived at a mountain called Gunung Malam,[220] he pitched his camp halfway up the slope of the mountain. At that moment, the captain of Makassar, Lin Nansheng (林南生), ordered his general, Lieutenant Xie Chenggong (謝成功), together with his vanguard leader, *Encek* Kanari (Anze Ganlanli, 安責干藍里), to lead several hundred Makassarese soldiers to Batavia. They detected that Kiai Tapa's robbers were camping on this hill, and immediately leading their vanguard soldiers via the back of the mountain they climbed to the top. Then, taking advantage of the terrain, they suddenly descended on the enemy.

---

219   In the secret resolution of 13 November 1750 (see De Jonge, *Opkomst*, 10.166) the initial defeats on the battlefield are described as follows: A small company of fifty-one European soldiers commanded by Ensigns Philippe and Liebe had, with eight hundred men provided by Ratu Sharifa, attacked the enemy. After Philippe and the headman of the Balinese soldiers were killed and the soldiers of Ratu Sharifa fled, the remaining Dutch soldiers—some forty in all—also had to withdraw with the loss of their field cannons. In an extensive article about the 'Great Bantam Rebellion', Robidé van der Aa describes how the Dutch troops, which were considerably weakened by the fighting that was going on in Central Java and recurring epidemics, continued to be beaten by Kiai Tapa's troops until they finally carried the day the next year. Curiously, Robidé van der Aa nowhere mentions the contribution by the Chinese lieutenants, who also do not figure in the Dutch documentation concerning the rebellion. See P.J.B.C. Robidé van der Aa, 'De groote Bantamsche opstand in het midden der vorige eeuw, bewerkt naar meerendeels onuitgegeven bescheiden uit het oud-koloniaal archief met drie officiëele documenten als bijlagen', *Bijdragen tot de Taal-, Land- en Volkenkunde van Nederlandsch-Indië* series 4, part 5 (1881): 1–127.

220   Gunung Munara, near Bogor.

> To descend from above already means half the victory!

Kiai Tapa and his men did not know where these soldiers were coming from, panicked, and fled away in disarray. Xie Chenggong chased them and killed many. The beaten Kiai Tapa ran away to Tanjung Kait, but when he looked behind he saw that his pursuers were far away. Just at that instant, Lin Jianlao led his soldiers and blocked the way out.

Kiai Tapa showed his formidable force and broke out fighting with all his might and the Chinese soldiers were unable to withstand him, so they gave way and withdrew.

> Excellent!

The defeat encouraged the two [Chinese forces] to join forces and obtain a victory. Kiai Tapa pursued them, killing them from behind, pushing all the way to a bridge.

> Where this bridge was, cannot be ascertained.

But Lin Jianlao and his troops held the bridge. At this dangerous moment, suddenly somebody harangued his soldiers and from the side of the road burst forward to help. When Jianlao saw this, he turned around and fought back against Kiai Tapa, who was now attacked from front and rear. Fearing there was an ambush, he panicked and ran away immediately, but where he went is unknown. Jianlao's army, together with Wang Rongshi and the captain of Makassar, Lin Nansheng, and his Lieutenant Xie Chenggong gained a complete victory and returned triumphantly. The king rejoiced, acknowledged their service, and gave them presents. He only grieved about the complete annihilation of the army of Commissioner Djoesit and native headman Djitlane. Thereupon Banten was pacified. The uprising of Banten lasted four years.[221]

In the eleventh moon of this year Secretary Huang Liangquan passed away. He had served only two months but I don't know where he was buried. Captain Huang Shinao immediately appointed Huang Ranguang (黃冉光, Oeij Tjamko) in his place.

On the fifteenth day of the second moon of Qianlong 17, *renshen* [壬申], 1752, there was at night a black cloud in the shape of a cross in the middle

---

221 In 1753, the High Government of Batavia recalled the exiled son of Sultan Zainul Arifin from Ceylon and put him on the throne as Sultan Zainal Asyikin. Henceforth Banten was considered a fief of the Batavian government.

of the moon. By the eighteenth day of the third moon, between 7 and 9 o'clock in the morning, heavy rain and hail started to fall from heaven and continued for three days. In the sixth month, the former Captain Huang Zhenguan's coffin was sent back to China to be buried there.

This is rarely seen!

In August of that year, an edict from the sovereign in the mother country arrived in Batavia formally investing Jacob Mossel with the title of great king of Batavia.[222] Lieutenant Lin Jianlao went to see the king to discuss the fact that Banten had recently been pacified and that there were many local affairs that had to be settled. He suggested that a captain be appointed to manage the affairs of the Chinese in Banten. The king immediately appointed Lin Yuguan (林語觀) to the position of captain, and Wang Rongshi sent a petition to appoint a lieutenant to assist him in arranging the affairs in Banten. The king immediately appointed Wang Xiangguan (王祥觀) to act as lieutenant in Banten.

Thereupon Lin Yuguan and Wang Xiangguan both prepared presents to give to the king. Together they went to Banten to assume their offices. Wang Xiangguan originally was a *shahbandar*; later he came to Batavia and Wang Rongshi made him undertaker, and three months later he became lieutenant.

At the time, Wang Rongshi took the initiative to send a petition asking not to auction off the opium tax so that the profits from it could be reserved for all the lieutenants' expenses. In addition, he asked that Chinese junks be permitted to trade with Makassar. The king and the councilors discussed this and very calmly decided to approve this.[223] So, from then on the junks from Xiamen could start trading with Makassar.[224] Because this was done thanks to the petition of Wang Rongshi, his merits were very great!

In the fourth moon of Qianlong 18, *guiyou* [癸酉], in May 1753, there was a man from Kotja (Coromandel) named Abu Bakar who petitioned the king to be given the position of captain of his own community. The king discussed it with the councilors and made a decision, and thereupon appointed Abu Bakar to the captaincy. When Boedelmeester Chen Shuguan had served his full term, he stepped down and stopped working. The great king immediately appointed Guo Heguan (郭賀觀, Que Hoko) in his place.

---

222   24 July 1752, *Plakaatboek*, 4.199.
223   Until then, sailing direct from China to Makassar had been strictly forbidden. See *Plakaatboek*, 5, 325 and 426 (28 January and 25 November 1746, respectively).
224   See *Plakaatboek*, 6.350–55, 8/15 May 1753.

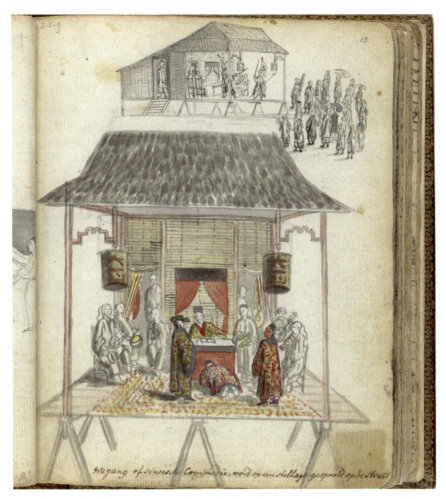

FIGURE 15   *Chinese* wayang *or street theater. Jan Brandes (Lutheran Minister, 1779–1785 in Batavia)*
RIJKSMUSEUM AMSTERDAM

Compared to all other officers then, Lin Jianlao rejoiced in special favours from the great king, but in addition to that he possessed a very steadfast and upright character. When the people did not listen to him, he would give them a tongue-lashing. The only person whom he did not dare to scold was the great king himself. One day he suddenly sent for somebody and asked him to perform a *wayang* (Chinese opera). But the head of the theatre troop had already agreed to play for other people, so he did not dare to agree. Thereupon, Lin Jianlao exploded in fury and asked the king to stop the play. The king and the councilors met and discussed and decided to add two tax farms, one on the Chinese theatre and the other one on *ronggeng*.[225]

In the third moon of Qianlong 19, *jiaxu* [甲戌], May 1754, an edict from the sovereign of the mother country arrived at Batavia elevating Jacob Mossel to the position of great king of Batavia and captain general.[226] The king thereupon issued a proclamation inside and outside the city to people of every kind to hang lanterns with decorations in front of the gates. That night it was feast everywhere. At Jakatra he gave a banquet and enjoyed food and drinks together with the councilors.

In the fifth moon, Boedelmeester Chen Shuguan died. In the ninth moon, Lieutenant Wang Rongshi died and was buried at the cemetery of the Japanese pavilion across the bridge on the left-hand side. The king immediately appointed Lin Chaiguan (林釵觀, Lim Theeko) lieutenant.[227] He also ordered Lieutenant Chen Yuansheng to go to Pasisir[228] to establish a shipyard with the name of Shunli Wu (順利塢, Prosperous Dock).

That year, Lin Chaiguan initiated the collection of funds for the construction of a temple at Ancol. This was an illustrious and spiritual place for prayers to ward off disaster; whatever is prayed for will be heard [by the deity]!

All merchants who came to Batavia, all went there with a sincere heart, to donate and worship.[229] Behind the temple there is a native holy grave, with a pagoda built by the Chinese. One is not allowed to use pork meat for sacrifices. Inside the temple on the left there is an effigy of Lin Chaiguan.[230] Up to the

---

225   See 6 December 1751, 'Regulations on Wayang plays and *tandak* (dancing)'; *Plakaatboek* 6.110. *Ronggeng* are Javanese dancing girls of pleasure.

226   This is incorrect. By resolution of 25 April 1754 the States General of the Netherlands bestowed on Jacob Mossel the rank and title of lieutenant general of the Dutch army. The appointment was made public on January 10 1755. *Plakaatboek*, 7.1.

227   Lin Chaiguan (Lim Theeko) was appointed on 8 November 1754 to succeed Ong Engsaij who had passed away. On 3 December 1754, his rent of the land Pondok Jagon was continued for six years at fifty rixdollars a year. Upon his death in 1764, it was concluded that he still owed 5,700 rixdollars to the company for the property. On 6 December 1764, Lim Djoenko and Lin Guoshi (Lim Kocko) were appointed executors of his 'dubious' if not insolvent inheritance.

228   North coast of Java.

229   The last two paragraphs under 1754 are taken from the Leiden manuscript.

230   Salmon and Lombard give an extensive description of the Dabogong Anxu Miao (大伯公安恤庙, Dabogong temple, Ancol) and also quote from various eyewitness reports by contemporary visitors. See *Les Chinois de Jakarta*, 87.

present day, clouds of incense billow forth. The native people also do not dare to slight this temple, because it has proved to be effective.

In the second moon of Qianlong 20, *yihai* **[乙亥], March 1755,** The king started repairing the city walls all around the city. He also built watergates and sluices at Zainiu Gangkou (宰牛港口, Cow-slaughter Port) and at the place where bamboo is sold (Maizhuzhichu, 賣竹之处). And at Maowuxu (茂物墟, Buitenzorg), he dug a canal all the way to Jishizhen (結石珍, Pasar Senen) to divert the water toward the Sunda Sea (順達洋). In this way, the paddy fields were irrigated and boats could also pass, to the benefit of all.

In the fourth moon, Boedelmeester Guo Heguan had served his full term and stepped down, and the king appointed Lin Chuguang (林初觀) in his place.

Captain Huang Shinao was then drunk day and night. From time to time he visited houses of pleasure and visited monks to banter and discuss Buddhist doctrine, or he went see friends to raise wine cups and chat. When in high spirits, he wrote poems singing of the wind and the moon. Full of wit he set out to write essays. He was courteous to the wise, and he loved scholars. Because he was carefree and relaxed everyday, he gave the Guanyinting temple the name Jinde Yuan (金德院, Temple of Golden Virtue) and hung these three characters on a placard above the entrance of the Guanyinting.[231]

> How joyful! To be happy without having any anxieties. One might call him a celestial on earth!

He truly had the style of a poet and a scholar, but he did not know how to manage the Company's affairs, and moreover he was in debt to the *weeskamer*. He had not met the time limit for paying back his debts. The secretary of the *weeskamer* had a bad character, and he therefore went to see king and asked him to arrest the captain and throw him into prison. The king approved and sent Captain Huang Shinao to jail.

> Huang Shinao served as captain five years and three months. When fortune comes to an end, sadness arrives.

The following officers were serving then: Captain Huang Shinao; Lieutenants Lin Jiguang (林緝光), Chen Yuansheng, Wang Rongshi, and Lin Jianlao— but Wang Rongshi had already died and Lin Chaiguan (林釵觀) replaced

---

231 For a description of the Jinde Yuan, see Salmon and Lombard, *Les Chinois de Jakarta*, 72–86.

him; Secretary Huang Ranguang; Soldaat He Cunguan; also Undertakers He Cunguan [he was soldaat as well], Su Quanguan, and Huang Lianguan.[232]

Lieutenant Lin Jiguang (Lim Tjipko) went to see the great king, and applied for the position of captain. The king approved, and thereupon appointed him, and sent a memorial to the sovereign in the mother country.[233] There was a man called Xu Fangliang (許芳良, Khouw Hong Liang) with a generous, gentle, and placid temper who applied for the position of lieutenant.[234] The king approved and appointed him. In the fifth moon, Lieutenant Chen Yuansheng returned to Batavia from Java's north coast.

---

232   He Cunguan seems to have had two functions.
233   Lin Jiguang (林緝光, Lim Tjipko) was appointed lieutenant on 3 June 1749. On 9 April 1754, he was given postponement of payment on a huge advance payment of 10,000 rixdollars given to him on 26 October 1751. (See on this issue also the resolution of 26 October 1753. In the resolution of 15 March 1763, he is said to be renting two sugar mills on the Concordia estate. The *water-fiscaal*—public prosecutor for affairs outside Batavia proper—was ordered to reclaim the money with force, if necessary.

Lin Jiguang's rise to captain was the result of nothing less than a palace revolution. On 21 August 1756, the lieutenants of the Chinese Council reported that many Chinese were staying in Batavia illegally, without paying their dues. Their efforts to combat these abuses were failing 'because the present Chinese Captain Huang Shinao (Oeij Tjilauw) undoubtedly is the root of this illicit and disobedient behaviour.... [He] is despised and has lost all credit because of his *méchant* (abominable) behaviour', which had led to irreparable subordination. Consequently, they asked for his immediate demotion and dismissal and for the appointment of Lin Jiguang is his place. The lieutenants also proposed that Xu Fangliang (Khouw Hong Liang) serve as lieutenant in Lin Jiguang's place.

The Batavian Diary of 19 February 1757 mentions in detail how this new Chinese captain was publicly introduced with much pomp and circumstance after the Governor General and Council had confirmed his nomination on 11 February. On 20 December 1757, it was decided to bestow on Captain Lin Jiguang (Lim Tjipko) and his successors the tax farm of the *du* (賭) and *dubo* (賭博), that is, gambling, at a fixed monthly payment of 300 rixdollars. See *Plakaatboek*, 7.244. This was to provide him with an extra source of income 'because it is well-known that the Chinese officers, by virtue of their office, have to incur considerable expenses'.

The resolution of 19 May 1769 expresses the government's great pleasure with this captain's administrative talents. He passed away on 23 January 1775. See Hoetink, 'Chineesche officieren', 67–71.
234   Xu Fangliang (Khouw Hong Liang), was a native of Zhangzhou (漳州). 'He was also of a liberal disposition and truly generous'. See Ong-Tae-Hae, *The Chinaman Abroad: or A Desultory Account of the Malayan Archipelago, Particularly of Java*, translated by W.H. Medhurst (Shanghai, 1849). He was given a two-year extension to collect the gambling hall tax. He owned two sugar mills at Karang Conggok (see resolution of 6 April 1753).

On the first moon of Qianlong 21, *bingzi* [丙子], **March 1756,** an edict from the sovereign of the mother country arrived formally appointing Lin Jiguang to the position of captain.

In the fourth moon of Qianlong 22, *dingchou* [丁丑], **June 1757,** Boedelmeester Lin Chuguang had served his full term and stepped down. The king appointed Shi Huaguan (施華觀, Sie Huako) in his place.

In the tenth moon of Qianlong 23, *wuyin* [戊寅], **December 1758,** the secretary Huang Ranguang, died and was buried at the Japanese pavilion cemetery. He served seven years, one month, and twelve days. Lin Jiguang recommended Hu Baoyao (胡保耀) for the position of secretary. The king approved and thereupon Hu Baoyao served in that function.

> Hu Baoyao was originally a monk and later became secretary. This is what is called escaping from Mohism and turning into a Confucian. Why did he do so?[235]

In the eleventh moon of the same year, Undertaker Huang Lianguan died and was buried at the western cemetery. He served fourteen years as undertaker.

At the time, the daughter of the great king married the *water-fiscaal*, (美色葛, meisege).[236] Two theatre pieces were performed in the warehouse. Within and outside the city, all households put lanterns and streamers in front of their doors to congratulate the *fiscaal* on the new marriage.

Together with eleven other men he was appointed *wijkmeester* (quartermaster) in the *Chinesche Kamp*, on 16 August 1754. He was (co)executor of the inheritance of Lieutenant So Tsoenseeng (resolution of 21 November 1755). His will was drawn up by Notaris Pieters Lammers on 18 September 1772, and according to the resolution of 2 October 1772, he had recently passed away. Bok Kinhi and Hiapko were the executors of his 'heavily indebted inheritance' (resolution of 10 December 1772). See Hoetink, 'Chineesche officieren', 116.

235   Mo Di was one of the earliest rivals of Confucius. This original utilitarian thinker proposed *jian ai* (love for everyone), an offensive idea to the Confucians who placed family loyalties first. On account of their commitment to rationality the Mohists were in many respects comparable with the early Greek philosophers.

236   On 24 April 1754, Geertruida Mossel married Mr. P.C. Hasselaar. It was an incredibly opulent affair, with 'two fountains that poured wine, to the joy of the people. In short, all that opulence, wealth, and happiness can show, could be witnessed here in its extremes'. Mossel, who on 30 December 1754 promulgated the strict 'Measures to rein in pomp and circumstance', should have looked back on his own family's conspicuous consumption with profound shame. See F.J.G. van Emden and Willem Brand, *Kleurig memoriaal van de Hollanders op Oud-Java* (Amsterdam: Strengholt, 1964), 58.

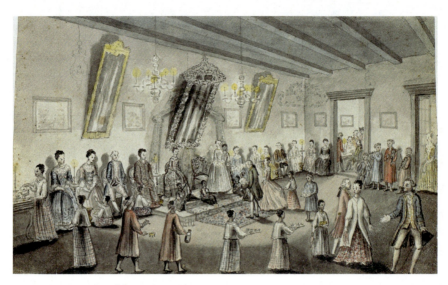

FIGURE 16   *Dutch wedding. Jan Brandes*
RIJKSMUSEUM AMSTERDAM

In the ninth moon of Qianlong 24, *jimao* [己卯], November 1759, Lieutenant Chen Yuansheng died and was buried at the Japanese pavilion cemetery. When Dai Biange (戴弁哥, Thee Poanko) of Buitenzorg heard about this, he descended to the city that very night and went to see the king to ask him for the position of lieutenant.[237] The king approved of this and installed him. At the time, the king and councilors met and discussed and decided to free Huang Shinao from prison and let him reside in his big house at Xinchi. Shinao's wife had engaged in lewd behaviour, and in the meantime had given birth to three children. ~ *How scandalous!* ~ When Huang Shinao checked his belongings, more than ten golden and silver objects were missing. He then discovered the hows and whys. He went to see the king and reported on his situation. The king thereupon ordered his wife locked up in jail on top of the castle wall, and then banished her to an island in perpetuity.[238]

---

237   Dai Biange (Thee Poanko) ran away when he could not repay his debts but was caught and died in jail. See resolution of 5 February 1768. CO 116–17. Regarding his flight, see below, Qianlong 31, sixth moon.

238   The unfaithful wife, Li Guanniang (李觀娘, Lie Quanio), was banished for five years to the isle of Edam in the Bay of Batavia, a sentence that was changed into banishment to Ceylon on account of her bad health. See resolution of the Governor General and Council, 16 October 1761; and Hoetink, 'Chineesche officieren', 67.

In Qianlong 25, *gengchen* [庚辰], 1760, Captain Lin Jiguang and the lieutenants met and decided to build one more Chinese cemetery. He asked the *nakhodas* of the junks, and the (Chinese) great merchants to subscribe according to their wealth and to buy the Gunung Sari garden from the king with the money collected.[239] In the garden there was a temple and a pavilion, and in the temple there were several stone statues that Chinese had put there in the past. Gunung Sari and the Longyan garden of Bazhilan were joined together.[240]

In the fourth moon of this year, Boedelmeester Shi Huaguan had served his full term and stepped down. The great king immediately appointed Chen Qiaolang (陳巧郎, Tankalong) in his place. Thereupon Qiaolang petitioned the king to forbid the Chinese to ride sedan chairs at their weddings. They would be fined 500 *wen* (文, rixdollars) for violating this,[241] and the money would be put into the *weeskamer* treasury. Qiaolang liked to line his own pocket, and with the public money he falsely helped the Dutch but harmed the Chinese. What was the point of that?

> *John Chinaman comments*: You showed no benevolence, you, Chen Qiaolang! You were not forthright and doing good, but you were good at robbing people's money! Riding a sedan chair at a wedding is the high point of the ceremony. To forbid sedan chairs means the beginning of the Chinese turning into barbarians. To fine 500 *wen* and pour the money into the *weeskamer*'s treasury will only urge the great king to mete out punishments and bring harm to our countrymen! This is spreading harm

---

239 The stele commemorating the foundation of the Gunung Sari cemetery has been saved. For a full translation of the text of this *beiwen*, see Claudine Salmon, 'Ancient Chinese Cemeteries of Indonesia as Vanishing Landmarks of the Past (17th–20th c.)', in Claudine Salmon, ed., 'Chinese Deathscapes in Insulindia' (Paris: Association Archipel, 2016), 31, 58–61.

240 'The Chinese captain was allowed to use the aftermost part of the land of Gunung Sari for tombs on the condition that two boundary pillars were erected next to the former course of the Great River. See resolution of 6 October 1761, *Realia* 1.122. This is the Sentiong temple, the former residence of Frederik Julius Coyett. See V.L. von de Wall, *Oude Hollandsche buitenplaatsen van Batavia* (Deventer: Van Hoeve, 1943), 29–48.

241 This is pure fantasy. Sedan chairs had already been forbidden on 30 December 1754, within the framework of the so-called 'measures to rein in pomp and circumstance' promulgated by Governor General Mossel. See *Plakaatboek*, 6.778. Trespassers were fined 300 *rixdollars*. At the request of Captain Lim Tsipko (20 November 1767) the fine was lowered to 50 *rixdollars*, and family members of the captain and lieutenants were allowed to use sedan chairs. See *Plakaatboek*, 8.318–19.

among our people. Ayah! The ways of our ancestors are gone! I cannot help making this point!²⁴²

In the third moon of Qianlong 26, *xinsi* [辛巳]**, May 1761,** the great king fell critically ill and on the fifteenth [day] he met with the councilors and ordered Petrus Albertus van der Parra to act as king and assume the throne.²⁴³ He passed away on the nineteenth and was buried in the great church. He had occupied the throne for eleven years and seven months. Van der Parra sent a memorial to the sovereign in the mother country. In the sixth moon, the former Captain Huang Shinao and his son boarded a junk and returned to China.

A sailing ship of the company brought the son of the king of Ceylon and his wife to Batavia. The great king and the councilors came out to receive him, and after meeting them with ceremonies in Batavia castle, he ordered that a residence be arranged [for them] in the garden of Damujiao (the Great Mauk) where the guests could stay, and he had a platoon of Dutch soldiers lined up as guards at the gate.²⁴⁴

Twelve men make a platoon.

In Qianlong 27, *renwu* [壬午]**, 1762,** Lu Langge (盧郎哥, Louw Nungko) petitioned the king asking him to follow the old rules, which provided for six lieutenants. The king approved of this and allowed Xu Cange (許燦哥, Khouw Tjiangko) and Lu Langge to be installed as lieutenants.²⁴⁵ Because Soldaat He Cunguan was in debt to the Dutch, they put him behind bars. Captain Lin

---

242 Commentary from the Leiden manuscript.
243 Petrus Albertus van der Parra was born in Colombo (Ceylon) on 29 September 1714. His family had already been living there for two generations. From the humble position of soldier (at the age of fourteen) he rose to the rank of junior merchant and then was sent to Batavia where he remained the rest of his life, continuing his career as merchant (1739), second secretary of the Council of the Indies (1741), first secretary (1747), extraordinary councilor (same year), ordinary councilor (1751), and various other honorary functions. He was appointed director general in 1755 and succeeded Governor General Mossel on 15 May 1761. He passed away on 28 December 1775 after fourteen years in office.
244 This was most likely Kroempty Pippit, or Krom Muen Tep Pippit (Thepphiphit), son of the second wife of King Boromakot of Siam (r. 1733–58). This son was exiled to Ceylon after he conspired against his brother, Ekathat, who succeeded to the throne. More or less involved in a failed attempt on the life of King Kirti Sri Rajasinha of Kandy in Ceylon, he was shipped to Batavia by the VOC. See L.S. Dewaraja, *The Kandyan Kingdom of Sri Lanka, 1707–1782* (Colombo: Lake House Investments, 1988), 119–28; and Lodewijk Wagenaar, *Galle, VOC-vestiging in Ceylon. Beschrijving van een koloniale samenleving aan*

Jiguang proposed that the king install another soldaat. The king approved and appointed Ye Jianguan (葉健觀). At the time, the king summoned all the lieutenants to make a proclamation to the Chinese, that if they did not have a residence permit, they should get the money and purchase it. If anybody was caught without a permit, then he would surely run into trouble.

On the thirtieth (day) of the eighth moon of Qianlong 28, *guiwei* [癸未], October 1763, an edict from the sovereign of the mother country officially arrived investing Petrus Albertus van der Parra with the title of king of Batavia. Thereupon the king issued a proclamation to people of all kinds (各色人等) within and outside the city that they should place lanterns and streamers in front of their doors. At Rejidou [Jakatra], he held a banquet with drinks in his garden to celebrate his glorious appointment.[246]

In the ninth moon of that year, Boedelmeester Chen Qiaolang broke the law and committed a crime. The authorities arrested him and threw him into jail.

> At the time the people felt miserable about him; the laws of the country could not tolerate him. The Heavenly principles are clear and transparent. They are perfectly matching!

Originally Chen Qiaolang and Chen Jingguan (陳景觀) had together contracted [to collect] the poll tax, yet they did not buy the company's residence permits but fabricated them themselves and falsely turned them into Company

---

de vooravond van de Singalese opstand tegen het Nederlandse gezag, 1760 (Amsterdam: De Bataafsche Leeuw, 1994), 22 and footnote 26.

245   During a meeting of the council of the Indies on 10 June 1762, Governor General Van der Parra mentioned that in recent years the number of Chinese had increased to an even greater number than in 1740, when a Chinese captain and six lieutenants were involved in the administration: Captain Lian Fuguang (Nihoekong), and Lieutenants Chen Zhongguan (Tan Tionko), Guo Weige (Que Oeijko), Huang Zhenge (Oeij Tsomko), Xu Jinguan (Khouw Tsinko), Lian Zhongguan (Niey Tjonko), and Huang Tige (Oeij Theeko).

Given that there were now only four lieutenants in service, he proposed appointing two more: Xu Cange (Khouw Tjiangko) and Lu Langge (Louw Nungko). Xu Cange owned two plots of land and possessed seven sugar mills about a seven—or eight—hour walk east of Batavia in the so-called Oosterveld. He passed away on 22 June 1770. His testament of 12 June 1770 mentions two sons, Kouw Hoe-tieeuw and Khouw Goan Kong.

In a resolution of 11 January 1743, Lu Langge had already been mentioned as a purveyor of knee timbers for ships before the 1740 uprising. See Hoetink, 'Chineesche officieren', 117–18.

246   According to the Batavia Diary, the official notice arrived on 1 June 1763. The great festivities around Van der Parra's official induction ceremony occurred on 29 September. For a detailed description, see Van Emden, *Kleurig memoriaal*, 60–64.

permits. This amounted to breaking the law. When the authorities found out, it was considered a serious matter. But Qiaolang had people of influence on whom he could rely. He was protected from within and the affairs were temporarily hushed up. Later on, because Zheng Xuanguan (鄭軒觀) from Cirebon accused the captain of Cirebon, Huang Wenlao (黃文老), Wenlao came to Batavia to draw up a document allowing Qiaolang to represent him. He gave money to Qiaolang to use. When the case had already been closed, Qiaolang still had [some of] Wenlao's money left over but did not return it to him. Wenlao then mounted another lawsuit and asked a Dutchman named Rousong[247] (柔悚) to represent him. To settle accounts with Wenlao, Qiaolang started to launder the money saying, 'After a certain councilor bribed me with a considerable amount of money, now yet another councilor swindled me'. The Dutchman Rousong became very angry and said, 'You have yourself swindled other peoples' money. How do you dare use the name of the councilors saying that they cheated you out of the money?' But because Qiaolang's case had already been closed, he could not use it to incriminate him. For this reason, he sought out the falsification of the permits and reported Qiaolang to the authorities; so the authorities arrested him and put him into jail.

> *John Chinaman comments*: 'Evil will be rewarded with evil! Heaven gives warnings—that is for certain! This evil creates people who live temporarily on earth, but there is still the inferno for bad people over there. Qiaolang, that beast, should be sitting there after his death'.

At the time, Wu Wenge (吳文哥, Gouw Boenko) sent a petition to the king for Chen Qiaolang's position. The king approved and made him boedelmeester. In the tenth moon, Lieutenant Lin Chaiguan died and was buried at the Japanese pavilion cemetery. He served nine years and eleven months.

Wu Wenge sent in a petition and asked for Lin Chaiguan's position.[248] The king approved and immediately promoted him to the position of lieutenant, and also appointed Wang Yiguang (王懿光, Ong Ingkong) boedelmeester.

The great king ordered Lieutenant Dai Bianguan to issue a proclamation to the Chinese living between Petuakan, the Angke River, and the garden of the king [Buitenzorg] saying that anyone wishing to purchase a residence permit must go to the residence of Dai Bianguan to report his name and surname. Those who had not yet paid the poll tax also had to register their age

---

247 Unidentified person. Perhaps his name was Joosten.
248 Boedelmeester Wu Wenge (Gouw Boenko) was appointed lieutenant to succeed Lin Chaiguan by a resolution of 30 December 1763. Liu Chengguang (Louw Sinkong) was appointed to fill the vacancy of boedelmeester. See Hoetink, 'Chineesche officieren', 118.

FIGURE 17 *The burning of the image of 'Twabakong' (Dabogong) and Chinese officers paying their respects during the Qingming festival. Jan Brandes*
RIJKSMUSEUM AMSTERDAM

and occupation in the population register, as evidence for their permits. When registering, every person had to pay one *ba*.[249] There were some Chinese who did not want to buy the permits. They stealthily put up small slips of paper saying, 'the captain falsely wants to cheat money out of us Chinese!' Therefore

---

249   A *ba* (友) is a *fanam*, equal to a *dubbeltje*, i.e. two *stuivers*.

Dai Bianguan felt embarrassed in his heart and did not dare to pocket even one *fanam*.[250]

When around that time Soldaat He Cunguan was released from prison, he went to see the captain. The latter immediately ordered him to serve as undertaker at the Chinese cemetery. The guarantor of Boedelmeester Chen Qiaolang, Chen Jingguan (陳景觀), and his accountant Wang Liguang (王利光) were both exiled to Ambon.

> If you have wicked intentions, the Heavenly principles are clear and transparent. One should receive the punishment of Heaven in revenge to warn later generations!

In Qianlong 29, *jiashen* [甲申], 1764, Lieutenant Lin Jianlao died and was buried at the Japanese pavilion cemetery, in front to the right of the gate. He served fourteen years. The great king immediately appointed Tang Enge (唐恩哥, Tung Ingko) lieutenant.[251] Captain Lin Jiguang went to see the king and asked to add a soldaat. The king approved and thereupon appointed He Cunguan to that position.

> Earlier, He Cunguan had already been a soldaat, but because he had embezzled a Dutchman's money, he had been arrested by this Dutch person. Now he wanted to be reinstated in his position. Having served as undertaker for three months, he became a soldaat again. From then on there were two soldaten.

In the eleventh moon of Qianlong 30, *yiyou* [乙酉], January 1765, Lieutenant Wu Wenguan died and was buried at Gunung Sari. He served one year and seven months plus nine days.

The king immediately appointed Huang Hengge (黃珩觀, Oeij Hingko) lieutenant.[252] In the tenth month, Soldaat He Cunguan died and was buried in the western graveyard.

---

250 On 30 March 1764, measures were taken against Chinese loitering in the Ommelanden of Batavia. See *Plakaatboek*, 7.753.

251 On 6 April 1764, Tang Enge was appointed lieutenant as a replacement for Lin Jiange, who had passed away. On 27 December 1768 he was granted the tax farm on Chinese theatre in combination with the tax farm on gambling houses.

252 Huang Hengge was appointed on 10 February 1765 to replace Wu Wenge (Gouw Boenko). The resolution of 20 March 1772 refers to him as one of the better-off Chinese in town.

In Qianlong 31, *bingxu* [丙戌], 1766, the lieutenants sent a petition to the king and asked him to allow them to contract alternately for the tax farms for gambling and theatre and use the revenues for their expenses.[253] The great king approved and then ordered that the first turn would be given to Lieutenant Xu Fangliang.

[This is how it works:] The one whose turn it is to run the tax farm must give every lieutenant 400 *wen* per person every year.[254] He should also pay the Company 2,800 *wen* every month from the gambling taxes collected. And from the theatre tax farm he should pay 600 *wen*. As regards the tax farm on opium, this will be contracted by two lieutenants for one year, and they have to pay 300 *wen* a year to the other four lieutenants. This is a regulation for eternity, and will go around over and over.

Boedelmeester Wang Yiguang had served his full term and stepped down. The great king immediately appointed Liu Chengguang (劉成光, Louw Sinkong) in his place. In the third moon, Soldaat Ye Jianguang passed away and was buried at Gunung Sari.

The captain asked the king to appoint another soldaat. The king approved and appointed Ye Huaguan (葉華觀). (He was Ye Jianguan's eldest son.) The captain also asked [the king] to appoint a secretary. The king assented and appointed Xu Zhongqi (徐仲奇).

The great king's character was charitable, but he also harmed people stealthily. The houses at Pasar Senen burned down, and there were also fires outside the West Gate. These were warnings from Heaven. This was a sign for the great king.

In the sixth moon, because Lieutenant Dai Bianguan had borrowed money from a Dutchman and on top of that from the former King Jacob Mossel, his creditors time and again urged him to repay his debts; but as he was unable to do so, he saw no alternative but to run away together with his accountant, I don't know where to. He served as lieutenant eight years.

Boedelmeester Liu Chengguang petitioned the king asking him for the open position of lieutenant.[255] The king asked for Captain Lin Jiguang's opinion. He answered, 'Liu Chengguang was born and raised in Batavia. He has never been

---

253 The placard of 7 December 1775 refers to this arrangement but does not note when it came into being. See *Plakaatboek*, 8.966.
254 One *wen* is equal to one rixdollar, i.e. 2½ guilders.
255 On 5 July 1764, Boedelmeester Liu Chengguang (Louw Sinkong) was appointed lieutenant to replace the fugitive Dai Biange (Thee Poanko). Wu Shuguan (Gouw Sieuko/Sienko) was appointed boedelmeester in his stead. See Hoetink, 'Chineesche officieren', 119.

back to China. So he does not understand Chinese norms and customs. I am afraid he is not able to fulfil that office'. Thus this case was laid to rest.

But when Chengguang heard about it, he immediately asked for an audience with the king and reported to him, 'Although I am not a son of China born and raised, still I am not in debt and I have not run away. Why can't I handle this position?' Because of this the king sympathised with him, and he immediately appointed him lieutenant and also appointed Wu Shuguan (吳樹觀) boedelmeester.[256]

Liu Chengguang could only become lieutenant because Dai Biangguan had dodged his creditors. Because he had been made into a laughing stock by the Dutch, the later generations should learn a lesson from this.

In the fifth moon of Qianlong 32, *dinghai* [丁亥], July 1767, Wainanwang (外南望, Banyuwangi)[257] east of Semarang was attacked by the British (Hongmao, 紅毛, Red Hairs) and occupied. The governor of Semarang sent a report to Batavia. The Great King summoned the councilors for a discussion and all said: The British are greedy people, we should lure them by promises of gain instead of fighting them. Thereupon he ordered the commanders to recruit Dutch soldiers and sent them with ships to Banyuwangi and handed them a secret plan. When the governor of Semarang heard that the Company's soldiers had already arrived, he also led soldiers there to combine forces. The Dutch chief first ordered people to go to the British to fob them off with sweet words and also to lure them with financial profit. The British indeed accepted the money, hoisted the sails, and departed. Thus this place returned under the governance of the Company, and, moreover, the troubles of war had been avoided.

To pick up my story again: Dai Bianguan and Dai Maoshi (戴毛獅, Thee Mosai) were originally relatives from the same stock. To begin with, Dai Maoshi was in charge of the poll tax, but because he ran debts on this tax farm, he was unable to clear his debts and had run away to Banyuwangi. But Dai Bianguan had originally run to Sillebar (West Sumatra), and afterwards he sailed on a British ship to this place [Banyuwangi] to live together with Dai Maoshi. At the

---

256 This is an interesting case, because it is a breakthrough in the outdated procedure that Chinese officers, and specifically the captains, would be chosen by the local elite together with the visiting *nakhodas* (supercargos) of the visiting junks from Amoy.

257 There was no such attack, but the English East India Company became increasingly interested in selling opium in Bali and to Chinese merchants residing at Balambangan on Java's Oosthoek (Eastern Salient), which was traditionally under Balinese influence. Menaced by British interference, the VOC decided to send an army of occupation in February 1767. The area was not pacified until 1772, after the Balinese were driven out of Java. See Van Deventer, *Geschiedenis*, 216–27.

time, the Company had issued an order to arrest these two people, but now they were discovered by the Dutch at this place. Therefore, native people were sent to capture them and take them home on a Company ship. Maoshi jumped into the sea and drowned.

How brave!

Dai Bianguan was brought to Batavia and thrown into jail, where he wasted away with a heavy heart. Afterwards his corpse was taken out to be buried.

Soldaat He Cunguan died and was buried at Gunung Sari. He served twenty-five years and seven months. The captain reported this to the Great King and asked him to fill the opening. The King approved and thereupon he appointed the nephew of He Cunguan, He Juge (何局觀), in his place. In the eleventh moon, Boedelmeester Wu Shuguan died and was buried at Gunung Sari. He served one year and seven months. The Great King thereupon appointed Wu Xiguan (吳喜觀) in his place.

In the fourth moon of Qianlong 33, *wuzi* [戊子], May 1768, Boedelmeester Shi Huaguan died and was buried in the western cemetery. The King immediately appointed Chen Caiguan (陳彩觀, Tan Tjaijko) in his place. In the sixth moon, Secretary Xu Zhongqi died and was buried at Gunung Sari. He served three years. The captain went to see the Great King to report, and at the same time he recommended Lin Kuazu (林跨祖). The King approved and appointed him.

On the ninth day of the eighth month of this year, at midnight, a light rain had started falling when suddenly there was a deafening thunderclap that made the peak of the roof of a house at the wall of the South Gate collapse.

Qianlong 34, *jichou* [己丑], 1769, On the western side of Batavia there is a market at Tangerang called Benteng. There is a Dutch fort garrisoned under a Dutch commander. Not far from this fort there was a bridge for the use of the Chinese and natives visiting the market. Because it was in disrepair due to its old age, and had been replaced by one of bamboo construction, the Company planned to build a new bridge instead. Stones were placed in the water to form the foundations of the bridge, whereupon workers were recruited to operate a watermill to remove the water, but that did not work. Thereupon ox-power was used to replace the manpower. Six hundred to seven hundred oxen died! The expenses for the Company in terms of money and provisions were incalculable.

When the bridge was ready, the toll at Xinwuli was auctioned off once every three years. The toll farmer was permitted to charge every passer-by on the bridge two *duiten* and those returning one *duit*.[258] This was fixed forever, without any change.

It took six years—from 1769 to 1774—to build this bridge until it was completed.[259]

In the tenth moon, Secretary Hu Baoyao died and was buried at Gunung Sari. The captain reported this to the King and asked him to appoint another person to replace him; the King approved and appointed Lin Chunguang (林春光).

In the eleventh moon, the captain again went to see the king and told him that the Chinese community wished to host a *Qi'anjiao* (祈安醮, pray for peace) festival, to set decorated paper vessels adrift, and to place at everybody's gate a lantern to bring good luck. He asked permission. The king approved and thereupon the captain together with all the lieutenants led the festival for three days and three nights, sent off decorated boats, and lit the lanterns, seeking peace for the whole territory.[260]

In the fourth moon of Qianlong 35, *gengyin* [庚寅], May 1770, Boedelmeester Wu Xiguan (吳喜觀) had served his full term and stepped down.[261] The King immediately appointed Gao Genguan (高根觀, Ko Kimko)[262] in his place. In the sixth moon Lieutenant Lu Langge died and was buried at Gunung Sari. He served nine years and three months. The Great King immediately appointed Zheng Longge (鄭隆, The Liongko) in his place.[263]

A big fire again occurred at Pasar Senen;[264] the houses of the Chinese were reduced to ashes. A gunpowder magazine near Xinwuli exploded toppling all the houses and killing people.

In the fifth moon, Lieutenant Xu Youzhang (許有章) died and was buried at Gunung Sari. Xu Youzhang also had another name, Canlao (燦老). He served altogether ten years and three months. The King immediately appointed Lin Delang (林德郎, Lim Teko) in his place.[265]

---

258 A *duit* is a copper coin.
259 See *Plakaatboek*, 8.569, 28 February 1769; and *Plakaatboek*, 8.817, 19 November 1773.
260 A *jiao* (醮) is a traditional Taoist purification ceremony.
261 According to VOC archives, this should be Wu Shuguan (吳樹觀, Gouw Sieuko).
262 Gao Genguan (Ko Kimko), a native of Xiamen, was appointed Chinese boedelmeester of Batavia in the fourth moon of Qianlong 35, May 1770. Gao Genguan served two consecutive terms until 1775. See Hoetink, 'Chineesche officieren', 121.
263 Appointed 26 May 1769. Ibid., 119.
264 Pasar Senen was situated about twelve kilometers south of VOC-Batavia. This area became the new centre of Batavia, called Weltevreden. Since 1930 its name changed into Batavia-Centrum, nowadays it is Jakarta Pusat. It is the area around Merdeka Square.
265 On 22 June 1770. Hoetink, 'Chineesche officieren', 119–120.

In the twelfth moon of Qianlong 36, *xinmao* [辛卯], February 1771, a big flood suddenly struck, immersing the feet of the city walls. The water receded after three days and three nights. In the tenth moon, Lieutenant Liu Chengguang died and was buried in Gunung Sari. He served six years. The king immediately promoted Chen Caiguan to lieutenant and also promoted Huang Junguan (黃郡觀, Oey Kinkong) to boedelmeester.[266]

In Qianlong 37, *renchen* [壬辰], 1772, because of famine, the price of rice was as expensive as pearls and there was a great drought. The surface temperature was high, like fire; many people died. In the second moon, Boedelmeester Huang Junguan died and was buried at Gunung Sari. He served one year minus three days.

The King appointed Hu Tanguan (胡探觀, Khouw/Ouw Tanko) boedelmeester but in the fourth moon he died and was buried at Gunung Sari. Hu Tanguan served only 40 days. The King appointed Tang Pianshe (唐偏舍) Boedelmeester. Tang Pianshe was the third son of Tang Enguan. On the fifteenth of the sixth moon the coffin of the former Lieutenant Xu Canlao was shipped back to China on the junk *Jinshun Wu* (金順䲹).

On the 15th of the ninth moon there was a lunar eclipse. After it was over it was clear again. 25 days later Lieutenant Xu Fangliang died and was buried at Gunung Sari. He had served 17 years, nine months and five days. The King immediately appointed Wu Panshui (吳泮水, Gouw Poan Soeij) lieutenant.[267] In the tenth moon Lieutenant Chen Caiguan died and was buried at Gunung Sari. He served one year and two months. The King immediately appointed Wang Jiguan (王藉觀, Ong Tjako) Lieutenant.[268] At the time Wang Jiguan had just married three days before he was appointed Lieutenant. This can be said to be double happiness. After 28 days he suddenly fell ill, died and was buried at Gunung Sari. Feelings of sadness follow a bout of pleasure!

The King ordered a stone bridge built outside the Large South Gate. The water under the bridge could flow to Binansia (檳榔社, Binlangshe).[269] On the ninth day of the eleventh moon, rain fell mixed with red sand. And on the fourteenth (day) of the twelfth moon, earth tremors occurred twice.

---

266 3 October 1769. Ibid., 119.
267 On 2 October 1772 the High government decided to appoint Wu Panshui (Gouw Poansoeij) to replace Lieutenant Xu Fangliang (許芳良, Kouw Hong Liang) who had died.
268 On 17 November 1772 the High government decided to appoint Wang Jiguan (王藉哥, Ong Tjako), to succeed Lieutenant Chen Caige (陳彩哥, Tan Tjaijko). Chen Caige had three sons and one daughter. His will is mentioned in the resolution of 23 June 1775. Executors were Tjoa Goatse, Ong Bouseng and the former Chinese captain of Ternate Ong Hiamko.
269 Resolution of the Governor General and Council, 6 October 1772, *Realia* 1.111.

After Lieutenant Wang Jiguan had been buried, the King immediately appointed Zheng Shege (鄭奢哥, The Tjako)[270] in his place.

On the seventh moon of Qianlong 38, *guisi* [癸巳], August, 1773, a missive came from the sovereign of the mother country announcing the birth of the crown prince, and at the celebration of the prince's first birthday, the king issued a proclamation that on the seventh [day] of the seventh moon, that is, 24 August, people of every kind should light lanterns and decorate [the front of their houses] with streamers for three days and nights to congratulate the crown prince on his first birthday. On that day, everyone followed the order and lit lanterns. The light dazzled the eyes like the sun. The Great King gave a banquet at the Jakatra garden and invited guests for drinks. Colourful banners were raised at the four gates. In the morning and evening, the big cannons were fired a thousand times.[271]

On the eleventh day of the third leap month, a big flood occurred flooding the feet of the city walls.

On the twenty-seventh, the sultan of Banten captured Bagoes Slinki and sent him to the Company to be dealt with. He was banished to Pulau Onrust. In the fourth moon, that is, the fifteenth of June, the Company sent people with more than ten presents to give to the sultan of Banten. So, the barbarian king was very pleased and accepted them. On the fifteenth [day] of the sixth moon, 2 August, the sultan captured three evil natives, one named Kuijiamijingwenlan (奎甲迷井文難), the second Yulaoyanyawang (裕嘮眼亞望), the third Yuyayanliujia (裕亞眼六甲). The native king [of Banten] gave orders to send them to Batavia tied up. The great king exiled all three of them to Lampong.[272]

In the fourth moon of Qianlong 39, *jiawu* [甲午], June 1774, Boedelmeester Tang Pianshe had served a full term and stepped down. The king thereupon appointed Lin Handan (林漢丹, Lim Hantan) in his place.

---

270 On 15 December 1772, the High Government decided to appoint the former boedelmeester of Semarang, Zheng Shege (The Tjako), to replace Lieutenant Ong Tjako (王藉哥), who had passed away.

271 Permission for illumination, fire works, et cetera, on the occasion of the first birthday of the stadtholder's heir, Willem Frederik, the future King Willem I (1772–1843), 1/14 June 1773, *Plakaatboek*, 8.798–99. The dates are a bit confusing here.

272 The place of banishment was not Lampung in South Sumatra but Robben Island, the same island where Nelson Mandela would reside many years later. Resolution of the Governor General and Council of 25 May 1773. 'Sent by the king of Banten, the rebels Ratoe Oedien and Bagoes Massar will be placed at Robben Island' (Cape of Good Hope); resolution of the Governor General and Council of 19 July 1773. 'The *Ingabeijs* (Javanese, *ngabehi* lower rank of nobility) Cheribon and Doeta Laijana and others will likewise be banished to the Cape'; *Realia* 1.99.

On the second day of the fourth moon, early in the morning (3:00 to 5:00 AM), an earth tremor occurred. Another one occurred on the second day of the twelfth moon. By the sixth day, early in the morning again a big quake occurred and by 3:00 to 5:00 in the afternoon there was a yellow colour in the sun. On the afternoon of the twenty-first there was again this yellow colour in the sun.

Captain Lin Jiguang passed away at about midnight on the twenty-second. His wife, called Mrs. Zheng (鄭氏), had already died, and her coffin was kept in their house, because she wanted to send both coffins back to China after her husband had died. When Captain Lin Jiguang died, his coffin was put next to his wife's. The following year, when it was heard that the officials in China were very tyrannical, an auspicious day was chosen and both were buried at Gunung Sari.

From the beginning of his lieutenancy until the end of his captaincy, Lin Jiguang served twenty-eight years and seven days. At the time, Lieutenant Tang Enge petitioned the King asking him to allow him to succeed to the captaincy. The King thereupon promoted him to the position of captain and appointed Cai Dunge (蔡敦哥, Swa Toenko) lieutenant.[273]

Between 7:00 and 9:00 in the morning of the seventh day in the first moon of Qianlong 40, *yiwei* **[乙未], February 1775,** a yellow colour showed in the sun. At that exact moment, it was reported that a ship had arrived bringing an edict from the mother country. The King and his councilors gathered together and opened it and said, 'The crown prince has already ascended the throne'.[274]

So, the great King issued a proclamation ordering people of all kinds to set up lanterns and streamers in front of their gates. On the eighth day of the first moon, 15 February, the Chinese and the native people placed lanterns and streamers. The king gave a banquet at Jakatra to entertain the headmen. Pennants were flown over the four gates. In the morning and evening, the cannons were fired to celebrate and congratulate the crown prince's assumption of the throne. In the third month of this year, the sovereign of the mother country sent an edict to Batavia approving the elevation of Captain Tang Enge to the position of captain.

---

273 On 31 January 1775, the High Government decided to appoint the oldest Lieutenant, Tang Enge (唐恩哥, Ting/Thung Ingko), to the captaincy because 'he possessed the right ability and enjoyed esteem', and appointed Cai Dunge (蔡敦哥, Swa Thoenko) Lieutenant. (For more details about Cai Dunge, note his appointment to the captaincy on 26 November 1784.) Ting/Thung Ingko had been appointed Lieutenant on 6 April 1764. His inauguration ceremony was extravagant. Hoetink, 'Chineesche officieren', 71–78, quotes in full the *Batavian Diary* of 3 April 1775. He passed away on 19 December 1775.

274 Stadtholder Willem V of Orange-Nassau (1748–1806).

By the fourth day of the third moon, the captain was riding the 'Five Holy Mountains' sedan chair carried by eight people and followed by a suite of of thirty-two men walking in pairs, with a retinue in front and behind playing a great din of drums and pipes banners so thick they hid the sun. The ten sounds confused the ears; a resplendent sight with flowery lamps lining the streets. All the lieutenants were escorting him, including the son who was in office, followed by two soldaten with whips. Moreover, lining the road the people of Batavia burned incense welcoming him. The captain first headed for Jakatra to be installed in his position at the palace of the king and then he entered via the Large South Gate ascending to the Gongtang[275] and formally acted upon his promotion. He then made a swing through town, his followers filling up the streets—it was difficult to estimate how many. Nothing as extreme as this had ever been seen since the founding of Batavia. Although they were heroes of their generation, where are they now? Six lieutenants then escorted him, in the following order:

1. Huang Hengge; 2. Zheng Longge; 3. Lin Delang; 4. Wu Panshui; 5. Zheng Shege; 6. Cai Dunge. The secretaries were Lin Kuazu and Lin Chunguang (林春光); the soldaten were Ye Huaguan and He Juge.

On the sixth day of the seventh moon, Lin Delang passed away and was buried at Gunung Sari. He served five years. The king appointed Wang Zhusheng (王珠生, Ong Tjoeseeng) in his place.[276] Zhusheng was the eldest son of the former Lieutenant Wang Rongshi.

In the past, in the fourth year of Longfei [龍飛], *jiwei* [己未], the rebellion of Batavia occurred.[277] The authorities had sentenced the former Captain Lian Fuguang and sent him in exile to Ambon to reside there. After he finally died in Ambon, his coffin was sent to Batavia this year, with the intention of burying

---

275   The office of the Kong Koan, or Chinese Council.
276   On 4 August 1775, the High Government decided to appoint Ong Soeseeng to replace Lieutenant Lim Theeko, who had passed away.
277   Only the Liem manuscript mentions the Longfei year period. Why did the author write Longfei 4 rather than Qianlong 4 or even better Qianlong 5? Ming adherents among the overseas Chinese often used this imaginary reign period in order to avoid using the reign periods of the invading Qing dynasty. The use of Longfei, 'Flying Dragon' in the meaning of 'ascending the throne' is based on the *Yijing* (Book of Changes). Throughout Chinese history, meritorious emperors of and on also were lauded with the Longfei *epitheton ornans*. See Ruan Yonghe (Yon Weng Woe 阮湧俐), 'Research on Southeast Asia Ming Adherents using the word "Long Fei", 东南亚明朝遗民使用"龙飞"之动机考证' Unpublished MA thesis, Xiamen University, 2017.

him with the ritual befitting his original position as captain. When the King heard about this, he forbade it. Because Lian Fuguang was found guilty, he had been [banished] to a faraway place. He should be buried according to the ritual befitting a poor person. Thereupon he was buried at the western cemetery.

> *John Chinaman comments*: Good has its reward and evil has its recompense. Like this it was proven! When Lian Fuguang began to serve as captain, and the Chinese were suffering, he did not show compassion for the people, but he spent a life of pleasure and banquets, enjoying his own pleasures. Later, he showed no intention of either rescuing the country or saving the people. If one million people were plunged into misery, this was all because this captain failed to protect the people and take responsibility. He deserved punishment by Heaven. So, when, after his death, his coffin returned to Batavia from a faraway place, it deservedly received the burial rites of poor people, to put the case before the public![278]

On the seventeenth day of the intercalary tenth moon, Captain Tang Enge died and was buried at the back of the temple in Gunung Sari. He served as lieutenant eleven years and as captain only nine months.

> *John Chinaman comments*: To ride the five mountain sedan chair carried by eight bearers, and to be escorted by followers as well, that is grand ceremony, proper to the court. When native officers overstep their authority with ceremonies in defiance of Heaven and behave irrationally, slight fortune is hard to face! You should not overstep your authority and show such ostentation. Then your vitality is drained. Thus the wrath of Heaven did not let you enjoy your position for a long time. Later generations should learn a lesson from this.

The Great King promoted Huang Hengge[279] to the position of captain and sent a memorial to the sovereign in the mother country. He also promoted Tang

---

278 This commentary is taken from the Leiden manuscript.
279 On 19 December 1775, the High Government decided to appoint to the captaincy the eldest Lieutenant, Huang Hengge (黄恒哥, Oeij Hingko), because 'he possessed the right ability, and enjoyed esteem among his people'. Huang was appointed *Wijkmeester* of the first 5 parts of *blok* O in the Westerveld on 23 August 1763. The city was divided up in quarters (*wijk* or *blok*) that were supervised by *wijkmeesters*. See Remco Raben, *Batavia and Colombo. The ethnic and spatial order of two colonial cities 1600–1800*. PhD thesis, Leiden University, 1996). His appointment to lieutenant followed on 19 February 1765. He passed

Pianshe to the position of lieutenant.²⁸⁰ That year Gao Genguan had served two full terms. On the twenty-ninth [day] of the tenth intercalary month the great king appointed Chen Fulao (陳富老, Tan Hoelo) boedelmeester to fill the vacancy [left by] Gao Genguan. On the third [day] of the eleventh moon, Lieutenant Zheng Shege died and was buried at Gunung Sari. (He served four years.)

In the twelfth moon, the Great King Petrus van der Parra passed away and was buried in the great church. He served fourteen years and one month. The councilors together bestowed the title of acting Great King on Jeremias van Riemsdijk to manage the country's affairs and sent a memorial to the sovereign in the mother country to inform him.²⁸¹ Only two days after he had assumed his position, he promoted former Boedelmeester Gao Genguan to the position of Lieutenant.²⁸²

This year Gao Genguan presided over a meeting of the six lieutenants, and proposed to the captain to establish a school of the lieutenants named Mingcheng Shuyuan (明誠書院) behind the temple (Guanyinting), where a tablet dedicated to Ziyang (紫陽; Zhu Xi, 朱熹) was venerated. Within the town was the Nanjiang Shuyuan (南江書院), where a statue of Ziyang was

---

away on in November 1784. His executors were Oeij Toatko and Lieutenant Lim Tjoenkong (14 June 1785 and 11 June 1793, respectively). See Hoetink, 'Chineesche officieren', 78–79).

280 On 19 December 1775, the High Government appointed Tang Pianshe (唐偏哥, Tung Pi-enko) to the position of Lieutenant.

281 Jeremias van Riemsdijk was born in Utrecht on 18 October 1712. On 24 September 1735, he arrived in Batavia with the rank of sergeant. He changed to the Company's civil service and, thanks to his family relations with Governor General Valckenier, his career took off with a flying start: junior merchant in 1736, merchant 1738, and second senior merchant in Batavia Castle and first senior merchant in 1742. Understandably everything came to a halt during the reign of Van Imhoff, but in October 1753 he was appointed extraordinary councilor and seven years later ordinary councilor. On 17 August 1764, he was appointed director general under Van der Parra. Van Riemsdijk was known for his great wealth and possessed no less than two hundred household slaves at his big mansion in Batavia. When he became governor general in 1775, he was already sixty-three years old. He passed away on 3 October 1777.

282 On 29 December 1775, the High Government decided to appoint former Boedelmeester Gao Genguan (Ko Kimko) to replace Lieutenant Zheng Shege (The Tjako), who had passed away. Gao Genguan drafted his will on 27 June 1787. His executors were Wang Zhusheng (Ong Tjoeseeng), Ko Tamko (高潭官), and Liouw Ikong (柳揚官); see resolution of 22 March 1791. For the disputes between the executors and his widow, Tan Sinnio (陳審娘), see the resolutions of 8 and 22 March and 21 June 1791.

also venerated, which was made into the captain's school. Both schools invited teachers to reside there to teach the poor students.[283]

> Every year in spring and autumn sacrifices were held, and people would drink to their hearts' content and bond their friendships with their writings. Two lieutenants and the secretary would supervise the proceedings and designate the best and second best students to reward them with tuition. The Nanjiang Shuyuan also functioned like this. So there was an abundance of scholarly environment. How refined!
>
> CHEN XUELAN (陳雪瀾) COMMENTS: From the Wanli period in the Ming dynasty, when we Chinese came to Batavia, until Qianlong 40, some 150 years passed. Although there were already captains, none ever thought about this [education]. Yet they built Buddhist temples and temples for [other] deities. That was just to pray for happiness and wealth; they had not given a thought to the care of the education of poor children. It is only because Mr. Gao Gen (高根先生) did not forget about the sacred learning of China while living in the uncivilised regions that the climate of learning did not vanish. This is to be praised and respected! The headmen of the Chinese a hundred years ago and a hundred years from now should bow their heads and feel embarrassed facing him! (Written as a token of respect in Guangxu [光緒] 20, *jiawu* [甲午, 1894] by Chen Xuelan of the later generation.)[284]
>
> XU YUNQIAO (許雲樵) COMMENTS IN TURN: The Mingcheng Shuyuan and the Nanjiang Shuyuan were established in 1775; they represent the earliest Chinese schools in the Nanyang. Therefore, Gao Gen is in fact the pioneer in the history of overseas Chinese education in the Nanyang.

In the fourth moon of Qianlong 41, *bingshen* **[丙申], May 1776,** Boedelmeester Lin Handan had served his full term and stepped down. On the twenty-eighth [day] of the fourth moon, the Great King appointed Gao Yonglao (高永老, Koinko) boedelmeester.

On the tenth [day] of the fifth moon, the exile of the criminal former Boedelmeester Chen Qiaolang had expired. When he returned from Ambon to Batavia, he had cut his hair and he sported a beard; wearing a sarong and

---

283 This paragraph about the founding of the school is taken from the Leiden and Yang Bodong manuscripts. Its contents do not conform with the earlier [wrong] statement in 1694 that Guo Junguan would have founded this school.

284 This comment is taken from the Yang Bodong manuscript.

tacking up his clothes in the barbarian manner, he had gone native. Ayah, what a pity! This is enough to prove that when he began to serve as boedelmeester and immediately proposed to punish Chinese brides riding in a sedan chair, he already intended to go native. And now he had done it! We can say that Chen Qiaolang fulfilled his wishes. We may also suppose that he felt very fortunate![285]

On the second [day] of the sixth moon of Qianlong 42, *dingyou* [丁酉], July 1777, Lieutenant Zheng Longge (鄭隆哥) died and on the ninth he was buried at Gunung Sari. (He served eight years.)

The King immediately appointed Yang Kuange (楊款哥, Njo Koangko) lieutenant.[286] On the fourth [day] of the ninth moon, the fourth of October, the Great King Van Riemsdijk passed away and was buried in the great church. (He served three years as great king).

The position of Great King was transferred to Reinier de Klerck to take charge of the country's affairs.[287]

On the fourth [day] of the tenth moon, Javanese natives from the east came sailing to Batavia in more than one thousand vessels led by their Javanese headmen. They came to congratulate the new Great King on his assumption of the throne. The King ordered people to go and have a look [at the situation] outside the castle. Discovering that there were so many Javanese, he worried that a rebellion might occur and ordered powder and cannon balls put in the cannons and dispatched soldiers to guard day and night, keeping a smouldering fuse close to the cannons at all positions. The authorities could not put their hearts at ease until the Javanese had returned home.

---

285   This paragraph is taken from the Leiden manuscript.
286   On 8 July 1777 the High Government appointed Yang Kuange (Njo Koangko) to the position of lieutenant.
287   Reinier de Klerck was born in Middelburg in 1710. After his third voyage to the East as third mate of the ship *'t Vliegend Hert*, he signed off at Batavia in July 1731 and continued his sailor's career in Asian waters for five more years. In 1737, he entered the Company's civil service and via various positions (also military ones) he ended up as governor of Java's Northeast-Coast. On 30 December 1748, he was appointed governor of Banda, and returned in 1750. In 1754, he served as president of the Chinese board of boedelmeesters, and one year later he was appointed extraordinary councilor and in 1770 councilor. He fulfilled various important functions before his appointment as director general in 1775. When he was appointed to the highest position on 4 October 1777, De Klerck—by then sixty-seven years old—remarked that he considered this promotion to be like 'mustard served after dinner'. He passed away on 1 September 1780. De Klerck was one of the founders and the first director of the Batavian Society for the Arts and Sciences (*Bataviaasch Genootschap van Kunsten en Wetenschappen*), established in 1778.

In the eighth moon of Qianlong 43, *wuxu* [戊戌]**, September 1778,** an edict from the sovereign in the mother country arrived in Batavia formally investing Reinier de Klerck with the Kingship. Boedelmeester Gao Yonglao died and was buried at Gunung Sari. The King immediately appointed Huang Mianshe (黃綿舍, that is, Oeij Biankong, 黃綿光) in his place. At the end of this year, the two Boedelmeesters Chen Fulao and Huang Mianshe sent a petition to the king asking him to let them handle the *shahbandar* tax farm. The king discussed this with the councilors and authorized the two boedelmeesters to manage this tax farm in turn, with the understanding that they would pay 4200 guilders monthly to the company.

In the ninth moon of Qianlong 44, *jihai* [己亥]**, October 1779,** Boedelmeester Wang Yiguang died on the twenty-third day and was buried on the twenty-seventh at Gunung Sari. On the night of the fifteenth of the tenth moon there was a lunar eclipse. The moon darkened to black but afterwards became bright again. On the eleventh of the eleventh moon, the captain of Lembang, Lin Xiangguan (林享觀) died at Batavia, and his coffin was returned to Lembang. On the sixteenth of the twelfth moon there was a heavy downpour that flooded the streets so that one could sail a boat through them. An earthquake occurred in the early afternoon and more then one hundred houses inside and outside of the city caved in, killing countless people. The flood did not begin to recede until the twenty-seventh.

In the fifth moon of Qianlong 45, *gengzi* [庚子]**, June 1780,** the Company wanted to impose a tax on the money remitted to China by the Chinese people, that is, one *fanam* for every guilder.[288] The revenues were to be used as income by the Chinese hospital for its expenses. Captain Huang Hengge and all the lieutenants went to see the king and asked him not to open the Chinese people's money envelopes, but the captain and his officers were willing to pay the money per household. This case remained dormant and was not touched upon again. This can be said to be the great virtue of the Chinese officers. As the King's health progressively deteriorated, he made a will and let director general Willem Alting replace him and manage the country's affairs, and sent a memorial to the sovereign in the mother country.

On the night of the first day of September, the Great King Reinier de Klerck passed away and he was buried on the fourth in the great church. He served two years and one month. On the fourth of September, Director General Willem Alting provisionally assumed the throne,[289] and on the fifteenth an

---

288 This means that a tithe was levied.
289 Willem Arnold Alting was born in Groningen on 11 November 1724. He studied law at the University of Groningen and set sail for the east arriving in Batavia with the position

edict from the sovereign in the mother country arrived formally investing him with the Kingship.[290] On the twentieth of September, the councilors of the Indies welcomed Willem Alting to enter the castle and ascend the throne. That night, fireworks were set off at Gunung Sari to celebrate and congratulate the new king at his ascendency. On the thirteenth [day] of the tenth moon, that is, on Wednesday, 20 November, the king ordered the inner and outer *temenggongs* to each send a police officer to the house of the captain and keep guard at the captain's meetings [=meetings of the Chinese Council] as a fixed rule forever.[291]

On the twenty-seventh [day] of the first moon of Qianlong 46, *xinchou* [辛丑], February 1781, the Great King Willem Alting received a missive from the sovereign in the mother country stating that on 20 December 1780 a declaration of war had been presented by the British, who wished to fight it out with the sovereign [Willem v] and the Estates General.[292] Now the sovereign of the mother country had already prepared the army to await the enemy, and ordered that all lands belonging to him should train soldiers and strictly guard the territory. King Willem Alting convened the councilors and all the headmen and issued a proclamation that all subject territories must prepare their weapons to keep out the British. He ordered the recruitment and training of soldiers, and the instruction of formation drills. In the west, upwards from Tong'ankou, wooden palisades were constructed with barracks inside, and downwards along the coast east of Tong'ankou palisades were raised with cannons on top, surrounded on the outside by a deep moat and with barracks manned by a garrison inside.

On the twentieth [day] of the fifth moon, 14 July, the [Chinese] junk *Shunyuan Wu* (順源鵤) caught fire and all its cargo was lost. The [junk's] *nakhoda* Gao Guishan (高圭山) returned to China on board of a Cantonese junk. In the sixth moon, July, the Company ordered all Dutch headmen and the descendants of the old headmen to drill how to use weapons, to prepare for war with the English. All the various native communities recruited soldiers to

---

of junior merchant on 30 July 1751. He became merchant in 1754, and second and first secretary of the High Government in 1756 and 1759, respectively. He was appointed ordinary councilor in 1772 and director general in 1777. He served as governor general from 2 September 1780 until 17 February 1797, when he retired. He passed away on 7 July 1800 on his estate Kampong Melajoe.

290 Long before telegraph came into use, it was of course impossible that the Gentlemen XVII would have formally invested Alting ten days after De Klerck's death.
291 The meeting hall, usually called Gongtang (Minnanhua *Kong Tong* 公堂) of the Chinese Council, Gongguan (Minnanhua *Kong Koan* 公館).
292 The British government initiated the Fourth Anglo-Dutch War (1780–84) on account of Dutch aid to the rebellious American Republic.

guard their areas. The [Chinese] officers went to see the King and asked him to let the Chinese also exercise with weapons to guard their own kampongs. Everyone wanted to earnestly stand watch. The King entered the great hall of the castle to meet with the councilors and make a decision. On the second day of the seventh moon, 20 August, he first gave fifty flintlocks to the captain, to let him drill the Chinese. On 13 September, he again furnished flintlocks to the lieutenants and boedelmeesters, who should all drill the Chinese. In the event that any Chinese were secretly colluding with the English, they were to be arrested and punished without pardon.[293] Chinese and natives should unite in a concerted effort!

FIGURE 18   *Drilling the Chinese militia at Batavia. Jan Brandes*
RIJKSMUSEUM AMSTERDAM

---

293   16 March 1784: 'Since the outbreak of the war, the officers of the Chinese nation have been provided with 450 flintlocks to exercise some of their nation in the use of arms'. See *Plakaatboek*, 10.708.

On the evening of the sixteenth of the eighth moon, there was a partial lunar eclipse, but the moon returned to its circular shape and brightness. This day, Wednesday, 3 October, the Dutch elite devoutly wished to attend church to pray to God hoping that the English would agree to a ceasefire and peace would return to the country. A day earlier, the soldaat [of the Kong Koan] was ordered to proclaim that on Wednesday afternoon at five o'clock, everyone should close the doors of their stores inside and outside the city. They should not make any noise. Boys and girls should not play in the streets. Anyone who violated this order would be punished. On the first day of the ninth moon, the [Chinese] officers went to worship at the temple (Guanyinting) praying for protection and peace in the country, harmony among the people, and an abundance of goods.

On the fifth day of the ninth moon, 20 October, a French vessel that was preparing to set sail also caught fire and all its cargo went down with it on the twenty-sixth of the ninth moon. On 11 November, the king ordered a commander to fit out several ships to sail to the mother country to enquire about the military situation with the English. At the time, the susuhunan of Mataram, who had heard that Batavia was preparing for war, also sent soldiers to assist the Company. The Great King [of Batavia] ordered a commissioner to direct several Dutch soldiers to go to Krawang and to wait for them there. On the seventh day of the tenth moon, 20 November, the first thousand Mataramese soldiers arrived. The commissioner and the Dutch officers directed them to be stationed at Jaga Monyet (Rijswijk). On the fourteenth of the tenth moon, 29 November, another thousand soldiers came from Mataram. The company provided them with provisions and ordered them to garrison in an open field at Jaga Monyet across the harbour. Together with the people who had come earlier they amounted to three thousand men. The Company again provided them with victuals but did not allow them to cause disturbances and make trouble. Among the guns they had brought along there were useless ones. The company exchanged them for better ones and let them train.

Moreover, owing to the exercises by the Chinese officers, the fusiliers were already well trained; their manoeuvring was already well coordinated.

On the first of December, the authorities visited the house of the Chinese captain to inspect the soldiers. The king gave the captain a large musket, a golden shield, and a uniform. Later they went to the houses of the lieutenants to inspect the exercises and bestowed on every one of them a decoration.

In this year the English occupied Bengal, Coromandel, and Calcutta, Padang, and other places. And in all these places they stationed soldiers to intercept the ships of the Company. Thus it was hard for the ships from the mother country to pass through to Batavia. The business of Batavia was depressed. Sugar and arak could not be sold. Activities at many sugar mills slowed down.

In Qianlong 48, *guimao* ([癸卯),] 8 January 1783, Lieutenant Wu Panshui died and was buried at Gunung Sari. He served eleven years. The king immediately promoted Boedelmeester Chen Fulao to the rank of lieutenant and appointed Chen Misheng (陳泌生, Tan Piseeng) boedelmeester in his place.[294]

Qianlong 49, *jiachen* [甲辰], 1784. Because the company lacked cash, paper money was introduced as currency. On the paper money were written the signatures of the authorities. Starting from 5 guilders, [the value of] this money went up to 10, 100, [and] 1000 guilders.[295] The backs of the paper money for circulation in Batavia had different pictures and colours. When this money was amply in use, there were some sly people—Huang Mengguan (黃猛觀), Cai Kunguan (蔡坤觀), Wang Zaisheng (王再生)—together with a black native named Chasen Blok, three Chinese and a native—who together counterfeited money to mix with other money and cheat people.[296] Because this secret plot was unveiled, Cai Kunguan and the others were found out and arrested and punished. Only Huang Mengguan slipped through the holes in the net and hid in the house of a native called *Tuan* Ayub. The authorities discovered this and threw them in jail and Huang Mengguan was immediately strangled. *Tuan* Ayub was sent in exile to a faraway place.

In this year, a Dutchman named Van Riemsdijk bought a large garden. In the middle was a big tower; originally it was an estate [belonging to one] of the authorities.[297] Along the side of a road bordering the garden, Van Riemsdijk then built brick houses that he rented out for Chinese to reside in. The authorities

---

294 On 2 December 1783, the High Government appointed Chen Fulao (Tan Hoelo) to the position of lieutenant to replace Gouw Poan Soei (Wu Panshui 吳泮水), who had passed away. Chen Fulao served as boedelmeester from 22 December 1775 until 2 December 1783. He proposed a plan to fight piracy that was subsequently approved on 28 June 1785. His widow, Oeij Tjoanio (Huang Zhaoniang 黃招娘), and Tan Tjeeuwsing were executors of his inheritance (resolution of 1 July 1791). His resolutions of 2 August and 19 December 1791 refer to his sons Tan Limseeng and Tan Tjoeseeng. See Hoetink, 'Chineesche officieren', 122.

295 Because of the outbreak of the war, the government was short of cash. 'Papers of Credit' were introduced as early as 2/6 December 1782 (see *Plakaatboek*, 10.632–36), and by 24 February 1784, denominations as large as 10,000 rixdollars were even brought into circulation (*Plakaatboek*, 10.705).

296 29 June 1784, 'Warning against counterfeited papers of credit', *Plakaatboek*, 10.720–22.

297 Willem Vincent Helvetius van Riemsdijk, son of former Governor General Jeremias van Riemsdijk. The tower was the former observatory of the clergyman J.M. Mohr. See De Haan, *Oud Batavia*, 151.

disapproved of this and confiscated half the houses for the company and let the company clerks live in them.[298]

Originally, the money from the *weeskamer* was used for Chinese and native orphans and disabled people. But this year the money was taken by the authorities to provide the Company clerks with their daily meals. This serves to show that the authorities were not fair.

At the time, the captain was Huang Hengge, the lieutenants were Zheng Shege, Wu Panshui, Zheng Longge, Cai Dunge, Wang Zhusheng, and Tang Pianshe. After Zheng Shege died, Gao Genguan replaced him [on 29 December 1775]. When Zheng Longguan died, Yang Kuange replaced him [on 8 July 1777]. When Wu Panshui died, Chen Fulao replaced him [on 2 December 1783]. The secretaries were Lin Kuazu and Lin Chunguang (林春光). Ye Huaguan and He Juge were the two soldaten. Huang Lianguan and Su Quanguan were the undertakers.[299]

Originally, all the affairs of the Chinese people were under the purview of the Chinese captain. The permits for the junks sailing to Makassar were issued by the captain. If Company ships wanted to enlist Chinese crewmembers, this was also taken care of by the captain. If the Company wanted to use white candles, only the captain could provide them. The supply of food for Pulau Onrust all was taken care of by the captain. All of these affairs provided great benefits.

By the time that Huang Hengge served as captain, issuance of permits for Makassar had already been taken over by Chen Shunguang (陳順光). After Chen Shunguang's death, the permits were publicly auctioned. The material supply for Onrust had already been taken over by [Lieutenant] Chen Fulao, after he asked the great king for permission. After Chen Fulao died, these transactions were included in the tax at the *boom*. When Chen Peilao (陳沛老) asked the king for the business of hiring [Chinese] crew members, he was apportioned six ships.

In the tenth month, Captain Huang Hengge died and was buried at Gunung Sari. He had served twenty-one years. His record of management was mediocre. The king immediately promoted Cai Dunge to the captaincy.[300]

---

298   This is not true. Van Riemsdijk actually put the houses at the disposal of the government. See De Haan, *Oud Batavia*, 647.

299   Huang Lianguan actually died in 1758.

300   On 26 November 1784, it was decided to appoint the oldest Lieutenant Cai Dunge to the position of captain. On 1 December 1784, Governor General Alting proclaimed the appointment of the new captain and asked the Chinese community to 'be obedient, and honor, aid, and assist' their headman. Before he came to Batavia in 1770, Cai had been

He appointed Huang Mianguang (黃綿光, Oeij Biankong) as lieutenant and Chen Shuiguan (陳水觀, Tan Soeyko) as boedelmeester. He ordered Chen Peisheng (陳沛生 *aka* Chen Peilao 陳沛老) to manage the Company ships. Originally the work of hiring the crews for the Company ships belonged to the Chinese captain, but when Huang Yanguan was captain, Chen Peisheng had already been apportioned six ships. However, after the captain passed away, all the affairs were managed by Chen Peisheng himself.[301]

FIGURE 19   *Chinese sailors staying over at the VOC-wharf in Amsterdam, Jacob de Vos, c. 1790*
RIJKSMUSEUM AMSTERDAM

---

tax farmer of the tolls of the in- and outgoing shipping at Ambon. (See the resolution of 10 May 1771.) Because the school for poor children at the Chinese hospital had been neglected by the captain, the lieutenants asked permission to open another one at Klenteng, outside the city; resolution of 9 March 1787. See Hoetink, 'Chineesche officieren', 79–80.

301   For the hiring of Chinese crews by the VOC, see Leonard Blussé, 'John Chinaman Abroad: Chinese Sailors in the Service of the VOC', in Alicia Schrikker and Jeroen Touwen, eds. *Promises and Predicaments, Trade and Entrepreneurship in Colonial and Independent Indonesia in the 19th and 20th Centuries* (Singapore: NUS Press, 2015), 101–112.

Qianlong 50, *yisi* [乙巳], 1785. In the past the Riau natives had taken up arms and laid siege to Malacca. The sovereign of the mother country had already dispatched troops to pacify them, but in this year Malacca was again besieged by the Riau natives, so Batavia was called in for assistance. Therefore, the king ordered his officers to lead the soldiers in Company ships to put them down. After several years of unsuccessful fighting, a memorial was sent to the sovereign in the mother country. He issued an order to send six warships and ordered high-ranking Dutch officers to lead the soldiers in battle. In one swift action, the siege was lifted and the commander of the Riau natives was killed, and singing triumphantly, the troops returned to Batavia. Thus, Malacca was completely pacified.[302]

In the eleventh moon of this year, Secretary Lin Kuazu resigned. Captain Cai Dunge recommended that Lin Rongzu (林榮祖) replace him. The king approved and then appointed him. (Lin Rongzu's grandfather was the former Captain Lin Mingguang; Rongzu was the eldest son of Lin Chunshe. Like grandfather like grandson!)

In the sixth month of Qianlong 52, *dingwei* [丁未], July 1787, a Chinese junk shipwrecked near Onrust. On the sixth day of the sixth moon, the Chinese junk *Sanhexing Wu* (三合興鵂) of the *nakhoda* Guo Huiguan (郭回觀) hoisted sail in the Bay of Batavia. After it had run only three *geng* (更), it was hit by a squall and ran aground on a reef and went down without a trace.[303] That year, Yang Chaoguan (楊朝觀) and Hu Chunguan (胡春觀), who with their followers, altogether eighteen men, had gone to Guoxi (過西, Padang) to smuggle opium, arrived at Batavia. They were unmasked by the people and reported to the *fiscaal*. He immediately dispatched his men to arrest them. All of them were banished to faraway places.

In Qianlong 53, *wushen* [戊申], 1788, at the Zainiu Gangkou (Cow-slaughter Port) outside the West Gate, there was an evil native named *Tuan* Haji who could recite the holy scripture. Innumerable people went to receive his

---

302 On 14 March 1783, Captain Commander Jacob Pieter van Braam left with a flotilla of warships for Asia to assist the VOC during the Anglo-Dutch War. Upon arrival in the Indonesian archipelago in 1784, Van Braam and his naval force were directed to the Riau Archipelago to quell the uprising of the Buginese and liberate Malacca. See Reinout Vos. *Gentle Janus, Merchant Prince: The VOC in the Malay World, 1740–1800*. (Leiden: KITLV Press, 1993), 165–86.

303 One *geng* is a maritime measure of distance expressed in time. Twenty-four hours are divided into ten geng. One *geng* equals about 50 Chinese *li* (approximately 25,000 meter). Consequently, three *geng* means that this particular junk had been under sail for some seven hours, or about 45 sea miles.

instructions. He lectured them like a father. They venerated him like heaven. Everybody called him an immortal. Upon hearing that, he spread heresies to deceive the people and said that he planned an uprising. The authorities made a plan and sent a native commander to trick him by saying that the company had a foreign barbarian book that nobody could make sense of. He said, 'We have heard about *Tuan* Haji's talents. The authorities have ordered me to accompany you to the castle in a carriage to have a look at the book'. Once Tuan Haji had stepped down from the carriage and entered the gate, he was bound up without ado, sent to sea, and drowned. At the same time, people were dispatched to his house, and all his household belongings were put up for auction. But there was a box with native holy writings, and without considering their own spending power, people bid against each other to lay their hands on it. The authorities surmised that there were devilish things inside these books. They thereupon did not allow that lot to be auctioned, and had the native books burned.[304]

On the sixteenth [day] of the eighth moon, Lieutenant Gao Genguan died and was buried at Gunung Sari. He served thirteen years.[305] The king immediately appointed Lin Handan in his place.[306] The Dutch built a theatre stage at Gangzaiwei (港仔尾), in town. Every Wednesday and Saturday Dutch plays were staged to entertain the elite and, moreover, to make a profit.

Qianlong 54, *jiyou* [己酉], **1789.** There were two men, Chen Yeti (陳夜提) and Guo Weiguang (郭委光), who together were counterfeiting money to circulate with genuine money. They were informed on by their female slave, who had stealthily taken their printing block. The authorities sent people to surround their house and arrest them. But because Yeti and his men had been forwarned, they had already run away. In the tenth moon, Lieutenant Chen Fulao died and was buried at Gunung Sari. He had served six years. He was good-natured and kind-hearted. He followed the crowd. He made a living as he wished; when he could make a profit, he did so. He was favoured by the great king, but he was illiterate and could not read a simple character.

---

304 For the persecution of the Arab Said Mochamad Ebenoe Abdullah, see De Jonge, *Opkomst*, 12.xx–xxxi. He was not thrown overboard but was exiled to Ceylon.

305 According to the *Gong An Bu* (公案簿, *Minutes of the Board Meetings of the Chinese Council*), Lieutenant Gao Genguan (高根官) died on the sixteenth of the eighth moon, Qianlong 52 (that is, 27 September 1787), 1.258; the *Gong An Bu* also mentions that Gao Genguan had his testament drawn up on 28 June 1787 (*Gong An Bu* 1.8–11).

306 Lin Handan (Lim Hantan) was appointed on 12 October 1773. He had served as boedelmeester from 1773 to 1775.

The king immediately appointed Huang Jilao (黃繼老 *aka* Huang Jige 黃繼哥, Oeij Geeko) in his place.[307]

In Qianlong 55, *gengxu* [庚戌], **1790.** The natives of Solo raised soldiers and invaded Semarang. The governor captured their leader and sent him bound up to Batavia Castle.

There was a temple at Ancol in Batavia. In former days [1754], Lieutenant Lin Chaiguan (林釵觀, Lim Theeko) had held a meeting and proposed to establish it, but he did not yet have a title to the land.[308] When the Company put the land up for auction this year, Lieutenant Wang Zhusheng proposed to collect money from the Chinese and to use the donated money to turn it into a place where the Chinese people could burn incense and pray. At the back, bordering on the port, he built a pagoda to provide people with a place to avoid the summer heat.

At an inland place called Kebun Jeruk (Suanganzai Yuan, 酸柑仔園), three native families conspired to forge guilders adulterated with tin and circulate them in Batavia. After some time, the authorities found out and arrested the counterfeiters and sentenced them all to death. Elsewhere inland at a spot called Sungai Atap (阿答港口) there was a robber called Murah. He hid fierce runaway slaves, and had amassed 400 to 500 of them. He robbed merchants and ran amuck; not a calm day passed by. He ordered his followers to cultivate the soil and carry out corvée labour. Some of those who could not bear the intolerably hard work ran away. He ordered his men to chase and kill them.

At that time, there were also some prisoners who had snuck away to that place. Among them there was one prisoner who felt some remorse and returned and reported on the situation in detail to the warden. The warden thereupon reported this to the authorities. These in turn dispatched the bailiff with twenty men. He did not anticipate that the robbers would put up such a brave resistance that three policemen were killed. The bailiff ran away to the house of a native in the neighbourhood at Lülanjiaoyi (律蘭礁逸), who thereupon recruited several hundred native soldiers to attack them, but again five men were killed whose heads were hung in the trees. Unable to see a way out,

---

307 The characterisation of Chen Fulao (Tan Hoelo) is taken from the Leiden manuscript. On 22 December 1789, the High Government appointed 'the present farmer of the duties on the in- and outgoing trade Huang Jige' to the position of lieutenant to replace Chen Fulao, who had passed away. He served for only a few months because he died before 28 September 1790. The executors of his inheritance were Huang Hengge (黃恒哥, Oeij Hongko) and the seventeen-year-old Oeij Tjoeijseng, presumably his son. See Hoetink, 'Chineesche officieren', 122.

308 Also known as Lin Qinge (林釵哥). This sentence was taken from the Leiden manuscript.

the bailiff headed back to town and drew up a detailed report. The authorities were furious and dispatched 800 Muslim soldiers and 34 Dutch soldiers and ordered them to attack the enemy and capture their chief and wipe out the robbers' lair. But Murah had already led his robbers into the mountains and escaped the army's vanguard. There was only an empty camp left behind. So, after they had set the camp afire, the soldiers returned [empty-handed].

Living inland at Pondok Gedeh there was a Dutch pastor named Padri Weiman who acted outrageously and behaved wantonly, in a very bad and unscrupulous manner. This year he was killed by people with a gun. That probably was also the revenge of Heaven!

There also was a boat from Gunung Sari that wanted to return to Krawang carrying coffee. When it arrived at the port, its crew saw a sandbank obstructing the ship. When they looked closely it turned out to be a dead giant whale lying there. Thereupon they returned to report this to Batavia. The commissioner ordered some natives sent to collect all the bones. There were several tens of them, four or five *zhang* (丈) in length; seven or eight people were needed to carry every bone back to the warehouse [castle]. Never had such a strange water animal been witnessed since the founding of Batavia.

On the nineteenth day of the fourth moon, Captain Cai Dunge died and was buried at Gunung Sari. He had served ten years as lieutenant and six years as captain. He was mediocre in his management, had no special talents, and could not even read a simple character. He hated other people's success and rejoiced in their losses. That was how his character was!

The king immediately promoted Lieutenant Wang Zhusheng to the position of captain.[309] Because the Boedelmeesters Chen Misheng and Chen Shuiguan had served their full term, they stepped down, and the king immediately appointed Chen Kuanguan (陳寬觀, Tan Koanko) and Lin Zhangsheng (林長生, Lim Tiangseeng) in their places. In the eighth moon of this year, Lieutenant Huang Jilao died and was buried at Gunung Sari. The king thereupon promoted Secretary Lin Chungong (林春公, Lim Tjoengkong) to lieutenant.

---

309 Wang Zhusheng (Ong Tjoeseeng/Soeseeng) was appointed lieutenant on 1 August 1775 and promoted to captain on 8 June 1790. In his place, Chen Baoge (Tan Poko) was appointed lieutenant. On 1 July 1790, Wang Zhusheng was formally installed in the presence of Lieutenants Tang Pianshe (Tung Pi-Enko), Yang Kuange, Huang Miangong (黃綿公, Oeij Biankong), Lin Handan, Huang Jige, and Chen Baoge. When he complained that he was harassed by the 'disrespectful, impertinent, and seditious behaviour' of Poa Kontong, the High Government banished the latter temporarily to the island of Edam in the Bay of Batavia. He was released on 4 October 1791, after Wang Zhusheng had died.

In Qianlong 56, *xinhai* [辛亥], 1791, the company filled up all the canals that crossed the city perpendicularly. Originally the water of the small canals in the city could circulate. Now the authorities built a dam and tore down the bridges, and filled up all the transverse canals [that crossed the town in East-West direction] and turned them into streets. Only the canals connecting the four corners remained; via them water could flow into the sea.

In the first moon of this year, Lieutenant Lin Handan died and was buried at Gunung Sari. He was in office for three years. The king immediately appointed Wu Zuanxu (吳纘緒, Gouw Tjiansie) lieutenant, and also appointed Wu Zuanshou (吳纘綬) secretary.[310] (Zuanxu and Zuanshou were both sons of [former Lieutenant] Wu Panshui.)

In the ninth moon, Captain Wang Zhusheng died and was buried near the Japanese pavilion. He had served fifteen years as lieutenant and only five months as captain. He managed the administration firmly and resolutely. He took a clear position on what to love and what to hate. The people respected him and asked him to establish a rule that the wives of the Chinese must distinguish themselves as such, and should honour the dress of us Chinese. So, Wang Zhusheng agreed, but he had already died before he carried that out. The great king immediately promoted Huang Mianshe[311] to the position of captain and promoted Chen Kuanguan to the rank of lieutenant[312] and appointed Chen Binglang (陳炳郎, Tan Peengko) boedelmeester.

During a meeting of the Council of the Indies in the castle that year, a councilor called Shenmi (神密)[313] proposed that native soldiers from Solo and

---

310   Wu Zuanxu (Gouw Tjiansie) was appointed 8 February 1791. According to the resolution of 14 February, he was coexecutor of the inheritance of the late Captain Wang Zhusheng.

311   Huang Mianshe (黃綿舍, *aka* Huang Miangong, 黃綿公) was promoted on 11 October 1791 and formally installed on 15 October 1791. On 27 December 1800, he sent a request to the High Government asking to be dismissed on account of his advanced age. He cited that he had served as boedelmeester from 1 June 1778 until 26 November 1784 and had been appointed lieutenant on 26 November 1784. He had served as captain for nine years, but in recent years he had turned deaf. Because he had difficulty breathing, he was often incapacitated for several days on end. Consequently, he prayed to be honourably dismissed so that he could spend the rest of his life in peace and enjoy a rest. He also asked that his son be awarded the title and rank of former boedelmeester. This last request was not awarded 'because the son had not any claim to such an honour'. Captain Huang died in early 1803. See Hoetink, 'Chineesche officieren', 82–85.

312   Chen Kuanguan was also appointed on 8 February 1791.

313   Johannes Siberg (1740–1817), son-in-law of Governor General Alting, was extraordinary councilor of the Indies and colonel of the citizenry. He was governor general from 1801 to 1805. The story that he would have paid the troops from Mataram from his own purse is

Mataram should help the company guard the territory of Batavia. The military expenditures for these soldiers amounted to too great a sum, so the other councilors had doubts about this. Therefore, they auctioned off Shenmi's household items, and because it was not enough they also auctioned off his son's goods. Shenmi thereupon sent a memorial to the sovereign in the mother country expressing his wish that a commissioner be delegated to Batavia to investigate who was right or wrong.[314]

Originally, all the hiring of Chinese crews for the Company's ships was controlled by the Chinese captain, but by 1784, all this business came under the control of Chen Peisheng. After Peisheng had died, his younger brother Chen Kenshi (陳墾使) continued to manage. Later on he drew up a contract and made Chen Yelang (陳燁郎) act as his agent to manage these affairs; but within a year Chen Kenshi had died, and Lieutenant Wu Zuanxu petitioned the authorities that he might walk away with control over all those matters. Yet all these fellows who contracted the hiring of Chinese crews for the Company ships acted cruelly and harshly. Although they made a lot of profit, they all remained without children. Very strange! This should be taken as a warning!

In the twelfth moon of Qianlong 57, *renzi* [壬子], February 1792, Lieutenant Chen Kuanguan died, and his coffin was transported to Semarang. ~ *Where was Chen Kuanguan's actual home? This should be looked into!* ~

The king thereupon appointed Lin Zhangsheng in his place, and appointed Huang Dongguan (黃董觀) boedelmeester.[315] In the seventh moon, Lieutenant Chen Baoge (陳報哥, Tan Poko) died and was buried at Gunung Sari. He had served two years as lieutenant. The king immediately promoted Chen Binglang lieutenant and appointed Dai Hongge (戴弘哥, Tee Honko) boedelmeester.[316]

One night this year, an island called Pulau Lambat (浮羅南抹) was robbed by pirates, who killed a Dutchman and his whole family and freed more than ten criminals. They also robbed another island called Pulau Dunlao (浮羅敦唠) where they killed three Chinese and took their possessions, cows, and horses, loading all of them aboard their ships and sailing away.

---

unfounded. Nor did he ask for the dispatch of commissioners general. These gentlemen, S.C. Nederburgh and S.H. Frijkenius, were appointed by the Gentlemen XVII on 23 May 1791 to investigate and redress abuses on the Cape of Good Hope and Java.

314 In reality, nothing like this happened.
315 Boedelmeester Lin Zhangsheng (林長生, Lim Tiangseeng) was appointed lieutenant on 12 March 1792.
316 Boedelmeester Chen Binglang (陳炳哥, Tan Peengko) was appointed lieutenant on 13 November 1792.

When the authorities heard about this they did not know what to do.[317] In the tenth moon, a VOC ship with a cargo of rice for Ceylon caught fire in the roadstead and burned out. The authorities also informed all Chinese and natives in town who possessed one thousand guilders to pay 2 percent—that is, twenty guilders—to the company. The authorities authorised the captain to manage these affairs and settle the accounts high and low according to this rule. The extracted money was called 'Relief for the treasury of the company'.[318]

There was a water-powered sawmill outside the city at Jiku (積古). It was used for sawing the company's timber. This year it was also put up for sale. All the very old trees standing in the town were cut down for unknown reasons. This year the company also put up for auction a new tax farm for textiles. All the incoming and outgoing textiles from the so-called Western quarters [*Wester kwartieren*, namely, the Indian subcontinent] had to pay taxes to the tax farmer.[319] The personnel at the *boom* should not interfere.

There also was a Dutchman called Duurkoop, a sugar mill owner at Tanjung, who died this year. There were about two thousand male and female slaves at the sugar mill. His agent wanted to take them all into town to auction them off. Among them were forty to fifty strong slaves who banded together to resist. They killed his accountant and the foreman, and ran away and hid in the mountain forest.[320] They plotted to cause trouble. When the Company heard about this, a commissioner was sent with more than a thousand Muslim soldiers and more than a hundred Dutch soldiers to go into the mountains to capture them. But they [the slaves] refused to obey. Therefore, the Company that very night brought out four cannons to exterminate them. But the commissioner felt compassion and asked the authorities to give him some more time. He planned to catch them alive by a delaying tactic. The virtue of Heaven caring for people's life was not violated. Afterwards, more than half of the runaway slaves were captured, and were henceforth put up for sale in town.

At the time, most of the rich Dutchmen and Chinese and big merchants did not dare to buy them, because they feared that among them there were still people who had the evil intention of waging another rebellion.

[Here the Liem manuscript stops.]

---

317 On 26 January 1793, already measures had been taken against the increase of piracy on Java's Northeast coast. See *Plakaatboek*, 11.500.
318 This was the so-called *Liberale gift*, which was levied on 8 November 1791. De Jonge, *Opkomst*, 12.308–309.
319 19 and 28 February 1793, *Plakaatboek*, 11.512, 521.
320 J.A. Duurkoop. See De Haan, *Oud Batavia*, 701.

On the twenty-fourth day of the first moon of Qianlong 58, *guichou* [癸丑], 5 March 1793, a big English chief came to Batavia.[321] Batavia's Great King Alting sent two councilors to the English ship and invited the English headman to land and enter the castle. The Englishman did not want to move, but it so happened that the sovereign in the mother country celebrated his birthday two or three days later, so on 8 March the king and the councilors went together to the castle and received the English chief. The English stayed at Batavia a bit longer than half a month before they hoisted their sails and went away.

But, in fact, this chief had prepared presents because they were on their way to China on a tribute mission to our emperor. Only when a junk arrived at Batavia at the end of this year did we understand why and how. The English brought along two carriages, one for the winter and one for the summer, and a celestial globe. They had mounted on it precious stones as in the shape of the sun and moon, and with pearls depicting the stars. The carriages had doors and windows big enough so that one could sit inside, and a carpet of golden thread large enough to fit in the imperial palace. There also was a comfortable chair with a machine inside whereby one could move the chairs left and right without anyone's help. Most ingenious! But because the British behaved insolently at the meeting with the emperor, they did not meet the emperor's sense of decorum, so they were cold-shouldered and treated with only ritual ceremony.

On the twenty-first day of the seventh moon, there was a partial solar eclipse, and afterwards the sky turned clear again. One day, two Dutch ships intended to sail to Ceylon but, arriving at Boximen (勃系門, Sunda Strait),[322] [and] one of them was captured by a French ship. The Company immediately fitted out five warships; on every ship there were forty Chinese together with the Dutch crew members. They chased them but were not able to catch up with the captured ship. Therefore, to avoid later troubles, the king issued an edict that if anybody met with Frenchmen henceforth, he had license to kill them.

Moreover, a ship belonging to Commissioner Rongqili (榮訖力) was captured by the French when it was halfway home from Surat. Together with two Chinese, the captain returned on a little boat to Batavia to report about this. On the twenty-second day of the eighth moon, 26 September, the commander

---

321 This refers to the Earl of Macartney, the first envoy to China who was on his way to the Middle Kingdom aboard HMS *Lion*. J.L. Cranmer-Byng, ed., *An Embassy to China: Being the Journal Kept by Lord Macartney during His Embassy to the Emperor Ch'ien-lung, 1793–1794* (London: Longmans, 1962).
322 See *Plakaatboek*, 11.556.

at Banten sent a missive to Batavia saying that four French ships had already arrived at Banten preparing to attack.

The Company immediately proclaimed that the Dutch military officers and the Chinese captain should prepare their weapons for a fight if it was necessary.

In addition to this, on the ninth of September Councilor Suqipo (速訖潑) died at his mansion at Pasar Senen.[323] On the second of October, Captain Huang Mianguang heard from a Hakka called Chen Xiuyi (陳秀義) that two Hainanese pirates were grouping together with Chinese in the mountains, though he did not know what they were up to. Captain Huang Mianguang reported this to the king, who immediately ordered Commissioner Rongqili to go to that place to investigate the actual situation. The commissioner at once invited Lieutenant Lin Zhangsheng to go to Waiwuluo (外勿洛) to make inquiries, but they were unable to find these two people. Later they were caught in an opium den in town, but not all their followers had been arrested yet.

On the eighth [day] of that same moon, Rongqili went again in the company of Lieutenants Wu Zuanxu and Lin Zhangsheng to Ninggangbu (寧崗蔀) to seize the remaining followers of the Hainanese pirates. They captured Liu Yasi (劉亞四) and Liu Yaqi (劉亞七) on the spot and handed them over to the authorities to deal with them. After they had been interrogated about the reason [they were hiding in the mountains], they said that they were worried and that they especially feared that the native mountain robbers would plunder them. They had therefore collected people and put up palisades around them to avoid danger. They had never even dared do evil.

On the ninth day of the tenth moon, 12 November, the authorities ordered the two Liu's to swear at the Chinese temple that they would not dare do anything evil or misbehave, and to implore the Company not to cast blame on them. If they did that, the Company would approve their request and release them.

That month, Chen Shunguang and all the Chinese officers sent a petition to the authorities asking to be issued guns to ward off robbers. The authorities approved and each officer was provided with twelve men and weapons.

On the twelfth day of the twelfth moon, a Thursday, Lieutenant Wu Zuanxu was promoted to lead the armed Chinese to the square in front of the Guanyinting to train them in the use of guns, and later to stand in formation and parade. The younger brother of Wu Zuanxu, Secretary Wu Zuanshou, formed the rearguard. All the way from the Chinese quarter (*Chinesche kamp*) they marched through the city to the residence of Captain Huang Mianguang,

---

323 Hendrick van Stockum.

where they saluted him with three volleys in the air. Afterwards they disbanded and all returned home to their own homes.

On the twelfth day of the eleventh moon, it was heard that the inspectors from the mother country had already arrived at Boximen (Sunda Strait). On the fourteenth they landed at Batavia.[324] People of all kinds went to welcome them properly dressed in a very ceremonious manner, as if they were receiving the sovereign of the mother country. When their ship arrived in the roadstead, the great king ordered all the ships anchored there to salute with their cannon to honor the inspectors upon their landing in Tong'ankou. The great king, the councilors, and all the officers together came out of the town to welcome the inspectors inside Batavia Castle, where a great banquet was set up with food and drink. He ordered the Dutch soldiers to stand in files on both sides as guards and to fire the cannons on the walls. The authorities also ordered the black devils [Mardijkers] and the Gaoshe [高奢, people from the Coromandel coast] to stand watch at the factory, and ordered the Chinese captains and lieutenants to collect more than a hundred colourful banners in front of the town hall to welcome them.

Outside the Large South Gate, the native soldiers stood on both sides aligned with long peaks all the way to Jaga Monyet. Such spectacular display was truly rare then. Also, on the twenty-eighth day of the same month, the inspectors brought the royal edict to Batavia Castle and proclaimed the appointment of Ban Laomi (班嘮嘧), great secretary of the factory, to serve as governor of Ambon,[325] and Maoge (貓格), Xinxi (新禧), Lun (倫), Baolao (報勞), Wan Linmeide (萬林媚德), Silimaozai's (泗里貓仔, Surabaya) Bei (杯), Meise (美色) and Geshashi (葛殺氏)—altogether eight people—to serve as councilors of the Indies.[326]

The poll tax of the Chinese was originally fixed at nineteen *fanams*. That year Captain Huang Mianguang petitioned [the Company] saying that the Chinese were poor and could not bear that tax. He begged for an amnesty

---

324 Commissioners General Mr. S.C. Nederburgh and S.H. Frijkenius arrived in Batavia on 15 November 1795.

325 Alexander Cornabé. See *Naamboek van den Hoog Edelen Gestrengen Heeren Commissarissen Generaal over geheel Nederlandsch Indië en Cabo de Goede Hoop, item van den Wel-Edelen Heeren der Hoge Indiasche Regeering zo tot, als buiten Batavia* (Batavia: Pieter van Geemen, 1786), 63.

326 Ibid., 12. The councilors' Chinese names seem to represent only surnames and are difficult to identify: Johannes Siberg, Adriaan de Bock (Maoge, Ba-keh), Jan Hendrik Wiegerman, Arnoldus Constantijn Mom (Bei, Poe?), Coenraad Martin Neun (Lun), Willem Vincent Helvetius van Riemsdijk (Wan Linmeide, Ban Lim-mi-tek), Godfried Christoffel Fetmenger, and Albertus Henricus Wiese (Meise, Bi-sek).

and a reduction of the tax. The great king approved and thereupon the poll tax was set at only 7.5 *fanams* per month—and 20 *fanams* per year in upland areas—and [collection of] all this was to be publicly auctioned. Furthermore, the *shahbandar* toll farms would also be taken back and publicly farmed out this year.[327]

> *John Chinaman comments*: The reduction of the payment of the poll tax was a favour for the poor. All this shows how, thanks to Captain Huang Mianguang's thoughtfulness, the king felt urged to spread his benefits to the people. Compared with him, shouldn't those stupid leaders of people die of shame?

That year the authorities proclaimed that a more than 500-year-old inscription had been found on a wall in France. The French king had ordered the stone slab taken down from the old wall. A Hebrew text was written on it in golden letters. Nobody could understand it. So the stone with the inscription was sent to England because there was a Jewish rabbi who could profoundly understand this text. He then explained the various things from this inscription and wrote them down and transmitted them as follows:

> In 1790, the French people plot to harm their king. Moreover, when the present Pope will die, there will be no successor.
> In 1791, the kings of the neighbouring countries of France will engage in a great war with the king of France.
> In 1792, these kings continue to fight hard, without end.
> In 1793, all the kings will continue to fight at other places resulting in many casualties.
> In 1794, the French will not honour the laws, and their behaviour will subsequently be in great chaos.
> In 1795, all the kings will be meted out a big punishment.

---

327   12 December 1793. See *Plakaatboek*, 12.615–19. In reaction to complaints by Chen Shuige (Tan Soey Ko), the farmer of the Chinese poll tax, Governor General Alting had ordered the Chinese captain and lieutenant to investigate why proceeds from this tax had dramatically declined. They reported that the number of Chinese in Batavia had decreased due to high mortality, the smaller number of newcomers from China, and the migration of many citizens from Batavia to the Ommelanden. It was decided to lower the tax from thirty-eight *stuivers* to fifteen *stuivers* a month. All Chinese farmers were exempt from the tax.

In 1796, both on land or at sea the war casualties will heap up even more.

In 1797, in the Jewish book Namo Xiqi (南無西訖), the [Book of Ezekiel; chapter 39], it is written that there will appear a Gog of the land of Magog who will engage in a big fight with the people of all kinds in the world. Nobody can resist him.

In 1798, all the countries of the world will fight with each other because they want to divide the world.

In 1799, the descendants of King Louis [of France] will receive the lawful power from Heaven and wipe out Gog from Magog.

In 1800, the peoples of all kinds in the world (各色人) will return in the fold of one government, and will all get along like brothers, be in accord with customs and laws, and hold in awe and veneration Heaven's will.[328]

In Qianlong 59, *jiayin* [甲寅], 1794, the government of Batavia prepared tributary presents and dispatched Councilor [Isaac] Titsingh in the company of the former supercargo of the Canton office [Andreas Everardus] Van Braam to go to China to bring tribute to the emperor. After their arrival in Guangzhou, they informed the local governor, who quickly sent a memorial to the emperor, who issued an imperial edict that they could proceed to Beijing to receive an audience with the emperor. They immediately were given an official title and went to Beijing. After they had been taught at the Board of Ritual how to practice the [obligatory] rituals, they were escorted to the [palace] for the audience.

Our emperor said China is unified and peaceful, majestic and magnificent, and he asked, 'Why can't you people from France and Holland who originally belong to the same trunk, be on good terms with each other, and why are you fighting each other incessantly?' The envoys answered in a polished and reverential and polite manner, to the satisfaction of the emperor. He praised Holland as a country that understands ceremony. 'Although this tribute embassy came from Batavia, and was not sent by the sovereign, still we can see that they use sage people!'

Thereupon when they returned home, the emperor ordered presents given to them in exchange and ordered all the local mandarins and military officers outside the capital where the envoys would pass to treat them with the utmost ceremony. Councilor Titsingh brought the presents from the emperor from

---

328 This commentary on contemporary global politics and the accompanying prophecy clearly refer to the French revolution, the beheading of King Louis XVI, and the emergence of Napoleon (Gog of Magog). The land of Gog and Magog and its people represented the chaos beyond civilisation.

Canton back to the mother country. Van Braam returned to Batavia to report on the completion of their task.

There was at the time a certain Zheng Chunguan (鄭春觀), born and raised in Batavia, who made a living using his big mouth. He was very good at planning strange tricks. He just trusted on his luck and his big mouth; there was nothing that he could not do. Sporting his carriage and clothing, he would hang out with the Dutch, but he was in debt to them many times over. He lived extravagantly for several decades; he did not even wink at the elders and betters of his own [Chinese] kind. Most of the rich Tang merchants had been persecuted and insulted by him. All the officers often wanted to indict him but were unable to do anything.

But now Chen Shunguang was being persecuted and his house was sealed up. Talking wildly, Zheng Chunguan said he would also continue to sue Shunguang's son [Boedelmeester] Chen Guosheng (陳果生).

As a result, Chen Shunguang exploded in rage, and not caring how much it would cost him, he undertook to purchase Zheng Chunguan's outstanding debts and bought them all up and thereupon sued him in turn. Now Zheng Chunguan could no longer protect himself.

Thereupon he gave his priceless objects and valuables big and small to his mother and wife to hide them. The remainder of his goods he moved to other places to be hidden. A large carved Buddha statue he hid underground, his house gods were moved elsewhere to be venerated. All alone, he asked to be allowed into the *miskin* (poorhouse), and he entered into a lawsuit with Chen Shunguang to contest him.

Chen Shunguang however kept his composure and secretly colluded with the Chinese officers and rich merchants and petitioned the great king, accusing Zheng Chunguan of his crimes and exposing the fact that he had hidden his valuables.

Thereupon they [the authorities] immediately searched for the hidden objects, and when these had been found they were auctioned off. When the statue was dug up, it was already missing its hands and feet. The authorities rendered a judgement. Because she had hidden objects, his mother was banished to the island of Dianmayu (點馬嶼, Pulau Damar)[329] for life. Zheng Chunguan and his wife were both exiled to Ceylon for life, without the possibility of return. He left only a young, blameless son in Batavia to continue his family's name. But after the boy had grown up, he died of swollen legs. Zheng Chunguan's family had no offspring evermore.

---

329 Pulau Damar is a remote island in the Banda Sea.

John Chinaman comments: Chen Shunguang has the highest reputation among the great merchants of the Batavian Chinese. He is a millionaire; his words carry enormous weight. High and low alike look up to him and respect him. Zheng Chunguang relied only on luck. He had a mouth as big as the barrel of a cannon. And by throwing eggs and stones he dared insult a great, rich merchant and persecuted him until he enraged Chen Shunguang. He was toppled in an instant. In the wink of an eye he became destitute and homeless. This was all because Zheng Chunguan darted like a moth to the flame. He brought his final misfortune upon himself. The Heavenly principles are clear and transparent. If you had not accumulated evil, you would not have hurt yourself.

This is directed at you, Zheng Chunguan! Because this Zheng Chunguan had long been leading a luxurious life and insulting lots of people, if he had not crossed Chen Shunguang, others would not have been able to do anything. If Chen Shunguang had not been thrown into a rage, then he would not necessarily have hit him. This really is a turn of destiny that they were made into opponents. Evil rebounds on wicked people. This Zheng Chun brought guilt upon himself and invited Chen Shunguang's punishment on him. But although for his own part Chen Shunguang spent a fortune, he in fact got rid of an evil for the people. That is his great achievement. Evil people are punished by Heaven.

Qianlong 60, *yimao* [乙卯]**, 1795,** our Chinese emperor abdicated. The title of the new emperor is Jiaqing [嘉慶].

The first year of Jiaqing [嘉慶], *bingchen*[丙辰]**, 1796.**

PART 3

Accompanying Texts

∴

CHAPTER 1

Brief Account of Galaba (噶喇吧紀略), by Cheng Xunwo (程遜我)

The natives call the coconut *galaba* (噶喇吧, *kelapa*). Since the Xuande [宣德] period of the Ming dynasty, when the eunuch Wang Sanbao (王三保)[1] descended to the Western Ocean, we Chinese call the place this, because there are many coconut trees. The Javanese people call it Jakatra (二噶礁喇), the Dutch people call it Batavia (目兜予, Betawi), so these names do not sound the same.

The lands of the Southern Ocean, all are countries, regions and islands surrounded by water. The towns are protected by walls and ditches, and well defended, but the one that controls all the foreign countries is Galaba of the Dutch, which can be called the most strategic one. In southern direction there are volcanoes, but to west, north, and east this country borders on the sea. The regions to the west are Banten, Palembang, Malacca, Ceylon, the Cape of Good Hope, and Aceh. Those to the east are Cirebon, Tegal, Pekalongan, Semarang, Gresik, Surabaya, Rembang, Banjarmasin, Makassar, Timor, Bima, Kupang, Banda, [and] Ternate. Their populations are all different from each other. They are all separated from each other by the sea, the farthest distance being more than ten thousand *li* (里), and all these places are under Dutch control.

The might and virtue of our dynasty extends in the four directions, the people from far away obey. The imperial decrees do not prohibit trading with them. Therefore the people from Zhangzhou, Quanzhou, Chaozhou, and Guangzhou vie with each other to go there considering how to meet the needs for commodities such things as food and drink, clothes, utensils and medicines (for instance, tea), Zhangzhou tobacco, silk socks, silk threads, flowered satin, silk ribbons, paper, porcelain, copper pots, *radix cyathulae*, longanfruit (龍眼), dry persimmon, Chinese olive, flour, ginseng, china root, and other medicines.

All people bring these commodities [to the Nanyang] for making a profit and look for the local products, for example, pepper, sappan wood, ebony, incense, benzoin, lignum aloes, sandalwood, ripe gharu (束香), *shuxiang*,

---

1 Wang Sanbao (王三保) refers to Wang Jinghong (王景弘) who was a eunuch of the Ming dynasty and vice-envoy of Zheng He's seven voyages to the Western Seas during the early of the 15th century.

gharu-wood (沉香), kyara wood (奇楠), camphor, white rattan, sleeping mats, elephant tusks, rhinoceros horns, deer sinews, bird's nests, trepang [bêche-de-mer], white sugar, sugar cubes, coconuts, betel nuts, lead, tin, pearls, diamonds, western linen, woollen cloth, flannels, bombazines, sulphur, opium, clove, nutmeg, wine, brandy, sago, peacock feathers, parrots and so on.

They buy them all up for making a profit. But those who are wealthy hoist the sails and set out and return triumphantly beating their drums. Those without means remain there. Although there are who have struck it rich, many forget about their home town, make a living, and sire children. Their number amounts to no less than 100,000 people.

When I was about twenty years old, I thought of clearing the debts of my father and braved the terrible cold of winter, and sailed the sea with the northern wind in southern directions, and with the Paracels (七洲) behind me, passed by Cochin (交趾, Tonkin), arrived at Champa, and from there, successively passing by the ports of Cambodia and Siam, we arrived in the Tioman Sea, from which emerge the Changyao (長腰, Bintan Is.) and Sow Head Mountains (Selayar Is.), and then arrived at a narrow sea strait, with many trees growing out of the water on both sides; the strait is three to four *li* wide. Close to the west it is shallow and muddy, on the eastern side it is deeper but with stones. The crew sounded the depth, with six or seven fathoms the ship could pass.

After three days of sailing we left the Narrow Strait [Bangka Strait] and arrived at Palembang. The Dutch use this place to search the Chinese vessels that are coming in and out. Thereupon we passed the Sanli Sea (三立洋)[2] and arrived at Wang Yu (王嶼, Pulau Onrust) with its windmills, Jiaban Island (甲版嶼, Pulau Kapal), Black Devils Island, Grassy Island, [and] White Island. They are scattered like stars all over the sky; they are a table in front of Batavia. Dingjiaolan (丁腳蘭, Tangerang), a sandbank on the west, and Lugutou (魯古頭, Coral Point), on the east, are like wings on both sides. When calculated from the north, the total distance is in all 240 *geng* (更). (One *geng* is 50 *li*).[3] If calculated over land, then this would amount to 12,000 *li*. Counted on my fingers, the voyage did not take more than thirty days.

The weather is burning hot, the nights are very short. The weather is not at all like China. Because the water flows out in a southerly direction, the land is low, the northern polar star has sunk below [the horizon]—all the stars sink below the horizon. The ancient sages say that the stars disappear below 36 degrees. This can be understood on the basis of this, and the southern polar star

---

2 The waters between Western Java, Sumatra, and Banka.
3 2 *li* equals 1 kilometre. Consequently 1 *geng* equals about 25 kilometres.

becomes visible. Therefore, the cold and the heat of winter and summer, and the length or the night and day, are all opposite to China.

All year long it is not cold; only during the sixth moon is it a little fresher. After the eighth moon the spring atmosphere begins. From the tenth until the end of the twelfth month the rain falls down without interruption. In the first moon, it is half rain and sun. From the second to the eighth month it is often dry. When you enter the roadstead, warships encircle the outer side. The merchant ships gather inside, patrol vessels sail around.

From the Tong'an (桶岸) canal one can cross over to Batavia. Very many people live on the western bank, and all kinds of trades are carried out there. On the eastern bank, the castle and the grasslands for the Dutch cattle are connected to each other; the access ways are forbidden for Chinese. If you enter from the western bank, near the North Gate there is a turning bridge office for inspection of the evasion of taxes. The bridge is opened for ships to go in and out. At night, the turning bridge is closed. At the side stands a water spy tower.[4] It is more than ten fathoms high, for observing the ships that are coming from afar. [From it one] can look over a distance of 300 *li*. This is the strategic passageway of the North Gate.

Inside the town there are many buildings. The streets are straight and the squares are wide. The middle of the street for horse and wagon is a bit elevated, the surface is covered with *lugushi* (魯古石, coral stone), thick like a spiral shell or a finger so that there is no dust on the street. On either side, the streets are paved with bricks for the people to walk on. Below the eaves of the roof a small ditch covered with planks is built to conduct the water flow. The markets are prosperous. The water of Shengmu Gang (聖墓港, Blandongan) flows from the south.[5] The water of Mangga Dua comes from the southeast, the Angke River comes from the southwest, and creating a confluence at the Small South Gate [Pintu Kecil], and from there flows northwards through the city. From the East Gate [Rotterdammerpoort] a canal connects with Ancol, and from the West Gate another canal connects Crocodile Pond (鱷仔潭). Together with the water from Mangga Dua it reaches to the southeast of the town, and divides into another canal, which is dug around the town. All these waters connect again at the North Gate and flow into the sea.

At the place where the canal narrows south of the city, a sluice has been built, the city wall saddles over it. North of the city the water surface is several fathoms wide, and in the middle of the town there are two bridges that span the river centre. The northern bridge is called the Weigh-House

---

4 This tower, the Uitkijk ['Look out'] still overlooks Pasar Ikan.
5 The canal from Klenteng (Tangerang) to Blandongan.

(秤官亭, *waag*), bearing the inscription *Haiguo Quanheng* (海國權衡), that is, 'The weight and balance of the sea countries'. A toll of 2 percent is levied apart from the tolls on rice, wine, and sugar resulting every year in more than 100,000 *liang* (兩), ounce, or tael, of silver].

The south bridge is placed next to a redoubt, big cannons cover the four directions. Within the walls many canals have been dug. Three horizontal canals and also three vertical ones connect with the big port. The ships can navigate in the canals; the bridges span them.

The people live in the eastern part of town; north of the town is the so-called Wangcheng (王城, King's Castle, Batavia Castle).

When the Dutch ships came to Batavia to trade in the past, they hoodwinked the Javanese headman, wishing to rent a piece of land as big as a cow hide. He gave permission, but the Dutch sliced the cowhide into fine strips and connected them into the surface area of the castle; later they captured Java, they made it into the palace of the king.[6]

Tuku kou (土庫口) is south of the castle, where the Dutch live. Pecinan (八芝蘭) is the Chinese quarter; Prinsenstraat (爵仔街) is where many Chinese silversmiths live. Pasar Gelap (暗澗) is where Chinese shops are situated, especially the evening market. Close to the port are the horse stables and gambling houses. Puzai (圃仔, Tanah Lapang) is another place where Chinese live. The gate of the *bicara* building (*Stadhuis*), the Dutch law court has a large square. The Dutch carry out the death sentence here. The Dutch live everywhere inside Pintu Besar and at the eastern edge of the city.

In the western part of the town there is Boom Street (泊面街); many Dutchmen live there. In Gangzaiwei (港仔尾, 'the tail of the port') there are many native houses rented out to the Chinese junks for use as warehouse. Mi Jian (米澗) is the rice market, where there is a rice official. To its side there are many houses of the Chinese. Then there is the Zao Jian (蚤澗), the flea market where fish is sold and a market official is stationed. Wan Jie (碗街, Porceleinmarkt), at the street crossing, is all inhabited by the Chinese; this is where most traders are. Zhushuxia (竹樹下, 'under the bamboos') is connected with Pintu Kecil; many Dutchmen live here.

If you leave the East and West Gates, both of which are at a distance of more than 10 *li* from the sea, you end up in the west at the Bridge Three (三角橋, Jambatan Tiga) and Crocodile Pond, and in an eastern direction at the Toa Pe Kong (大伯公) Temple at Ancol (This is the Tudigong Temple of the Chinese).

---

6 The same story is told in the *Kai Ba Lidai Shiji*. See note 18, p. 55.

Only outside the [large] South Gate and Small South Gate do people [of different ethnicities] live together. The plain and wooded hills vary a bit in height. This is where the Chinese and the natives live together. Close to town, merchants live at Ashenjiao (森腳, Asenka), Zhonggangzai (中港仔, Tongkangan), Bachaguan (八茶礶, Patekoan), Hongxitou (洪溪頭, Angke), Nianliujian (廿六間, Jilakien)—all outside the Small South Gate (Pintu Kecil). At Banjiaojian (班蕉澗, Pancoran), the water from the mountains comes from afar, but it is saved in a reservoir, and an aqueduct leads the water from above to below. The natives come to get the water with their ships. The people of Batavia all drink this water. At the side, there is a water-powered sawmill. Wenjiaolai (蚊茭賴, Mangga Dua) and Pancoran are outside the Large South Gate. These are the places where goods are stored and traded, just like at the five cities [in China]. Around the city is the countryside like Damojiao (大末腳, Mauk). To its side are the public cemetery and the Bao'en Si (報恩寺, Bao'en Temple, where Guanyin is venerated).

Then there are Jiaobo (茭泊, Depok), Rundayang (閏達洋, Kampong Sunter), Helanying (荷蘭營, the Dutch camp], Gandongxu (干冬墟, Meester Cornelis), Wangjiaosi (望茭寺, Bekasi), Shi'er Gao Di (十二高地, 'The Twelve Highlands'), Zhihe Ashen (芝荷阿森, Cisau, near Tangerang), Benlu Zouma (奔鹿走馬, Serong and Tjiomas), all in the south. Furthermore, there are Dingjiaolan (Tangerang), located at the west side, and Lugutou (Coral Point), which is located to the east, and so on. At all these places, sugar mills have been established. In the sugar mills there are the *budie* (廍爹, Potia) millers, who run the mill; *caifu* (財副, managers), who take care of the books and the apparatus; and the *manlü* (蠻律, mandors), who supervise the workers.

Moreover, there are pleasure gardens and ponds of the high officials and rich merchants scattered here and there. They come on Sunday to relax at these places. Every seven days there is worship; they do not engage in business, but enjoy themselves. Those who come by road use carriages; these carriages have four wheels and the cabin hangs on both sides in two leather straps, and [they are drawn by] precious horses of the same colour and strength, with gilded decorations. Those who come over the water travel in decorated ships and are accompanied by pipes and drums. In the gardens you can see peacocks showing their tails, parrots that have learned to speak, roses that produce sent, elixir of life (仙丹, *xiandan*) flowers bursting in glorious bloom, coconut trees towering to the skies, jackfruit in clusters on the trees, [and] enjoy drinking. All this gladdens the heart while making poems; it truly gives one great pleasure!

But I felt apprehensive about being able to stay here long, because all these kinds of natives are ferocious and tough. Swords, halberds, spears and guns, scare those who travel abroad. All the towns I have passed through are surrounded by ditches and forts and are all very strictly controlled and very severely checked. The guardsmen on clear and sunny days carry a rifle, but when it rains they hold a spear. They change watch every two hours without stopping; at night they do not rest.

They use self-striking clocks that chime at the hour. The Chinese midnight period is their one o'clock; daybreak is at five o'clock. When it is already twelve, then the afternoon starts. At six o'clock the evening begins. After nine o'clock the night watch begins and people cannot go out. All the sentry guards are stationed by their officer at their respective positions and every two hours they change the watches.

At the gate they place drawbridges; they are opened and closed at set times. At six in the morning, the castle hands out the keys to open the gates and lower the drawbridges. At six at night they hoist the bridge and close the gates, and return the keys to the castle.

If the passers-by want to cross, soldiers with weapons stand there like trees in line. Our Chinese live in peace and tranquillity, but when they see this scene, they shiver all over though it is not cold. When the law is handled too strictly, one should not run counter to its sharp edges. When we enter a country, we should ask after the dos and don'ts, how can we afford not knowing the laws one by one.

Here I give a survey of the ranking of their officials. The king is called *kapitein wu* (甲必丹勿, *kapitein mor*).[7] He holds the political power. The vice king [the director general] manages the finances. Their subordinates are called *zhima* (知禡, *dienaar*). The second king commands the forces and the horses. His subordinate is the *majoor* (馬腰). The law officials are called the heads of the *bicara* (嘧喳嘮, council); there are two [councils, i.e. of justice and of the aldermen] for the Dutch, and one [council/board of aldermen] for the Chinese and all kinds of natives.

The officer who deals with the incoming and outgoing ships is called *shahbandar* (沈萬達). He who supervises the maritime prohibitions is called the [*zee-*]*fiscaal* (美色葛). The one who supervises the hinterland affairs [Ommelanden] is called *commissaris* (公勃柵里); he who takes charge of the details in and outside the town is called *temenggong* (淡板公). Subservient to them there are those in charge of the money, pepper, iron, rice, wine, clothing. Everybody manages his own affairs; they cannot meddle in other's affairs. The *secretary* (諸葛礁) is the petty official in charge of writing. The *dashi* (達氏, *soldaat*) takes care of the deliveries. The *notaris* (梁礁) makes contracts and writes legal documents for others. The *gouverneur* (公班律) is the official who governs large regions. The *da beiluo* (大杯螺, chief factor) is in charge of small

---

7   From Portuguese "Capitão Mor", great chief.

places. The *kapitein* (甲必丹) is the head of the Chinese. Under him are two *luitenants* (雷珍蘭), and under them four more. Moreover as regards the manager of inheritances, the *boedelmeester* (撫直迷), every year one is chosen and he is replaced every three years.

All these officials are part of the administrative system and they are all based on the bureaucratic system of their country, which governs Batavia. Holland is situated in the northwest. By sea the voyage is three months.[8]

The Chinese Zhou Guangmei (周光美, Thebitsia) was good friend of Governor General Van Hoorn.[9] He has been to Holland and after he came back he told many details about it.

According to their law and discipline the throne is handed over to a worthy person. When the king dies, their officers high and low congregate and all write down their own opinion. Then they all scrutinize this together. The man with most prestige then takes the position. They use people according to their merits. Day by day they accumulate their achievements, from small to big. They venerate their ruler and are loyal to their superiors already for many generations. In fact, already more than 1,750 years!

When eating and drinking they all look up to heaven and pray. They sprinkle wine on the soil because the ten thousand things originate from heaven and earth. They bury people of their own family together and mark off the ground with a wall. They build the grave with bricks and cover it with a stone slab. On it is an iron ring; after somebody has died they stick a pole through the ring and lift it, and lower the coffin with a rope into the grave, and then cover it again and mark it with chalk. They build a temple in the middle. They call it a praying hall (禮拜). It is some twenty *zhang* (fathoms) high. Every seven days they gather together and read aloud the Bible. Their puberty rites and marriages they announce publicly because the origin of man is in the ancestors. Apart from this they have no sacrifices.

When they see the Chinese venerate statues made of mud and burn paper money they almost die of laughter. They don't care about evil deities. They make 366 (!) days into one year. Every month has thirty or thirty-one days. They have no intercalary month.

On the first day of every month of the Dutch calendar, the [Chinese] captain hoists a flag for three days on end to inform the people that they can purchase their residence permit [i.e. poll tax]. Ten days after the winter solstice is the beginning of the New Year. During the three days before the beginning of the New Year they auction all sorts of tax farms. The contractors must pay the taxes

---

8   This is rather optimistic. The average voyage took twice as long, i.e. six months.
9   See part 2, notes 95 and 119, p. 86 and 97.

for the first four months in advance. Ten days after 'Grain Fills',[10] they fire the big cannons.

In the past, Holland occupied Java on that day.[11] Since then, every year they fire the big cannons on top of the walls and those in the ships and the redoubts along the road. It does not matter how many hundred or thousand shots are fired one after the other on that day. When they have been fired, they again pour gunpowder in them and use earthen dummies to show their happiness and also because preparedness avoids peril. Although the first and fifteenth days of the Dutch month do not correspond with the full moon and the new moon, yet the solar terms have not the smallest deviation. This is also a manner to coordinate the right months and days.

Weights and measures are publicly proclaimed. Four times a year they mark them to unify them. If it [a weight] does not bear a mark, it cannot be used. When the marks are full, then the weight is cancelled and made again. This is the same as our ancient tradition of weights and measures.

Robbers and thieves must be punished with different punishments. In case of burglary the punishment is inserting the candle; that is, they put them on the *jiangjunzhu* (將軍柱, literally, the pile of the commander) with an iron stick from behind in the backbone, cut off eating and drinking, and let them die; or they bind them on a wooden bench and beat them dead with an iron stick. In the case of stolen goods, they hang the stolen goods around the neck of the thief, pull down his underclothes and lash him with split rattan until blood and flesh flow out, and heat up an iron stamp and brand him and exile him to another place.

He who kills somebody pays with his life with the original murder weapon. He who kills with a knife is knifed himself; he who kills with a gun is shot himself.

Adultery is punished with imprisonment. Those engaging in adultery with a Dutch or Chinese woman when they are found out are placed in prison, men and women in different locations. In the case of a slave girl, it is not punished.

Sodomy is punished by drowning. Young and old are each placed in a barrel, which is covered and closed up with nails so that they penetrate the inside. Then they are pushed over the road and finally drowned in the sea.

Incest is punished with castration. Insubordination is punished by cutting off a hand. Arsonists have another punishment: setting a house afire is punished with [a fine of] thirty *liang* (两, taels of silver). There is a punishment on

---

10 'Grain fills' (Xiaoman) is one of the year's twenty-four solar periods, and falls on May 20, 21 or 22.

11 Here the author refers to the occupation of Jayakarta in 1619. 30 May 1619 is considered the day of establishment of Batavia and was celebrated as such.

breaking the curfew at night. Those who are caught after nine o'clock without light or a light permit are fined eighteen *liang*. Those who have no money to pay are punished with the cat with seven tails.

There [also] is a punishment on those without a residence permit. A hawker who does not have a hawking permit is punished twelve *liang*. No matter what colour of skin he has, whoever does not possess a poll tax permit pays seven *liang* and two *qian* (錢).[12] The person who cannot pay up awaits flagellation with the big cat with seven tails.

Smuggling is prohibited. The Dutch government is called the *Compagnie* (公班衙; Malay: *Kompeni*). Cloves, betel nuts, clothes, and opium—everything that comes from the government—is all publicly auctioned. If someone is found out to be engaged in private trade, the smuggled goods are confiscated and the culprit is exiled.

Those who flee because of debts are punished. Those debtors who are caught when running away are chained and set to forced labour. Generally speaking, criminals are put in the big and the second black hole where they cannot see the sky, sun, and moon.

He who owes goods is taken prisoner, bound up, and put under arrest. He is not shackled, but he is kept inside and cannot go out. Every month he has to pay jail residence money of one *liang* and two *qian*. If he cannot return the debt completely in twenty-four months, the person to whom he owes the money will have to pay one *liang* and two *qian* a month and the debtor will be put in chains and set to forced labour.

Punishments are meted out throughout the four seasons. There is no rule for suspension or pardon [of punishment]. Alas!

The nets of the law are very strict, and yet cases of adultery and robbery resulting in death are following one upon the other. He who debauches another's wife or concubine will be killed upon discovery. When someone's wife or concubine has an illicit relation, [the adulterers] may plot against [the husband] and have him killed. In these cases the bed and home provide a motive for murder. If you are robbed you may be killed, but if you happen to run across an amuck maker than you can also die. When natives are angry and want to commit suicide and kill all people that they encounter, that is called *fanmu* (反目, amuck). If you see someone running amuck, you had better run away! There are a lot of lethal places beyond one's doors!

In Dutch law, if you are caught at the scene of the crime, even 10,000 pieces of gold will not reduce your punishment. If family members of the victim accuse you of murder, the chief justice investigates proofs, oaths, witnesses

---

12 A *qian* is a copper coin equal to 1/10 of a *liang*.

(削是, *xueshi*),[13] and the accused. The law does not bear that hapless people pay with their lives. Even if corpses are piling up outside the door, those within the house do not want to be involved. Therefore, it is not risky to kill people.

The *li* (禮, moral propriety) is maintained before anything happens. The law is executed after bad things have happened. The guiding principle of the Dutch is to aim for the enrichment of the country, and morality is not cared about. So, if husband and wife do not get well along with each other, then they order them to divorce. The official concerned makes the attestation of divorce. Thus, the husband is no husband and the wife is no wife.

If a father dies without a will, his son cannot receive the inheritance. In the event someone dies without a will, his or her belongings are seized and given to the hospital for the disabled and the orphans. In that case, the father is no father and the son is no son. They stash up tons of opium to trade it to the natives. This is how those above rob those below. They collect taxes on gambling; they establish gambling dens everywhere. This is nothing else than 'a ruler ripping off his own people'. Rich people without conscience enjoy themselves with prostitutes and this is not outlawed. This is leading people into lascivity. These slave girls for sale are cruising the streets in their several hundreds and are called *guili* (龜李, *kuli*). They are for hire, and those without self-respect take the opportunity to promote lascivious behaviour.

Because those in charge do not have the skill of good guidance, the common people don't feel shame in their hearts. Therefore, although their law can control the neighbourhoods close to the roadways, it has difficulty reaching the surrounding territory in all directions. Moreover, the Chinese captain is not good in his own conduct. In the beginning, the captain and the governor general held the right to decide on the life and death of the Chinese. Later, he [the captain] only collected the weigh-house taxes and the tax on the Chinese junks, and gave half of it to the governor general. Is this not oppressing one's own [people]?

In the beginning he was selected on his merits and worked together with the inner and outer city law officers (*temenggongs*], but later he acquired his position by bribing with his fortune and only managed everything for the governor general. He supplied all food and clothing. Now, on the contrary, he [the Chinese captain] is serving the *temenggongs*. Is this not a shame for one's own [people]?

Because the Dutch see that the Chinese daily increase in numbers, they gradually have come to despise them, and increasingly exploit them and extort them. They levy taxes on lumbering, on the sugar mills, on the arrack factories,

---

13   From Malay *saksi*.

and on the *warongs* (阿郎) (*dianpu* (店鋪, shops) in Chinese). If you want to have a theatre performance, then twelve *liang* must be paid for the floor space of the stage. As for the taxes that people must pay, there are such expenses as the monthly poll tax, amounting to nineteen *fanam* per month.[14] Then there is the tax for the new immigrants (新客, *xinke*). Although one may reside [here] for quite some time, one still has to pay the *commissaris* six *fanams*.

Then there is the sea pass; those who ship goods by water have to pay one *liang* and two *qian* a month. Besides this, one also has taxes on marriages and on burials. Both the marriage and death certificates cost 6 *liang*. Then there is the business tax. For edible goods and groceries one *fanam* per day; the tax for the lamp permit, used while walking at night; [and finally] the inland pass— those who go inland pay six *fanams* to the *commissaris*.

They even have permits for marriage and death, a marriage certificate costs 6 *liang*, a death certificate 6 *qian*. They rely on these taxes to make profit. The poor have no means to live. Therefore, those who have no permits are fined. Then there are those who run away with other people's goods. Then there are those who secretly buy smuggled goods. Here are those who rob when they see someone's wealthy; the rich do not examine their own behaviour. They vie with each other in lecherous behaviour in order to amuse themselves. This is a situation that inevitably meets doom.

When I arrived, I was a young man who did not know anybody. So, I wished to be hired by people for work. One day, I reached the mountains carrying a weapon to protect myself and I passed a thick forest where I saw the bones of dead people spread out. I could not stay there one day.

Afterwards I went to Semarang and thereupon Batavia. I made a living ploughing my tongue [teaching]. There often were people who invited me to marry their daughter. But I stuck to what my father had said when I left: 'You must remember that you can leave home because of poverty, but you cannot indulge in another pleasure place and forget your hometown and your duty!'

Within seven years' time, I had completely cleared the old debt [of my father] and returned in a relaxed manner. Two years later, in the year *wuwu* [戊午, 1738], I was invited by Mr. Zhou (周老夫子) from Xichang (西昌). At that time a friend of mine, Zeng Junbi (曾君弼), was still at Batavia. I wrote a letter to him inviting him over and told him: 'Batavia has a pestilential atmosphere without end. The *Qingque huanglong* (青雀黃龍) ship has already half gone down.[15] This is perhaps because Heaven hates that the Chinese live in Batavia. O, my friend, come back quickly!"

---

14 One *fanam* is equal to 3 *fen* (*qian*) and 5 *li*, or two Dutch *stuivers*.
15 'Fresh and green yellow dragon'.

In the autumn of *gengshen* [庚申, 1740] there were two narrow-minded people who could not bear the Dutch cruelties and headed for disaster by pushing for a rebellion. Thereupon, several tens of thousands of people, no matter [whether they were] good or bad, were all butchered. Among the people from Zhangzhou, Quanzhou, Chaozhou, and Guangzhou, fathers cry for their sons, brothers cry for their younger brothers, wives cry for their husbands. In every homestead, one can hear one's neighbours crying. Although the products of Batavia are abundant, the pearls, diamonds, agates, and corals are in no way enough to be placed in the mouths of the murdered people. Western linen, woollen cloth, flannels, bombazines are not enough to serve as shrouds for their bodies as big as whales. Cups of rhinoceros horn, chopsticks made of ivory, edible birds' nests, grape wines are not enough to make offerings to the enormous burial place. They died in vain facing the sharp swords, or wasted away in the mountains, or floated as drowned corpses in the sea.

I was fortunate to be in a situation to foresee this, but I commiserate with those who were unable to avoid the disaster. What a tragedy! Together with my friends, I went to Beijing to pay a visit to Mr. Cai Geshan [蔡葛山, *aka* Cai Xin (蔡新)]. When he heard that I had visited Batavia he asked me to write down my account. Thereupon I wrote this account to submit to him.

Supplement

When I was in Beijing, after I had composed the 'Brief Account of Galaba', I submitted it to Mr. Cai Geshan. Because its contents were not without lacunae, after my return home I wrote several supplementary notes and added them to the original text.

A Supplement on the Customs

Galaba originally belongs to Java, but later on it was occupied by the Dutch and Java and all the various natives belonging to it are also vassals of the Dutch. Because there are various people, each with different customs, therefore I must make three different supplements on their customs.

The Dutch

Dutch people have white faces, yellow eyes, and their noses are shaped like fish hooks. They don't grow beards and their hair is a bit red and about one foot long. They cut and arrange it in such a way that the tail is curled. But there are also those who have razed their hair, and wear a periwig made from the hair of a cow tail. If they marry a Serani woman, another type of black devil, their children also have black hair.[16]

Most Dutch women have a narrow waistline. When they are young, they put a bamboo corset around their waist, wide on the upper side and narrow below. After some time, it [the narrow waist] becomes natural. Their character is changeable, now fierce, then meek, so that most husbands fear their wives. If he has a wife, he does not dare to take a concubine. They often go for a walk arm in arm by moonlight. In the street they kiss each other, as if there was nobody around. When the husband dies, the widow marries immediately, as many deaths means as many marriages. She folds up the inheritances of her several husbands. Lusting for money, young lads marry old ladies, so that 'the old tree produces flowers'. Those who see it ridicule it.

The Dutch hat is made of felt with a flat top and round rim. They squeeze it in a triangular shape with their hand. When they meet they take it off for a polite greeting.

Their clothing is of different colours, but they wear black while mourning. Their upper and lower cloth is short, with many buttons on the breast. On the foreside of their jacket they have pockets to put away things. Their garments are all lined.

The points of their leather shoes have no indented profiles; their socks are made of silk, with the shape of the foot, so they are not wide. The women wear blue gauze covering their hair bun. They wear long dresses, tied at the waist, that reach the ground. They have silk stockings and woollen slippers, as if in the style of mandarins.

The Dutch like to live in storied houses; the windows are high and wide. On the outside they are made of glass and carved on the inside, allowing the light to pass through on both sides. The gate has one door which is cut into an upper and lower half. The walls are white and black, and in the four seasons change colour. Every week [the floors] are scrubbed with water. The interior of their house is clean, quiet and cool, how pleasant!

The Dutch invite guests or they let guests come by themselves. The host invites the guest to sit down by the table on which they lay a white [table]cloth; they also put white cloth [napkins] on the knees of the guests. Then they place delicious food, most of it roasted, there are various kinds of wine, every person has a dish and cup, and one spoon and a fork, [and], moreover, a spittoon, but I have not seen them spit in it—and furthermore an empty dish because one should not throw bones to the dogs.

---

16   Serani, Eurasian.

The Dutch are exceptionally ingenious. They make the quadrant, they plumb the depth [of the sea], they set the time by measuring the sun, they also have windmills and watermills for sawing wood, clocks that sound by themselves, and all those special skills. They construct houses and build ships with extraordinarily meticulous technical skill. When the ships reach the end of their service life, they scrap them and do not wait until they fall apart.

The Javanese
Java belongs to Holland, but the people, amounting to several hundred thousand, have established their country in Mataram. Yet Cirebon, Pekalongan, Tegal, Semarang, Surabaya, Lampong, Gresik, and Buitenzorg (Bogor) are all places that are controlled by the Dutch. In appearance, the Javanese look a bit like the Chinese, but their face is very dark. Their upper garments are short, reaching down to the waist. Below they wear a *doupeng*-like (斗蓬, cloak) cloth as a skirt. They call it *man* (襷).

The king is called *susuhunan* (顙孫蘭). He is assisted by the *adipatih* (二把致). The people pay one silver piece a year and no other taxes. They have the so-called tiger punishment. They order the prisoner to fight a tiger with a sword. If the prisoner wins, he is released; but if the tiger wins, he dies.

The year begins with a month, but there are no days. They set the calendar by observing the number of stars at night. Their local products—silver, rice, oil, tobacco, sugar, cotton, fish, salt, striped mats, white rattan, birds' nests—are sufficient to supply several regions. It is actually a wealthy country.

Various Barbarians
The various barbarians are all robbers who have been seized to be put on sale as slaves. There are also people among the Chinese who buy them. Those slaves who stay and are employed for a long time may accumulate some surplus, buy themselves free, and set up their own homestead. Their appearance is not the same. But the Malays are the best looking, close to the Chinese, and after them the Makassarese and Balinese. The Bacan, Keling, Bugis, Lingga, and the Bengalis are unbearably ugly. Their mood is also different from us people.

CHAPTER 2

Selections from the *Biography of Cai Xin* (蔡新傳)[1] and from *Historical Materials in the First Historical Archive of China Concerning the Debates about Banning the Overseas Trade to the Nanyang during the Qianlong Period*[2]

In the previous chapters, it was mentioned how discussions were held at the Chinese court as to how the trade with the Nanyang (南洋), and more specifically the trade with Batavia, should be dealt with in the aftermath of the massacre of 1740. The following report by Cai Xin and the three memorials to the throne by provincial and local military and civil officials throw light on the way in which information relevant to these issues was gathered in the coastal regions. They also show what solutions these officials proposed.

Particularly interesting are the references made to the wilful arrest of Chinese by Batavian authorities in the summer of 1740. On the proposal of the former governor of Ceylon (西壟, Xilong), Van Imhoff, Chinese were rather indiscriminately arrested with the intention of banishing them to Ceylon. Although frequent references can be found in Dutch sources about the banishment of Chinese criminals to Ceylon and the Cape of Good Hope, nowhere is it suggested that these exiles were enlisted in the local militia as discussed in the first three entries. These memorials stress that that the Chinese emperor need not have any strong feelings about the fate of the victims of the massacre because they should not be considered subjects but rather as disloyal people who in remaining abroad and creating families through marriages with local women ignored imperial orders. The author of the third memorial sings a different tune: he enumerates one by one why it should be unwise to impose a new ban on overseas trade to the Nanyang.

---

1 *Guangxu Zhangzhou Fu Zhi* (光緒漳州府志) chapter 33 *renwu* (人物) [biographies] 6.
2 Lu Jing (盧經) and Chen Yanping (陳燕平), eds. 'Qianlong nianjian yi jin Nanyang maoyi shiliao' (乾隆年間議禁南洋貿易史料) Historical Materials in the First Historical Archive Concerning the Debates about Banning the Overseas Trade to the Nanyang during the Qianlong Period], *Lishi Dang'an* [Historical Documents], (2002) 2. 23–35.

a) *A selection from the biography of Cai Xin.*

In Qianlong 6, the barbarians of Galaba (噶剌吧) murdered the Chinese merchants. The high officers of Fujian province memorialized to the throne about this asking to forbid the merchants to trade with the Nanyang and to persecute the Dutch, but no decision had yet been taken. Because he knew that Cai Xin cared about the economy, Sub-Chancellor of the Grand Secretariat Fang Bao (方苞) sent him a letter asking for advice.

Cai Xin then replied as follows: What happened in the Nanyang is truly wrong. But these Chinese merchants originally were disobedient to the law. Because they lived there for a long time at that place they put themselves beyond the pale. Although they are called Chinese, in fact they are not different from the various barbarians of that place. If we consider this, taking all the bearings on this case, it brings no damage to our civilisation.

More than one hundred junks sail [every year] to the Nanyang from Fujian and Guangdong. It costs about 10,000 *jin* (金) to build a big ship, and 4,000 to 5,000 *jin* for a small one. Once you forbid them to sail abroad, then all these ships will be useless. Then the people will lose 500,000 to 600,000 in investments. At ports for maritime trade like Xiamen (廈門) and Guangzhou (廣州) are stored commodities with a value of several millions. If you suddenly stop this commerce, then the businesses will certainly go bankrupt and the goods will be wasted. And the people will also lose several millions of savings.

Regarding the [overseas] shipping, a great number of poor people depend on it for a living. Once you stop it, the merchants have no capital, the farmers have no products. They will probably become destitute and homeless; innumerable people will lose their livelihood. This is the present problem. But after a few years the damage will be even greater. The regions of Fujian and Guangdong both use foreign money. If we count how much money comes in every year, it will amount to almost 10 million taels.

If you forbid it altogether, suddenly from now onwards not only will life become more difficult for the people day by day, but the national economy will also suffer a deficit. This is what I gravely worry about.

I think we do not need to stop the trade right now. But we should order officials to interview [the traders] when the ships come back and find out whether they [the Dutch] already have regrets about this, and [tell them] to be more attentive to the merchants. In that case, they [the Dutch] will not dare to harm the Chinese merchants. If so, why then should we punish them? In case they will even lightly bully them [the Chinese merchants] then we will just forbid the trade with Galaba. But we should still let our people go to other places such

SELECTIONS FROM THE BIOGRAPHY OF CAI XIN   221

as Cambodia (君代嗎, Jundaima), Sonkhla (宋腒勝), Johor (柔佛]) and Ligor (六昆).³

Therefore, the proposal to forbid the trade was not carried out.

b) *The Provincial Military Commander Wang Jun* (王郡) *of the Fujianese Naval Forces presents a memorial to the throne to report about his investigation into the affair of the massacre of the Han [Chinese] merchants in the country of Galaba. Qianlong 6, seventh moon, eleventh day [21 August 1741].*⁴

[23] Provincial Military Commander Wang Jun of the Fujianese Naval Forces sincerely presents a memorial to report about what he has heard about the situation in the country of Galaba [Batavia].

I am stationed in Xiamen, which on the inside is a thoroughfare of travelling merchants and on the outside connects with the overseas barbarians. To fulfil the tasks at the coastal border that the emperor has entrusted on me, I devote all my attention to the personal investigation of all business that comes and goes by ship.

According to my investigation, Galaba is the farthest place for overseas shipping, but the trade with Galaba is also the most prosperous. On the sea route, distance is measured by *geng* (amounting to 60 *li* per *geng*), and Galaba is 280 *geng* from Xiamen, that is, a distance of 18,800 *li*.⁵

That country is situated very far away. In the past, it did not present tribute. The merchants frequently go there and don't care about the risks due to its distance, because it is a place where very many goods are collected and traded with every country. Those who have gathered capital in abundance marry there and settle down, siring boys and girls. Generation upon generation they have increased to over ten thousand people, and although they are called Han people, in reality, over time they have become barbarians, the so-called locally born [*peranakan*].⁶ Since the ban on the Nanyang trade was rescinded

---

3 Three ports on the Malay Peninsula.
4 Lu Jing (盧經) and Chen Yanping (陳燕平), eds. 'Qianlong nianjian yi jin Nanyang maoyi shiliao' (乾隆年間議禁南洋貿易史料), Historical Materials in the First Historical Archive Concerning the Debates about Banning the Overseas Trade to the Nanyang during the Qianlong Period), *Lishi Dang'an* (Historical Documents), (2002) 2. 23–35.
5 One *li* equals 500 meters.
6 *Peranakan* is an often used term for mestizo Chinese born and raised in the Indonesian archipelago.

in the past,[7] that country has enjoyed trading with the Han Chinese, and those who lived there for a long time are elected *kapitan* to manage the trade, and for years on end they have traded with us without problems.

After our ocean junks left the past winter, in the fourth and fifth moon there emerged a rumour about the massacre of the Han Chinese merchants in Galaba. Your humble servant was very surprised, but because it is far away overseas I could not investigate the real facts. It was not yet convenient to report about it. But in the beginning of the seventh moon the ships that had gone to Galaba came back one after another. When I interviewed them extensively then I began to know the true story, but there was not relation with our Chinese merchants. As a matter of fact, the peranakan who have been residing for a long time in Galaba, obey their law, and pay taxes, and live together peacefully.

The country of Galaba originally was governed by the Javanese (烏鴉, Wuya) barbarians, but later on it was occupied by the king of Holland (賀蘭, Helan). If, according to Dutch law, there are Chinese who break the law, they are banished to a place called Ceylon. Ceylon is related to the mother country of Holland and is situated very far away from Batavia. Because the neighbouring barbarians created a disturbance and Dutch power could not defeat them, the Dutch therefore sent convicted *peranakan* Chinese to defeat them, allowing them to perform meritorious service to atone for their crimes, and thereupon let them return to Galaba. These Han people vied with each other to enrol in the army and defeated the rebels in battle after battle. The Dutch worried that if the Chinese returned to Galaba, Ceylon would probably be harassed by the rebels again, but at the same time the atonement order for their crimes could not be changed.

Therefore, the Dutch wished to select the strongest Chinese from Galaba to replace those who had been sent earlier to Ceylon, but the Chinese without a criminal past did not want to go. Relying on their large number and their wealth, they planned to resist, but it was discovered by the Dutch authorities.

Then around the nineteenth of the eighth moon last year, the headman of the Dutch took the Chinese by surprise and attacked them with gunfire, burning and killing almost all of them. Only slightly more than a thousand fled from Galaba to the hinterland, a mountain called Gangjiayu (綱加嶼)[8] At a distance of about 30 li, there are fields to cultivate and land to live in; but in

---

7 The maritime trade with the ports of the Nanyang was formally opened by the Kangxi Emperor in 1684.

8 綱加嶼 is probably a misreading for Wangjiayu 網加嶼, Bangka island, situated east of Sumatra. In reality, the rebels withdrew inland. Most likely Wangjiaosi (望茄寺, Bekasi) is meant.

the surrounding area there are the Javanese subjects of the original ruler, who provided food to them so that they would not starve.

The Dutch authorities then very much regretted their behaviour. So, when our ships arrived, they welcomed them; but they only remained even more on their guard. Regarding the trade, the Dutch sought out a Han Chinese from Semarang to act as captain and fixed their minds on peace. Given the fact that affairs calmed down, and that this country [Holland] sent two vessels to see the Chinese junks off [to China],[9] so that they did not have to worry about their safety, we know that in the end the Dutch do not dare harm the Chinese merchants. At the time when every Chinese junk was leaving, the barbarians on all sides consoled the Chinese merchants saying that business next year would continue as in old days and so on. This was what the merchants on the ships agreed on.

According to my inquiry, Semarang is also ruled by the Dutch. When they heard of the massacre at Batavia, some Chinese over there want to seek trouble with the Dutch, but when they saw that they had no chance of winning, they retreated into the mountains. This is the information that the returning junk people had heard.

I have investigated [the claim] that the ships that returned to Xiamen from places in the Nanyang like Cambodia, Sonkhla, Johor, and Ligor all obtained rich profits, and only those who traded with Batavia were less profitable.

Considering the upheavals of last year, [24] ships from every country all go to other places to engage in business, but if our Chinese ships sail to that country [Batavia], there are no rich people to attract them. Now the king of Batavia also regrets this very much and fears that his harbour will fall into decay, so that there will be no taxes to collect and that his port will gradually become a deserted place. So, he enticed the sailors with sweet words, telling them that business will be like last year and that those who fled to the mountain forests will not be not be oppressed in the future.

I have investigated the affairs of the situation overseas to be correct and to agree in every detail. Our merchants returned peacefully, so there is almost nothing to be worried about that.

Your humble servant carefully drew up this report, respectfully dispatching my Squad Leader of the Back Camp Ma Jun to send it to the court. I prostrate myself before the Emperor's wise checks and orders

The Emperor signed 'In order'. Prince Yizheng (議政王) and the ministers discussed it.

---

9 That is, to protect them from pirates.

c) *The acting general of Fuzhou, Celeng (策楞, Tsereng), and others report to the throne about the massacre of the Chinese merchants in the country of Galaba and petitions to ban the Nanyang trade. Qianlong 6, seventh moon, fifteenth day [25 August 1741].*

The acting general of Fuzhou and the temporary acting governor of Fujian and Zhejiang provinces, Celeng, and the grand coordinator of Fujian and the provincial administration commissioner of Guangdong, Wang Shu (王恕), report because of a confidential affair.

We have ascertained that Galaba in the Nanyang belongs to Holland and is situated at a distance of 280 *geng* from Xiamen. According to calculations measuring distances at sea, one *geng* corresponds with 60 *li*. So Galaba is at a distance of 16,800 *li* from China. It is an out-of-the-way region located far away overseas. In the fifty-sixth year of his reign [1717], the former Emperor Kangxi decreed that because there were many Han Chinese congregating in Luzon and Galaba, these places had become lairs for pirates. After the nine chief ministers and the provincial military commanders of Fujian and Guangdong had petitioned to forbid trade with the Nanyang, the people from Fujian trading abroad were forbidden to return to the ancestral soil, but the former emperor allowed those who had gone abroad before Kangxi 56 to return within three years.

Many returned home in accordance with the order, yet not a few people remained behind. When in Yongzheng 5 [1727] the prohibition was lifted, the former governor Gao Qizhuo (高其倬) petitioned to set a timetable for people to come back, but the former emperor did not allow this. In the first year of Qianlong, the former governor of Fujian and Zhejiang, Hao Yulin (郝玉麟), again forwarded the same petition to the throne saying that those who had left after Kangxi 56 should not return, but if there were people who had left before that date and wanted to return they should be allowed to return. This time, on the fifteenth of seventh moon, the emperor gave his permission, and following this the petition was carried out.

But unexpectedly, the stupid people desiring profits and a good life had all gotten married and raised children. Although the emperor allowed them to return, in the end they did not all come back. This is why there are still Han people sojourning in Batavia.

This year in the fifth moon, we and Provincial Military Commander Depei (德沛) heard one story after another that in the intercalary sixth moon of last year the barbarians of Galaba had massacred those Han merchants. But because we are separated by a wide ocean, I feared that the tidings were hard to believe, and we did not yet dare to report this to the throne.

Subsequently, I secretly ordered Circuit Intendant Wang Pilie (王丕烈) and Naval Commander Liang Xupian (梁須梗) to interrogate traders returning from Batavia. Thereupon they transmitted the following message:

In the intercalary sixth moon of last year, the headman of the barbarians received an order from his sovereign to transfer Han people to Ceylon to be employed over there. We have heard that Ceylon belongs to the mother country of Holland and that it is situated far away from Galaba. In the past, Han criminals were sent over there. Recently in Ceylon, all sorts of barbarians were causing trouble, but the Dutch could not overcome them and they wanted the Chinese to help them to suppress [the rebels], and promised they would send them [the Chinese] back after they had obtained merits. The Chinese battled several times and won, but when the Dutch also wanted those without crimes to replace them, some several hundred people were sent; but once they had gone nobody came back.

In the eighth moon, when they again recruited them, there was in Batavia a captain taking care of the Chinese trade, Lian Fu (連富觀, Lian Fuguang), who was levying a poll tax on all the trading people in Batavia, collecting money every month. Because in the past there was no precedent for such recruitment, he started to argue with the Dutch. Then the headman of the Dutch arrested Lian Fu and seized able-bodied Chinese. How many people were arrested from the sixth until the eighth moon is hard to estimate. Thereupon the panic-stricken Chinese cried out against injustice and stopped trading. And then there was a man called Xu (許) who served as *kapitan* in Batavia who used to have disagreements with Lian Fu.[10] Availing himself of the situation, he planned to revolt with the Han Chinese.

Thereupon that night, the Dutch only lashed out, closing the city gates and firing their guns, setting houses afire everywhere. By the nineteenth of the eighth moon, all the Chinese men, women, young and old within the city had been killed. Many were also killed among those living outside the town; altogether more than 10.000 were wounded and the rest fled to Gangjiayu (Bekasi) to hide.

Among all the ships that went over there last year there were six from Fujian, four from Guangdong, and three from Zhejiang. They were all escorted by the barbarian chief into the harbour. They took away the rudders and allowed only thirty people from every ship to come ashore, and let them reside in Tong'ankou (桶岸口) outside the walls to trade. The others were not allowed to go ashore. After the trading season was over, they were sent back to their ships.

---

10 This may have been Lieutenant Xu Jinguan (許進觀).

Every junk has already returned peacefully. They have not suffered any harm. Because of this uprising, those barbarians fear that the court will forbid further trade and that they [the barbarians] will fall into poverty. Consequently, they consoled the crews in many ways when the junks returned to China.

Moreover, based on the report of Provincial Military Commander Wang Jun of the Fujianese naval forces, all the ships [that sailed] to Batavia were escorted out by the barbarians, who repeatedly expressed their desire that they would come to trade next year, as of old. Because that barbarian country is a nexus of trade for every country in the Southern Seas, if it plunges into chaos, the ships will all go elsewhere, and those barbarians will not reap any taxes. Therefore, they especially patted the Chinese traders on their backs for the sake of next year's trade.

We have scrutinised this from beginning to end and we add a plan. Those people who were hurt by the barbarians had all lived for a long time in Batavia. When the prohibition was lifted the last time, the emperor time and again mercifully forgave them. They did not come back; they gave up their home country. According to our laws, they all have committed a severe crime. Now, many people have been killed; this is terrible but it is their own fault.

Because Galaba is very far away, separated [from here] by the wide ocean, they dare carelessly commit atrocious things. This is really hateful. But our dynasty covers heaven and earth with kindness. We will not condemn the barbarians, because these killed people who were acting against the law by staying over. But the cruelty and greediness of the barbarians are hard to fathom. If they later hurt the trading ships, then it cannot be compared with those who overstayed, and it will certainly create great trouble.

We think in many ways if we do not use the example of Kangxi 56 and forbid overseas trade in order to frighten them [the Dutch] and wait until their hearts will change again and they repent and implore us for help, then we will ask you to show your imperial kindness. This is the way to apply the carrot and the stick judiciously on the barbarians. Moreover, we can trade with all the countries in the Eastern Ocean if you tolerate the several tens of Nanyang junks trading again as they like. That will also greatly enhance the guarding of the coastal defence.

d) *The Chief Investigating Censor of Guangdong Li Qingfang* (李清芳) *sets out the reasons why the trade with the Nanyang should not be forbidden. Qianlong 6, twenty-fifth day of the eighth moon [4 October 1741].*

Your humble servant observes that the barbarian countries of the Nanyang are not the same: Countries like Cambodia, Sonkhla, Johor, and Ligor are all places where merchants go to trade. The trade with the Nanyang is not exclusively focused on Galaba. Now, regarding what happened in Batavia: they cruelly hurt our people who remained there. If we want to prohibit merchants to trade with the Nanyang, is that not like [saying] we don't want to eat because of a hiccup?

Moreover, after prohibitions are issued, many people will be discomforted. I have found out that every year, one out of ten ships goes to the Eastern Ocean while nine out of ten sail to the Western Ocean. All the customs offices of Jiangnan, Zhejiang, Fujian and Guangdong receive very many taxes from this trade. If you put into effect a prohibition on trade, then the taxes of the four provinces will run short. The taxes amount to no less than several hundred thousand taels annually. That will amount to a loss for the treasury. That is the first issue.

All this is the trade of the common people. All of them first purchase and then sell. They first prepare to collect merchandise; year upon year they trade in it. Now, if you suddenly ban the trade, then the travelling merchants must certainly run into problems. That is the second issue.

The export items of the hinterland are tea, big and small oranges, porcelain, quicksilver, and so on. They trade these commodities in exchange for silver. If you forbid the trade in these products from the hinterland, they will be redundant and of no use. Every year, several millions of taxes will be lost and after one or two years the treasury will run empty. This is the third issue.

Every year no less than 100 ships, each carrying several hundreds of merchants, helmsmen, and sailors, amounting altogether to several hundred thousand men, do not eat our local rice. If the ban on trade is promulgated, then a hundred thousand men cannot eke out a living, and their family capital for a while cannot do away with the old and seek new plans. Then they will consume at home, whereupon the price of rice will rise in the interior. That is the fourth issue.

Moreover, the Nanyang is at a distance of 12,000 *li* from China, situated far away in the seas. Your humble servant believes that in the past, according to the historical annals, these lands never caused problems for our country. Therefore, the Yongzheng Emperor already understood this well and lifted the ban on overseas trade. The imperial mercy spreads wide, pacifying the four seas. Since Yongzheng 5, when the ban was lifted, until now, more than ten years have passed and the sea has remained tranquil and the people's livelihood happy. I have not heard that bad elements seek to make problems around the islands, and it is even more tranquil than before. Therefore, the opening of overseas trade is obviously beneficial for the hinterland. I humbly believe that if you order that ships temporarily should not go to trade to Galaba [while] waiting till they [the Dutch] come pray for [us to] resume trade, we should not stop the trade with other countries, but let them trade as of old. Then the merchant ships can sail without any worries, and it will benefit our country's well-being.

Your humble servant has another reason for a request. The provinces of Fujian and Guangdong have narrow land and many people. The local [agricultural] output is insufficient to feed the people. I have heard that since this spring the price of rice has risen. I have noted that in the petition of Yongzheng 5 to open trade, the following was said: The foreign countries all belong to rice-producing places, so the ships are ordered to bring back rice according to their size when they are sailing home. I only fear that it is a document from long ago. I respectfully hope that Your Majesty will order the provincial commanders to abide by the original proposals and carry them out. Then the livelihood of the coastal people will benefit even more.

Whether my proposal is proper or not, I prostrate myself before the Emperor's wise checks and orders.

The Emperor signed 'In order'. Prince Yizheng (議政王) and the ministers discussed it.

CHAPTER 3

Selections from *The Chinaman Abroad: An Account of the Malayan Archipelago, Particularly of Java,* by Ong-Tae-Hae (王大海, Wang Dahai), translated by W.H. Medhurst

[In the following section Medhurst's antique spelling of the Minnan dialect has been preserved but the Mandarin pronunciation has been added.]

Batavia (噶喇吧 Kat-la-pa, *Galaba*)¹ is a fertile country on the sea-shore, an extensive region in the extreme south-west. Setting sail from A-moy (廈島 Hāy-tó, *Xiamendao*) we pass by the 七洲 Seven Islands, or Paracels, leave Cochin-China (安南, An-lâm, *Annan*) and Cambojia (港口 Káng-k'haó, *Gangkou*) to the right, as well as the straits of Malacca (蔴六甲 Mwâ-lak-kah, *Maliujia*) and Palembang (巨港 Koò-kang, *Jugang*), steer through the straits of Banca (三笠 San-lak, *Sanli*) until we arrive at 嶼城 [*Yucheng*, Island City] the fortified island of Onrust, and then anchor in the roads of Batavia. It is calculated that the voyage is about 280 ship's watches, each watch comprising 50 le,² making together 14,000 *li*, after sailing over which we arrive at Batavia.

The city faces the north, and is bounded on the south by a range of volcanoes, as a sort of screen, beyond which is the Southern Ocean. To the left lies Bantam (萬丹 Bān-tan, *Wandan*) and to the right Cheribon (井裡汶 Chaíng-lé-būn, *Jingliwen*), while before it are spread out the fortified islands. The gates of the city are strong, and the walls high; the territory is extensive, and the streets are wide; merchandise is abundant, and all [page 2] the tribes of foreigners assemble there; truly it is a great emporium.

But the situation is low, and the climate sultry, all the four seasons being as warm as our summer, while the hot winds are very oppressive and exposure to them occasions sickness.

---

1 The names of these place are all give according the Hokkeen pronunciation, the writer having been a native of that province. We shall therefore follow, in a great measure, the orthography of the Fuh-keen Dictionary.

2 About 250 le [*li*] go to a degree, which would give as the distance 56 degrees; much too large a calculation; shewing the Chinese writer's ignorance of geography, as well as the slowness of junk sailing.

The river water is however cool and pleasant, and bathing in it keeps off disease. Their rainy season accords with our spring, and their dry season with autumn. They gather in only one harvest in the year, though the soil is rich and fertile. Plowing and sowing are easily performed, and the price of rice is moderate, so that the people are rich and well-fed. But articles of commerce generally come from the neighboring states, being conveyed to Batavia for the purpose of traffic, and are not the production of the place itself.

The regions subject to the government of Batavia are Pakalongan (北膠浪 Pōk-ka-lōng, *Beijiaolang*), Samarang (三寶壟 Sam-pa-lang, *Sanbaolong*), Grissee (竭力石 Kéet-lek-sek, *Jielishi*), Surabaya (四裡貓 Soò-lé-bâ, *Silimao*), Benjarmasin (馬辰 Má-sin, *Machen*), Makassar (望加錫 Bāng-ka-seak, *Wangjiaxi*), Amboyna (安汶 An-būn, *Anwen*), Banda (萬瀾 Bān-lân, *Manlan*), Ternate (澗仔底 Kàn-á-te, *Jianzaidi*), Bantam (萬丹 Bán-tan, *Mandan*), Malacca (蔴六甲 Mwâ-lak-kah, *Maliujia*), and so forth, to the amount of several scores.

The virtuous influence of our (Chinese) Government extending far, all the foreigners have submitted, and thus mercantile intercourse is not prohibited. Those who ply the oar and spread the sail, to go abroad, are principally the inhabitants of the Fujian and Guangdong provinces, who have been in the habit of emigrating, for the space of 400 years; from the early part of the 明 Bêng (Ming) dynasty (AD 1400) up to the present day, while those of our countrymen who have remained and sojourned in those parts, after propagating and multiplying, amount to no less than 100,000.

The territory of Batavia originally belonged to the Javanese, but the Dutch, having by stratagem and artifice got possession of the revenues, proceeded to give orders and enact laws, until [page 3] squatting down all the sea coast, they have exacted duties, issued passports, guarded ingress and egress, put down robbers, and brought the natives under their entire control.

The Hollanders have long noses, and red hair, they are deep-schemed and thoughtful, and hence they acquire such an influence over the natives. Their kingdom has been established about eighteen hundred years; they make no use of an intercalary moon; their months have sometimes upwards of thirty days, which are made up by cutting off the excrescencies and supplying the deficiencies of our intercalary moons. The beginning of each year occurs ten days after the winter solstice. The government officers all receive orders from their sovereign in Europe, and the ruler of Batavia does not presume to follow his own inclinations.

They have a Governor (大王 Tuā ông, *Dawang*) and a Lieutenant-Governor (二王 Je ông, *Erwang*); there are Members of Council (相柄 Sëang-pâing, *Xiangbing*) and Directors (伽頭 Kay-t'haôu, *Jiatou*), with Land and Water Fiscals (美色葛 Bé-sek-kat, *Meisege*), and inner and outer Tomonggongs or

Magistrates (淡板公 Tām-pán-kong, *Danbangong*), Factors (杯突 Poey-tut, *Beitu*), Commandants (公勃壟 Kong-put-lang, *Gongbolong*), and such like titles; these are divided off to superintend different districts, and take precedence, either higher or lower, according as their districts are great or small. The chief of the Javanese (爪亞 Jaóu-á, *Jiaya*) dwells in the interior, at a place called the Dalam (覽內 Lám-laē, *Lannei*) or palace of the Sultan of Solo; he takes the title of Susuhunan (巡欄 Sûn-lân, *Xunlan*), which resembles that of Grandee (單于 Sëen-ê, *Chanyu*) in the Han dynasty, or that of K'han (可汗 K'ó-hān, *Kehan*) in the Tông (Tang) dynasty; the other native chiefs, in every place, all call themselves Sultan (史丹 Soó-tan, *Shidan*) and invariably acknowledge the Susuhunan (巡欄 Sûn-lân, *Xunlan*) of the palace (覽內 Lám-laē, *Lannei*), as their liege lord. Amongst their officers, they have Adipatis (二把智 Jē-pá-tè, *Erbazhi*), Tomonggongs (淡板公 Tām-pán-kong, *Danbangong*), and Patis[3] (把低 Pá-te, *Badi*); [page 4] these have each of them assistants, like our great officers in China, who transact business for them; their elevation and depression, as well as their appointment to or dismissal from office, all depend upon the will of the Dutch. From the Swan-tek (宣德, *Xuande*) reign period of the 明 Bêng dynasty (AD 1430) when Ong-sam-pò [*Wang Sanbao*] and Taīng-hô [*Zheng He*] went to the western ocean, to collect and purchase valuable articles, to the present day, the flowery nation have not ceased going and coming for commercial purposes. After the winter solstice, they ply their oars from the island of Amoy. when in about 20 days, they may arrive at the city of Batavia (吧 Pa); there the streets are lined with shops, and the markets thronged with barbarians; high and low holding mutual intercourse, so that it may be truly said, "profit abounds in those southern seas." Our rich merchants and great traders, amass inexhaustible wealth, whereupon they give bribes to the Hollanders, and are elevated to the ranks of great Captain (甲必丹 Kap-pit-tan, *Jiabidan*), Lieutenant (雷珍蘭 Lûy-tin-lân, *Leizhenlan*), Commissioner of insolvent and intestate estates, or Boedelmeester (武直迷 Boó-tit-bêy, *Wuzhimi*), Secretary (朱葛礁 Choò-kat-tat, *Zhugejiao*), and such like appellations; but all of them take the title of Captain.

When the Chinese quarrel or fight, they represent their cause to the Captain, before whom they make a low bow, without kneeling, and call themselves his "juniors". The rights and wrongs, with the crookeds and straights of the matter, are all immediately settled, either by imprisonment or flogging, without giving the affair a second thought. With respects to flagrant breaches of the law and great crimes, together with marriages and deaths, reference must invariably be made to the Hollanders. Those who journey by water and land, must all be

---

3 These are all Javanese titles of nobility.

provided with passports, to prevent their going and coming in an improper way; from this may be inferred how strict the Hollanders are in the [page 5] execution of laws, and how minute in the levying of duties. The life of man, however, is not required at the hand of his next neighbor;[4] but Europeans lay great stress on evidence, requiring the witnesses to submit to examination, and to take oath by cutting off a fowl's head, before they dare to settle a matter or decide a case; thus when men are killed, they are either thrown out into the streets, or suffered to float down the streams, everyone being silent without enquiry, and nobody daring to stand forward as a witness. Alas! alas! that the important affair of human life should after all be treated so lightly.

With respect to the Dutch, they are very much like the man who stopped his ears while stealing the bell.[5] Measuring them by the rules of reason, they scarcely possess one of the five cardinal virtues;[6] the great oppress the small, being overbearing and covetous, thus they have no benevolence; husbands and wives separate, with permission to marry again, and before a man is dead a month his widow is allowed to go to another, thus they have no rectitude; there is no distinction between superiors and inferiors, men and women are mingled together, thus they are without propriety; they are extravagant and self-indulgent in the extreme, and thus bring themselves to the grave, without speculating on leaving something to tranquillize and aid their posterity, thus they have no wisdom.[7] Of the single quality of sincerity, however, they possess a little. As it respects the manners of the natives, with their uncouth forms, their singular appearances, dwelling in hollow trees, and residing in caverns, with their [page 6] woolly hair and tattooed bodies, their naked persons and uncooked food, and all such monstrous and unheard of matters, it is scarcely worth while wasting one's breath upon them.

The situation of Batavia (吧 *Ba*) is low, and the dwelling-houses are very close together; but when you get out into the kampongs (監光 kam-kong, *Jianguang*) or villages, you meet with the gardens and parks of the Hollanders,

---

4 In China when a dead body is found, the nearest inhabitants are taken up, and required to discover the culprit; the Chinese writer laments that it is not so in Batavia.

5 Intimating that they try to hide their vices from themselves, and think that they are as much concealed from others. They have a story in China, that while a man was stealing a bell, he stopped his own ears, to prevent his hearing the noise, and then thought that others were also deaf to the sound.

6 The five cardinal virtues among the Chinese are benevolence, righteousness, propriety, wisdom, and truth.

7 Note from editors: Wang Dahai ignores the existence of Dutch inheritance law and the special arrangements that were made by the *boedelmeesters* and *weeskamer*, not to speak of the charity organisations of the Protestant church.

adjoining one another, for miles together. There you have high galleries and summer pavilions, bridges and terraces, so elegant and beautiful, as almost to exceed the compass of human art; the extreme skill and cleverness displayed in erecting them no pen can describe. Every seven days there is a 禮拜 [*libai*, worship] ceremony-day or sabbath, when, from nine to eleven in the morning, they go to the place of worship, to recite prayers and mumble charms; the hearers hanging down their heads and weeping, as if there was something very affecting in it all; but after half an hour's jabber they are allowed to disperse, and away they go to feast in their garden-houses, and spend the whole day in delight, without attending to any business. Then you may see the dust of the carriages and the footsteps of the horses all along the road, in one unbroken succession, presenting a very lively scene.

I should say that these lands of the Western Ocean have something agreeable in them, and something to be lamented. The climate is not cold, and the whole year is like a continual summer; all the flowers are in bloom during the four seasons; in the time of our winter and spring the nights are rainy and the days fine, truly this is an enchanting state of things and very agreeable. In their manners Europeans aim to be polite, and affect an elegant air; they seem delighted at meeting with their friends, and are lavish in their compliments to one another; if a man in his poverty make application to them, they do not reject him, whether he be of the same clan or only distantly connected, they do not look [page 7] strangely upon him. When young people see a stranger, they compliment him with a bow, and when menials meet their masters, they honor them by kneeling; this is according to the liberality of human feeling displayed in ancient times, and is truly praiseworthy. The soil is rich and fertile, and necessaries are cheap and easily procured; a peck of rice can be bought for a few cash, fowls and ducks are cheaper even than vegetables, and for a mere trifle you can obtain an attendant; this is a cheap state of things, and very agreeable. But there are no writings of philosophers and poets, wherewith to beguile the time; nor any friends of like mind, to soothe one's feeling; no deep caverns or lofty towers, to which one could resort for an excursion; all which is very much lamented....

[page 8] [*On the appointment of the Chinese captain of Semarang*]

Whenever any of the Chinese are appointed to be Captains a representation must be made to Europe. The new Kap-pi-tan (甲必丹, *Jiabidan*) then selects a lucky period, and assembles his relatives and friends, the guests in his family, and visitors from the villages, amounting to some score of persons, when on the appointed day a Hollander approaches bringing the order. The Kap-pit-tan and his friends go outside the door to receive him; the Hollander enters, and stepping up into the middle of the hall, stands conspicuous, and opening the order, reads it; then pointing to heaven above, and earth beneath, he says, "This man is polite, intelligent, and well-informed regarding the principles of things, hence he is promoted to be a Kap-pit-tan; you elderly gentlemen, what think you of it?" All the people then with one voice exclaim, "Very good, most excellent!" The Hollander then shakes hands with all of them, and this ceremony being completed, they all return to their seats; the European then taking the Kap-pit-tan by the hand, leads him up the steps to the middle of the hall where they pay compliments to each other; and this is the way in which the Dutch get our people into their net. The [page 9] power of the Kap-pit-tan of Batavia is divided, and the profits of the situation are uncertain; but the authority of the Semarang Kap-pit-tan is fixed, and his profits more regular in their returns. The boiling of the sea to make salt, and the cultivation of the fields to produce revenue, are all the perquisites of the Kap-pit-tan. Thus it is that a person who fills this office, can amass stores of wealth....

[page 22]

蘇某之妻 The Wife of One Soo (*Su*)

In the city of Chang-chow (漳州, *Zhangzhou*) in Fokien [*Fujian*], outside the eastern gate, in the (深青) deep green village, there dwelt a man belonging to the clan of 蘇 Soo, who went to trade across the western ocean; he there married a wife, but being unsuccessful in business, after several years returned, and died in his native land. His western wife hearing the news, and knowing that his family was poor, his parents old, and his children young, resolved to venture alone across the sea, to visit her husband's home, and support and nourish her aged mother-in-law; in doing this, she carried to the utmost the duties of filial piety, and instructed the children, till they grew up to maturity. Alas! Female constancy and rectitude, even if sought for in the flowery land of China, is not often to be found, how much less can we expect it in wild and uncivilized parts of the world. Truly, it is enough to awaken one's respect and perpetual admiration. It is a pity that we are not acquainted with her surname, or we would record it here.

The Wife of 連捷公 Ne-Tseet-Kong (*Lian Jiegong*)

The wife of Nê-tsëet-kong, was a woman of a beautiful countenance, and happening to live about the time of the Batavian rebellion, was taken by a rich and powerful man, who desired to obtain her for his wife. The lady pretended compliance, but requested leave first to sacrifice to her husband on the river, when she would put on the bridal dress, [page 23] and go through the marriage-ceremony; but when she had finished the sacrifice, she threw herself into the water, and was drowned.

連木生 Ne-Bok-Seng (*Lian Musheng*)

Nê-bok-seng dwelt in a plantain garden, on the banks of the 聖墓港 (*Shengmu Gang*) Holy Grave Canal, where he separated himself from common pursuits, and employed time his time in copying books; he was fond of the flute and violin, could make poetry, and was a skilful player at chess; in all of which he excelled. Every Sunday his country-seat was thronged with friendly visitors, and he had something of the spirit of our famous 北海 Pok Haè (*Beihai*), who was so celebrated for entertaining his friends. The trees in his garden were beautifully verdant, the flowers and fruits were blooming and luxuriant: the weeping willow swept the surface of the water, while the cedars and firs shot up to the heavens. There was a gallery called the moon gallery, and a bridge called the crescent arch: there was also a bamboo grove and a fish pond: the grove was shady, the paths were serpentine, and the whole had an elegant appearance. Bok-seng himself was quiet and still, like the chrysanthemum flower, while his bosom was full of bright ideas; truly he might be considered the retired scholar of the age.

陳豹卿 Tan-Pa-K'heng (*Chen Baoqing*)

Tan-pà-k'heng, whose name was 曆 Lek [*Li*] was an inhabitant of the 石美 [*Shimei*, "Stone Beauty"] beautiful stone village in the prefecture of 漳州 Chang-chow. He was naturally shrewd, and well acquainted with human nature; his first cousin 暎 Yang was the Captain China of Samarang. Pa-k'eng went to inquire after his relative, and was soon enabled to assist him in his business. After a time Yang died, and K'heng [page 24] succeeded to his office. He soon obtained several scores of trading vessels, which he despatched to different ports, and gained, wherever they touched, cent per cent profit. Before many years had expired, he became the richest man in all the country, when he kept his singing-boys, and trained his dancing-girls; he had a sumptuous table spread before him and hundreds of females waiting at his side. When I first arrived at Samarang, I observed a native officer of the rank of Tomonggong (淡板公 Tām-pán-kong), paying a visit to Pa-k'hèng. His train consisted of several hundred horsemen, who came in grand procession, but on their arrival at the outer gate, they alighted; and on entering approached on their knees, while Pa-k'hèng sat exalted, until they came near, when he greeted them with a slight inclination of his head. Most assuredly, to attain such an extent of elevation in a foreign land, shows what the flowery Chinese are capable of.

In Batavia there used to be a large building, called the Samarang factory, where, on the arrival of the Chinese junks, those new-comers who wished to proceed to Samarang, took up their residence, until they found vessels ready to take them on thither; these, whether of the same or different clans, whether well or ill-recommended, were all received and recorded; after which every man was employed according to his ability, and placed in the situation best adapted for him. Both Chinese and foreigners received assistance from Pa-k'hèng, and his merchants and factors were without number. Trading vessels thus accumulated in Samarang, and mercantile commodities were abundant, above all other places in the western ocean: but when our hero died, the merchant ships came to an anchor, the busy mart was still, and silence and solitude pervaded Samarang. How true is the proverb, that 人傑地靈, a man of talent is the soul of a place.

許芳良 K'hoe-Hong-Leang (*Xu Fangliang*)

K'hoé-hong-lëâng was a native of 漳州 Cheang-Chew [*Zhangzhou*] and became Captain China of Batavia; he was also of a liberal disposition, and truly generous. There was at that time one 蔡錫光 Ch'hwà-sek-kong [*Cai Xiguang*], who resided in his family, and experienced an instance of his generosity. It seems that of all the fruits of Cheang-chew, the 棕梨 brown pear is considered the most delicious; but it is never obtained in great quantities, and when the Chinese junks arrive they merely bring two or three specimens. The largest of these are sold for a hundred reals, and the smallest for twenty, all of which are generally sent up, by great and influential persons, as presents to the Governor General of Batavia. Hong-lëâng purchased a couple of these, and entrusted them to Sek-kong, intending to send them to the governor: but Sek-kong, thinking that they were only common productions, sliced them up, and presented them to his patron. Hong-lëâng said composedly, "此誠故鄉中珍果也,實希得嘗,悉呼其客及家人共嘗之. This is indeed one of the most delicious fruits of our native place, and is rarely to be obtained, let all my guests and inmates be called to partake of it."

Amboyna produces the oil of cloves, which is generally kept in small glass bottles; the largest of which are worth a hundred reals; one day Sek-kong, whilst wiping the table, accidently broke one of these, when the fragrance diffused itself through all the house; and it being impossible to conceal the fact, he informed his patron. Hong-lëâng merely said, "生毀有數,何必較也. The preservation and destruction of things are determined by fate; why need you mention it."

In Batavia, when guests are invited, they use crystal vessels and dishes, even the tea-cups are all of glass, each set of which is worth one or two hundred reals. One day, when they were entertaining some friends, a slave-girl, by a slip [page 26] of the hand, broke a whole set: whereupon the maid prostrated herself on the ground, and begged to be put to death. Hong-lëâng said: "無須進內,但云我悮碎可矣. Never mind! go in, and tell your mistress that I broke it by mistake." For, according to the custom of Batavia, the slaves are treated very cruelly; the men-servants are indeed subject to the master's controul, but the women-servants are under the superintendence of the mistress. Thus, had not Hong-lëâng adopted this plan, the slave-girl would have been in danger of her life.

At that time all those belonging to the clan of 許 K'hoé (*Xu*) were people of respectability, of which Hong-lëâng used to boast. It being reported to him, however, that one of his clan was doing the work of day-labourer, Hong-lëâng sent for him, and said: "Since you are a relation of mine, you ought, on your arrival at Batavia, to have waited on me immediately; why should you stand in your own light?" The Captain then took him into his employ, and in a few years he became a rich man. Of such acts of generosity there are frequent instances, all of which it would be impossible to particularize.

CHAPTER 4

Jialaba (甲喇吧, Galaba), by Gu Sen (顧森)[1]

In the beginning of the Qianlong reign, I had a neighbour whose family name was Yin (殷); sailing the sea was his trade. One day I met him in a teahouse and asked him about the conditions overseas. He told me that the sea ships use *geng* (更) for counting distances, he said the distance to the Western Ocean is about 320 *geng*. About 20,000 li [里]. The name of that place is Sunda Jialaba (甲喇吧, Galaba). It is a marketplace where traders collect like spokes of the wheel.

This country has three kings, who separately manage their affairs. But they are governed by a general who governs another place.[2] The great king is in charge of rites and music; that is, the government of the country.[3] The second king is in charge of finance.[4] The third king is in charge of justice.[5] Therefore the people only fear the third king.

When Chinese junks arrive in Galaba, they hand over their goods to their manager [*comprador*], and store it in a big warehouse, which is surrounded by a wooden stockade. When you have sold your goods he asks you: "What would you like to buy?" And he immediately purchases it for you; the visiting trader does not have to manage these affairs. This is very fair and without deceit.

The men in this country all join the militia. Those who do business in the market are all women! So they collect the poll tax from the husbands of the local women, and that is moreover a heavy tax.

Chinese are called *Tangren* (唐人). If a woman marries a Chinese, she does not have to pay taxes. So, when a ship arrives, there are often old ladies who bring along young girls, who are nicely made up and put up for sale. Their price is very low. They only do not allow them to be taken back to China. After you marry a girl, she does not only work hard, but if you let them go to the *pasar* to trade, they can all take care of the business.

---

1 An extract from *Yun'an Yiwen* (雲庵遺文), quoted in Chen Yusong's preface to Xu Yunqiao's revised and annotated edition of the *Kai Ba Lidai Shiji*.
2 The stadtholder of the United Provinces of the Netherlands.
3 The governor general.
4 The director general.
5 The chief councilor of justice.

There is rice and salt in abundance in this place. The price of foodstuffs is low; one *jin*[6] of pork meat only costs 10 *fanams*.[7] All other things are like that. If you want to entertain guests, you should first tell your wife; then, on that day, she goes out early in the morning to buy things, and thereupon starts cooking. So, when the guests arrive, you can immediately regale them with food, without delay. If you count how much you have spent, it does not amount to more than two or three *qian*.

Justice in that country is quite different from ours. Outside the town, they have built a stage in the fields. They call it the execution stage. It is made like the stage of our [Chinese] theatre. At the end of every month, an official leads the criminals onto this stage. The people gather together below to watch. Then he orders the criminal to reveal on stage the bad things he has done. After he has done so, the punishment is meted out.

For instance, in the case of theft, he lets him show on the stage what and how he has stolen. And then, when the performance is over, he makes him take off his clothes so that he is nude, binds his two hands, and with two crude rattans the outer ends of which are cut into several whips, two people beat him left and right on the upper body. If it is a heavy crime, they are beaten a hundred times. After the beating, blood and flesh drip down. This is their version of flogging in China.

In case of murder, they also take off the criminal's clothes and bind his head. Two people both take a spear, they both stick the spears from below in his breast. This is like beheading in China.

If there are even more serious crimes than these, they put a pile of timber seven to eight feet high on the stage, and on top of it they place an iron pestle about two feet high. On the top of it, there is a barb, and then they cut open his behind and hang the skin on this iron rack and pull him down with force. And make the angle stick out of the neck. That man sits on top of this pike, feels all kinds of pain, and his hands and feet mill around. Sometimes it takes several days before they die. This is like our *guazui* (剮罪, 'cutting into pieces').

There is also another punishment whereby they bind him to a stick, and put firewood under him and burn him alive, but this is not very often carried out.

The people of that country are good at using cannons, and they are also good at swimming. Just before they arrive at their country, there is an island in the middle of the sea. That sea is called Longtan (龍潭, Dragon Pool). When they [the Dutch] first arrived in this country, there were countless dragons at

---

6 One *jin* equals one pound.
7 One *fanam* is equal to 3 *qian* (*fen*) and 5 *li*, or two *stuivers* (ten cents).

this place.[8] Later these people often fired their great cannons at these animals, so that the dragons became scared and all moved to another place. In the past twenty or thirty years, there are no more left.

Watchmen stationed on this island make a long iron chain that they have put into the sea. When they see ships from other countries pass by, swimmers bind this iron chain to their rudders. The people on the island then pull them in with a windlass, and when the ship comes nearby they steal its cargo, and they say that it has been sent by Heaven: *Tian songlai* (天送來).

Several thousand Chinese (華人, *huaren*) reside in that country. They are all involved in sugarcane cultivation. They choose an able man to act as their headman and call him the Tang Da (唐大, misreading for: 甲大, *jiada*, captain). The Tang people are all under his control.

Later, a king from another country passed by this place.[9] When he saw how prosperous they were, he found out that, because Chinese cultivate sugarcane, traders come to trade in droves. Because of this he wished to borrow from the third king several hundred people to reside in his country and teach them how to cultivate. The third king approved of this. He ordered the Chinese captain to dispatch them in groups.

But the Chinese captain disagreed. Thereupon the third king became angry; he threw the Chinese captain into jail. The Tang people thereupon were in turmoil, and picked a fight with the people of that country. In the beginning, the Tang people were winning, but because the people of that country used big cannons, and the Tang people did not possess any, more than half were wounded and killed.

Later on, following the order of the general [in Holland], the Chinese captain was released and he was ordered to soothe the Chinese. From that moment, they were pacified.

When this event was made known in China, the high officials of the coastal regions sent a memorial to the emperor. They considered that although these Chinese were people from our country, they had turned their back on our government and gone far away. The emperor issued an edict saying: Don't interfere. Mr. Yin witnessed this disaster at that place; he was very scared and did not go there anymore.

Mr. Yin also said: To the Eastern Ocean is only 36 *geng*, this is about 2,000 li. He also had been to that country [Manila]. The food is very expensive there, and the people behave very arrogantly over there. It cannot at all be compared to Galaba.

---

8   Probably crocodiles.
9   This probably refers to Gustaaf Willem, Baron van Imhoff, who wanted to send Chinese to Ceylon, and the Chinese rebellion that ensued.

Appendices

Appendix 1: The Appointment of Captain Tsoa Wanjock

Resolution of Governor General and the Councilors of India, 14 June 14, 1678[1]

Because the captainship of the Chinese at this city has remained vacant since the passing away of Siqua in the year 1665, and has been taken care of by his widow, and since recently several requests have reached us from the oldest and most established inhabitants of this town, to be allowed again as in former times [to have] a man and not a woman as head of their nation, and because in the same way this is observed by the other native inhabitants, and because it is considered certainly for the general welfare not only useful but also necessary,

Therefore, after several deliberations it has been agreed to engage in the election of a new captain and head of the Chinese. Tsoa Wanjock has been elected as the most capable for this position. He is one of the oldest inhabitants and has lived here over forty years. He is considered the most flexible, most popular, and most eminent among the people of his nation and, moreover, his [vested] interests inside and outside the town are considered important.

But because the requests of the Chinese also incline towards a situation in which they will be provided with some headmen of lower rank in addition to the captain, so, considering that they also belong to the oldest and most eminent [of their nation], have been nominated Limsisay to the position of lieutenant and Litsoeko to the position of ensign.[2]

It is believed that with this election the Chinese in general will be quite contented and can also be put in better order, so that they can serve, in the case of unforeseen events, in the protection of this city, along with other native citizens, a task for which they have even somewhat voluntarily presented themselves.

Daghregister gehouden int Casteel Batavia vant passerende daer ter plaetse als over geheel Nederlandts-India, 29 juni 1678, *p. 327*

Today around nine in the morning there arrived at the castle of Batavia the Chinese Tsoa Wanjock, Limsisay, and Litsoeko, mobbed by a large concourse and following of

---

1 Hoetink, 'Chineesche officieren', 28–30.
2 The *Kai Ba Lidai Shiji* does not refer to a *vaandrig* (ensign) but to a *soldaat* (soldier).

Chinese inhabitants, who were, according to their fashion, all dressed up in their best outfits and accompanied by many flags and silk bows of various colours and musicians playing all kinds of Chinese instruments. On 14 June, these gentlemen were elected by the Council of the Indies respectively to the positions of captain, lieutenant, and ensign (*vaandrig*) to administer those of their nation who reside here.

Having spent awhile inside with the governor general, they reappeared outside on steps of the large assembly hall, where they were solemnly authorized in their respective functions by the fiscal of the Indies, the bailiff, the *landdrost* (sheriff of the Ommelanden), as well as two delegated *schepenen* (aldermen of the city council) in the following way: first in Dutch, by merchant Joan van Hoorn, first clerk of the general secretariat, and thereupon in Chinese by the Chinese merchant Tenglauw, with the following words:

> Rijklof van Goens, Governor General, and the Council of the Indies, representing the General Netherlands Chartered East-India Company in the Orient, salutes all those who see or hear this proclamation:
>
> Because the captaincy of the Chinese inhabitants of this city of Batavia has remained vacant since the passing away of Siqua in 1665 and has been partly been taken over by his widow, and because now again for some time various requests have been made by the older and most [representative] Chinese inhabitants to be allowed again as in former times [to have] a man and no longer a woman as the chief of their nation, which indeed is deemed necessary for the general welfare,
>
> Therefore, this council has agreed after deliberation to elect from various proposed Chinese as captain, headman and advocate of the Chinese nation Tsoa Wanjock, who has lived here for more than forty years and about whose experience and amiability among his countrymen we are pleased. Consequently, we nominate and authorize him on this occasion to act as captain, and, on the recommendation of the Chinese nation, we add Limsisay as Lieutenant and Litsoeko as ensign to assist him. We confer on Captain Wanjock and his two inferiors the same powers as his predecessor, Siqua, that is, to settle in our name all small affairs among the Chinese citizenry and to remit all large and dubious cases to the authorities concerned and furthermore to conduct themselves as a pious, attentive captain and mediator should.
>
> We ordain and order all high and low officers and especially those of the Council of Justice of this town to recognize and acknowledge Tsoa Wanjock and also to properly deal with all cases that apply to his office, and exhort all Chinese citizens of this town, who are residing here or will come to reside in the future, to show him in his official status all proper obedience, honour, assistance, and

APPENDIX 1: THE APPOINTMENT OF CAPTAIN TSOA WANJOCK   245

favours, because we feel that this should be so to the service of the convenience of the General Company and the well-being of our Chinese citizenry.

Acted at Batavia, in the castle, on the island of Greater Java, 29 June 1678.

Signed Rijcklof van Goens

Beneath was attached the Company's seal pressed in red sealing wax and on orders of the aforementioned gentlemen

Signed by Joan van Hoorn, clerk.

After this proclamation had been acclaimed with loud voices by those of their nation, the Chinese officers were again directed into the room of the governor general where, after a short stay, they were handed over the above appointment, and were conducted, after having been taken leave of by the aforementioned officers and representatives, to the town hall in the city where the assignment was again read to the people by the clerk of the board of aldermen, Jacob van Dam, and the Chinese merchant Tenglauw.

From there the procession proceeded on foot or on horseback accompanied by the sound of all kinds of musical instruments to the house of Captain Wanjock where a table stood prepared and the delegates and their further company were regaled with a collation, and whereupon everybody returned home after having been cheered.

Appendix 2: Name Lists

TABLE 1 *Governors General during the VOC period*

No.	Dutch name	Chinese name	Year of appointment	Term of service	Further remarks
1	Pieter Both	庇直物	1610	1610–1614	Retires and drowns on the way home.
2	Gerrit Reijnst	呀力能氏	1614	1614–1615	†Batavia.
3	Laurens Reael	咾能是禮豁	1615	1615–1619	Retires and returns to Holland, †1637.
4	Jan Pietersz Coen	然庇得郡	1619	1619–1623	Founder of Batavia. Returns to Holland.
5	Pieter de Carpentier	庇得葛邊值	1623	1623–1627	Retires and returns to Holland, †1659
6	Jan Pietersz Coen	然庇得郡	1627	1627–1629	Returns from Holland. †Batavia.
7	Jacques Specx	惹谷習白氏	1629	1629–1632	Retires, returns to Holland. † unknown
8	Hendrik Brouwer	應得力物勞凡	1632	1632–1636	Retires and returns to Holland. †1643, Chili.
9	Antonie van Diemen	安多哹伴慮宜	1636	1636–1645	†Batavia.
10	Cornelis van der Lijn	高哩哹伴禮僯	1645	1645–1650	Retires and returns to Holland. †1679, Alkmaar
11	Carel Reiniersz	膠慮螺哹氏	1650	1650–1653	†Batavia.
12	Joan Maetsuijcker	裕安嗎西吃	1653	1653–1678	†Batavia.
13	Rijklof van Goens	螺吉祿伴牛氏	1678	1678–1681	†Batavia.
14	Cornelis Janszoon Speelman	高裡年然是必蠻	1681	1681–1684	†Batavia.

No.	Dutch name	Chinese name	Year of appointment	Term of service	Further remarks
15	Johannes Camphuijs	裕亞那敢回氏	1684	1684–1691	Retires, †1695, Batavia.
16	Mr. Willem van Outhoorn	冥實弟微唧伴烏道郎	1691	1691–1704	Retires, †1720, Batavia.
17	Joan van Hoorn	裕安伴烏倫	1704	1704–1709	Returns to Holland. †1711, †Amsterdam.
18	Mr. Abraham van Riebeeck	冥實阿壟伴慮默氏	1709	1709–1713	†Batavia.
19	Christoffel van Swoll	吉慮羅氏多勃伴一忻	1713	1713–1718	†Batavia.
20	Hendrik Swaardecroon	應得力些裡吉倫	1718	1718–1725	Retires, †1728, Batavia.
21	Mattheus de Haan	嗎得厘罕	1725	1725–1729	†Batavia.
22	Mr. Diederik Durven	冥實弟螺力伴勞物	1729	1729–1732	Is recalled. †1740. Delft.
23	Mr. Dirk van Cloon	冥實弟螺力邦吉壟	1735 (1732)	1735–1737 (1732–1735)	†Batavia.
24	Abraham Patras	阿勿壟巴得勞	1737 (1735)	1737–1739 (1735–1737)	†Batavia.
25	Adriaan Valckenier	阿慮安伴吉哞	1739	1739–1740	Retires and is accused of manslaughter. †1751, Batavia.
26	Johannes Thedens	裕亞禮地寧	1741	1741–1742	Governor general *ad interim*. Retires, †1748, Batavia.
27	Gustaaf Willem baron van Imhoff	呀實礁微瑯貓郎伴熊木	1742	1742–1750	†Batavia.
28	Jacob Mossel	惹閣毛述	1750	1750–1761	†Batavia.

TABLE 1 *Governors General during the VOC period* (cont.)

No.	Dutch name	Chinese name	Year of appointment	Term of service	Further remarks
29	Petrus Albertus van der Parra	敝得律豁微突伴螺巴嘮	1761	1761–1775	†Batavia.
30	Jeremias van Riemsdijk	勞冥實得	1775	1775–1777	†Batavia.
31	Reinier de Klerck	奎螺力	1777	1777–1780	†Batavia.
32	Mr. Willem Arnold Alting	沃力丁	1780	1780–1796	Retires,†1800, Batavia.
33	Mr. Pieter Gerardus van Overstraten	胡勃實達丹	1796	1796–1801	†Batavia.

SOURCE: XU YUNQIAO, PREFACE, "THE EARLY ACCOUNTS OF CHINESE IN BATAVIA, A REVISED AND ANNOTATED EDITION" (開吧歷代史紀校注), IN *NANYANG XUEBAO* (南洋學報), IX(1), 1953, 13–15; DE HAAN, *OUD BATAVIA*, 759; VAN RHEDE VAN DER KLOOT, *DE GOUVERNEURS-GENERAAL*, PASSIM.

NOTE: W.A. ALTING WAS THE LAST GOVERNOR GENERAL IN THE *KAI YAOLAOBA LIDAISHI QUANLU* (開咬咾吧歷代史全錄), THE LIEM MANUSCRIPT, PP. 2B–3B.

APPENDIX 2: NAME LISTS   249

TABLE 2   *Chinese* Kapiteins (*Captains*) *in Batavia during the* VOC *period*[a]

No.	Name according to the *Kai Ba Lidai Shiji*	Name according to Dutch sources	Year of appointment according to Dutch sources	Term of service according to the *Kai Ba Lidai Shiji*	Appointed by (Governor General)
1	蘇明光 Su Mingguang	Bencon	11 October 1619	1620–1631	Coen
2	林六哥 Lin Liuge	Lim Lacco	21 Juli 1636	Not mentioned	van Diemen
3	潘明岩 Pan Mingyan	Bingam	4 Maart 1645	1631–1637	van Diemen
4	顔二官 Yan Erguan	Siqua	10 April 1663	1637–1648	Maetsuijcker
5	顔二娤 Yan Erya	Gan Dji Nyai	No records	1648–1655	van Goens
6	蔡煥玉 Cai Huanyu	Tsoa Wanjock	14 Juni 1678	1655–1669	van Goens
7	郭郡哥 Guo Junge	Queeconko	3 Augustus 1685	1669–1686	Camphuijs
8	林敬官 Lin Jingguan	Limkeenqua	10 Juni 1695	1686–1706	van Outhoorn
9	陳穆哥 Chen Muge	Tambocco	11 April 1707	1706–1726	van Hoorn
10	郭昂官 Guo Maoguan	Quebauqua	3 Maart 1719	1726–1733	Swaardecroon
11	郭春官 Guo Chunguan	Que Tjoenqua	6 Januari 1733	1733–1738	van Cloon
12	連富光 Lian Fuguang	Ni Hoekong	11 September 1736	1738–1740	Patras
13	林明哥 Lin Mingge	Lim Beenko	28 Juni 1743	1742–1746	van Imhoff
14	黃箴哥 Huang Zhenge	Oeij Tsomko	21 April 1747	1746–1751	van Imhoff
15	黃市鬧 Huang Shinao	Oeij Tsjilauw	7 Juli 1750	1751–1755	van Imhoff
16	林緝哥 Lin Jige	Lim Tjipko	27 Augustus 1756	1755–1774	Mossel

TABLE 2 *Chinese* Kapiteins (*Captains*) in Batavia during the VOC period (cont.)

No.	Name according to the *Kai Ba Lidai Shiji*	Name according to Dutch sources	Year of appointment according to Dutch sources	Term of service according to the *Kai Ba Lidai Shiji*	Appointed by (Governor General)
17	唐恩哥 Tang Enge	Ting/Tung Ingko	31 Januari 1775	1774–1775	van der Parra
18	黃恒哥 Huang Hengge	Oeij Hingko	19 December 1775	1775–1784	van der Parra
19	蔡敦哥 Cai Dunge	Swa Toenko	26 November 1784	1784–1790	Alting
20	王珠生 Wang Zhusheng	Ong Tjoeseeng	8 Juni 1790	1790–1791	Alting
21	黃綿公 Huang Miangong	Oeij Biankong	11 October 1791	1791–1800	Alting

a Throughout the original text, the honorifics that follow the Chinese names such as -*guan*, -*guang*, -*gong*, -*ge*, -*lao*, -*sheng*, -*shi* and -*she* (觀 or 官，光，公，哥，老，生，使 and 舍) are alternatively used. Here we have assembled per person the most commonly used versions. For instance: Su Mingguang (蘇明光) instead of Su Minggong (蘇明公), Tang Enge (唐恩哥) instead of Tang Enguan (唐恩觀), Huang Jilao (黃繼老) instead of Huang Jige (黃繼哥), and Huang Mianshe (黃綿舍) instead of Huang Mianguang (黃綿光). In Minnanhua, *guang* 光 has the same sound as *gong* 公, namely 'kong.'

SOURCES: B. HOETINK, "CHINEESCHE OFFICIEREN TE BATAVIA ONDER DE COMPAGNIE", IN *BIJDRAGEN TOT DE TAAL-, LAND- EN VOLKENKUNDE VAN NEDERLANDSCH-INDIË*, VOL 78, NO. 1 (1922), P.9; XU YUNQIAO, "THE EARLY ACCOUNTS OF CHINESE IN BATAVIA, A REVISED AND ANNOTATED EDITION" (開吧歷代史紀校注), IN *NANYANG XUEBAO* (南洋學報), IX(1), 1953, PP. 15–16; *KAI BA LIDAI SHIJI* (開吧歷代史紀), THE LEIDEN MANUSCRIPT, PP. 11B–12B.

TABLE 3   *Chinese* Luitenanten *(Lieutenants) in Batavia during the* VOC *period*

No.	Name according to the *Kai Ba Lidai Shiji*	Name according to Dutch sources	Year of appointment according to Dutch sources	Term of service according to the *Kai Ba Lidai Shiji*	Appointed by (Governor General)
1	林時使 Lin Shishi	Lim Si Say	14 June 1678	No records	van Goens
2	李祖哥 Li Zuge	Li Tsoeko	16 May 1679	No records	van Goens
3	黃舅哥 Huang Jiuge	Oeij Koeko	12 January 1682	No records	Speelman
4	郭包哥 Guo Baoge	Que Pauko	3 August 1685	No records	Camphuijs
5	林敬官 Lin Jingguan	Lim Keenko	4 August 1685	No records	Camphuijs
6	王五哥 Wang Wuge	Ong Gouko	26 March 1694	No records	van Outhoorn
7	郭喬哥 Guo Qiaoge	Que Kiauko	10 June 1695	No records	van Outhoorn
8	陳穆哥 Chen Muge	Tambocco	16 June 1702	1685–1706	van Outhoorn
9	郭訓哥 Guo Xunge	Que Hoenko	5 May 1705	1632–1651	van Hoorn
10	李容哥 Li Rongge	Lie Joncko	5 May 1705	1686–1707	van Hoorn
11	何蓮哥 He Liange	Ho Lienko	10 June 1707	1669–1685	van Hoorn
12	林春哥 Lin Chunge	Lim Tsoenko	28 June 1720	1698–1725	Swaardecroon
13	林森哥 Lin Senge	Lim Somko	28 June 1720	1689–1712	Swaardecroon
	蔡威觀 Cai Weiguan	No records	No records	1689–1698	—
14	陳榮公 Chen Ronggong	Tan Eengkong	28 December 1725	1707–1729	de Haan
15	陳忠官 Chen Zhongguan	Tan Tionqua	28 December 1725	1727–1740	de Haan

TABLE 3   *Chinese* Luitenanten (*Lieutenants*) in Batavia (cont.)

No.	Name according to the *Kai Ba Lidai Shiji*	Name according to Dutch sources	Year of appointment according to Dutch sources	Term of service according to the *Kai Ba Lidai Shiji*	Appointed by (Governor General)
16	連祿哥 Lian Luge	Ni Locko	8 July 1729	1706–1727	Durven
17	王應使 Wang Yingshi	Ong Eengsaij	8 July 1729	1707–1734	Durven
18	楊成光 Yang Chengguang	Io Seenkong	21 October 1729	1729–1739	Durven
19	連富光 Lian Fuguang	Ni Hoekong	6 February 1733	No records	van Cloon
20	李和哥 Li Hege	Li Hoko	23 June 1733	1707–1735	van Cloon
21	郭威哥 Guo Weige	Que Oeijko	12 March 1734	1712–1737	van Cloon
22	楊簡哥 Yang Jiange	Nio Kanko	31 December 1734	1737–1740	van Cloon
23	黃篏哥 Huang Zhenge	Oeij Tsomko	28 September 1736	1736–1740	Patras
24	許進官 Xu Jinguan	Khouw Tsinqua	27 May 1738	1736–1740	Valckenier
25	連鐘官 Lian Zhongguan	Ni Tonqua	13 June 1738	1725–1739	Valckenier
26	黃提哥 Huang Tige	Oeij Theeko	26 January 1740	1734–1736	Valckenier
27	黃篏哥 Huang Zhenge	Oeij Tsomko	28 June 1743	1742–1746	van Imhoff
28	陳怡哥 Chen Yige	Tan Iko	28 June 1743	1742–1749	van Imhoff
29	林國哥 Lin Guoge	Lim Kocko	7 May 1745	1747–1748	van Imhoff
30	蘇俊生 Su Junsheng	Tsou Tsoen Seeng	21 April 1747	No records	van Imhoff
31	陳遠生 Chen Yuansheng	Tan Wang Seeng	10 December 1748	1749–1759	van Imhoff

APPENDIX 2: NAME LISTS

No.	Name according to the *Kai Ba Lidai Shiji*	Name according to Dutch sources	Year of appointment according to Dutch sources	Term of service according to the *Kai Ba Lidai Shiji*	Appointed by (Governor General)
32	黃市鬧 Huang Shinao	Oeij Tsilauw	10 December 1748	No records	van Imhoff
33	林緝哥 Lin Jige	Lim Tjipko	3 June 1749	1748–1755	van Imhoff
34	王榮使 Wang Rongshi	Ong Eng Saaij	29 December 1750	1751–1754	Mossel
35	林健哥 Lin Jiange	Lim Kienko	15 June 1751	1751–1764	Mossel
36	林釵哥 Lin Chaige	Lim Theeko	8 November 1754	1754–1763	Mossel
37	許芳良 Xu Fangliang	Khouw Hong Liang	27 August 1756	1755–1772	Mossel
38	戴弁哥 Dai Biange	Thee Poanko	18 December 1759	1759–1766	Mossel
39	許燦哥 Xu Cange	Khouw Tjiangko	10 June 1762	1762–1770	van der Parra
40	盧郎哥 Lu Langge	Louw Nungko	10 June 1762	1762–1770	van der Parra
41	吳文哥 Wu Wenge	Gouw Boenko	30 December 1763	1763–1765	van der Parra
42	唐恩哥 Tang Enge	Tung Ingko	6 April 1764	1764–1774	van der Parra
43	劉成光 Liu Chengguang	Louw Sinkong	5 July 1764	1766–1771	van der Parra
44	黃珩哥 Huang Hengge	Oei Hinko	19 Febuary 1769	1765–1775	van der Parra
45	鄭隆哥 Zheng Longge	The Lionko	26 May 1769	1770–1777	van der Parra
46	陳彩哥 Chen Caige	Tan Tjaiko	3 October 1769	1771–1772	van der Parra
47	林德哥 Lin Dege	Lim Teko	22 June 1770	1770–1775	van der Parra

TABLE 3   *Chinese* Luitenanten (*Lieutenants*) in Batavia (cont.)

No.	Name according to the *Kai Ba Lidai Shiji*	Name according to Dutch sources	Year of appointment according to Dutch sources	Term of service according to the *Kai Ba Lidai Shiji*	Appointed by (Governor General)
48	吳泮水 Wu Panshui	Gouw Poansoei	2 October 1772	1774–1783	van der Parra
49	王藉哥 Wang Jige	Ong Tjako	17 November 1772	Dies suddenly after only 28 days in office	van der Parra
50	鄭奢哥 Zheng Shege	The Tjako	15 December 1772	1772–1775	van der Parra
51	蔡敦哥 Cai Dunge	Swa Thoenko	31 January 1775	1774–1784	van der Parra
52	王珠生 Wang Zhusheng	Ong Soeseeng	4 August 1775	1775–1790	van der Parra
53	唐偏哥 Tang Piange	Tung Pienko	19 December 1775	1775–?	van der Parra
54	高根哥 Gao Genge	Ko Kimko	29 December 1775	1775–1787	van der Parra
55	楊款哥 Yang Kuange	Njo Koanko	8 July 1777	1777–?	van der Parra
56	陳富老 Chen Fulao	Tan Hoelo	2 December 1783	1783–1789	Alting
57	黃綿公 Huang Miangong	Oeij Biankong	26 November 1784	1784–1791	Alting
58	林漢丹 Lin Handan	Lim Hantan	12 October 1787	1788–1791	Alting
59	黃繼哥 Huang Jige	Oeij Geeko	22 December 1789	1789–1790	Alting
60	陳報哥 Chen Baoge	Tan Poko	8 June 1790	1790–1792	Alting
61	林春公 Lin Chungong	Lim Tjoengkong	26 October 1790	1790–1791	Alting
62	吳纘緒 Wu Zuanxu	Gouw Tjiansie	8 February 1791	1791–1800	Alting
63	陳寬哥 Chen Kuanshi	Tan Koanko	11 October 1791	1790–1791	Alting

APPENDIX 2: NAME LISTS

No.	Name according to the *Kai Ba Lidai Shiji*	Name according to Dutch sources	Year of appointment according to Dutch sources	Term of service according to the *Kai Ba Lidai Shiji*	Appointed by (Governor General)
64	林長生 Lin Zhangsheng	Lim Tiangseeng	16 March 1792	1792–1809	Alting
65	陳炳哥 Chen Bingge	Tan Peengko	13 November 1792	1792–1808	Alting
66	黃董哥 Huang Dongge	Oeij Tamko	9 January 1793	1791–1793	Alting
67	戴弘哥 Dai Hongge	Tee Honko	1795	1791–1809	Alting
68	吳科哥 Wu Kege	Gouw Kocko	20 April 1798	1793–1812	van Overstraten
69	陳水哥 Chen Shuige	Tan Soeijko	27 December 1800	1800–1809	van Overstraten

SOURCES: B. HOETINK, "CHINEESCHE OFFICIEREN TE BATAVIA ONDER DE COMPAGNIE", IN *BIJDRAGEN TOT DE TAAL-, LAND- EN VOLKENKUNDE VAN NEDERLANDSCH-INDIË*, VOL 78, NO. 1 (1922), PP. 88–95; XU YUNQIAO, "THE EARLY ACCOUNTS OF CHINESE IN BATAVIA, A REVISED AND ANNOTATED EDITION" (開吧歷代史紀校注), IN *NANYANG XUEBAO* (南洋學報), IX(1), 1953, PP. 16-18; *KAI BA LIDAI SHIJI* (開吧歷代史紀), THE LEIDEN MANUSCRIPT, PP. 13B-16B. *KAI YAOLAOBA LIDAISHI QUANLU* (開咬咾吧歷代史全錄), THE LIEM MANUSCRIPT, P. 6B; *KAI BA LIDAI SHIJI* (開吧歷代史紀), THE LEIDEN MANUSCRIPT, PP. 22B-23B; LU ZIMING (陸子明), *LIREN BAGUO GONGTANG SHUJI TIMINGLU* (歷任吧國公堂書記題名錄), IN XU YUNQIAO, "THE EARLY ACCOUNTS OF CHINESE IN BATAVIA, A REVISED AND ANNOTATED EDITION" (開吧歷代史紀校注), IN *NANYANG XUEBAO* (南洋學報), IX(1), 1953, PP. 20-21.

TABLE 4   *Chinese Boedelmeesters (Curators) in Batavia during the VOC period*

Year	Name according to *Kai Ba Lidai Shiji*	Name according to Dutch sources	Year of appointment according to *Kai Ba Lidai Shiji*	Term of service according to *Kai Ba Lidai Shiji*	Term of service according to Dutch sources
1640	—	Bencon (蘇鳴崗)	—	—	R.B. 860, 441 1640.06.02 to
	—	Tellouw	—	—	1641.05.31
1641	—	Bencon	—	—	R.B. 861, 122 1641.06.01 to
	—	Conjock	—	—	1642.06.06
1642	—	Bencon	—	—	R.B. 861, 481 1642.06.07 to
	—	Bingsam	—	—	1643.05.31
1643	—	Bencon	—	—	R.B. 862, 113 1643.06.01 to
	—	Nootsangh	—	—	1644.06.02
1644	—	Conjocq	—	—	R.B. 862, 452 1644.06.03 to
	—	Jocqhey	—	—	1645.06.02
1645	—	Conjock	—	—	R.B. 863, 43 1645.06.03 to
	—	Goyko	—	—	1646.06.10
1646	—	Goyko, alias Singon	—	—	R.B. 863, 268 1646.06.11 to
	—	Doctor Isaack (*Chinese Christian Isaac Loccon*)	—	—	1647.06.07
1647	—	Conjocq	—	—	R.B. 863, 432 1647.06.08 to
	—	Khopeco	—	—	1648.06.06
Closed 1648.06.06 to 1655.11.04					
1655	—	Conjock	—	—	R.B. 867, 349 1655.11.05 to
	—	Soetse	—	—	1656.10.19

APPENDIX 2: NAME LISTS   257

Year	Name according to *Kai Ba Lidai Shiji*	Name according to Dutch sources	Year of appointment according to *Kai Ba Lidai Shiji*	Term of service according to *Kai Ba Lidai Shiji*	Term of service according to Dutch sources
1656	—	Conjock	—	—	Valentyn, IV, 407
	—	Soetse	—	—	1656.10.20 to 1657.06.06
1657	—	Conjock (*Deceased in office*)	—	—	R.B. 869, 138 DRB 1656–57, 171
	—	Soetse	—	—	1657.06.02 to 1658.05.31
1658	—	Soetse	—	—	R.B. 870, 106 1658.06.01 to 1659.06.06
1659	—	Soetse	—	—	R.B. 871, 100 DRB 1659, 118
	—	Sanjock	—	—	1659.06.07 to 1660.06.04
1660	—	Soetse	—	—	R.B. 872, 71 1660.06.05 to
	—	Sanjock	—	—	1661.06.04
1661	—	Sanje (*Succeeded by Khopeko 6 months*)	—	—	R.B. 873, 99 DRB 1661, 175 1661.06.05 to 1662.06.01
	—	Wanjock (蔡煥玉)	—	—	
1662	—	Wanjock	—	—	R.B. 875, 123 1662.06.02 to
	—	Khopeko	—	—	1663.05.31
1663	—	Khoupeko	—	—	R.B. 875, 123 DRB 1663, 224
	—	Saqua (*Limsaqua*)	—	—	1663.06.01 to 1664.06.06

TABLE 4   *Chinese* Boedelmeesters (*Curators*) *in Batavia* (cont.)

Year	Name according to *Kai Ba Lidai Shiji*	Name according to Dutch sources	Year of appointment according to *Kai Ba Lidai Shiji*	Term of service according to *Kai Ba Lidai Shiji*	Term of service according to Dutch sources
1664	—	Soeko (李祖觀)	—	—	R.B. 876, 242 DRB 1654, 229; 1655, 130 1664.06.07 to 1665.06.04
	—	Wanjock	—	—	
1665	—	Soeko	—	—	R.B. 877, 180 DRB 1665, 131; 1666–67, 81 1665.06.05 to 1666.06.03
	—	Wanjock	—	—	
1666	—	Gisay (*Sisai* 林時使)	—	—	R.B. 878, 166–167 DRB 1666–67, 81 1666.06.04 to 1667.06.02
	—	Khopeko	—	—	
1667	—	Gisay	—	—	R.B. 879, 96–97 DRB 1666–67, 287 1667.06.02 to 1668.05.30
	—	Khopeko	—	—	
1668	—	Gisay	—	—	R.B. 880, 137 DRB 1668–69, 102 1668.06.01 to 1669.06.06
	—	Soeko (李祖觀)	—	—	
1669	—	Soeko	—	—	R.B. 881, 130 DRB 1668–69, 339 1669.06.07 to 1670.06.05
	—	Wanjock	—	—	

APPENDIX 2: NAME LISTS

Year	Name according to *Kai Ba Lidai Shiji*	Name according to Dutch sources	Year of appointment according to *Kai Ba Lidai Shiji*	Term of service according to *Kai Ba Lidai Shiji*	Term of service according to Dutch sources
1670	—	Wanjock	—	—	R.B. 882, 97
	—	Lim Saqua	—	—	DRB 1670–71, 90
					1670.06.06 to
					1671.06.04
1671	—	Lim	—	—	R.B. 883, 125
					DRB 1670–71,
	—	Soeko	—	—	352
					1671.06.05 to
					1672.06.02
1672	—	Soeko	—	—	R.B. 884, 150;
					885, 177
	—	Wanjock	—	—	DRB 1672, 148
					1672.06.03 to
					1673.06.01
1673	—	Wanjock	—	—	R.B. 885, 178
					DRB 1673, 136
	—	Gisay (林時使)	—	—	1673.06.02 to
					1674.06.01
1674	—	Gisay	—	—	R.B. 886, 148
					DRB 1674, 148
	—	Lim Zaqua	—	—	1674.06.02 to
					1675.06.06
1675	—	Limsaqua	—	—	R.B. 887, 101
					DRB 1675, 153
	—	Wanjock	—	—	1675.06.07 to
					1676.06.04
1676	—	Wanjock	—	—	R.B. 888, 101
					DRB 1676, 122
	—	Gisay (林時使)	—	—	1676.06.05 to
					1677.06.03

TABLE 4   *Chinese* Boedelmeesters *(Curators) in Batavia* (cont.)

Year	Name according to *Kai Ba Lidai Shiji*	Name according to Dutch sources	Year of appointment according to *Kai Ba Lidai Shiji*	Term of service according to *Kai Ba Lidai Shiji*	Term of service according to Dutch sources
1677	—	Gisay	—	—	R.B. 889, 113
	—	Soeko (李祖觀)	—	—	DRB 1677, 163; 1678, 286 1677.06.04 to 1678.06.02
1678	—	Soeko	—	—	R.B. 890, 143 DRB 1678, 289
	—	Tanhonqua	—	—	1678.06.03 to 1679.06.03
1679	—	[Oeij] Koeko (黃舅觀)	—	—	R.B. 891, 243 DRB 1679, 235–236
	—	Que-Sieuqua	—	—	1679.06.04 to 1680.05.31
1680	—	[Oeij] Koeko	—	—	R.B. 892, 370 DRB 1680, 320
	—	Quesieuqua	—	—	1680.06.01 to 1681.06.06
1681	—	Bondziqua	—	—	R.B. 893, 301 DRB 1681, 322–323
	—	Limzinqua	—	—	1681.06.06 to 1682.06.05
1682	—	Bondsiqua	—	—	R.B. 896, 619 DRB 1682-I, 728
	—	Limzinqua	—	—	1682.06.06 to 1683.06.04

APPENDIX 2: NAME LISTS 261

Year	Name according to *Kai Ba Lidai Shiji*	Name according to Dutch sources	Year of appointment according to *Kai Ba Lidai Shiji*	Term of service according to *Kai Ba Lidai Shiji*	Term of service according to Dutch sources
1683	—	Quedsieuqua alias Jouko	—	—	R.B. 897, 380 1683.06.05 to 1684.06.01
	—	Limkeko (林敬觀) (*Limkeenqua alias Jacob*)	—	—	
1684	—	Quedsiqua	—	—	R.B. 898, 197 1684.06.02 to 1685.06.01
	—	Limkeko	—	—	
1685	—	Bonsiqua (*Succeeded by Limjako 10 months*)	—	—	R.B. 899, 245 1685.06.02 to 1686.05.30
	—	Quepauqua (郭包觀)	—	—	
1686	—	Quepauqua	—	—	R.B. 900, 254 1686.05.31 to 1687.06.05
	—	Lim Jako	—	—	
1687	—	Lim Jako	—	—	R.B. 901, 306 1687.06.06 to 1688.06.01
	—	Tanjongqua	—	—	
1688	—	Tantsjongqua	—	—	R.B. 902, 259–260 1688.06.02 to 1689.06.02
	—	Limsinqua	—	—	
1689	—	Limsinqua	—	—	R.B. 903, 240 1689.06.03 to 1690.06.01
	王悟觀 Wang Wuguan	Ong Gouko	1696	1696–1699	

TABLE 4   Chinese Boedelmeesters (Curators) in Batavia (cont.)

Year	Name according to Kai Ba Lidai Shiji	Name according to Dutch sources	Year of appointment according to Kai Ba Lidai Shiji	Term of service according to Kai Ba Lidai Shiji	Term of service according to Dutch sources
1690	—	Ong Gouko	—	—	R.B. 904, 271
	—	Tswa-wiko	—	—	1690.06.02 to 1691.05.31
	郭郡觀 Guo Junguan	Queeconko	1690	1690–1693	—
1691	—	Tswa Wiko	—	—	R.B. 905, 262 1691.06.01 to 1692.06.05
	—	Limkeko	—	—	
1692	—	Limkeko	—	—	R.B. 907, 383 1692.06.06 to 1693.06.05
	—	Ong Gouko	—	—	
1693	—	Ong Gouko	—	—	R.B. 908, 327 1693.06.06 to 1694.06.03
	—	Lim Jako	—	—	
1694	—	Lim Jako	—	—	R.B. 909, 373–374 1694.06.04 to 1695.06.03
	—	Lim Sinqua	—	—	
1695	—	Limsinqua (Succeeded by Bepeequa 4.5 months)	—	—	VOC 710, 412 D.R.B. 2514, 367 1695.06.04 to 1696.05.31
	—	Tsoayqua (Tsoa Uwqua)	—	—	
1696	—	Tsoa-Uwqua (Deceased in Office 8 months)	—	—	R.B. 912, 302 1696.06.01 to 1697.06.04
	—	Bepeequa	—	—	
1697	—	Bepeequa	—	—	R.B. 913, 257 1697.06.05 to 1698.06.05
	—	Pousaaqua	—	—	

APPENDIX 2: NAME LISTS 263

Year	Name according to *Kai Ba Lidai Shiji*	Name according to Dutch sources	Year of appointment according to *Kai Ba Lidai Shiji*	Term of service according to *Kai Ba Lidai Shiji*	Term of service according to Dutch sources
1698	—	Pousako (*Pausako*)	—	—	R.B. 914, 199 1698.06.06 to 1699.06.04
	—	Ong Gouko	—	—	
1699	—	Ong Gouko	—	—	R.B. 915, 177 1699.06.05 to 1700.06.03
	—	Bepequa	—	—	
1700	—	Bepequa	—	—	R.B. 916, 253 1700.06.04 to 1701.06.02
	—	Li-Joncko (李容哥)	—	—	
1701	—	Li-Joncko	—	—	R.B. 917, 179 1701.06.03 to 1702.06.01
	—	Pausaqua	—	—	
1702	—	Pausaqua	—	—	R.B. 918, 257 1702.06.02 to 1703.06.07
	—	Tio Jino / Tio Iunio	—	—	
1703		Tyo Iunio	—	—	R.B. 919, 273 1703.06.08 to 1704.06.05
	—	B[e]pequa	—	—	
1704	—	Nio Jonko / Liejonko (李容哥)	—	—	R.B. 920, 344 1704.06.06 to 1705.06.04
	—	Gou Oulauw (*Deceased in office*)	—	—	
1705	—	Gouw Lienko / Holienko (何蓮觀)	—	—	R.B. 921, 372 1705.06.05 to 1706.06.03
	魏惠觀 Wei Huiguan	Goey Hoey Kong	1696	1696–1699	

TABLE 4   *Chinese* Boedelmeesters (*Curators*) *in Batavia* (cont.)

Year	Name according to *Kai Ba Lidai Shiji*	Name according to Dutch sources	Year of appointment according to *Kai Ba Lidai Shiji*	Term of service according to *Kai Ba Lidai Shiji*	Term of service according to Dutch sources
1706	—	Gouw Lienko / Holienko	—	—	R.B. 924, 393 1706.06.04 to 1707.06.02
	—	Goey Hoey Kong	—	—	
	—	Tanlianko	—	—	
1707		Tanlianko			R.B. 925, 434 1707.06.03 to 1708.05.31
	周美爹 Zhou Meidie	Tsieuw Bitia (*Thebitsia*)	—	—	
	郭昂觀 Guo Maoguan	Que Bauqua (*Quebauko*)	1712	1712–1715	
1708	—	Tsieuw Bitia	—	—	R.B. 928, 425 1708.06.01 to 1709.05.30
	—	Que Bauqua	—	—	
	李俊觀 Li Junguan	Litsoenqua (*Lie Tsjoenqua*)	1693	1693–1696	
1709	—	Litsoenqua	—	—	R.B. 929, 233 1709.05.31 to 1710.06.05
	—	Goey Hoey Kong (魏惠觀)	—	—	
	陳財觀 Chen Caiguan	Tan Sayko	1699	1699–1702	
1710	—	Goey Hoey Kong	—	—	R.B. 930, 249 1710.06.06 to 1711.06.04
	—	Tan Sayko	—	—	
	—	Lim Som Ko (林森觀)	—	—	

APPENDIX 2: NAME LISTS 265

Year	Name according to *Kai Ba Lidai Shiji*	Name according to Dutch sources	Year of appointment according to *Kai Ba Lidai Shiji*	Term of service according to *Kai Ba Lidai Shiji*	Term of service according to Dutch sources
1711	—	Lim Som Ko	—	—	VOC 727, 412
	—	Tanlianko	—	—	D.R.B. 2535, 422
	—	Que Bauqua	—	—	1711.06.05 to 1712.06.02
1712	—	Tanlianko	—	—	VOC 728, 347
	—	Que Bauqua	—	—	D.R.B. 2537, 343–344
	葉敬觀 Ye Jingguan	Jap Keengko	1718	1718–1720	1712.06.03 to 1713.06.01
1713	—	Jap Keengko	—	—	VOC 729, 312
	—	Goey Hoey Kong (魏惠觀)	—	—	1713.06.02 to 1714.05.31
	—	Tan Sayko	—	—	
1714	—	Goey Hoey Kong	—	—	D.R.B. 2541, 614 1714.06.01 to 1715.05.30
	—	Tan Sayko	—	—	
	—	Que Bauqua	—	—	
1715	—	Que Bauqua	—	—	R.B. 939, 366
	王鞍觀 Wang Anguan	Ongwako	1715	1715–	1715.05.31 to 1716.06.04
	連祿觀 Lian Luguan	Nilocko	1699	1699–1702	

TABLE 4 *Chinese* Boedelmeesters (*Curators*) *in Batavia* (cont.)

Year	Name according to *Kai Ba Lidai Shiji*	Name according to Dutch sources	Year of appointment according to *Kai Ba Lidai Shiji*	Term of service according to *Kai Ba Lidai Shiji*	Term of service according to Dutch sources
1716	—	Ongwako	—	—	R.B. 941, 332
	—	Nilocko	—	—	1716.06.05 to
	—	Goey Hoey Kong (魏惠觀)	—	—	1717.06.03
1717	—	Goey Hoey Kong	—	—	VOC 733, 392–393
	—	Tanliongko	—	—	1717.06.04 to
	—	Lihoeyko	—	—	1718.06.02
1718	—	Tanliongko	—	—	VOC 734, 315
	—	Lihoeyko	—	—	1718.06.03 to
	—	Limtsoenko (林春哥)	—	—	1719.06.01
1719	—	Limtsoenko	—	—	VOC 735, 430
	王泰觀 Wang Taiguan	Ongthayko	1714	1724–1727	1719.06.02 to 1720.06.06
	李援觀 Li Yuanguan	Liwanko	1712	1712–1715	
1720	—	Ongthayko	—	—	VOC 736, 366
	—	Liwanko	—	—	1720.06.07 to
	康敬觀 Kang Jingguan	Kungkeengko	1702	1702–1705	1721.06.05

APPENDIX 2: NAME LISTS   267

Year	Name according to *Kai Ba Lidai Shiji*	Name according to Dutch sources	Year of appointment according to *Kai Ba Lidai Shiji*	Term of service according to *Kai Ba Lidai Shiji*	Term of service according to Dutch sources
1721	—	Kungkeengko	—	—	VOC 737, 199
	—	Goey Hoey Kong (魏惠觀)	—	—	1721.06.06 to 1722.06.04
	陳財觀 Chen Caiguan	Tan Sayko	1726	1726	
1722	—	Goey Hoey Kong	—	—	VOC 738, 197–198
	—	Tan Sayko	—	—	1722.06.05 to
	王成功 Wang Chenggong	Ongseenko	1714	1714–1718	1723.06.03
1723	—	Ongseenko	—	—	VOC 739, 182
	—	Que Tsoenko (郭春官)	—	—	1723.06.04 to 1724.06.01
	李裕觀 Li Yuguan	Litsoeko	1715	1715–	
1724	—	Que Tsoenko	—	—	VOC 740, 271 1724.06.02 to
	—	Li Tsoeko	—	—	1725.05.31
	—	Li Tsianko	—	—	
1725	—	Li Tsiangko	—	—	VOC 741, 257
	陳忠舍 Chen Zhongshe	Tan Tionqua	1714	1714–1720	1725.06.01 to 1726.06.06
	—	Ongseenko	—	—	

TABLE 4 Chinese Boedelmeesters (Curators) in Batavia (cont.)

Year	Name according to *Kai Ba Lidai Shiji*	Name according to Dutch sources	Year of appointment according to *Kai Ba Lidai Shiji*	Term of service according to *Kai Ba Lidai Shiji*	Term of service according to Dutch sources
1726	—	Tan Tionqua	—	—	VOC 742, 341
	—	Ongseenko	—	—	1726.06.07 to
	—	Nilocko (連祿觀)	—	—	1727.06.05
1727	—	Tan Tionqua (陳忠舍)	—	—	VOC 743, 358 1727.06.06 to
	林養生 Lin Yangsheng	Limjenko	1727	1727–1731	1728.06.03
	—	Nilocko	—	—	
1728	—	Lim Inko (Limjenko, Lim Janko)	—	—	VOC 744, 277 1728.06.04 to 1729.06.02
	陳天生 Chen Tiansheng	Tan Tien Seeng	1720	1720–1725	
	陳進光 Chen Jinguang	Tan Tsinkong (alias Gouw Tsing Kong, Gouw Sinkong)	1731	1731–1732	

APPENDIX 2: NAME LISTS

Year	Name according to *Kai Ba Lidai Shiji*	Name according to Dutch sources	Year of appointment according to *Kai Ba Lidai Shiji*	Term of service according to *Kai Ba Lidai Shiji*	Term of service according to Dutch sources
1729	—	Tan Tsinkong (陳進光) alias Gouw Singkong	—	—	VOC 745, 357 1729.06.03 to 1730.06.01
	—	Tan Tien Seeng (陳天生)	—	—	
	—	Gouw Goankong (吳元光)	—	—	
1730	—	Gouw Goankong	—	—	VOC 746, 625 1730.06.02 to 1731.05.31
	康政舍 Kang Zhengshe	Kung Tsiangko	1737	1737–1738	
	連富光 Lian Fuguang	Nihoekong	1723	1723–1726	
1731	—	Kung Tsiangko	—	—	VOC 747, 759–760 1731.06.01 to 1732.06.05
	—	Nihoekong	—	—	
	許純觀 Xu Chunguan	Khouwsoenko (*No assumption*)	1705	1705–1712	
1732	邱祖觀 Qiu Zuguan	Khoe Tsouwko	1705	1705–1712	VOC 749, 990 1732.06.06 to 1733.06.04
	—	Li Hooko	—	—	
	許屬觀 Xu Shuguan	Khou Tsiocko	1738	1738–1740	

TABLE 4   Chinese Boedelmeesters (Curators) in Batavia (cont.)

Year	Name according to *Kai Ba Lidai Shiji*	Name according to Dutch sources	Year of appointment according to *Kai Ba Lidai Shiji*	Term of service according to *Kai Ba Lidai Shiji*	Term of service according to Dutch sources
1733	— — —	Hoet Siauwko Li Hooko Khou Tsiocko (*VOC 753, 1031*) Succeeded by Oey Somko (*11 months*) and Ni Goan Kong (*5 months*)	— — —	— — —	VOC 751, 826–827 1733.06.05 to 1734.06.03 (renewed)
1734	— 連元光 Lian Yuanguang 陳賞光 Chen Shangguang	Oey Tsomko (黃篆哥) Nigoang Kong Tan Tsiangko	— 1726 1736	— 1726–1729 1736–1738	VOC 753, 1037 1734.06.04 to 1735.06.02
1735	— — 陳振光 Chen Zhenguang	Nigoang Kong Tan Tsiangko Tan Tsinko (*Succeeded by Oey Eengko, 4 months*)	— — 1738	— — 1738–1740	VOC 755, 1017–1018 1735.06.03 to 1736.05.31

APPENDIX 2: NAME LISTS

Year	Name according to *Kai Ba Lidai Shiji*	Name according to Dutch sources	Year of appointment according to *Kai Ba Lidai Shiji*	Term of service according to *Kai Ba Lidai Shiji*	Term of service according to Dutch sources
1736	黃應觀 Huang Yingguan	Oey Eengko (*Deceased in Office*)	1702	1702–1705	VOC 757, 655 1736.06.01 to 1737.06.06
	連蓮光 Lian Lianguang	Nilienkong	1729	1729–1732	
	—	Tan Hoeko	—	—	
1737	—	Nilienkong	—	—	VOC 757, 655 1736.06.01 to 1737.06.06
	—	Tan Hoeko	—	—	
	李驛觀 Li Yiguan	Li Jaco	1738	1738–1740	
1738	—	Li Jaco	—	—	VOC 761, 664 1738.06.06 to 1739.06.04
	連捷光 Lian Jieguang	Nitsietkong	1729	1729–1735	
	黃燕觀 Huang Yanguan	Oey Inko	1733	1733–1736	
1739	—	Oey Inko	—	—	VOC 763, 838 1739.06.05 to 1740.06.02
	—	Nitsietkong	—	—	
	黃恭使 Huang Gongshi	Oey Kionko	1738	1738–1740	

TABLE 4   Chinese Boedelmeesters (Curators) in Batavia (cont.)

Year	Name according to Kai Ba Lidai Shiji	Name according to Dutch sources	Year of appointment according to Kai Ba Lidai Shiji	Term of service according to Kai Ba Lidai Shiji	Term of service according to Dutch sources
1740	—	Oey Inko	—	—	VOC 765, 539
	連福光 Lian Fuguang	Ni Hocko	1739	1739–	1740.06.03 to 1741.06.01
	王寬使 Wang Kuanshi	Ong Khoangsay	1740	1740–1742	
	—	(VOC 768, 488) Johannes van Hoogstede, Roeland Blaas, and Gabriel van Gheeren took office	—	—	
1741	—	—	—	—	—
1742	蘇俊觀 Su Junguan	Souw Tsoenseeng	1742	1742–1745	—
1743	—	—	—	—	—
1744	—	Souw Tsoenseeng	—	—	VOC 773, 390–391
	施標觀 Shi Biaoguan	Sie Piauwko	1745	1745–1747	1744.06.05 to 1745.06.03
1745	—	Souw Tsoenseeng	—	—	VOC 775, 336 1745.06.04 to
	—	Sie Piauwko	—	—	1746.06.02
1746	—	Lou Saenseeng	—	—	VOC 776, 295
	—	Sie Piauwko	—	—	1746.06.03 to 1747.06.01
1747	—	Sie Piauwko	—	—	VOC 777, 379
	林椿舍 Lin Chunshe	Lim Thoenko	1748	1748–1751	1747.06.02 to 1748.06.10

APPENDIX 2: NAME LISTS 273

Year	Name according to *Kai Ba Lidai Shiji*	Name according to Dutch sources	Year of appointment according to *Kai Ba Lidai Shiji*	Term of service according to *Kai Ba Lidai Shiji*	Term of service according to Dutch sources
1748	— 黃燕觀 Huang Yanguan	Lim Thoenko Oey I. Enko	— 1747	— 1747–	VOC 778, 123 1748.06.11 to 1749.06.02
1749	— —	Lim Thoenko Oey I. Enko	— —	— —	VOC 779, 161–162 1749.06.03 to 1750.06.04
1750	— 陳疏觀 Chen Shuguan	Ong Eengsay (王應使) Tan Sauko	— 1751	— 1751–1754	VOC 780, 257 1750.06.05 to 1751.06.07
1751	— —	Tan Souko Lim Ki-Enko (林健哥)	— —	— —	VOC 781, 173 1751.06.08 to 1752.06.01
1752	— 郭賀觀 Guo Heguan	Tan Souko (陳疏觀) Que Hoko	— 1753	— 1753–1755	VOC 782, 125 1752.06.02 to 1753.06.04
1753	— —	Tan Souko Que Hoko	— —	— —	VOC 783, 318 1753.06.05 to 1754.06.30
1754	— —	Que Honko Lim Theeko (林釗哥)	— —	— —	VOC 784, 509 1754.07.01 to 1755.06.05
1755	— — 林初光 Lin Chuguang	Lim Theeko Lu Hako —	— — 1755	— — 1755–1757	VOC 785, 345 1755.06.06 to 1756.06.17 —

TABLE 4   Chinese Boedelmeesters (Curators) in Batavia (cont.)

Year	Name according to Kai Ba Lidai Shiji	Name according to Dutch sources	Year of appointment according to Kai Ba Lidai Shiji	Term of service according to Kai Ba Lidai Shiji	Term of service according to Dutch sources
1756	— —	Lim Theeko Lu Hako	— —	— —	VOC 786, 178 1756.06.18 to 1757.06.09 (renewed)
1757	— 陳巧郎 Chen Qiaolang	Lu Hako Tankalong	— 1760	— 1760–1763	VOC 787, 104–105 1757.06.10 to 1758.06.08
1758	— —	Lu Hako Tankalong	— —	— —	VOC 788, 87 1758.06.09 to 1759.06.07
1759	—	Tankalong	—	—	VOC 789, 104 1759.06.08 to 1760.06.02
1760	— —	Lu Hako Tankalong	— —	— —	K.R.B. 790, 488–489 1760.06.03 to 1761.06.01
1761	施華觀 Shi Huaguan —	Sie Huako Tankalong	1757 —	1757–1760 1760–1768	VOC 791, 472 1761.06.02 to 1762.06.07
1762	王懿光 Wang Yiguang 吳文哥 Wu Wenge	Ong Ingkong Gouw Boenko	1763 1763	1763–1770 1763	VOC 792, 166 1762.06.08 to 1763.06.06
1763	— —	Ong Ingkong Gouw Boenko	— —	— —	VOC 793, 153 1763.06.07 to 1764.06.04

APPENDIX 2: NAME LISTS   275

Year	Name according to *Kai Ba Lidai Shiji*	Name according to Dutch sources	Year of appointment according to *Kai Ba Lidai Shiji*	Term of service according to *Kai Ba Lidai Shiji*	Term of service according to Dutch sources
1764	— 劉成光 Liu Chengguang	Ong Ingkong Louw Sengkong	— 1766	— 1766	VOC 794, 159 1764.06.05 to 1765.06.03
1765	—	[Ong Ingkong] [Louw Sengkong]	— —	— —	VOC 795, 140 1765.06.04 to 1766.06.02 (not mentioned)
1766	— 吳樹觀 Wu Shuguan	Ong Ingkong Gouw Sieuko	— 1766	— 1766–1767	VOC 796, 273 1766.06.03 to 1767.06.01
1767	— — 吳喜觀 Wu Xiguan	Ong Ingkong Gouw Sieuko —	— — 1767	— — 1767–1780	VOC 797, 539 1767.06.02 to 1768.06.01 —
1768	— — 陳彩觀 Chen Caiguan	Ong Ingkong Gouw Sieuko [Tan Tjaijko]	— — 1768	— — 1768–1771	VOC 798, 428 1768.06.02 to 1769.06.05 —
1769	— —	Ong Ingkong Gouw Sieuko	— —	— —	R.B. 1048, 519 1769.06.06 to 1770.06.11 (renewed)
1770	黃郡觀 Huang Junguan 高根觀 Gao Genguan	Oey Kinkong Ko Kinko	1771 1770	1771–1772 1770–1775	VOC 800, 153–154 1770.06.12 to 1771.06.10

TABLE 4   *Chinese* Boedelmeesters *(Curators)* in Batavia *(cont.)*

Year	Name according to *Kai Ba Lidai Shiji*	Name according to Dutch sources	Year of appointment according to *Kai Ba Lidai Shiji*	Term of service according to *Kai Ba Lidai Shiji*	Term of service according to Dutch sources
1771	—	Oey Kinkong	—	—	VOC 801, 195 1771.06.11 to 1772.06.03
1772	— 胡探觀 Hu Tanguan	Ko Kinko Khouw Tanko [Ouw Tanko]	— 1772	— 1772–	VOC 802, 295–296 1772.06.04 to 1773.06.08
1773	唐偏舍 Tang Pianshe 林漢丹 Lin Handan	Tiung Pienko Lim Hantan	1772 1774	1772–1774 1774–1776	VOC 803, 322 1773.06.09 to 1004.06.06
1774	— —	Tiung Pienko Lim Hantan	— —	— —	VOC 804, 202 1774.06.07 to 1775.06.07
1775	— —	Tiung Pienko Lim Hantan	— —	— —	VOC 805, 195 1775.06.08 to 1776.06.13
1776	陳富老 Chen Fulao 高永老 Gao Yonglao	Tan Hoelo Koinko	1775 1776	1775–1783 1776–1778	VOC 806, 398 1776.06.14 to 1777.06.02
1777	— —	Tan Hoelo Koinko	— —	— —	VOC 807, 588–589 1777.06.03 to 1778.06.01
1778	— 黃綿舍 Huang Mianshe	Tan Hoelo Oey Biankong	— 1778	— 1778–1784	VOC 808, 789 1778.06.02 to 1779.05.31
1779	— —	Tan Hoelo Oey Biankong	— —	— —	VOC 809, 554–555 1779.06.01 to 1780.06.07

APPENDIX 2: NAME LISTS   277

Year	Name according to *Kai Ba Lidai Shiji*	Name according to Dutch sources	Year of appointment according to *Kai Ba Lidai Shiji*	Term of service according to *Kai Ba Lidai Shiji*	Term of service according to Dutch sources
1780	— —	Tan Hoelo Oey Biankong	— —	— —	VOC 810, 510–511 1780.06.08 to 1781.06.20
1781	— —	Tan Hoelo Oey Biankong	— —	— —	VOC 811, 666–667 1781.06.21 to 1782.06.13
1782	— —	Tan Hoelo Oey Biankong	— —	— —	VOC 812, 428 1782.06.14 to 1783.06.05
1783	— —	Tan Hoelo Oey Biankong	— —	— —	VOC 813, 357 1783.06.06 to 1784.06.07
1784	— 陳泌生 Chen Misheng	Oey Biankong Tan Piseeng	— 1783	— 1783–1790	VOC 814, n.p. 1784.06.08 to 1785.06.06
1785	— 陳水觀 Chen Shuiguan	Tan Piseeng Tan Soeyko	— 1784	— 1784–1790	VOC 815, 736–737 1785.06.07 to 1786.06.28
1786	— —	Tan Piseeng Tan Soeyko	— —	— —	VOC 816, 865–866 1786.06.29 to 1787.06.07
1787	— —	Tan Piseeng Tan Soeyko	— —	— —	VOC 818, 917 1787.06.07 to 1788.06.09
1788	— —	Tan Piseeng Tan Soeyko	— —	— —	VOC 820, 783–784 1788.06.10 to 1789.06.18

TABLE 4   Chinese Boedelmeesters (Curators) in Batavia (cont.)

Year	Name according to *Kai Ba Lidai Shiji*	Name according to Dutch sources	Year of appointment according to *Kai Ba Lidai Shiji*	Term of service according to *Kai Ba Lidai Shiji*	Term of service according to Dutch sources
1789	— —	Tan Piseeng Tan Soeyko	—	—	R.B. 1110, 2185–2186 1789.06.19 to 1790.06.14 (renewed)
1790	— —	Tan Piseeng Tan Soeyko	—	—	R.B. 1114, 443–444 1790.06.15– (renewed)
	陳寬觀 Chen Kuanguan	[Tan Koanko]	1790	1790–1791	VOC 824, 979 1790.06.15– (not mentioned)
	林長生 Lin Zhangsheng	[Lim Tiangseeng]	1790	1790–1792	—
1791	陳炳郎 Chen Binglang	[Tan Peengko]	1791	1791–1792	VOC 827, 126 1791.06.21– (not mentioned)
1792	黃董觀 Huang Dongguan	[Oeij Tamko]	1792	1792–1793	Oost Indisch Comité 66 (unknown)
	戴弘觀 Dai Hongguan	[Tee Honko]	1792	1792–1795	—
1793	—	—	—	—	Oost Indisch Comité 70 (unknown)
1794	—	—	—	—	—
1795	陳果生 Chen Guosheng	—	1795	1795–1799	—

APPENDIX 2: NAME LISTS 279

SOURCES:

1. Chinese sources
(1) *Kai Yaolaoba Lidaishi Quanlu* (開咬吧歷代史全錄), the Liem manuscript, pp. 6a–6b;
(2) *Kai Ba Lidai Shiji* (開吧歷代史紀), The Leiden manuscript, pp. 18b–21b;
(3) Xu Yunqiao, 'The Early Accounts of Chinese in Batavia, a revised and annotated edition' (開吧歷代史紀校注), in *Nanyang Xuebao* (南洋學報), IX(1), 1953, pp. 18–20.

2. Dutch sources
(1) B. Hoetink, 'Chineesche Officieren te Batavia onder de Compagnie', *Bijdragen tot de Taal-, Land- en Volkenkunde van Nederlandsch-Indië*, deel 78, 1/2de Afl. (1922): blz. 8–9, 88–95.
(2) Hsin Samuel Cha, 'Collegie van Boedelmeesters of Batavia in the Seventeenth and Eighteenth Century' (draft only).

R.B. = Net-generale resoluties en—incidenteel—net-secrete resoluties. Grotendeels met inhoudsopgaven. Gedeeltelijk kopie, 1613–1810, Archief van de Gouverneur-Generaal en Raden van Indië (Hoge Regering) van de Verenigde Oostindische Compagnie en taakopvolgers, 1612–1812, nr. 853–1182. Arsip Nasional Republik Indonesia, Jakarta.

DRB = J.A. van der Chijs, et al., eds. *Dagh-Register gehouden in't Casteel Batavia van't passerende daer ter plaetse als over geheel Nederlandts-India, 1624–1682*, 30 delen (Batavia: G. Kolff, 1887–1931).

D.R.B. = Journalen ('Daghregisters'). Grotendeels met inhoudsopgaven en/of alfabetische indices. Minuut, net en kopie, 1640–1806, nr. 2457–2622. Arsip Nasional Republik Indonesia, Jakarta.

Valentyn IV = F. Valentyn, *Oud en Nieuw Oost-Indiën, Vervattende een Naaukeurige en Uitvoerige Verhandelinge van Nederlands Mogentheyd in de Gewesten ...*, deel IV/A (Dordrecht: Joannes van Braam / Amsterdam: Gerard onder de Linden, 1724).

VOC = K.R.B. = Kopie-resoluties van gouverneur-generaal en raden. Gedeeltelijk met inhoudsopgaven, 1637–1791, Verenigde Oostindische Compagnie (VOC), 1602–1795 (1811), nr. 661–827. Nationaal Archief, Den Haag.

TABLE 5 *Chinese Secretaries of the Kong Koan (Chinese Council) of Batavia during the rule of the VOC*

No.	Name	Year of appointment	Term of service	Remarks
1	黃市鬧 Huang Shinao	1750	1750–1751	Less than a year, to be promoted Captain.
2	黃良全[(1)] Huang Liangquan	1751	1751.10–1751.12	Dies after two months in office.

TABLE 5 *Chinese Secretaries of the Kong Koan (Chinese Council) of Batavia* (cont.)

No.	Name	Year of appointment	Term of service	Remarks
3	黃冉光 Huang Ranguang	1751	1751–1758	
4	胡保耀 Hu Baoyao	1758	1758–1769	Originally a monk, then disrobed and turned into secretary.
5	徐仲奇 Xu Zhongqi	1766	1766–1768	Two secretaries from then on.
6	林跨祖 Lin Kuazu	1768	1768–1785	
7	林春光 Lin Chunguang	1769	1769–1790	
8	林榮祖 Lin Rongzu	1785	1785–	A grandson of Captain Lin Mingguang (林明光), the eldest son of Boedelmeester Lin Chunshe (林椿).
9	吳纘綬(2) Wu Zuanshou	1791	1791–1799	The second son of Lieutenant Wu Panshui (吳泮水), younger brother of Captain Wu Zuanxu (吳纘緒).

SOURCES: *KAI YAOLAOBA LIDAISHI QUANLU* (開咬咾吧歷代史全錄), THE LIEM MANUSCRIPT, P. 6B; *KAI BA LIDAI SHIJI* (開吧歷代史紀), THE LEIDEN MANUSCRIPT, PP. 22B-23B; LU ZIMING (陸子明), *LIREN BAGUO GONGTANG SHUJI TIMINGLU* (歷任吧國公堂書記題名錄), IN XU YUNQIAO, "THE EARLY ACCOUNTS OF CHINESE IN BATAVIA, A REVISED AND ANNOTATED EDITION" (開吧歷代史紀校注), IN *NANYANG XUEBAO* (南洋學報), IX(1), 1953, PP. 20–21.
NOTES: (1) HUANG LIANGQUAN (黃良全) WAS CALLED HUANG JINLIANG (黃金良) IN THE REVISED AND ANNOTATED EDITION OF XU YUNQIAO, BUT WAS KNOWN AS HUANG LIANGQUAN (黃良全) IN THE LEIDEN AND LIEM MANUSCRIPTS.
(2) WU ZUANXU (吳纘緒) AND WU ZUANSHOU (吳纘綬) WERE CALLED WU ZUXU (吳組緒) AND WU ZUSHOU (吳組綬) RESPECTIVELY IN THE LEIDEN MANUSCRIPT AND IN THE REVISED AND ANNOTATED EDITION OF XU YUNQIAO.

APPENDIX 2: NAME LISTS

TABLE 6   *Chinese* Soldaten (*Soldiers*) *during the VOC period*

No.	Name	Year of appointment	Term of service	Remarks
1	林蓮觀 Lin Lianguan	1633	1633–1684	Served fifty-three years until his death.
2	洪石光 Hong Shiguang	1684	1684–1728	Served forty-four years until his death.
3	郭扶觀 Guo Fuguan	1728	1728–1740	Served twelve years until the rebellion in 1740.
4	遊添觀 You Tianguan	1738 1742	1738–1740 1742–	Served two years until the rebellion, but entered into service again in 1742.
5	何忖觀 He Cunguan	1740 1742	1740 1742–1767	In prison for debt, then served three months as undertaker.
6	葉華觀 Ye Huaguan	1766	1766–1791	
7	何局觀 He Juge	1767	1767–1791	Nephew of He Cunguan (何忖觀).
8	許富哥 Xu Fuge	1791	1791–1793	
9	許誦哥 Xu Songge	1793	1793–1808	

SOURCE: *KAI BA LIDAI SHIJI* (開吧歷代史紀), THE LEIDEN MANUSCRIPT, PP. 24B–25A.

TABLE 7   *Chinese Undertakers in Batavia during the VOC period*

No.	Name	Year of appointment	Term of service	Remarks
1	黃石公 Huang Shigong	1650	1650–1685	The first Chinese undertaker in Batavia.
2	顏經觀 Yan Jingguan	1685	1685–1728	The Chinese officers created a new cemetery and appointed the eldest son of Yan Jingguan as undertaker in 1728.

TABLE 7 *Chinese Undertakers in Batavia* (cont.)

No.	Name	Year of appointment	Term of service	Remarks
3	顏巒觀 Yan Luanguan	1728	1728–1745	The eldest son of Yan Jingguan. Father and son both were undertakers.
4	黃聯觀 Huang Lianguan	1745	1745–1758	In 1745, the Kong Koan (Chinese Council) of Batavia established three cemeteries, and appointed three undertakers to take charge of them. The first undertaker Huang Lianguan was in charge of the Eastern cemetery (東塚), the second undertaker He Cunguan of the Western cemetery (西塚) and the third undertaker Su Quanguan of the Japanese pavilion (日本亭) cemetery.
5	何忖觀 He Cunguan	1745 1763	1745–1760 1763–	The second undertaker in charge of the Western cemetery (西塚). After his death in 1767 there were only two undertakers left.
6	蘇全觀 Su Quanguan	1745	1745–	The third undertaker in charge of the Japanese pavilion (日本亭). In 1760, the Kong Koan (Chinese Council) of Batavia established another cemetery at Gunung Sari.
7	許燦觀 Xu Canguan			

SOURCE: *KAI BA LIDAI SHIJI* (開吧歷代史紀), THE LEIDEN MANUSCRIPT, PP. 25B–26A.

APPENDIX 2: NAME LISTS   283

TABLE 8   *Non-Chinese names in the* Kai Ba Lidai Shiji

Mandarin Spelling	Chinese Characters	Original Name	Remarks
Alang Chengjiang	阿郎成江	Aru Sinkang	The King of the Bugis in Makassar
Alü'an Banjinian	阿慮安伴吉哷	Adriaan Valckenier	Governor General
Anduonian Ban Lüli	安多哷伴慮宜	Antonio van Diemen	Governor General
Anze Ganlanli	安責幹藍裡	Intje Kanari	Makassarese warrior
Awulong Badelao	阿勿壟巴得勞	Abraham Patras	Governor General
Badenü Weiman	巴得女碨蠻	Padri Weiman	Dutch individual
Banlaomi	班嘮嘧	Alexander Cornabé	Governor of Ambon
Bananmaohan	巴南貓罕	Panembahan	Royal title of the ruler of Mataram
Ban Wulan	伴勿覽	Andreas Everardus van Braam Houckgeest	Supercargo at Canton and emissary to the Qing court.
Baolao	報嘮	?	Member of the Council of the Indies, 1793
Bazhili Baoyushi	巴直裡包鬱氏	?	Jewish rabbi
Bei	杯	Mom?	Member of the Council of the Indies, 1793
Bide Gebianzhi	庇得葛邊值	Pieter de Carpentier	Governor General
Bidelü Huoweitu Ban Luo Baluo	敝得律豁微突伴螺巴嘮	Petrus Albertus van de Parra	Governor General
Bizhi Guiyou	庇之龜幼	Pieter Erberfeld	Freeburgher and presumed conspirator
Bizhi Wu	庇直物	Pieter Both	Governor General
Bolishi Putaoya	勃栗氏葡萄衙	Willem IV of Orange Nassau	Dutch Stadtholder
Dashe	大舍	Toassa	Pirate chief
Duan Yayu	緞亞裕	Tuan Ajoeb	Javanese exile
Ema'e	蕚嗎蕚	Gog of the land of Magog	Biblical figure
Ganpei	矸呸	?	Ceylonese Prince
Gaolinian Ban Li Lin	高哩哖伴禮僯	Cornelis van der Lijn	Governor General
Gaolinian Ran Shibiman	高裡年然是必蠻	Cornelis Janszoon Speelman	Governor General

TABLE 8   *Non-Chinese names in the* Kai Ba Lidai Shiji *(cont.)*

Mandarin Spelling	Chinese Characters	Original Name	Remarks
Geshashi	葛殺氏	?	Member of the Council of the Indies, 1793
Jiaolü Luonianshi	膠慮螺哖氏	Carel Reiniersz	Governor General
Jililuoshiduobo Ban Yixin	吉慮螺氏多勃伴一忻	Christoffel van Swoll	Governor General
Kuijiamijingwennan	奎甲迷井汶難	?	Villain from Banten
Kui Jiaoba	奎礁罷	Kiai Tapa	Muslim elder from Banten
Kuilaozhen	奎勝陣	Kiai Radin?	Javanese
Kuiluoli	奎螺力	Reinier de Klerck	Governor General
Lannan Wang	蘭難王	Herman Willem Daendels	Governor General
Laochu Shinüba	唠廚失女巴	Ratu Fatima	Wife of the Sultan of Banten
Lao Mingshide	勞冥實德	Jeremias van Riemsdijk	Governor General
Lao Mingshide Mei lang	唠冥實德袂郎	Willem Vincent Helvetius van Riemsdijk	Landowner, son of the G.G.
Laonengshi Lihuo	咾能是禮豁	Laurens Reael	Governor General
Laoyi Wang	荖逸王	Louis XVI	King of France
Laozhen	勝陣	Radin	Bantenese headman
Lun	倫	Neun?	Member of the Council of the Indies, 1793
Luojilu Ban Niushi	螺吉祿伴牛氏	Rijklof van Goens	Governor General
Made Li Han	嗎得厘罕	Mattheus de Haan	Governor General
Maoge	貓格	de Bock?	Member of the Council of the Indies, 1793
Maolao	毛勝（唠）	Murah	Robber chief
Maowushi Wang	貓兀氏望	Ratu Bagus Buang	Bantenese rebel
Maolishilin	貓厘士㷠	?	Bantenese person
Meise	美色	Wiese?	Member of the Council of the Indies, 1793

APPENDIX 2: NAME LISTS

Mandarin Spelling	Chinese Characters	Original Name	Remarks
Mingshidi Along Ban Lümoshi	冥實弟阿壟伴慮默氏	Mr. Abraham van Riebeeck	Governor General
Mingshidi Luoli Bang Jilong	冥實弟螺力邦吉壟	Mr. Dirk van Cloon	Governor General
Mingshidi Luoli Ban Laowu	冥實弟螺力伴勞物	Mr. Diederik Durven	Governor General
Mingshidi Weilang Ban Wudaolang	冥實弟微啷伴烏道郎	Mr. Willem van Outhoorn	Governor General
Ran Bide Jun	然庇得郡	Jan Pietersz Coen	Governor General
Raoshi Bazhili	饒氏巴直裡	?	Jewish Rabbi
Rege Xibaishi	惹各習白氏	Jacques Specx	Governor General
Rege Maoshu	惹閣毛述	Jacob Mossel	Governor General
Rilaonian	日嘮哖	Djitlane	Native captain
Ronghua	絨滑（戎滑）	Kapitein Jonker	Ambonese Captain
Rongqili	榮訖力	Sebastiaan Nederburgh?	Commissioner General
Shenmi	神密	Johannes Siberg	Member of the Council of the Indies
Shilao'erlanzhao	史勞爾藍罩	Selalilada alias Wijaya Krama	Ruler of Jayakarta
Rousong	柔悚	Joosten?	Dutchman
Suqipo	速訖潑	Hendrick van Stockum	Member of the Council of the Indies
Tisheng	提陞	Isaac Titsingh	Member of the Council of the Indies
Wan Linmeide	萬林媚德	W.V.H. van Riemsdijk?	Member of the Council of the Indies, 1793
Wo Liding	沃力丁	W. Arnold Alting	Governor General
Xiandali	仙達裡		Muslim holy man
Xinnao Ming	新嶢明	Justinus Vinck	Landdrost
Xinxi	新禧	?	Member of the Council of the Indies, 1793
Yaguo	牙國	J.[acob?] A. Duurkoop	Dutch estate owner
Yali Nengshi	呀力能氏	Gerrit Reijnst	Governor General

TABLE 8   *Non-Chinese names in the* Kai Ba Lidai Shiji *(cont.)*

Mandarin Spelling	Chinese Characters	Original Name	Remarks
Yashijiao Weilang Maolang Ban Xiongmu	呀實礁微瑯貓郎伴熊木	Gustaaf Willem baron van Imhoff	Governor General
Yawumaoge	亞務貓葛	Abubakar	Gujarati Gaptain
Yingdeli Wulaofan	應得力物勞凡	Hendrik Brouwer	Governor General
Yingdeli Zhalijilun	應得力柵裡吉倫	Hendrik Swaardecroon	Governor General
Yuan Andelao	袁安得勝	Wang Abdullah	Captain Melayu
Yu'an Ban Wulun	裕安伴烏倫	Joan van Hoorn	Governor General
Yu'an Maxichi	裕安嗎西吃	Joan Maetsuijcker	Governor General
Yulaoyanyawang	裕嘮眼亞望	?	Bantenese rebel
Yushi	宇實	Djoesit	Commissioner, officer.
Yuya Lidining	裕亞禮地寧	Johannes Thedens	Governor General
Yuya Yanliujia	裕亞眼六甲	Doeta Laijana	Bantenese rebel
Zixin	字信	Djisim	Balinese Captain

TABLE 9   *Place Names in the* Kai Ba Lidai Shiji

Western Name	Name in Chinese
Alkmaar	亞六馬
Ambon	安汶
Amoy (Xiamen)	廈門
Amsterdam	奄失覽、暗濕覽
Angke	洪溪
Ancol	安恤
Bali	峇（貓）厘
Banda	萬達
Banjarmasin	馬辰
Banka	邦加
Banten	萬丹
Banyuwangi	外南望（夢）、外南旺
Batavia	勿礁維、吧城
Bekasi	望加寺
Belitong (Billiton)	勿裡洞

APPENDIX 2: NAME LISTS

Western Name	Name in Chinese
Bengal	望絞剌
Benteng	文登（丁）
Blandongan	聖望（墓）港
Bogor, Buitenzorg	茂物（兀）、冒冗山、務兀墟、尾陳
Bugis	武訖（吃）
Calcutta	高實踏
China	唐山（中國）
Cirebon	井里汶
Ceylon	西琅（郎、啷）
Cochin	龜靜國
Delft	螺納
Dordrecht	茗律
Eastern Cemetery	東塚
Eindhoven	蔭裡寅
English People	紅毛人
Enkhuizen	應魁順
Fengyang prefecture	鳳陽府
France	荷蘭西
Fukien (Fujian)	福建
Glodok	戈（高）勞屈
Grenoble, France	吃力勿螺予
Guangdong	廣東
Gunung Sari	牛郎丗（些）里
Hebrew (Jewish) people	奚勿留氏
Heerlen	亞以寧
Holland	和蘭、和
Hoorn	和倫
Ikan, Pasar	魚潤
Jagalan	宰牛巷
Jaga Monyet	惹呀毛吃
Jakarta	如吉礁、如吉得勝、裕吃礁
Jalan Directeur Generaal	二王街
Jalan Panjang	吃浪班讓
Jambatan Lima	五腳橋
Jambatan Tiga	三角橋
Japanese pavilion	日本亭
Java	爪亞（鴉）、爪哇
Jilakien	廿六間

TABLE 9   *Place Names in the* Kai Ba Lidai Shiji (cont.)

Western Name	Name in Chinese
Kaap de Goede Hoop (Cape of Good Hope)	鴿牛嶼（鴨地）
Kali Besar	大港墘
Kali Berang	甲裡武郎
Kampung Melayu	鑒光每勝由
Kalapa, Kelapa	噶喇吧、咬咾吧、吧國
Kelapa Dua	咖嘮吧賴（咬嘮吧賴）
Klenteng	觀音亭
Kodjah (Gujarat)	高（戈）奢
Kota Shi (Xinchi)	高踏屎（新池）
Kramat	加覽（南）抹
Krawang	茄老旺（膠荖汪）
Krokot, Krukut	高勞屈
Lembang	覽旁
Longyan garden	龍眼園
Lugutou (Coral Point)	魯古頭
Madura	未流嘮
Makassar	望加錫（孟加錫）
Malaka (Melaka)	麻六甲
Mangga Dua	蚊加賴，望加賴
Mataram	覽內
Mayoran	馬蟯蘭（嗎腰蘭）
Melayu	無勝由
Mocha	木膠
Muak	大木腳、大末脚
Onrust	王嶼
Padang	巴（把）東、過西
Pancoran	班蕉蘭
Patekoan	八茶罐
Pecinan	八（班）芝蘭
Pekojan	八戈然
Petuakan	八廚沃間
Pinangsia	檳榔社
Pintu Besar	大南門
Pintu Kecil	小南門

Western Name	Name in Chinese
Prinsenstraat	爵仔街
Pulau Lambat	浮羅南抹
Pulau Tunda	浮羅敦嘮
Portuguese	勃直吃氏、葡萄衙
Rembang	南望
Riau	廖內
Rotterdam	茗四覽、老置覽
Rotterdammerpoort	東門
Semarang	三寶壠
Schiermonnikoog	是在鴼
Selebar	實螺潑
Senen, Pasar	結石珍
Siam	暹羅
Smids straat	打鐵街
Sulo	梭羅
Sunda	順達
Sunda Sea	順達洋
Sunda Strait	勃系門
Sungai Atap	阿答港口
Surabaya	泗裡末（泗水）
Surat	思嘮知
Sweden	綏嶙
Tanah Abang	丹藍望
Tangerang	丁腳蘭（文登）
Tanjung	丹絨
Tanjung Kait	丹絨加逸
Ternate	澗仔抵
Toko Tiga	三間土庫
Tong'ankou (at the river mouth)	桶岸口
Utrechtsche poort	西門
Vierkantspoort	北門
Western Cemetery	西塚
Xiamen (Amoy)	廈門
Xinchi (New Pond, Kota Shi)	新池
Xinwuli (West of river mouth)	欣勿力

Appendix 3: Glossary of Malay and Dutch Terms in *Kai Ba Lidai Shiji*

Mandarin	Chinese Characters	Origin Malay	Origin Dutch	English
Anda	安哒	Antar	Garant	Collateral
Ba	犮(鈸)	Fanam	Fanam	Twenty pennies
Banqilan	班奇蘭(邦奇蘭)	Pangeran	Prins	Prince
Baxian	八仙	Persen	Procent	Percent
Bomian	泊面	Pabean	Boom	Custom house
Budie	廊爹(蔀爹)	Potia	Suiker molenaar	Sugar miller
Choukui	抽奎	Cukai	Belasting heffen	Levy a tax
Dagou	大狗	Sekaut	Schout	Sheriff
Danbangong	淡板公	Temenggung	Hoofd; Baljuw	Headman; Bailiff
Dashi	達氏	Soldadu	Soldaat	Soldier
Dawang	大王	Gubernur Jenderal	Gouverneur-generaal	Governor General
Duan	緞	Tuan	Mijnheer	Mister
Emanlü	鵝蠻律	Gubernur	Gouverneur	Governor
Emanlü rendelao	鵝蠻律仁得勝	Gubernur Jenderal	Gouverneur-generaal	Governor General
Fang	鈁	Kupang	Stuiver (Penning)	Penny
Fenpai	分派	Utusan	Gezant	Envoy
Gandao	干刀	Kantor	Kantoor	Office
Gaopi	高丕	Kopi	Koffie	Coffee
Gongbanya	公班衙	Kompeni	[Verenigde Oost-Indische] Compagnie (VOC)	East India Company
Gongbolong	公勃壟	Komandan	Commandant	Commander
Gongmanlü	公蠻律	Gubernur	Gouverneur	Governor
Gongboxie(sa)li	公勃些(卅)里	Komisaris	Commissaris	Commissioner
Guasa(sha)	掛卅(沙)	Kuasa	Volmacht	Authority
Jiaban chuan	甲板船	Kapal	(Retour) schip	East Indiaman

APPENDIX 3: GLOSSARY OF MALAY AND DUTCH TERMS

Mandarin	Chinese Characters	Origin		English
		Malay	Dutch	
Jiabidan (Jiada)	甲必丹(甲大)	Kapitan	Kapitein	Captain
Jiabidan rendelao	甲必丹仁得勝	Kapitan Genderal	Kapitein-Generaal	Captain General
Jian	澗	Gang	Gang	Narrow street
Jianguang	鑒光	Kampung	Kampong	Village
Kuiwei	奎維	Orang Kaya	Voorname	Man of prowess
Landelü	蘭得律	Landrad	Landraad	Native court of justice
Langying	郎迎	Ronggeng	Dansmeisje	Female dancer
Laoshen	勞申	Losin	Dozijn	dozen
Laojun	老君	Dukun	Dokter	Doctor
Lei	鐳(雷)	Duit	Duit	Copper coin
Leizhenlan	雷珍蘭	Letnan	Luitenant	Lieutenant
Liangjiao	梁礁	Notaris	Notaris	Notary
Lilong	黎壟	Lelang	Veiling	Auction
Maowei han	貓味蚶	Babi ham	Varkensham	Pork ham
Mazai	傌仔	Béa	Pacht	Tax farm
Meisegan	美色甘	Miskin (Rumah)	Weeskamer	Orphans Chamber
Meisegan Zhu	美色甘朱	Sekretaris Weeskamer	Secretaris van de Weeskamer	Secretary of the Weeskamer
Meisegan Bingcuo	美色甘病厝	Rumah sakit miskin	Weeskamer ziekenhuis	Weeskamer hospital
Meisege	美色葛	Piskal	Fiscaal	Public prosecutor
Meisejin	美色（僅）近	Miskin	Armenhuis	Poor-house
Michalao	嗹喳嘮	Bicara	Raad	Council
Michalao Cuo	嗹喳嘮厝	Gedung bicara	Raad (van Justitie)	Courthouse
Pu	贌	Pajak, Pak	Pacht	Tax farm
Reya	喏牙	Jaga	Wacht	Guard
Sezainian	色仔哖	Serani	Serani	Eurasian
Shafang	卅鈁	Syahbandar	Shahbandarij	Business tax
Shenwanda	沈萬達	Syahbandar	Shahbandar	Harbour-master

(cont.)

Mandarin	Chinese Characters	Origin		English
		Malay	Dutch	
Shidan	史丹	Sultan	Sultan	Sultan
Shijiao	詩礁	Sita	Confiscatie	Confiscation
Shisunlan (Xunlan)	史孫蘭(巡欄)	Susuhunan (Sunan)	Soesoehoenan [van Mataram]	Ruler of Mataram
Shuangbing	雙柄	Skepen	Schepen	Alderman
Tuku	土庫	Toko	Factorij / Kasteel	Factory / Castle
Wuliwo	勿裡窩	Baliu	Baljuw	Sheriff
Wuzhimi	武直迷	Budelmister	Boedelmeester	Curator of wills
Xilan	息夳(畣)	Selam	Islamiet	Muslim
Yapian	鴉片	Afiun	Opium	Opium
Zhebu	蔗廊(蔗蔀)	Pengilingan gula	Suikermolen	Sugar mill
Zhugejiao	朱葛礁	Sekretaris	Secretaris	Secretary

Bibliography

Bataviaasch Genootschap van Kunsten en Wetenschappen, ed. *Realia. Register op de generale resolutiën van het kasteel Batavia 1632–1805*. Leiden: Kolff, 1882. 3 vols.

Berg, van der, N.P. 'Het toneel te Batavia in vroegeren tijd'. In *Uit de dagen der Compagnie, geschiedkundige schetsen*, 97–191. Haarlem: Tjeenk Willink, 1904.

Blussé, Leonard. 'The Caryatids of 17th-Century Batavia: Reproduction, Religion and Acculturation under the VOC'. In *Strange Company*, 156–71.

Blussé, Leonard. 'Jakarta: Erberveld-monument, de nieuwe kleren van de koningin van het oosten'. In *Plaatsen van herinnering*, vol. 2, *Nederland in de zeventiende en achttiende eeuw*, edited by Maarten Prak, 390–99. Amsterdam: Bert Bakker, 2006.

Blussé, Leonard. 'Doctor at Sea: Chou Mei-yeh's voyage to the West (1710–1711)'. In *As the Twig is Bent...: Essays in Honour of Frits Vos*, edited by Erica de Poorter, 7–30. Amsterdam: J.C. Gieben, 1990.

Blussé, Leonard. 'Driemaal is scheepsrecht. Batavia 1619, 1627–1629'. In *Belaagd en belegerd*, edited by Herman Amersfoort, Hans Blom, Dennis Bos, and Gijsbert van Es, 147–69. Amsterdam: Balans, 2011.

Blussé, Leonard. 'John Chinaman Abroad: Chinese Sailors in the Service of the VOC'. In *Promises and Predicaments, Trade and Entrepreneurship in Colonial and Independent Indonesia in the 19th and 20th Centuries*, edited by Alicia Schrikker and Jeroen Touwen, 101–12. Singapore: NUS Press, 2015.

Blussé, Leonard. 'One Hundred Weddings and Many More Funerals a Year: Chinese civil society in Batavia at the end of the eighteenth century'. In *The Archives of the Kong Koan of Batavia*, edited by Leonard Blussé and Chen Menghong, 8–28.

Blussé, Leonard. *Strange Company: Chinese Settlers, Mestizo Women and the Dutch in VOC Batavia*. Dordrecht-Holland: Foris, 1986.

Blussé, Leonard. 'Trojan Horse of Lead: the Picis in Early 17th Century Java'. In *Between People and Statistics. Essays on Modern Indonesian History*, edited by F. van Anrooy, 33–48. The Hague: Martinus Nijhoff, 1979.

Blussé, Leonard. 'The VOC and the Junk Trade to Batavia: A Problem in Administrative Control'. In *Strange Company: Chinese Settlers, Mestizo Women and the Dutch in VOC Batavia*, 97–155. Dordrecht-Holland: Foris, 1986.

Blussé, Leonard. 'Wills, Widows and Witnesses: Executing Financials Dealings with the Nanyang—A glimpse from the notebook of the Dutch Vice-Consul at Amoy, Carolus Franciscus Martinus de Grijs'. In *Maritime China in Transition 1750–1850*, edited by Ng Chin-keong & Wang Gungwu, 317–34. Wiesbaden: Harrasowitz Verlag, 2004.

Blussé, Leonard, and Chen Menghong. *The Archives of the Kong Koan of Batavia*. Leiden: Brill, 2003.

Blussé, Leonard, and Wu Fengbin. *The Chinese Community of Batavia at the End of the Eighteenth Century.* 包樂史，吳鳳斌：*18世紀末吧達維亞唐人社會*. 廈門：廈門大學出版社, 2002.

Brommer, Bea. *To My Dear Pieternelletje, Grandfather and Granddaughter in VOC Time, 1710–1720.* Leiden: Brill Hes & De Graaf, 2015.

Brug, van der, P.H. *Malaria en Malaise. De VOC in Batavia in de achttiende eeuw.* Amsterdam: Bataafse Leeuw, 1994.

Chen Menghong. *De Chinese gemeenschap van Batavia, 1843–1865: Een onderzoek naar het Kong Koan-archief.* Leiden: Leiden University Press, 2011. See www.leidenuniv.nl, library, catalogues, kong koan archive.

Chijs, van der, J.A. *Nederlandsch-Indisch Plakaatboek 1602–1811.* Batavia: Landsdrukkerij 1885–1900. 17 volumes.

Colenbrander, H.T. *Jan Pietersz Coen, Bescheiden omtrent zijn verblijf in Indië.* 's-Gravenhage: Nijhoff, 1919–53.

Cushman, Jennifer. 'Duke Ch'ing-fu deliberates: a mid-century reassessment of Sino-Nanyang commercial relations'. *Papers on Far Eastern History* 17. Canberra: Australian National University, 1978.

Deventer, van, M.L. *Geschiedenis van de Nederlanders op Java*, vol. 2. Haarlem: Tjeenk Willink, 1887.

Dewaraja, L.S. *The Kandyan Kingdom of Sri Lanka, 1707–1782.* Colombo: Lake House Investments, 1988.

Douglas, Carstairs. *Chinese–English Dictionary of the Vernacular or Spoken Language of Amoy, with the Principal Variations of the Chang-chew [Tsiangtsiu] and Chin-chew [Quanzhou] Dialects.* London: Trübner, 1873; with *Supplement* by Thomas Barclay Shanghai: The Commercial Press: 1923. Taipei: SMC Publishing Co (reprint).

Emden, van, F.J.G., and Willem Brand. *Kleurig memoriaal van de Hollanders op Oud-Java.* Amsterdam: Strengholt, 1964.

Erkelens, Monique. *The Decline of the Chinese Council of Batavia: The Loss of Prestige and Authority of the Traditional Elites amongst Chinese Community between 1900–42.* PhD diss., Leiden University, 2013. See www.leidenuniv.nl, library, PhD theses.

Feddersen, C. *Principled Pragmatism, VOC Interaction with Makassar 1637–68 and the Nature of Company Diplomacy.* PhD diss., Leiden University, 2016.

Fruin-Mees, W. *Geschiedenis van Java.* Weltevreden: Commissie voor de Volkslectuur, 1920.

Gaastra, F.S. *The Dutch East India Company. Expansion and decline.* Zutphen: De Walburg Pers, 2003.

Guangxu Zhangzhou Fu Zhi (光緒漳州府志) The Local Gazetteer of Zhangzhou sub-prefecture of the Guangxu reign. [1877].

Haan, de, Frederik. *Oud Batavia, gedenkboek uitgegeven ter gelegenheid van het driehonderdjarig bestaan der stad in 1919.* Batavia: Kolff, 1922.

Heydt, J.W. *Allerneuester Geographisch- und Topographischer Shau-Platz von Africa und Ost-Indien.* Wilhermsdorf: In Verlag des Authors, 1744.

Hibino Takeo (日比野丈夫). 'ジャカルタの牛郎沙里義塚碑につい, A Study of the Inscription of Gunung Sari Cemetery in Djakarta', 南方文化 *Nampo-Bunka, Tenri Bulletin of South Asian Studies*, (1975) 1–2: 41–55.]

Hoetink, B. 'Chineesche officieren te Batavia onder de Compagnie'. *Bijdragen tot de Taal-, Land- en Volkenkunde van Nederlandsch-Indië* 78: (1922): 1–136.

Hoetink, B. 'Ni Hoekong, kapitein der Chineezen te Batavia in 1740'. *Bijdragen tot de Taal-, Land- en Volkenkunde van Nederlandsch-Indië* 74 (1918): 447–518.

Hoetink, B. 'So Bing Kong. Het eerste hoofd der Chineezen te Batavia'. *Bijdragen tot de Taal-, Land- en Volkenkunde van Nederlandsch-Indië* 73 (1917): 344–415, and 79 (1923): 1–44.

Hoetink, B. 'De weduwe van kapitein Siqua'. *Chung Hwa Hui Tsa Chih* 2:1 (1918): 16–25 and 2:2 (1918): 98–107.

Hoëvell, van, W.R., and P. Meijer, eds. 'Chronologische geschiedenis van Batavia, geschreven door een Chinees, uit het Chineesch vertaald door W.H. Medhurst'. *Tijdschrift voor Neêrlands Indië* 3: 2 (1840): 1–145.

Hsu Yun-Tsiao (Xu Yunqiao), ed. '開吧歷代史紀, The Early Accounts of Chinese in Batavia (a revised and annotated edition)'. 南洋學報, *Journal of the South Seas Society* 9:1 (1953): 1–63.

Hsu Yun-Tsiao (Xu Yunqiao). 'Baguo Gongtang yu Huaqiao Shiliao' (吧國公堂與華僑史料) 'The Chinese Council of Batavia and Overseas Chinese sources' in 南洋學報, *Journal of the South Seas Society* (1955) 12, 17–22.

Hummel, Arthur W. *Eminent Chinese of the Ch'ing Period (1644–1912)*. Washington: United States Printing Office 1943. 2 vols.

Iwao Seiichi (岩生成一). 'ジャカルタの「新建養済列福戸捐金姓氏」の碑, On the Inscription of the *Yang-chi-yuan* 養濟院 (Chinese Hospital) in Jakarta', 南方文化 *Nampo-Bunka, Tenri Bulletin of South Asian Studies* (1975) 2, 13–25.

Iwao Seiichi (岩生成一). 'ベンコン一族の墓碑, Tombstones of Captain Bencon's family', 南方文化 *Nampo-Bunka, Tenri Bulletin of South Asian Studies* (1989) 16: 129–136.

Jackson, Jason Baird. 'The Story of Colonialism, or Rethinking the Ox-Hide Purchase in Native North America and Beyond'. *Journal of American Folklore* 126:499 (2013): 31–54.

Jonge, de, J.K.J. *De Opkomst van het Nederlandsch gezag in Oost-Indië. Verzameling van onuitgegeven stukken uit het Oud-Koloniaal Archief.* 's-Gravenhage: Nijhoff, 1862–1909.

Kanumoyoso, Bondan. *Beyond the City Wall: Society and Economic Development in the Ommelanden of Batavia, 1684–1740.* PhD diss., Leiden University, 2011.

Knaap, Gerrit. *Kruidnagelen en Christenen. De VOC en de bevolking van Ambon 1656–1696.* Leiden: KITLV, 2004.

Krom, N.J. *Gouverneur Generaal Gustaaf Willem van Imhoff*. Amsterdam: P.N. van Kampen, 1941.

Kuhn, Philip. *Chinese among Others: Emigration in Modern Times*. Lanham: Rowman & Littlefield, 2008.

Kuiper, Koos. *The Early Dutch Sinologists (1854–1900), Training in Holland and China, Functions in the Netherlands Indies*. Leiden: Brill, 2017.

Kuiper, Koos. 'The Chinese Name for "Holland": 和兰，荷兰，贺兰– a Historical Survey,' in Xu Quansheng 许全胜, Liu Zhen 刘震编, *Neilu Ou-Ya lishi yuyan lunji——Xu Wenkan xiansheng guxi jinian wen ji* 内陆欧亚历史语言论集——徐文堪先生古稀纪念文集, (Yu Taishan 余太山主编) Ou-Ya lishi wenhua wenku 欧亚历史文化文库 (Lanzhou: Lanzhou daxue chubanshe 兰州大学出版社, 2014), 72-98.

Li Minghuan. 'A Portrait of Batavia's Chinese Society Based on the Tandjoeng Cemetery Archives'. In *The Archives of the Kong Koan of Batavia*, edited by Leonard Blussé and Chen Menghong, 80–105. Leiden: Brill, 2003.

Liem Thian Joe. *Riwajat Semarang 1416–1931*. Semarang: Boekhandel Ho Kim Yoe, 1933.

Lohanda, Mona. *The Kapitan Cina of Batavia 1837–1942, A History of Chinese Establishment in Colonial Society*. Jakarta: Djambatam, second edition, 2001.

Lombard, Denis, and Claudine Salmon. 'Les Chinois de Jakarta; Temples et vie collective'. Paris: Maison de Science de l'homme, 1977.

Lu Jing (盧經), Chen Yanping (陳燕平), Wang Che (王澈), eds. '乾隆年間議禁南洋貿易案史料', Historical Materials in the First Historical Archive Concerning the Debates about Banning the Overseas Trade to the Nanyang during the Qianlong Period, *Lishi Dang'an, Historical Records* (2002) 2: 23–35.

Lukito, Hendra. *Riwayat Kapitan Tionghoa Pertama di Batavia Souw Beng Kong (1580–1644) Konservasi, Pelestarian dan Pengakuan Makamnya sebagai situs vaga budaya*. Jakarta: Yayasan Kapitan Souw Beng Kong, 2013.

Macartney, George. *An Embassy to China; Being the Journal Kept by Lord Macartney During His Embassy to the Emperor Ch'ien-Lung, 1793–1794*. Edited by J.L. Cranmer-Byng. London: Longmans, 1962.

Masselman, George. *The Cradle of Colonialism:* New Haven, Yale University Press, 1963.

Medhurst, W.H. *The Chinaman Abroad: An Account of the Malayan Archipelago, Particularly of Java*. London: 1850.

Medhurst, W.H. 'Chronologische Geschiedenis van Batavia, geschreven door een Chinees'. *Tijdschrift voor Neêrland's Indië* 3:2 (1840): 1–145.

Naamboek van den Hoog Edelen Gestrengen Heeren Commissarissen Generaal over geheel Nederlandsch Indië en Cabo de Goede Hoop, item van den Wel-Edelen Heeren der Hoge Indiasche Regeering zo tot, als buiten Batavia. Batavia: Pieter van Geemen 1786.

Nakamura Takashi (中村孝志). 'バタビィア華僑の徴税請負制度について, The Contract System in Tax Collection by the Chinese Merchants in Batavia', 東洋史研究 *Toyoshi Kenkyu* (1969) 28 -1, 52–79.

Newman, Andrew. 'The Dido Story in Accounts of Early Modern European Imperialism—An Anthology.' *Itinerario* 41:1 (2017): 129–50.

Ng Chin-keong. 'The Case of Ch'en I-lao: Maritime Trade and Overseas Chinese in Ch'ing Policies, 1717–1757'. In *Emporia, Commodities and Entrepreneurs in Asian Maritime Trade, c. 1400–1750*, edited by Roderick Ptak and D. Rothermund, 373–99. Stuttgart: Steiner, 1991.

Nie Dening, Wu Fengbin, Chen Menghong, Hou Zhenping and Leonard Blussé, et al., eds. 聶德寧，吳鳳斌，陳萌紅,侯真平，包樂史，*Gong An Bu (Minutes of the Board Meetings of the Chinese Council 1787–1920)*. 吧城華人公館(吧國公堂)檔案：公案簿, 1787–1920. 廈門：廈門大學出版社, 15 vols., 2002–17.

Niemeijer, Hendrik E. *Batavia. Een koloniale samenleving in de 17de eeuw*. Amsterdam: Balans, 2005.

Ong-Tae-Hae. *The Chinaman Abroad: or a Desultory Account of the Malayan Archipelago, particularly of Java*, translated by W.H. Medhurst. Shanghai: 1849.

Raben, Remco. *Batavia and Colombo: The Ethnic and Spatial Order of Two Colonial Cities, 1600–1800*. PhD diss., Leiden University, 1996.

Raffles, Thomas Stamford. *The History of Java*. 2 vols. 1817. Reprint Oxford: Oxford University Press, 1965–78.

Reid, Anthony, ed. *Slavery, Bondage & Dependency in Southeast Asia*. St Lucia: University of Queensland Press, 1983.

Remmelink, W.G.J. *Emperor Pakubuwana II, Priyayi & Company and the Chinese War*. Leiden: KITLV, 1991.

Rhede van der Kloot, van, M.A. *De Gouverneurs-Generaal en Commissarissen-Generaal van Nederlandsch-Indië 1610–1888, historisch-genealogisch beschreven*. 's Gravenhage: W.P. van Stockum, 1871.

Rietbergen, P.J.A.N. *De eerste landvoogd Pieter Both (1568–1615)*. Zutphen: Walburg Pers, 1987.

Robidé van der Aa, P.J.B.C. 'De groote Bantamsche opstand in het midden der vorige eeuw, bewerkt naar meerendeels onuitgegeven bescheiden uit het oud-koloniaal archief met drie officiële documenten als bijlagen'. *Bijdragen tot de Taal-, Land- en Volkenkunde van Nederlandsch-Indië* 29:1 (1881): 1–59, 60–100, 101–106, and 107–27.

Ruan Yonghe (Yon Weng Woe 阮湧俰), 'Research on Southeast Asia Ming Adherents in using the word "Long Fei", 东南亚明朝遗民使用"龙飞"之动机考证' Unpublished MA thesis, Xiamen University 2017.

Salmon, Claudine. 'Ancient Chinese Cemeteries of Indonesia as Vanishing Landmarks of the Past (17th–20th c.)'. In Claudine Salmon, ed. 'Chinese Deathscapes in Insulindia'. *Archipel* 92 (2016): 23–62.

Salmon, Claudine. 'Un Chinois à Java (1729–1736)'. *Bulletin de l'École française d'Extrême-Orient* 59 (1972): 279–318.

Salmon, Claudine. 'The Massacre of 1740 as Reflected in a Contemporary Chinese Narrative'. *Archipel* 77 (2009): 149–54.

Salmon, Claudine. 'Women's Social Status as Reflected in Chinese Epigraphs from Insulinde (16th–20th Centuries)'. *Archipel* 72: 1 (2006): 157–94.

Salmon, Claudine. 'Hsu Yun Tsiao (1905–1981)', *Archipel* (1983) 25, 3–5.

Salmon, Claudine. *Ming Loyalists in Southeast Asia, As Perceived though Various Asian and European Records*. Wiesbaden: Harrassowitz Verlag, 2014.

Salmon, Claudine. 'Wang Dahai and his View of the 'Insular Countries (1791)'. In Ding Choo Ming & Ooi Kee Beng, eds. *Chinese studies of the Malay World, A Comparative Approach*. Singapore: Eastern University Press, 2003, 31–67.

Salmon, Claudine, and Denys Lombard. *Les Chinois de Jakarta: temples et vie collective*. Paris: Editions de la Maison des Sciences de l'Homme, 1980.

Shapiro, Judith. *Mao's War Against Nature*. Cambridge: Cambridge UP, 2001.

Sidharta, Myra. 'The Role of the Go-Between in Marriages in Batavia'. In *The Archives of the Kong Koan of Batavia*, edited by Leonard Blussé and Chen Menghong, 46–59. Leiden: Brill, 2003.

Stapel, F.W. *De Gouverneurs-Generaal van Nederlandsch-Indië in beeld en woord*. Den Haag: Van Stockum, 1941.

Talens, Johan. *Een feodale samenleving in koloniaal vaarwater. Staatsvorming, koloniale expansie en economische onderontwikkeling in Banten, West-Java (1600–1750)*. Hilversum: Verloren, 1999.

Tan Yeok Seong (陳育崧, Chen Yusong). 'The Chinese in Batavia and the Troubles of 1740' (English version) in *Journal of the South Seas Society* (1953) Volume IX-I, 1–68.

Valentijn, François. *Oud en nieuw Oost-Indiën*. 5 vols. Dordrecht: Johannes van Braam, 1724–27.

Vermeulen, J. Th. *De Chineezen te Batavia en de troebelen van 1740*. Leiden: Eduard IJdo, 1938. English translation: Tan Yeok Seong. 'The Chinese in Batavia and the Troubles of 1740'. *Journal of the South Seas Society* 9:1 (1953): 1–68.

Vermeulen, J. *Eenige opmerkingen over de rechtsbedeeling van de Compagnie in de 17de en 18de eeuw voor de Chineesche samenleving*, lezing voor het China-instituut te Batavia, [s.n.], 1939. 11–12. English translation: Y.S. Tan. 'Some Remarks about the Administration of Justice by the Compagnie in the 17th and 18th century in respect of the Chinese Community'. *Journal of the South Seas Society*, 12:2 (1956): 4–12.

Vos, Reinout. *Gentle Janus, Merchant Prince: The VOC in the Malay World, 1740–1800*. Leiden: KITLV Press, 1993.

Wagenaar, Lodewijk. *Galle, VOC-vestiging in Ceylon. Beschrijving van een koloniale samenleving aan de vooravond van de Singalese opstand tegen het Nederlandse gezag, 1760*. Amsterdam: De Bataafsche Leeuw, 1994.

Wall, van de, V.I. *Oude Hollandsche buitenplaatsen van Batavia*. Deventer: Van Hoeve, 1943.

Wang Dahai (王大海), Yao Nan (姚楠) ed. *Haidao Yizhi [Island Memories]*, 海島逸志, 香港: 學津書店出版, 1992.

Wilkinson, Endymion. *Chinese History: A Manual*. Cambridge: Harvard University Press, 2000.

Wu Fengbin, Nie Dening, and Xie Meihua. *The Chinese Marriages in Jakarta: Marriage Registrations of Chinese in Batavia 1772–1919*. Xiamen: Xiamen University Press, 2010. [In Chinese—吴凤斌，聂得宁，谢美华编纂：雅加达华人婚姻，1772–1919 年吧城唐人成注註冊簿. 厦门：厦门大学出版社，2010.]

Zhang Xie (张燮). *Dong xi yang kao* (東西洋考 A Study of the Eastern and Western Oceans), Beijing: Zhonghua Shuju, 1981. [First published in 1618].

Zhou Kai (周凱). *Xiamen Zhi* (廈門誌 Xiamen Gazetteer), Taipei 1961, [First published in 1832]. 5 vols.

Index of Personal and Geographical Names

Page numbers in italic refer to tabular matter. **Page numbers in bold** refer to illustrations.

Abbis, Henry 134n
Abu Bakar 156
Abu'l Fatah 72n
Aceh 205
Agung, Sultan 59n, 68n
Alang Chengjiang (Aru Sinkang) 113; *283*
Alkmaar, Neth. 70; *286*
Alting, Willem Arnold 181–82, 186n, 192n, 195, 198n; *248, 250, 254, 255, 285*
Amat, Enci 110n
Ambachtskwartier (handicraft quarter) 10
Ambon 71–72n, 92n, 187n; Chinese officials in: 114n, 179, 197; Dutch in: 53n, 73n; exiles to: 103, 119, 136, 147–48, 168, 176; *286*
Ambonese 11, 82, 94, 113, *285*
American Republic 182n
Americas 6, 51n
Amsterdam 84n, 118; chamber of the VOC: 51n, 53n, 61n; natives of: 52n, 53n, 61, 73, 76, 97, 99n, 116; *286*
Ancol 158, 190, 207, 208; *286*
Angke River (Hongxi) xi, 62, 127, 166, 207, 209; *286*
Anze Ganlanli *See* Kanari, *Encek*
Aru Palaka 71n, 75n, 82n, 86n
Aru Sinkang *See* Alang Chengjiang
Arung Palaka *See* Aru Palaka
Asenka (Ashenjiao) 209
Ashenjiao *See* Asenka
Asia 6, 8, 12, 55n, 56n; Dutch in: 8, 51, 188n

Baarle, van, Hendrick 112n
Babok 125
Bacan 218
Bachaguan (Patekoan) 209; *288*
Bacheng (Batavia) x *note*
Bagoes Massar 174n
Bagoes Slinki 174
Bagoes, *Enci*/ *Encek* 110n
Bali 11, 19, 71, 137, 170; *286*
Balinese 11, 23, 218; cemetery: 77; soldiers: 71, 82, 103, 113, 153, 154n; wives: 18–19, 23, 68n, 72–73
Bananmaohan *See* Panembahan

Banda Is. 54, 97, 180, 205, 230; *286*
Bandanese 11
Bangka Is. (Wangjiayu) 222n
Bangka Strait (Sanli) 206, 229
Banjarmasin 145–46, 205; *286*
Banjiaojian *See* Pancoran
Ban Laomi 197
Banlong 137
Bantam *See* Banten
Banten (Bantam; Wandan) 3, 5, 7–8, 95, 205; Batavia vs.: 94; *boom* in: 140; Chinese in: 37, 59, 64n, 156; Dutch in: 51–52, 55, 96, 99; English and: 56n, 75n; French at: 196; fugitives in: 131; Great Banten Rebellion: 154n; internal disputes: 67, 80, 151; missions to: 97, 151; pacification of: 152–56; river to: 107; *shahbandar* at: 141; war with (1656): 110n; *286*
Banten Lama (Old Banten) 96n
Bantenese *284, 286*
Banten, sultan of 31, 40, 54, 58n; threatened: 72, 118, 120, 148–49; and Dutch: 147, 174
Banyuwangi (Wainanwang) 170; *286*
Bao'en Si (Bao'en Temple) 209
Baolao 197
Batavia (Betawi) 3–4, 58n, 76n; administration in: 10, 17, 22, 29, 33, 61, 71–72n, 152, 211, 230, 234; banishment to: 77n, 120; and Banten: 37, 64n, 67n; bay of, 52, 87, 148, 162, 188, 191; buildings in: 37, 64, 76, 236; cemeteries in: 21; Chinese community in: x, xv, 8, 10, 17–18, 23, 26, 38, 77–78, 198; Chinese-Dutch relations in: 7–11; Chinese massacre at: 47, 116n, 123–24, 128–33, 176–77; Chinese reaction to massacre at: xii, 47–48, 135, 220–28, 240; Chinese rebellion in: 39, 122–28, 144, 176; Chinese trade with: 9–10, 59–61, 68n, 134, 179, 184, 219–28; customs in: 237; design of: 8, 121, 207; Dutch in: 3, 6, 230; English and: 75, 195; environment of: 7, 12–17, 108, 215, 229, 232; environs of: 11, 206; founding of: 36, 51n, 54, 58n, 212; goods at: 11, 120, 216, 227, 230; immigration to: 38;

Kapitan Melayu in: 109–10n; money in: 185, 190; morphology of: 3, 47; name of: x–xi, 3, 52n, 205; neighborhoods of: 10, 104n, 139n, 142n, 172, 177n, 190n, 208, 232; population of: 6, 10, 15; slavery in: 10–11; social services in: 22–23; taken by Dutch: 216; women in: 17–18, 20, 23, 212; writing about: xi–xiii, 25–47; *286*
Batavia Castle (Wangcheng) 76; 164, 197; officials of: 103n, 110n, 114n, 178n; prisoners in: 39, 116n, 119n, 134n, 136n, 190
Batavia-Centrum 172n
Bazhilan *See Pecinan*
Bei 197
Beijiaolang *See* Pekalongan
Beijing xi *note*, 47, 199, 216
Bekasi (Wangjiaosi) 3, 209, 222n, 225; in Chinese massacre: 127, 132, 137; *286*
Bencon *See* Su Mingguang
Bengal 113, 114n, 116, 151n, 184; Bengalis, 218; *287*
Benlu Zouma (Serong and Tjiomas) 209
Benteng 127, 171; *287*
Bepeequa/Bepequa *262, 263*
Betawi *See* Batavia
Bima 205
Binansia (Binlangshe) 173
Bingam *See* Pan Mingyan
Bingsam *256*
Binlangshe *See* Binansia
Blaas, Roeland 272
Black Devils Is. 206
Blandongan (Shengmu Gang) 207; *287*
blok O, Batavia 142n, 149n, 177n
blok P, Batavia 104n
Bock, Adriaan de (Maoge, Ba-keh) 197; *284*
Bogor (Buitenzorg; Maowuxu, Weichen) 3, 137, 154n, 159, 162, 218; gardens at: 143–44, 166; *287*
Boin, Michèle xiii
Bok Kinhi 161n
Boleshi Putaoya 146–47
Bomao Shan 105
Bomian (Boom) 75; *290*
Bondsiqua/Bondziqua/Bonsiqua *260, 261*
Boni kingdom 71n, 86n
Book of Ezekiel *See* Namo Xiqi
Boom Street 208
Boreel, Isabella Sophia 118n

Both, Pieter 51–53; *246, 283*
Boximen (Sunda Strait) 195, 197
Boycko 64n
Braam Houckgeest, van Andreas Everardus 199
Bridge Three (Jambatan Tiga) 208; *287*
British *See* English
Brouwer, Hendrik 62n, 65–67; *246, 285*
Buang, Ratu Bagus *See* Maowushi Wang
Bugis 71, 113, 188, 218; soldiers: 82, 103, 113, 153; *283, 287*
Buitenzorg *See* Bogor
Buru 77n
Buton 11

Cai Dunge (Swa Thoenko/Toenko) 175–76, 186, 188, 191; *250, 254*
Cai Geshan 47, 216 *See also* Cai Xin
Cai Huanyu (Tsoa Wanjock) 38, 76–78, 80, 243–45; *249*
Cai Kunguan 185
Cai Weiguan 90, 95; *251*
Cai Xin (Cai Geshan) xi–xii, 47, 216, 219–20
Calcutta 184; *287*
Cambodia (Gangkou [Harbour]; Jundaima) 5, 206, 221, 223, 227, 229
Camiri 81n
Camphuijs, Johannes 58n, 87–94; *247, 249, 251*
Canlao *See* Xu Youzhang
Canton 182, 199–200 *See also* Guangzhou
Cao Cao 152
Cao Mo 129
Cape of Good Hope 6, 99, 116, 193, 205; banishment to: 174, 219; Valckenier arrested at: 135, 138; *288*
Caron, François 73n
Carpentier, de, Pieter 61; *246, 283*
Carthage 55n
Cassem 81n
Celebes *See* South Sulawesi
Celeng (Tsereng) 224
Ceylon (Xilong) 100, 164, 222, 225; Chinese exiled to: 107, 121, 162, 200, 219, 240n; Dutch rule in: 112, 150, 225; governors of: 13, 76, 84, 118; non-Chinese exiled to: 109, 111, 148, 155, 164, 189; unrest in: 113, 118–20, 146, 149, 222, 225; Van Imhoff in: 118–20, 149–50, 240; *243, 287*
Cha Hsin, Samuel xvi

INDEX OF PERSONAL AND GEOGRAPHICAL NAMES

Champa 206
Chang-chow/Cheang-chew *See* Zhangzhou
Changyao (Bintan Is.) 206
Chaozhou 205, 216
Chasen Blok 185
Chen Baoge (Tan Poko) 191n, 193; *254*
Chen Bingge/Binglang (Tan Peengko) 192, 193; *255, 278*
Chen Caige/Caiguan (1) (陳財觀/才觀) (Tan Sayko) 96, 104, 115, *264–65*, 267
Chen Caige/Caiguan (2) (陳彩觀) (Tan Tjaijko/Tjaiko) 171, 173, *253, 275*
Chen Canlang (Tansjauko) 88
Chen Fulao (Tan Hoelo) 178, 181, 185–86, 189–90; *254, 276, 277*
Cheng Rijie/Xunwo xi–xii, 27, 42, 47, 205
Chen Guosheng 200; *278*
Chen Jingguan 165, 168
Chen Jinguang (Gouw Singkong/Gouw Tsing Kong/Tan Tsinkong) 109; *268–69*
Chen Kenshi 193
Chen Kuanguan/Kuanshi (Tan Koanko) 191–93; *254, 278*
Chen Menghong xiv, 26n
Chen Misheng (Tan Piseeng) 185, 191; *277, 278*
Chen Muge (Tambocco) 88–90, 97–98, 100, 104; *249, 251*
Chen Naiyu 28, 40n, 42, 44–45, 47
Chen Peisheng/Peilao 186–87, 193
Chen Qiaolang (Tankalong) 163, 165–66, 168, 179–80; *274*
Chen Ronggong (Tan Eengkong) 98, 106; *251*
Chen Shangguang (Tan Tsiangko) 115; *270*
Chen Shuguan (Tan Souko/Sauko) 152, 156, 158; *273, 289*
Chen Shuige (Tan Soeijko/Soeyko) 187, 191, 198n; *255, 277*
Chen Shunguang 186, 196, 200–201
Chen Tiansheng (Tan Tien Seeng) 101, 103, 113; *268–69*
Chen Xiuyi 196
Chen Xuelan 44, 150, 179
Chen Yeti 189
Chen Yilao/Yige (Tan Iko) 19, 137, 141, 145, 148–49; *252*
Chen Yuansheng (Tan Wang Seeng) 149, 152n, 153, 158–60, 162; *252*

Chen Yusong (Tan Yeok Seong) 42, 44–45, 48, 238
Chen Zhenguang (Tan Tsinko) 122, 124; *270*
Chen Zhongshe/Zhongguan/Zhongge (Tan Tionqua/Tionko) as boedelmeester: 98, 100–101, 105; as lieutenant: 98n, 114, 122, 165n; imprisoned: 133, 136; *251, 267–68*
Cheribon (Jingliwen) 174n, 229
China (Tangshan) 5–6; archives in: 25, 33, 181, 232, 239; Batavia compared with: 206–207, 209; culture in: 8, 92, 179; emigrants from: 7–7, 10, 17–18, 198; Europeans in: 6, 28; families in: 23, 32, 68, 148n, 199; Ming/Qing transition in: 34, 68–70; missions to: 195; names for: 53, 68–69, 88; reaction to massacre in: xii, 47–48, 135, 220–28, 240; remittances to: 9, 18, 181; trade: 5, 32, 54, 60, 156; *287 See also* Chinese massacre; Chinese massacre, reaction to; Tangshan
Chinatown 5–6, 14, 16
Chinese (Tangren) 13, 15, 53; administration of: 67, 123–24, 240; in Batavia: x, xiv–xv, 59–60, 62, 165; boedelmeesters, 38, 91, 107, *256–79*; bravery of: 40, 128, 152; and building of Batavia: 8; cemeteries and burials: 20, 74, 105, 232; crew: 5, 40, 186–87, 193, 195, *287*; cuisine, 19; descriptions of Batavia: viii, x–xii; in Dutch East Indies: 80, 89n, 106, 145–46, 233; families of: 148n; hospital: 74, 91, 92, **94**; immigrants: 6, 8–9, 18, 38, 149, 198, 215; language: ix–xi, 52n; residence of: 141; *251–55*; marriage: 10, 18–19, 68; morals and virtue of: 37–38, 72, 79, 93, 181, 232; names for: 53, 238; officers: **167**, 170; overseas: xii, 4–5, 9, 22, 30–32, 34, 176, 179, 240; quarters: 142, 208–209; records: 7, 25, 39; relations with Dutch: 7; soldiers: 154–55, **183**–84; taxation of: 67, 70, 74, 92; trade: 5, 8, 32, 53–54, 59–60, 156 *See also* cemeteries, Chinese; Chinese massacre; Chinese rebellion; taxes and taxation
Chinese kamp 14, 16, 142n, 161n, 196
Chinsura 151n
Chu, empire of 125
Chuangwang (Li Zicheng; Dashing Robber) 69

INDEX OF PERSONAL AND GEOGRAPHICAL NAMES 303

Cibayu (Zhibayu) 82
Ciji Donggong temple 32n
Cirebon 11, 143, 166, 205, 218; officials in, 88–89, 98, 106n; unrest in: 137; *287*
Cisau *See* Zhihe Ashen
Cleve, Duchy of 84n
Clive, Robert 151n
Cloon, van, Dirk 112–14; *247, 249, 252, 285*
Cochin (Tonkin) 103–104, 206; *287*
Cochin-China (Annan) 229
Coen, Jan Pietersz 53, 67, 76; and Chinese: 6, 8, 15, 59–60; founds Batavia: 3, 6, 18, 55–56, 58–59; as governor general: 53–55, 61–62, 69; *246, 249, 285*
Comiry estate 89n
Concordia estate 160n
Confucius 30, 161
Conjock/Conjocq *256–57*
Coral Point *See* Lugutou
Coromandel (Kotja) 73n, 84n, 86n, 104n, 113n, 151n, 156, 184, 197
Crocodile Pond 207–208
Culemborg, Neth. 67n

Dabogong Anxu Miao (Dabogong temple in Ancol) 158n
dagou 108; *290*
Dai Biange/Bianguan (Thee Poanko) 162, 166, 168–71; *253, 278*
Dai Hongge/Hongguan (Tee Honko) 193; *255, 278*
Dai Maoshi (Thee Mosai) 170–71
Damojiao/Damujiao (Mauk) 209, 113, 164
Danlan Wang cemetery (Tanah Abang) 101, 103, 143; *289*
Dashe (Toassa) 113; *283*
Dashing Robber *See* Chuangwang
Delft, Neth. 51n, 105n; *247, 287*
Deli, North Sumatra 29
Depei, Provincial Military Commander 224
Depok *See* Jiaobo
Deshima, Japan 87n, 135n
Dianmayu (Pulau Damar) 200
Dido 60n
Diemen, van, Antonie 66–71; *246, 249, 283*
Diestgate, Batavia 149n
Dingjiaolan *See* Tangerang
Djisin, Captain 71

Djitlane (Rilaonian) 153–55; *285*
Djoesit (Yushi) 153–55; *286*
Doeta Laijana 174n; *286*
Dongzhong 74
Dordrecht 63, 103n; *287*
Dragon Pool *See* Longtan
Durven, Diederik 32, 105–12; *247, 252, 285*
Dutch (Hollanders) administration: 19–23, 26, 28, 124, 205, 213, 231–32; amorality of: 214, 232; appearance of: 18, 52n, 79, 216–17, 230; archives: xiii, 33; calendar: 33; and Chinese trade: 59–60; deceive *susuhunan* of Mataram: 85–86; diplomatic relations of: 55n, 85; houses of: 62, 232; in Java: x *note*, 3–8, 15–16, 54–58, 216, 230; ingenuity of: 218; interpreters: x–xi *note*; language: 31; punishments of: 208, 212–14; quarters: 208–209; relations with Chinese: 7–8, 11, 13, 15, 17, 37, 41, 72, 123, 214; scholars: 30; seize Batavia: 52n, 57–59, 212; ships: 8, 77; sources: 38–30, 219; terminology: 6n, 64n, 66n, 205; theater: 189; trade: 3n, 5, 51; wedding: 162; weights and measures: 71n *See also* Chinese massacre; currency; Dutch East India Company; law
Dutch camp *See* Helanying
Dutch Republic 3n, 8, 86n, 118n
Duurkoop, J. A. 194; *285*

East Africa 6
East China Sea 6
Eastern Ocean (Dongyang) 5–6, 226–27, 240
Eastern Salient *See* Oosthoek
East Gate (Rotterdammerpoort) 77, 84, 88, 207–208
Edam Is. 87n, 148n, 162n, 191n
Eluowu garden 113, 119
English (British) 52, 58n; designs on Batavia: 54n, 56, 58m, 75, 182–84; Banten and: 54n, 56n, 67; described: 170; Fourth Anglo-Dutch War, 182; in Bengal: 151n, 184; in Napoleonic Wars: 14, 24; visit Batavia: 40, 195; *287 See also* Red-haired barbarians, 170
Enkhuizen, Neth. 51n, 151n; *287*
Erberfeld, Pieter 101–102; *283*
Erkelens, Monique 25n

Eurasian *See* Serani
Europe   5, 8, 40
Europeans   10, 114, 154, 232–33; in Asia: 6, 8, 10; debarred from China: 28

Fang Bao/Pao   47, 220
Fatahillah, Prince   3
Fengyang prefecture   70; *287*
Fetmenger, Godfried Christoffel   197n
Formosa (Taiwan)   60n, 64n
Fort Jacatra   21
Fortress Victoria   53
Fort Speelwijk   96n
France   198–99; *287*
French   56, 58, 184, 195–96, 198–99; *284, 287*
Friederichstadt, Germany   135n
Frijkenius, S. H.   193n, 197n
Fujian (Min)   17–18, 20–21, 31, 60n, 228; authors from: xi, 47–48; honorifics in: 66n; trade of: 5–10, 36, 220–221, 224–26, 230, 234; *287*
Fuzhou   224

Galaba (Batavia)   x, 32n, 224–26; Chinese accounts of: 205–18, 219–28, 238–40; Dutch in: 52–53, 55–56, 58, 62; etymology of: x *note*, 52n, 205; trade of: 221, 227–28
Galaba Dua   105
Galaba garden   121
Gan Dji Nyai *See* Yan Erya
Gandongxu (Meester Cornelis)   209
Gangjiayu   222, 225
Gangzaiwei   189, 208
Ganwang Shan cemetery   101, 109
Gao Genge/Genguan/Gen (Ko Kimko/Kinko)   93n, 172, 178–79, 186, 189; *254, 275, 276*
Gao Guishan   182
Gaolaoqu Garden *See* Krokot
Gao Qizhuo   224
Gaoshe   197
Gao Yonglao (Koinko)   179   181; *276*
Gauw *See* Gouw
Germany   84n
Geshashi   197
Gheeren, van, Gabriel   272
Gisay (Sisai) *See* Lin Shishi
Glodok   65, 68, 104; *287*
Goa   6, 84n

Goens, van, Rijklof   37, 71n, 84–86, 244–45; *246, 249, 251, 284*
Goey Hoey Kong *See* Wei Huiguan
Gou Oulauw   263
Gou Sinseeng *See* Xu Jinguan/Jinsheng
Gouw Boenko *See* Wu Wenge
Gouw Goankong   269
Gouw Kocko *See* Wu Kege
Gouw Lienko/Holienko   263–64
Gouw Poan Soei/Poansoei *See* Wu Panshui
Gouw Sieuko/Sienko *See* Wu Shuguan
Gouw Singkong/Gouw Tsing Kong/Tan Tsinkong *See* Chen Jinguang
Gouw Tjiansie *See* Wu Zuanxu
Gowa kingdom *See* Makassar
Goyko (Singon)   256
Grassy Is.   206
Great River *See* Grote Rivier
Green Canal *See* Kali Borong
Grenoble, France   115; *287*
Gresik   205, 218
Groene Gracht *See* Kali Borong
Groningen, Neth.   181n
Groningen, University of   181n
Grote Rivier   81n, 89n, 143n, 163n
Guangdong   220, 224–28, 229; *287*
Guangxu   179
Guangzhou   199, 205, 216, 220 *See also* Canton
Guanyinting (klenteng)   81, 159, 178, 184, 196
Gujarat   139n, 142; *288*
Gulf of Siam   5
Gunung Malam   154
Gunung Sari   182, 191; burials at: 168–69, 171–73, 175–78, 180–81, 185–86, 189, 191–93; cemetery: 21, 163, 282n; *287*
Guo Baoge (Que Pauko/Quepauqua)   81n, 88n; *251, 261*
Guo Chunguan (miller)   132
Guo Chunguan (Que Tjoenqua/Tsoenko)   102, 113, 114, 119; *249, 267*
Guo Fuguan   105, 114, 122; *281*
Guo Heguan (Que Hoko/Honko)   153n, 156, 159; *273*
Guo Huiguan   188
Guo Junge/Junguan (Queeconko)   75, 80–82, 87, 89–93, 179n; *249, 262*
Guo Liuguan   81

Guo Maoguan (Que Bauqua/Quebauko/
    Quebauqua)   98–99, 104–105, 108, 113, 145;
    249, 264–66
Guo Qiaoge/Qiaoguan (Que Kiauko)   74, 81,
    84, 90n; *251*
Guo Shou   131
Guo Weige (Que Oeijko)   99, 104, 165n; *252*
Guo Weiguang   189
Guoxi *See* Padang
Guo Xunge (Que Hoenko)   66, 72–74, 81, 90;
    251
Gu Sen   xii, 18, 48, 238
Gusti, Panembahan Pangeran   147–48

Haan, de, Mattheus   17n, 103, 105–106; *247,
    251, 284*
Haase, de, Elias   133n
Hainanese   196
Haji, Sultan   67–68
Hakka   196
Hao Yulin   224
Hasselaar, Cornelis   112n
Hasselaar, P. C.   161n
He Cunguan   171; as soldaat: 142, 160, 164,
    168; as undertaker: 144; as lieutenant: 153;
    281–82
Heerenstraat   144n
He Haiming   42
He Juge   171, 176, 186; *281*
Helan *See* Holland
Helanying (Dutch camp)   209
He Liange (Ho/Gouw Lienko)   69, 73, 81;
    251
Hendrickz, Wouter   112n
Heurnius, The Rev. Justus   8n
Hiapko   161n
Hirado, Japan   62n, 65n
Hoet Siauwko   *270*
Hoetink, B.   29, 44, 60n
Hoëvell, van, W. R.   28
Hohendorf, van, Johan Andreas   137n
Ho Lienko/Holienko *See* He Liange
Holland (Helan)   33, 39, 51, 150, 199, 211;
    holdings in Asia: 218, 222, 224, 225; Zhou
    Meidie in: 86–87; *287*
Hollanders *See* Dutch
Hongmao fan   52, 144 *See also* Red-haired
    Barbarians

Hongqiao (Jambatan Merah)   103
Hong Shiguang   88, 90, 104–105; *281*
Hongxi *See* Angke
Hoogstede, van, Johannes   *272*
Hoorn, Neth.   51n, 54, 61; *209*
Hoorn, van, Joan, governor general   86n,
    92n, 96–99, 211; clerk: 244–45, *247, 249, 251,
    286*
Hoorn, van, Pieter   97n
Hoorn, van, Pieternel   92n
Huai, king of Chu   125–26
Huan, Duke   93n
Huang Banguan   127, 132–33
Huang Chengguan   152
Huang Daban   137
Huang Dongguan/Dongge (Oeij Tamko)
    193; *255, 278*
Huang Gongguan   121
Huang Gongshi (Oey Kionko)   122, 128; *271*
Huang Hengge (Oeij Hingko/Oeij Hongko/
    Oei Hinko)   168, 176–77, 181, 186, 190n;
    250, 253
Huang Jige/Jilao (Oeij Geeko)   190, 191; *254*
Huang Jinliang *See* Huang Liangquan
Huang Jiuge (Oeij Koeko)   80; *251, 260*
Huang Juguan   73, 90, 93
Huang Junguan (Oey Kinkong)   173; *275–76*
Huang Liangquan (Huang Jinliang)   153, 155;
    255n, 279, 280n
Huang Lianguan   144, 153, 160–61, 186; *282*
Huang Luanguang   142
Huang Mengguan   185
Huang Mianshe/Mianguang/Miangong
    (Oeij/Oey Biankong)   35–36, 181, 187, 192,
    196–98; *250, 254, 276, 277*
Huang Ranguang   153n, 155, 160–61; *280*
Huang Shigong   75, 81, 88; *281*
Huang Shinao (Oeij Tsjilauw)   149n, 151–53,
    155, 159, 162, 164; *249, 253, 279*
Huang Tige/Tiguan (Oeij Theeko)   114–115,
    141n, 165; *252*
Huang Wenlao   166
Huang Yanguan (Oey Inko/Oey I. Enko)
    boedelmeester: 113, 115, 137, 146; during
    Chinese uprising: 133, 137; *270, 271, 272,
    273*
Huang Yingguan (Oey Eengko)   96–97, 108;
    271

Huang Zhaoniang (Oeij Tjoanio)   185
Huang Zhenge/Zhenguan (Oeij/Oey Tsomko/Tsiomko/Tjomko/Somko)   142n, 144n, 145n, 152n, 156; captain: 144–46, 151, 153; imprisoned: 133, 136; lieutenant: 114–15, 122, 136n, 141, 145, 165; *249, 252, 270*
Hu Baoyao   161, 172; *280*
Hu Tanguan ([Ouw Tanko], Khouw Tanko)   173; *276*

Imhoff, van, Gustaaf Willem, Baron   **140**, 151–52; and Batavian Chinese: 13, 120, 122–25, 219, 240n; in Ceylon: 118–19, 149; character of: 32, 118, 138; and Chinese massacre: 32, 127–8, 130, 133, 138; governor general: 39, 139–43, 145–49, 178n; and Valckenier: 38–39, 133–35, 138–39, 150; *247, 249, 252, 253, 285*
India   6, 10–11, 71n, 103, 194; Dutch officials in: 92n, 100n, 112
Indian Ocean   6, 8
Indians   10–11, 139
Indonesian archipelago   5, 7, 14, 109, 188; Chinese in: 10–11; mestizo society in: 18–19, 221n
Indonesia, Republic of   3, 25
Indonesians   31, 41
Io Seenkong *See* Yang Chengguang
Ironsmith Street (IJzermids-straat)   127
Isaack, Doctor (Isaac Loccon)   *256*
Island City *See* Yucheng

Jabotabek   3
Jaga Monyet (Rijswijk)   184, 197; *288*
Jakarta   viii, 3–4, 52n, 172; *287 See also* Jakatra
Jakarta Pusat   172n
Jakatra   52–54, 77, 147, 165; Dutch in: 56, 58 *See also* Jakarta
Jalan Panjang   62; *287*
Jambatan Lima   *287*
Jambatan Merah *See* Hongqiao
Jambatan Tiga *See* Bridge Three
Jambi, Sumatra   114n
Japanese   xiii, 6, 16, 87
Japanese pavilion   144, 148, 152, 158, 161–62, 166, 168, 192; *282, 287*
Jap Keengko *See* Ye Jingguan

Java   5, 7–8, 59, 133; abuses in: 193n; Balinese driven from: 170n; central: 7, 14, 82, 118, 154; Chinese in: 27, 47–48; described: 229–34; Dutch in: 14, 208, 212, 216; east: 72, 170n; exploration of, 51–52, 99n; northern, 143, 158n, 159n, 160; piracy in: 194n; sailing to: 8–9; *288 See also* East Java; central Java
Javanese (Wuya)   56, 81, 174n, 180, 223; and Batavia: 10–11, 14; dancers: 158n; described: 218; society: 11, 14; soldiers: 57–58, 153; *283, 284*
Jayakarta   3, 52, 55, 59n, 212; destruction of: 15, 58; *285*
Jiaban Is. (Pulau Kapal)   206
Jiangnan   227
Jiaobo (Depok)   209
Jiaoning Gang *See* Mookervaart
Jiaqing Emperor   201
Jiku   194
Jilakien (Nianliujian)   127, 209; *287*
Jin Chaomei   108
Jincheng   76
Jinde Yuan (Temple of Golden Virtue)   81n, 159
Jingliwen *See* Ceribon
Jishizhen *See* Pasar Senen
Jocqhey   *256*
John Chinaman (Tangrenshi)   44–45, 69; comments: 69, 72, 75, 76, 78, 79–80, 85, 87, 92, 101, 112, 122, 163, 166, 177, 198, 201
Johor   146n, 221, 223, 226
Jong, de, Jacob   104n
Jonker, Captain   31, 71, 72n, 94–95
Jugang *See* Palembang
Jundaima *See* Cambodia

Kaempher, Engelbert   87n
Kalapa/Kelapa   xi *note*, 3, 45n, 52n, 54, 205; *288*
Kali Borong (Groene Gracht; Green Canal)   144
Kampong Baru   143n
Kampong Melajoe   182n
Kampong Sunter *See* Rundayang
Kampung Melayu   62; *288*
Kanari, *Encek* (Anze Ganlanli)   154
Kang Jingguan (Kungkeengko)   96–97, 105, 116; *266–67*

INDEX OF PERSONAL AND GEOGRAPHICAL NAMES 307

Kang Zhengshe (Kung Tsiangko)   116; 269
Kangxi emperor   97n, 224
Karang Conggok   160n
Kartasura   83n
Kebun Jeruk *See* Suanganzai Yuan
Kelapa Dua   288
Keling   218
Kemayoran   144
Khoe Etnio   145n
Khoe Tsouwko *See* Qiu Zuguan
Khopeco/Khopeko/Khoupeko   *256–58*
Khou Tsiocko *See* Xu Shuguan
Khouw Goan Kong   165n
Khouw Hoe-tieeuw   165n
Khouw Hong Liang/K'hoe-Hong-Leang *See* Xu Fangliang
Khouw Soenko/Khouwsoenko *See* Xu Chunguan
Khouw Tanko *See* Hu Tanguan
Khouw Tjiangko *See* Xu Cange
Khouw/Kou Tsinqua *See* Xu Jinguan/Jinsheng
Khouw Tsouwko *See* Qiu Zuguan
Kiai Tapa (Kui Jiaoba)   148n, 151, 153–55; *284*
Kiay Aria Martinata   89n
Kirti Sri Rajasinha   164n
Kleine Zuiderpoort *See* Small South Gate
Klenteng (Tangerang)   187n, 207n; *288*
Klerck, de, Reinier   24, 180n, 181, 182n; *284*
Ko Kimko/Kinko *See* Gao Gen/Genge/Genguan
Koinko *See* Gao Yonglao
koning Amsterdam *See* Sibori, Sultan
Kota Shi   58; *288*
Kotjias   139
Kou *See* Khouw
Kramat   154; *288*
Krawang   184, 191; *288*
Kroempty Pippit (Krom Muen Tep Pippit, Thepphipphit)   164n
Krokot (Gaolaoqu)   93, 101, 139; *288*
Krokot River   95n, 141n
Krom Muen Tep Pippit *See* Kroempty Pippit
Kuhn, Philip   36
Kuijiamijingwennan   174; *284*
Kuilaozhen   101
Kuiper, Koos   xn, xiv, xvi
Kungkeengko *See* Kang Jingguan

Kung Tsiangko *See* Kang Zhengshe
Kupang   205; *290*

Lagundi   76n
Lammers, Pieters   161n
Lampong   174, 218
Lannei *See* Mataram
Lapacang   125
Lariki, Ambon   92n
Lembang   62, 181; *288*
Leuven, Spanish Neth.   76n
Lian Fuguang (1) (連富光, Ni Hoekong, Nihoekong)   32; as boedelmeester: 102–104, 119, 122, 136, 269; as captain: 106, 120–22, 165n, 249; character of: 38, 123–24; and Chinese massacre: 123, 128–30, 133, 136, 136n; as lieutenant: 98n, 102, 114, 252; punishment of: 176–77; relatives of: 95n, 98n, 102, 106, 119; wealth of: 102, 103, 120; *249, 252, 269*
Lian Fuguang (2) (連福光, Ni Hocko)   122; *272*
Lian Huaiguan   125, 126n, 127
Lian Jieguang/Jiegong (Ni Tsietkong/Nitsietkong/Ne-Tseet-Kong)   112, 131, 234; *271*
Lian Lianguang (Nilienkong)   106, 112, 133, 136, 142; *271*
Lian Luge/Luguan (Ni Locko/Nilocko)   as boedelmeester: 96–98; relatives of: 102, 106, 112, 119; as lieutenant: 97, 104; *252, 266, 268*
Lian Yuanguang (Nigoang Kong/Ni Goan Kong/Nigoangkong)   104, 106; *270*
Lian Zhongguan (Ni Tonqua)   103–104, 114, 122, 165n; *252*
Liang Xupian   225
Liebe, Ensign   154n
Lie Joncko *See* Li Rongge
Lie Quanio *See* Li Guanniang
Liem Ho Soei (Lin Herui)   xvi, 45
Ligor   221, 223, 226
Li Guanniang (Lie Quanio)   162n
Lihan   82
Li Hege (Li Hoko)   98, 114n, 115n; *252*
Lihoeyko   266
Li Hoko *See* Li Hege
Li Hooko   269–70

Li Jaco *See* Li Yiguan
Lijn, van der, Cornelis   70–75; *246, 283*
Li-Joncko/Liejonko   *263*
Li Junguan (Litsoenqua/Lie Tsjoenqua)   95, 96; *264*
Lim   *259*
Lim Beenko/Lim Bing Kong *See* Lin Mingguang/Mingge
Lim Djoenko   158n
Lim Hantan *See* Lin Handan
Lim Inko/Limjenko/Lim Janko *See* Lin Yangsheng
Limjako/Lim Jako   *261–62*
Lim Keenko, Jacob/Limkeenqua/Limkeko *See* Lin Jingguan
Lim Kienko/Ki-Enko *See* Lin Jiange/Jingguan
Lim Kocko *See* Lin Guoshi
Lim Lacco/Limlacco *See* Lin Liuge
Lim Saqua/Limsaqua/Lin Zaqua   *259*
Limsinqua/Lim Sinqua/ Limzinqua   *260–62*
Lim Si Say *See* Lin Shishi
Lim Somko/Som Ko *See* Lin Senge
Lim Teko *See* Lin Dege/Delang
Lim Theeko *See* Lin Chaige/Chaiguan
Lim Thoenko *See* Lin Chunshe
Lim Tiangseeng *See* Lin Zhangsheng
Lim Tjipko *See* Lin Jige
Lim Tjoengkong *See* Lin Chungong
Lim Tsoenko/Limtsoenko *See* Lin Chunge
Lin Chaige/Chaiguan/Qinge (Lim Theeko)   158, 176n, 190; *253, 273–74*
Lin Chengjiu   149
Lin Chuguan   125, 126n, 127
Lin Chuguang   159, 161; *273*
Lin Chunge/Chunguan (Lim Tsoenko)   95, 98n, 99n, 103, 114n, 119n; *251, 266*
Lin Chungong (Lim Tjoengkong)   191; *254*
Lin Chunguang   172, 176, 186; *280*
Lin Chunshe (Lim Thoenko)   141n, 148, 152, 188; *272–73, 280*
Lin Cuipu   44, 45; comments by: 107, 119, 123, 138
Lin Dege/Delang (Lim Teko)   172, 176; 253
Lingga   218
Lin Guoge/Guoshi (Lim Kocko)   141, 145–46, 148–149, 152n, 158; *252*
Lin Handan (Lim Hantan)   174, 179, 189, 191, 192; *254, 276*

Lin Jiange (Lim Kienko/Ki-Enko)   153, 168n; *253, 273*
Lin Jiguang/Jige (Lim Tjipko)   as lieutenant: 148, 153, 159–60; as captain: 161, 163, 168–69, 175; *249, 253*
Lin Jingguan (Jacob Lim Keenko/Limkeenko/ Limkeenqua/Lim Keko)   80–82, 89–90, 93, 97, *249, 251, 261–62*
Lin Jiuru   44, 45
Lin Kuazu   171, 176, 186, 188; *280*
Lin Lianguan   66, 73, 81–82, 87; *281*
Lin Liuge/Liuguan (Lim Lacco/Limlacco)   37, 64, 65; *249*
Lin Mingguang/Mingge (Lim Beenko/Lim Bing Kong)   140, 141n; as captain: 36, 141, 144; descendants: 148, 188; *249, 280*
Lin Nansheng   154–55
Lin Qinge *See* Lin Chaige
Lin Rongzu   188; *280*
Lin Senge/Senguan (Lim Somko/Som Ko)   90, 114n, 117n; *251, 264–65*
Lin Shishi (Lim Si Say, Gisay)   66n, 78n; *251, 258–60*
Lin Yangsheng (Lim Inko/Limjenko/ Lim Janko)   105, 109; *268*
Lin Yuguan   156
Lin Zhangsheng (Lim Tiangseeng)   191, 193, 196; *255, 278*
Liouw Ikong   178n
Li Qingfang   226
Li Rongge (Lie Joncko)   89–90, 98; *251*
Li Tsianko/Tsiangko   *267*
Li Tsoeko/Litsoeko *See* Li Zuge *and* Li Yuguan
Litsoenqua/Lie Tsjoenqua *See* Li Junguan
Liu Chengguang (Louw Sengkong/Sinkong)   166n, 169–70, 173; *253*
Liu Yaqi   196
Liu Yasi   196
Liwanko *See* Li Yuanguan
Li Yiguan (Li Jaco)   121–22; *271*
Li Yuanguan (Liwanko)   99, 105; *266*
Li Yuguan (Litsoeko)   98–100, 112; *267*
Li Zicheng *See* Chuangwang
Li Zuge (Li Tsoeko/Soeko)   78n, 243–44; *251, 258–60*
Loccon, Isaac *See* Isaack, Doctor   *256*
Longchiyan temple   32n
Longtan (Dragon Pool)   239

Longyan garden 163; burials in: 80, 99, 104, 112, 115; *288*
Louis XVI 199; *284*
Lou Saenseeng 272
Louw Nungko *See* Lu Langge
Louw Sinkong *See* Liu Chenguang
Lu Guo (Lu State) 129n
Lugutou (Coral Point) 206, 209
Lu Hako *273–74*
Lu Langge (Louw Nungko) 164, 165n, 172; *253*
Lun 197
Lu State *See* Lu Guo
Luzon 6, 224
Lülanjiaoyi 190

Macao 6
Macartney, George, 1st Earl 40, 195n
Maetsuijcker, Joan appoints Yan Erya captain: 37; as governor general: 68n, 76–78, 80, 82, 84, 88; *246, 249, 286*
Maizhuzhichu 159
Ma Jun 223
Makassar (Kingdom of Gowa) 205, 230; as Dutch allies: 154–56; Chinese in, 80, 90–91, 93, 154; Makassarese: 218; *283, 288*; trade with: 157, 186; wars with Dutch: 71–73, 75, 86n, 94, 113, 115; *288*
Malabar 84, 103, 104n
Malacca (Maliujia) 28, 53n, 188, 205, 229, 230; captains of: 34
Malacca, Strait of 229–30
Malay peninsula 5, 221
Malays 11, 13; 31; appearance of: 218; captain: 109–10, 153; language: 25n; terms: 31, 52n, 64n, 127n, 139n, 147, 213; *290–92*
Maliujia *See* Malacca
Maluku *See* Moluccas
Manchus 34, 69
Mandela, Nelson 174
Mangga Dua (Wenjiaolai) 15, 60, 62, 207, 209; cemetery at: 21, 64, 72; *288*
Mangku Bumi 118n
Manhattan 60n
Manila 6, 8, 14, 240
Manipa 31, 71n
Manzano Moreno, Eduardo 7n
Maoge 197

Maowushi Wang (Ratu Bagus Buang) 148, 151–52; *284*
Maowuxu *See* Bogor
Mardijker (black devil) 10, 13, 139, 197, 217
Marunda River 72n
Mataram (Lannei) 59; attacks Batavia: 7, 54n, 58n, 151n, 110n; Chinese rebels in: 81n, 137; civil war in: 14, 82–85, 118n; expeditions against: 94, 136–37; seat of Javanese rule: 218, 231; supports Dutch: 184, 192–93; susuhunan of: 52n, 72n; *283, 288, 292*
Medhurst, Walter H. 69n, 77n, 90, 92; *The Chinaman Abroad:* xii, 26, 48, 160n, 229; translation of *Kai Ba Lidai Shiji:* 28, 42, 45, 47, 126, 147
Meester Cornelis *See* Gandongxu
Meise 197
Merdeka Square, Batavia 172n
Mexico 6
Middelburg 51n, 180n
Mijer, Pieter 28
Mi Jian 208
Ming Taizu 70
Moluccas (Maluku; Spice Islands) 53–54, 58n, 71n
Mom, Arnoldus Constantijn (Bei, Poe?) 197n; *283*
Mookervaart Canal (Jiaoning Gang) 12, 107n
Moreno, Eduardo Manzano 7n
Mossel, Geertruida 161n
Mossel, Jacob 152–53, 163n, 164n, 169; as Van Imhoff's successor: 118n, 149, 151, 156, 158; *247, 249, 253, 285*
Murah 190–91; *284*

Nagasaki, Japan 6, 87n
Namo Xiqi (Book of Ezekiel) 199
Nanyang (Southern Ocean) 47, 179, 205, 219–27, 229
Narrow Strait *See* Bangka Strait
Nederburgh, S.C. 193n, 197n; *285n*
Netherlands Indies 29
Neun, Coenraad Martin (Lun) 197n; *284*
Niai d'Siko 68n, 72n
Nianliujian *See* Jilakien
Niemeijer, Henk 17n
Nieuw Amsterdam (New York) 60n

Nieuwe/Brabantsche Compagnie 51n
Nigoang Kong/Nigoangkong/Ni Goan Kong
    See Lian Yuanguang
Ni Hocko See Lian Fuguang (2)
Ni Hoekong/Nihoekong See Lian Fuguang (1)
Nilienkong See Lian Lianguang
Ni Locko/Nilocko See Lian Luge/Luguan
Ninggangbu 196
Nio Jonko 263
Nio Kanko See Yang Jiange
Nirenberg, David 7n
Ni Tonqua See Lian Zhongguan
Ni Tsietkong/Nitsietkong See Lian Jieguang
Njo Koangko/Koanko See Yang Kuange
Nootsangh 256
North Gate 76, 207

Oei Hingko/Oeij Hongko See Huang Hengge
Oeij See also Oey
Oeij Biankong/Oey Bian Kong See Huang
    Mianshe/Mianguang/Miangong
Oeij Geeko See Huang Jige/Jilao
Oeij Hingko/Oeij Hongko/Oei Hinko See
    Huang Hengge
Oeij Tamko See Huang Dongge
Oeij Tjie (Tsi) Lauw See Huang Shinao
Oeij Tjoanio (Huang Zhaoniang) 185n
Oeij Toatko 178n
Oeij Tsjilauw See Huang Shinao
Oeij Tsomko See Huang Zhenge
Oey See also Oeij
Oey Eengko See Huang Yingguan
Oey Giok Po 45
Oey Inko/Oey I. Enko See Huang Yanguan
Oey Kinkong See Huang Junguan
Oey Kionko See Huang Gongshi
Oey Tsomko/Tjomko/Somko See Huang
    Zhenge
Old Banten See Banten Lama
Ommelanden 40, 210, 244; development of:
    11–12; migration to: 10, 198n
Ong Eengsaij/Eengsay See Wang Yingshi
Ong Eng Saaij See Wang Rongshi
Ong Gouko See Wang Wuge
Ong Ingkong See Wang Yiguang
Ong Khoangsay See Wang Kuanshi
Ong Ongko See Wang Wanguan
Ongseenko See Wang Chenggong
Ong Soeseeng See Wang Zhusheng

Ongthayko See Wang Taiguan
Ong Tjako See Wang Jige/Jiguan
Ong Tjoeseeng See Wang Zhusheng
Ongwako See Wang Anguan
Oosterveld 165n
Oosthoek (Eastern Salient of Java) 170n
Orange Garden See Suanganzai Yuan
Outhoorn, van, Willem 92–93, 96; 247, 249,
    251, 285
Ouw Tanko See Hu Tanguan
Overstraten, van, Pieter Gerardus 248, 255,
    284

Padang (Guoxi) 184, 188; 288
Padri Weiman 191; 283
Pajajaran 3
Pakojan 127
Pakubuwana II (susuhunan) 14
Palembang (Jugang) 114n, 205–206, 229
Pamanukan 81n
Pancoran (Banjiaojian) 209
Panembahan (Bananmaohan) 120, 147n,
    148n, 283
Pan Mingyan (Bingam) 64–66, 68; 249
Paracels 206, 229
Parang Mountains 105n
Parian, Manila 6
Parra, van der, Petrus Albertus 164–65, 178;
    248, 250, 253, 254, 283
Pasar Gelap 208
Pasar Ikan 207n
Pasar Senen (Jishizhen) 62, 159, 169, 196
Pasisir (North Coast of Java) 143, 158
Patani 110n
Patekoan See Bachaguan
Patras, Abraham 114–16; 247, 249, 252, 283
Patuakan 166
Pausaqua 263
Pearl River 6
Pecinan (Bazhilan) 78, 163, 208; burials in:
    80, 99, 104; 288
Pekalongan (Pakalongan; Beijiaolang) 26,
    48, 205, 218, 229–30
Pekodjaan (Pekojan) quarter, Batavia 139n
Penang 28
Persian Gulf 6
Philippe, Ensign 154n
Philippines 5, 6
Pintu Kecil See Small South Gate

Poa Kontong   191n
Pondok Gedeh   191
Pondok Jagon   153n, 158n
Porcelain Street (Porceleinmarkt; Wan Jie)   130, 140, 208
Portuguese   6, 18, 53–54, 55n, 84n; Portugese Buitenkerk: 102n, 105n; names: 139, 145n, 210; *289*
Pousaaqua/Pousako/Pausako   *262–63*
Prince Rotterdam   77n, 88n
Prinsenstraat   144, 208; *289*
Prosperous Dock *See* Shunli Wu
Puger, Pangeran   83n
Pulau Damar *See* Dianmayu
Pulau Dunlao   193
Pulau Kapal *See* Jiaban Is.
Pulau Lambat   193; *289*
Pulau Onrust (Wang Yu; King's Is.)   206; exiles to: 148, 174; fortress on: 150, 229; as storage depot: 68, 186, 188; *288*
Pumao Shan cemetery   93
Putra, Pangeran   120n
Puzai *See* Tanah Lapang

Qi state   129n
Qiu Zuguan (Khouw Tsouwko)   22, 31, 97, 99, 101; *269*
Quanzhou   205, 216
Que Bauqua/Quebauko/Quebauqua *See* Guo Maoguan
Quedsiqua   *261*
Queeconko *See* Guo Junge/Junguan
Que Hoenko *See* Guo Xunge
Que Hoko/Honko *See* Guo Heguan
Que Kiauko *See* Guo Qiaoge
Que Oeijko *See* Guo Weige
Que Pauko/Quepauqua *See* Guo Baoge
Quesieuqua/Que-Sieuqua (Jouko)   *260–61*
Que Tjoenqua/Tsoenko *See* Guo Chunguan

Radin (Laozhen)   131–32, 134; *284*
Raffles, Thomas Stamford   24
Ratoe Oedien   174n
Ratu Sharifa Fatima   147–48, 154n
Reael, Laurens   53–54; *246, 284*
Red-haired Barbarians (Hongmao fan)   52, 144, 170, 230
Reede tot Drakestein, van, Hendrik Adriaan   100n

Rees, Germany   84n
Reijnst, Gerrit   51–53; *246*
Rejidou   147, 165 *See also* Jakatra
Rembang   205; *289*
Reiniersz, Carel   73–76; *246, 283*
Rhinocerosgracht   92n
Riau   188; *289*
Riebeeck, van, Abraham   99–100; *247, 284*
Riebeeck, van, Jan   99n
Riemsdijk, van, Jeremias   178–80, 185, 186n, 197n; *248, 284*
Riemsdijk, van, Willem Vincent Helvetius (Wan Linmeide, Ban Lim-mi-tek)   185–86, 197n; *284, 285*
Rijswijk *See* Jaga Monyet
Robben Island   174n
Robidé van der Aa, P. J. B. C.   154n
Rongqili, Commissioner   195–96
Rotterdam   5n, 86n, 100n, 101; *289*
Rotterdammerpoort *See* East Gate
Rousong   166; *285*
Rujijiao   52n, 58n *See also* Jakarta, Jakatra
Rundayang (Kampong Sunter)   209

Said Mochamad Ebenoe Abdullah   189n
Salak Mountains   143n
Salemba (Jiananmo)   131
Salmon, Claudine   19, 21n, 27n, 48n
Sanje   *257*
Sanjock   *257*
Sanli Sea   206, 229
Saqua   *257*
Schinne, van, Isaak   133n, 138n
Schlegel, Gustaaf   29
Seiichi, Iwao   24n
Selayar Is. *See* Sow Head Mountains
Semarang (Samarang)   170, 190, 205; Chinese authors in: 48, 215; Chinese exiles in: 81n, 88, 133; Dutch rule in: 84, 218, 223, 230, 233–36; king of Mataram in: 82, 84–85; in Mataram civil war: 82, 133, 136; rises against Dutch: 136–37; road to: 143; *289*
Senthiong Temple   21
Serani (Sezainian; Eurasian)   101, 217; *291*
Serong *See* Benlu Zouma
Seven Islands *See* Paracels
Sezainian *See* Serani
Shanghai   28
Shengmu Gang *See* Blandongan

Shenmi *See* Siberg, Johannes
Shi Biaoguan (Sie Piauwko)   144, 146; *272*
Shi'er Gao Di (The Twelve Highlands)   209
Shi Huaguan (Sie Huako)   161, 163, 171; *274*
Shilao'erlanzhao (Selalilada)   55; *285*
Shunli Wu (Prosperous Dock)   158
Shunzhi Emperor   70
Siam   164n, 206; *289*
Siam, Gulf of   5
Siberg, Johannes   192–93, 197n; *285 See also* Shenmi
Sibori, Sultan (koning Amsterdam)   77n
Sidharta, Myra   xiv, xvi
Sie Huako *See* Shi Huaguan
Sie Piauwko *See* Shi Biaoguan
Silimaozai (Surabaya)   197
Sillebar (West Sumatra)   170
Singapore   14
Singon *See* Goykow
Siqua *See* Yan Erguan
Sisai *See* Lin Shishi
Small South Gate (Kleine Zuiderpoort; Pintu Kecil)   68, 127, 130, 143, 207–209; *288*
So Bing Kong *See* Su Mingguang
Soeko *See* Li Zuge
Soetse   *256*
Solo   14, 190, 192, 231
Songsisai (Songyashi)   131
Sonkhla   221, 223, 226
Sopeng kingdom   71n
South China   8
South China Sea   5–6
South Gate (Large Gate, Pintu Besar)   63, 127, 171, 173, 197, 208–209; *288*
South Sulawesi (Celebes)   86n
Southeast Asia 4   14, 30; Chinese in: xii, 5, 7n, 72n
Southern Ocean *See* Nanyang
Souw Beng Kong *See* Su Mingguang
Souw Tsoenseeng *See* Su Junsheng
Sow Head Mountains (Selayar Is.)   206
Specx, Jacques   iv, 62–66; *246, 285*
Speelman, Cornelis Janszoon   71n, 72n, 75n, 82n, 86–87; *246, 251, 283*
Spice Islands *See* Moluccas
Spring and Autumn Period   129n
Stevin, Simon   8
St. Martin, de, Isaac   95n

Stockum, van, Hendrick (Suqipo)   196n; *285*
Suanganzai Yuan (Kebun Jeruk; Orange garden)   154, 190
Su Junsheng/Junguan (Souw/Tsou Tsoenseeng/Tsoen Seeng)   153; as boedelmeester: 137, 142, 148; as lieutenant: 141, 144, 145, 152; *252, 272*
Sukabumi   42
Sulawesi   11, 86
Su Mingguang (Bencon/So Bing Kong/Souw Beng Kong)   64, 78n; as captain: 15, 36–37; and Mangga Dua: 21, 60, 64; and weights: 69n, 71n; *249, 256*
Sumatra   5, 29, 204, 206, 222; Dutch in: 72n, 170
Sumbawa   11
Sunda Kalapa/Kelapa/Jialaba/Galaba   x *note*, 3, 52n, 238
Sunda Sea   159; *289*
Sunda Strait   76; *289 See also* Boximen
Sungai Atap   190; *289*
Suqipo *See* Stockum, van, Hendrick
Su Quanguan   144, 153, 160, 186; *282*
Surabaya (Silimaozai)   82n, 143, 197, 205, 218, 230; *289*
Surat   195; *289*
Swaardecroon, Hendrik   100–103, 105; *247, 249, 251, 285*
Swa Thoenko/Toenko *See* Cai Dunge
Swedes   56, 58; *289*
Swoll, van, Christoffel   99–100; *247, 284*

Taiwan *See* Formosa
Tambocco *See* Chen Muge
Tanah Abang *See* Danlan Wang   101, 143; *289*
Tanah Lapang (Puzai)   208
Tan Eengkong *See* Chen Ronggong
Tang Enge (Ting/Thung/Tung Ingko)   38, 40, 168, 175, 177; *250, 253*
Tangerang (Dingjiaolan)   127, 171; and Chinese rebellion: location of: 3, 113, 206–207, 209; *289*
Tangerang River   143n
Tang Piange/Pianshe (Tiung Pienko/Tung Pienko/Pi-enko)   173–74, 178, 186, 191; *254, 276*

INDEX OF PERSONAL AND GEOGRAPHICAL NAMES 313

Tangren *See* Chinese
Tangrenshi *See* John Chinaman
Tangshan   68–69, 83, 88, 104, 134 *See also* China
Tan Hiamtse   78n
Tan Hoeko   271
Tan Hoelo *See* Chen Fulao
Tanhonqua   260
Tan Iko *See* Chen Yilao/Yige
Tanjongqua/Tantsjongqua   261
Tanjung   62, 75, 81–82, 194; 289
Tanjung Kait   154, 155; 289
Tanjung Priok   72n
Tankalong *See* Chen Qiaolang
Tan Koanko *See* Chen Kuanshi
Tanlianko   264, 265
Tan Limseeng   185n
Tanliongko   266
Tan Peengko *See* Chen Bingge/Binglang
Tan Piseeng *See* Chen Misheng
Tan Poko *See* Chen Baoge
Tan Sauko/Souko *See* Chen Shuguan
Tan Sayko *See* Chen Caige/Caiguan (1)
Tansjauko *See* Chen Canlang
Tan Soeijko/Soeyko *See* Chen Shuige
Tan Tien Seeng *See* Chen Tiansheng
Tan Tionko/Tionqua *See* Chen Zhongshe/Zhongguan/Zhongge
Tan Tjaijko/Tjaiko *See* Chen Caige/Caiguan (2)
Tan Tjeeuwsing   185n
Tan Tjoeseeng   185n
Tan Tsiangko *See* Chen Shangguang
Tan Tsinko *See* Chen Zhenguang
Tan Tsinkong *See* Chen Jinguang
Tan Wang Seeng *See* Chen Yuansheng
Tee Honko *See* Dai Hongge
Tegal   82n, 205, 218
Tellouw   256
Temple of Golden Virtue *See* Jinde Yuan
Ternate   72n, 173n, 205, 230; Prince Rotterdam, envoy from: 31, 77, 88; 289
Thebitsia *See* Zhou Meidie
Thedens, Johannes   135–36, 139, 146; 247, 286
Thee Mosai *See* Dai Maoshi
Thee Poanko *See* Dai Biange
The Lionko *See* Zheng Longge
Thepphipphit *See* Krom Muen Tep Pippit

The Tjako *See* Zheng Shege
Timor   89n, 205
Ting/Thung/Tung Ingko *See* Tang Enge
Tio/Tyo Jino/Iunio   263
Tioman Sea   206
Titsingh, Isaac   199; 285
Tiung Pienko/Tung Pi-enko *See* Tang Pianshe
Tjien-sit   125
Tjiomas *See* Benlu Zouma
Toa Pe Kong Temple (Dabogong or Tudigong Temple)   158n, 167, 208
Toassa *See* Dashe
Tong'an canal   207
Tong'an, Fujian province   60n
Tong'ankou   134, 143, 182, 197, 225; 289
Tongkangan (Zhonggangzai)   209
Tonkin *See* Cochin
Trunajaya   72n, 82n, 83
Tsereng *See* Celeng
Tsoa Uwqua *See* Tsoayqua
Tsoa Wanjock *See* Cai Huanyu
Tsoayqua (Tsoa Uwqua)   262
Tsou Tsoenseeng/Tsoen Seeng *See* Su Junsheng
Tswa-wiko   262
Tuan Ayub   185
Tuan Haji   188–89
Tudigong Temple *See* Toa Pe Kong Temple   208
Tuku/Tuku kou   208; 292
Tung Pienko *See* Tang Piange
Twelve Highlands *See* Shi'er Gao Di

Utrecht   178n
Utrechtsche poort   289

Valckenier, Adriaen   118, 178; arrest: 133–36, 138, 150–51; and Chinese massacre and rebellion: 32, 38–39, 139, 144, 149–50; as governor general: 114n, 115–17, 120–21; 247, 252, 283
Valentijn, François   8, 12, 77n, 95n
Vietnam   5
Vinck, Justinus   120n; 285
Vlissingen   51n

Wainanwang *See* Banyuwangi
Waiwuluo   196

Wajo kingdom   71n
Wan Abdoel Bagoes   110n
Wandan *See* Banten
Wandoellah   109–12
Wang Anguan (Ongwako)   99, 100, 103; *265–6*
Wang Chenggong (Ongseenko)   100–101, 109; *267*
Wang Chenggong   100–101, *267–68*
Wang Dahai (Ong-Tae-Hae)   18, 20, 69; *Haidao Yizhi*: xii–xiii, 26, 28, 48, *229–37*
Wang Faguan   73, 91
Wangjiaosi *See* Bekasi
Wang Jie   20, 96
Wang Jige/Jiguan (Ong Tjako)   173n; *254*
Wang Jun   xii, 221, 226
Wang Kuanshi (Ong Khoangsay)   124; *272*
Wang Liguang   168
Wang Pilie   225
Wang Rongshi (Ong Eng Saaij)   153–56, 158–59, 176; *253*
Wang Sanbao (Wang Jinghong)   205, 231
Wang Shu   224
Wang Taiguan (Ongthayko)   103, 105; *266*
Wang Wangguan/Wangge   79–80
Wang Wuge/Wuguan (Ong Gouko)   88, 95–96; *251, 261–63*
Wang Xiangguan   156
Wang Yiguang (Ong Ingkong)   166, 169, 181; *274–75*
Wang Yingshi (Ong Eengsaij/Eengsay)   98, 104, 114; *252, 273*
Wang Yu *See* Pulau Onrust
Wang Zaisheng   185
Wang Zhusheng (Ong Tjoeseeng/Soeseeng)   176, 178, 186, 190–92; *250, 254*
Wangjiayu *See* Bangka Is.
Wan Jie *See* Porcelain Street
Wanjock   *257–59*
Wan Linmeide   197
Weichen *See* Bogor
Wei Huiguan (Goey Hoey Kong)   95–96; *263–67*
Weltevreden   172n
Wenjiaolai *See* Mangga Dua
Western Ocean (Xiyang)   5, 233, 238; Chinese traders to: 227, 234, 236; Wang Sanbao to: 205, 231

Western quarters (*Wester kwartieren*)   194
Westerveld, Batavia   104n, 149n, 177n
West Gate   76, 108, 127, 169, 188, 207–208
Wettum, van, B.A.J.   44
White Is.   206
Wiegerman, Jan Hendrik   197n
Wiese, Albertus Henricus   197n
Wijaya Krama (Shilao'erlanzhao)   60n; *285*
Willem IV, Stadtholder   34n, 51n, 146n; *283*
Willem V, Stadtholder   34n, 51n, 175n, 182
Wonokerto   83n
Wu Kege (Gouw Kocko)   *255*
Wu Panshui (Gouw Poan Soei/Poansoei/Poansoeij)   35, 173, 176, 185–86, 192; *254, 280*
Wu Shuguan (Gouw Sieuko/Sienko)   169n, 170–72; *275*
Wu Wenge (Gouw Boenko)   166, 168; *253, 274*
Wu Xiguan   275
Wuya *See* Javanese
Wu Zuanshou   35, 36, 192, 196; *254, 255n, 280*
Wu Zuanxu (Gouw Tjiansie)   192–93, 196; *254, 280*

Xiamen (Amoy)   xi, 9, 20, 32, 66n, 156, 224; distance from Batavia: 221, 224, 229, 231; trade at: 220, 223; *286*
Xichang   215
Xie Chenggong   154–55
Xilong *See* Ceylon
Xinchi   55, 58, 102, 105, 162
Xinnao Ming   120; *285*
Xinwuli   111, 143, 171–72; *289*
Xinxi   197
Xiong   125
Xuantian Shangdi temple   81–82
Xu Cange (Khouw Tjiangko)   **20**, 164, 165n; *253*
Xu Chunguan (Khouw Soenko/Khouwsoenko)   97, 99–100, 108; *269*
Xu Fangliang (Khouw Hong Liang/K'hoe-Hong-Leang)   160, 169, 173, 236; *253*
Xu Fuge   *281*
Xu Jinguang/Jinsheng (Khouw/Kou Tsinko/Tsinqua, Gou Sinseeng)   115, 122, 165n, 225; *252*
Xu Shuguan (Khou Tsiocko)   120–21; *269–70*

INDEX OF PERSONAL AND GEOGRAPHICAL NAMES

Xu Songge *281*
Xu Youzhang (Canlao) 172
Xu Yunqiao (Hsu Yun-Tsiao) x *note*, xiii, 33, 42, 44–45
Xu Zhongqi 169, 171; *280*

Yan Erguan 19, 23, 37, 68–69, 72; *249 See also* Siqua
Yan Erya 19, 72–74, 77; *249*
Yang Bodong 42, 44, 150, 152, 179n
Yang Chenggong/Chengguang (Io Seenkong) 106–107, 114, 122, 124; *252*
Yang Jiange (Nio Kanko) 117, 122; *252*
Yang Kuange (Njo Koangko/Koanko) 180, 180n, 186, 191; *254*
Yang Ying 42
Yan Jingguan 105, 114; as undertaker: 88, 90, 104, 114, 122; *281*, *282*
Yan Luanguan 105, 114, 122; *282*
Yaolaoba (Kalapa) 45n, 51
Yecheng (coconut town) *see* Sunda Kalapa x
Ye Huaguan 169, 176, 186; *281*
Ye Jingguan (Jap Keengko) 101–102, 113; *265*
Yijing (Book of changes) 176n
Yin, Mr. 48, 238, 240
Yizheng, Prince 223, 228
Yogyakarta 14
You Tianguan 120–22; *281*
Yucheng (Island City) 229
Yulaoyanyawang 174
Yushi *See* Djoesit
Yuyayanliujia 174

Zain al-Abidin, Pangeran Putra (Panembahan) 120n

Zain Al-Arifin 120n
Zainal Asyikin 155n
Zainiu Gangkou (Cow-slaughter Port) 159, 188
Zainul Arifin 155n
Zao Jian 208
Zeeland 51n
Zeelandia Castle 55n
Zeng Junbi 215
Zhangpu County 47
Zhangzhou merchants from: 160, 205, 216, 234, 236; writers from: xii, 47–48
Zhang Zitian 42
Zhaoyalan 97
Zhejiang (Zhe) 224–25, 227
Zheng (Mrs. Lin Jiguang) 175
Zheng (Ms. Wang Jie) 96
Zheng Chunguan 40, 200–201
Zheng He 5, 205n, 231
Zheng Longge (The Lionko) 172, 176, 180, 186; *253*
Zheng Shege (The Tjako) 174, 176, 178, 186; *254*
Zheng Xuanguan 166
Zhibayu *See* Cibayu
Zhihe Ashen (Cisau) 209
Zhonggangzai *See* Tongkangan
Zhongguo (China) 42n, 69
Zhou Guangmei *See* Zhou Meidie
Zhou Meidie/Zhou Guangmei/Thebitsia/ Tsieuw Bitia) 86–87, 89, 97n; *264*
Zhou, Mr. 215
Zhushuxia 208
Zhu Xi *See* Ziyang
Ziyang (Zhu Xi) 178
Zwaardecroon, Henricus *See* Swaardecroon, Henricus

Subject Index

Page numbers in italic refer to tabular matter. **Page numbers in bold** refer to illustrations.

adipatih 218
Angke massacre *See* Chinese massacre (1740)
archives x–xi, 219; Dutch: 33; Kong Koan: xii–xiii, 16, 24–25, 28n, 39, 45; VOC: 17, 29, 32, 38, 48, 64n
Arsip Nasional Republik Indonesia 17
Asian Library of Leiden University 28, 36

ba (unit of currency) 167n
Baguo Yuanzhu Beiji (Inscription of Donors from Kalapa) 32n
baljuw (inner *temenggong*; police officer) 64n, 74; 292. *See also temenggong*
Banda (ship) 51n
Bataviaasch Genootschap van Kunsten en Wetenschappen 42, 44, 180n
Bataviaasch Genootschap ms. 42, 44
Bataviasche Statuten 17, 67n, 76n
bicara (assembly, council, Raad, *stadhuis*) 73–74, 78, 208, 210; *291*
Biography of Cai Xin ix, 47, 219–28
board of aldermen (*schepenbank, schepen(en)*) 107, 145n, 210, 244–45; function of: 15–16; consults with governor general: 67, 76n, 86; *292*
board of curators (*boedelkamer*) 22–23, 38
Board of Ritual 199
bode (messenger) 66n
boedelkamer See board of curators
boedelmeester (inheritance curator) xiii, 22–24, 36, 38–39, 91n, 92, 107; privileges of: 152, 183; lists of: 44–45; *256–78, 280, 292*
boom (*pabean*) 75, 134n, 140, 194; taxes collected at: 90, 142–43, 186; *290*
bridges 130, 143, 150, 192, 207–208; building of: 59, 61, 84, 150, 171–73; in gardens: 233, 235; drawbridges: 84, 127, 210;
Brief Account of Galaba 27, 42, 47, 205–18. *See also Galaba Jilüe*
budie (*potia*; sugar miller) 209; *290*

caifu (manager) 209
calendars 33–34, 218

Cambridge University 30n
Canal 8, 128; built: 3, 159, 192, 207–208; named: 12, 144, 207, 235. *See also* watergate
candle (Judas chair) 108, 212
capitão mor 210n
captain (*jiabidan, jiada; kapitein*) 69, 142; appointment of: 23, 38, 59–60, 231; functions of: 15, 114n, 186, 187n, 194, 196, 198, 211, 214, 231; lists of: 44–45, *249–50*; outside of Batavia: 97, 153, 155, 166, 173; privileges of: 68–69, 91, 107, 163n; qualifications of: 145n, 170n, 175n, 177; *249–50, 279, 285, 286, 291*
Casa de Misericórdia 22
Catholic Church 22, 28
cemeteries 16, 20n, 38, 44, 105n, 144; *281–82*; Balinese: 77; Company: 72, 74; Eastern: *287*; Gunung Sari: 163; Japanese pavilion: 144, 148, 152, 158, 161, 162, 166, 168; Western: 161, 168, 171, 177; *282, 289*. *See also* cemeteries, Chinese
cemeteries, Chinese 209; establishment of: 74–75, 105, 144, 163; *281–82, 287, 289*
The Chinaman Abroad: or a Desultory Account of the Malayan Archipelago ix, 48, 229–37
Chinese Annals of Batavia vii, 27, 37, 40. *See also Kai Ba Lidai Shiji*
Chinese Council *See* Kong Koan/Gongguan
Chinese massacre 128–33, 136, 144n; causes of: 123–25, 138; Chinese accounts of: xi, 38, 47, 176–77, 220–28; Dutch account of: 150
Chinese massacre, reaction to xii, 47–48, 135, 220–28, 240
Chinese Raad *See* Kong Koan/Gongguan
Chinese rebellion, accounts of 36, 38–39, 122–28, 134, 216, 222; causes of: 123–24, 138–39, 149, 216, 240; Dutch response to: 14, 138–39; officers' involvement in: 136, 176–77; rebels flee: 14, 222n
Chongxing Longchi Beiji (Inscription for Rebuilding Longchiyan Temple) 32n
Chronologische Geschiedenis van Batavia 42

SUBJECT INDEX 317

clerk (*klerk; schrijver*)   67n, 144n
clothing   96, 217; in Batavia: 79, 106–107; and Chinese massacre: 122–23, 125; Indonesian: 179–80, 218; 138
Collegie van Boedelmeesters (board of curators)   23
commissaris der inlanders (commissioner for native affairs)   64, 74, 210, 215; *291*
convivencia   7, 13, 41
council of justice (*Raad van Justitie*)   15, 16, 76n, 105n, 106n, 141n, 144n, 210, 244; *291*
Council of the Indies (*Raad van Indië*)   113, 141n, 165n, 192n; appoints Chinese captains: 37, 64n, 65n, 89n, 104n, 114n, 145n, 244; appoints lieutenants: 95n, 244; elects governors general: 62, 74n; part of High Government: 16, 51
crews   Chinese: 40, 186–87, 193, 195; Dutch: 8, 195
currency   Chinese: 84, 215n, 239n; Dutch: 65n, 96–97, 108, 167n, 185, 215n, 239n

da beiluo (chief factor)   210
Dabogong See Twabakong
dacing See weights and measures
Daghregisters   10n, 48, 68n, 150, 243
dashi   69, 210; *290. See also soldaat*
deforestation   11–12, 62
dienaar [*Compagnies*] *See zhima*
difangzhi See local gazetteer
director general (second/vice king)   54n, 64, 210, 238n
Dongyang Xiyang system   5
doupeng (cloak)   218
du/dubo See gambling
dubbeltje (unit of currency)   65n, 96, 167n
duit (unit of currency)   172; *291*
Dutch Royal Library (Koninklijke Bibliotheek)   25n

earthquakes   70, 78, 101, 173, 175, 181
East India Company (English) *see* English East India Company
East Indiaman (*retour schip*) *See jiaban chuan*
Echols Collection, Cornell University   45
eclipse   173, 181, 184, 195
Edict of Nantes   114n
English East India Company   54n, 170n

Ensign *See vaandrig*
Estado da India   6, 22
estates (manors)   Chinese: 81n, 89n, 160n; Dutch: 100n, 113n, 142, 182n, 185; Malay: 110n
estates (property)   22–23, 231. *See also* boedelmeester

factories   113n, 114, 236; in Batavia: 52n, 54n, 55n, 197, 208; in Japan: 62n, 87n, 135n; *292*
fanam (unit of currency)   minting of: 96; prices in: 215, 239; taxes in: 67, 71, 181, 197–98; value of: 65n, 167n, 215n, 239n; *290*
fanmu (amuck)   213
fen See qian
fengshuishi (geomancer)   21
fines   71, 140, 163, 212, 213, 215
fiscaal (*water-fiscaal, zee-fiscaal; meisege*)   64, 160–61, 210, 230; *291*
fishponds (*rawa*)
flooding   12, 100–101, 173–74, 181
folktales, Taiwanese   60n
Fourth Anglo-Dutch War   14, 40, 182n
French Revolution   41, 199
Friends of the Kong Koan Foundation   25n, 45
fu (wealth)   120
funerals   21–22, 26, 78, 114; taxes on: 74n, 92

Galaba Jilüe   xi, 27, 42, 47. *See also Brief Account of Galaba*
galaba/kalapa (coconut)   x *note*, 205
gambling (*du/dubo*)   111, 137, houses: 68–69, 208, 214; tax on: 22, 69, 79, 142, 160n, 168n, 169, 214
-ge See honorifics
geng (unit of time/distance)   188n, 221, 238; distances in: 206, 221, 224, 238, 240
Gentlemen XVII   18, 115n, 135n, 182n, 183n; accept Reael's resignation: 53n; administration of VOC: 34, 51n; appoint governors general: 39, 65n, 70n, 76n, 86n, 100n, 103n, 113n, 118n; block appointments: 62n, 74n, 106n; honourable discharges by: 87n, 118n; and married Chinese: 148n; recall Durven: 112n
-gong See honorifics

gong'an bu (minutes of the Kong Koan) 16, 25–26, 30, 32
Gongguan *See* Kong Koan/Gongguan
Gongtang *See* Kong Koan/Gongguan
gouverneur (*emanlü, gongmanlü*) 210; *290*
governor general 16, 34, 64, 92n; duties of: 51, 60–61, 214, 238; lists of: 44–45, 48; *246–48, 250–55, 283–90*. *See also* great king
'grain fills' (solar period) 212
grand secretariat viii, ix, 220
Great Bantam Rebellion 154
'Great Disturbance' 124. *See also* Chinese massacre
great king 64, 78, 89, 238; bad behavior of: 102–103, 107, 111, 130. *See also* governor general
-guan, -guang See honorifics
Guangxu Zhangzhou Fu Zhi 47
Guanyin 208. *See also* Guanyinting
guazui (cutting into pieces) 239
guilder 65, 181, 185, 194; forging of: 190; value of 55n, 169n
guili See slavery: girls

Haidao Yizhi (Anecdotes about the Sea Islands) xii–xiii, 26, 28, 48
haijin See trade prohibitions
Han dynasty 72, 231
Hanlin Academy 47
High Government (*Hoge Regering*) 104n, 109n, 136, 155n; appointments of: 173n–178n, 180n, 185n, 190n; composition of: 16, 51n; decisions of: 17, 91n
Historical Materials in the First Historical Archive ... 18, 219
The History of Japan (Kaempher) 194
The History of Java (Raffles) 24
Hokkien *See* Minnanhua
honorifics 66n, 80n; *250n*
hoofdgeld See poll tax
hospitals 94, 128, 187n; and Chinese community: 21, 38; boedelmeesters and: 23, 92; records of: 16, 24; funding of: 23, 74n, 91–92n, 181, 214; restoration of: 24; establishment of: 91–93; *291*
Huaqiao Congshu 42
Huaqiao Kai Ba Lidai Shilüe 42

immigrants, Chinese (*orang baru*) 6, 8–9, 38, 198n, 215
ingabeijs (*ngabehi*) 174
inheritance curator *See boedelmeester*
inscriptions 24n, 30, 102, 198, 208; taxes on: 21, 74n; and Xiamen-Batavia ties: 32
Institute for Research in Humanities (Jimbun Kagaku Kenkyujo) Kyoto University 47
interest rates 65, 66, 91, 132
'Island memories' *See Haidao Yizhi*

jiaban chuan (East Indiaman) 52n; *290*
jiabidan See captain
jiada See captain
Jialaba (Batavia) ix, 48, 238–40
jian ai (love for everyone) 161
jiangjunzhu (pile of the commander) 212
jiao ritual 40, 172
jin (unit of currency) 220
jin (unit of weight) 73n, 239
jinshi (advanced scholar) degree 47
Jin Shun Wu (junk) 173
Journal of the South Seas Society *See Nanyang Xuebao*
Judas chair *See* candle
justice 112, 238–39

Kai Ba Lidai Shiji 7n, 12n, 26; characteristics of: 30–31; dates in: 33–34, 64n; Dutch boedelmeesters ignored: 23n; editions and manuscripts: x, xiii, 28, 30, 42–45, 238n; as historical text: 37–41, 47–48; on taxes: 22; terminology in: 243; women in: 19–20; writing of: x–xi, 27, 35–36
Kai Yaolaoba Lidaishi Quanlu x note, xvi, 45
kampong (camp) 232; Chinese: 142, 183; native: 3, 11, 21, 127; *291*
kantoor (office) 64; *290*
Kapitan Melayu 109–10n
kapitein See captain
kapitein wu (*kapitein mor*) 210. *See also* governor general
king (*wang*) 34
klenteng (temple) 81. *See also* Guanyinting
klerk See clerk 67n
Kong Koan/Gongguan (Chinese Council; Chinese Raad; Kong Tong/

SUBJECT INDEX 319

Gongtang) 176, 182, 184; function of: 15–17, 19; and burials: 21; marital records of: 19, 26; and *Kai Ba Lidai Shiji*: 27, 35, 41–42, 48; Medhurst and: 28; formal beginning of: 36, 39; *279–80, 282*. See also archives; secretary
Kong Koan archive   xiv–xvi, 25, 28, 45
Kong Koan ms.   42, 44–45
Kong Tong/Gongtang See Kong Koan/Gongguan
kraton   54n, 58–59
kuli See slavery: girls

landdrost (outer *temenggong*; bailiff)   64, 74, 244; *286*. See also *temenggong*
law   59, 61, 97, 107, 210; Chinese: 17, 20, 152n, 226; Dutch: 8, 17, 67n, 68n, 76, 211, 213–14, 222, 232; Dutch-Roman law: 11, 16;
Leiden ms.   **43**, 44–45, 143; commentary from: 164n, 177n; text from: 57, 62, 65, 93, 158n, 179n, 180n, 190n
Leiden University   25–26, 29; students at: 53n, 92n, 99n, 105n
Leiden University Library   25, 28, 36, 44–45
li (moral propriety)   214
li (unit of currency)   239n
li (unit of measure)   188n, 206n, 221n
liang (unit of weight)   208, 212–15; value of: 213n
Liberale gift See Relief for the treasury of the company
Liem manuscript   **46**, 47, 54, 143, 194; date of: 40; contents of: 45; as source of translation: 57n, 70n, 176n
lieutenant (*luitenant*)   78, 91, 110, 153, 156; appointment of: 66, 68–69, 98, 149n, 164–65, 231; arming of: 183–84; eligibility for: 23; perquisites: 107, 163n, 169; lists of: 36, 44–45; responsibilities of: 179, 244; *251–55, 280, 291*
Lion, HMS   195n
literatus   xi, xii, 42, 47
local gazetteer (*difangzhi*)   30
London Missionary Society   28
Longfei period   34, 176
lugushi (coral stone)   207
luitenant See lieutenant

majoor   210
malaria   10n, 12, 107n, 108
man (skirt)   218
manager (*mandor; caifu; comprador*)   91, 209, 238
mandor See *manlü*
manlü (*mandors*)   91, 209
Measures to restrain display of pomp and circumstance (*Reglement ter beteugeling van pracht en praal*)   151, 161, 163n
meisegan See *weeskamer*
meisege See *fiscaal*
merchants   xii, 48, 65, 200–201; after Chinese massacre: 220–28; Chinese: 5, 60, 226–28, 231, 236; Dutch: 8, 54n, 236; English: 134n, 170; Indian: 139; pirates and robbers and: 113, 190; residences of: 209; role of, in Batavia: 15, 65, 88–89; slaves and: 194; and temple building: 158, 163
messenger See *bode*
mestizo   18, 101, 221n
Metamorfoze programme (of the Dutch Royal Library)   25n
midui See taxes, on rice
militia   67, 114n, **183**, 219, 238
Ming dynasty   5, 33, 66, 176, 205
Mingcheng Shuyuan (school)   93, 178–79
Minnanhua (Minnan dialect, Hokkien)   132n, 229; pronunciation: xi *note*, xiii *note*, 108n; words: 31, 45n, 53n, 58n, 60n, 91n, 182n
Mohism   161
monsoons   6, 8, 9
morality   37–40, 72, 214
mosquitoes   12, 21, 108n

nakhoda   144, 163; recommend captains: 65, 88–89n, 170
Nanjiang Shuyuan (school)   178–79
Nan Ming (Southern Ming) reign period   34
Nanyang Xuebao (Journal of the South Seas Society)   27, 42, 44
Napoleonic Wars   14
National Library of Indonesia   45
notaris (notary)   23, 210; *291*

oath of purge (*eed van purge*)   145n, 152n
Ode of Galaba   42, 44–45

opium   22, 120, 170; tax on: 141n, 143, 156, 169, 214; trade in: 188, 206, 213–14; *292*
Opium Sociëteit   151n
opperbewindhebber (supreme director)   34, 51n
orang baru See immigrants, Chinese
orphanage (*weeshuis*)   91n, 92
orphans   23, 91, 186, 214
orphans chamber *See weeskamer*
Oud en Nieuw Oost-Indiën (Valentijn)   8

pabean See boom
pachten   77, 79; *291*. *See also* taxes
pangeran (*panjilan*; prince)   52–53, 58, 82; *290*
papers of credit   185n
pasar (market)   22, 84, 238
payung (umbrella)   87, 107, 124, 151, 153
peranakan   19, 37, 221–22
Perang Cina (Chinese War)   14
permits   40, 186, 213, 215. *See also* residence permits
piracy   5, 113, 193, 223–24; in Java: 185n, 194n, 196
plakaat, plakaten   17, 97
plantations   3, 11, 29, 121; Chinese revolt and: 13, 16, 125
poll tax (*hoofdgeld*)   22, 152, 215; collection of: 15, 142, 211, 225, 238; nonpayment of: 120, 213; rate of: 67, 70n, 197–98; tax farm for: 79, 142, 165, 170, 198. *See also* residence permits
potia See budie
prices   food: 215, 239; rice: 120, 173, 227–28, 230; slaves: 238; trade goods: 157
Prins erfstadhouder   146n
'Provincial Military Commander Wang Jun of the Fujianese Naval Forces sincerely presents a memorial'   ix, 221–23
public prosecutor   64, 160. *See also fiscaal*
punishment   capital: 95; divine: 31, 40, 54, 131–32, 166, 168, 177, 191, 201; Dutch: 107–108, 212–14, 239; Javanese: 218; for overseas trade: 10, 220; wooden horse as: 135–36, 151

Qi'anjiao (pray for peace) festival   172
qian (*fen*; unit of currency)   213, 215, 239
Qianlong reign period   34, 48, 176n

Qiaowu Xunkan journal   42
Qing dynasty   66, 69; dating of: 33–34, 176; restrictions on movement: 10, 20, 38
Qingming festival   167

Raad van Indië See Council of the Indies
Raad van Justitie See council of justice
ratu   147; *284*
ratu bagus   148n
rawa (fishponds)   12, 108n
rebellion   38, 40, 69, 103; in Banten: 148, 150–51, 154, 174; in Bengal: 113, 116; Bugis: 113; Captain Jonker's: 94; in Ceylon: 113, 119, 222, 225; Erberfeld's: 102; fear of: 180, 194; Trunajaya's: 71, 81, 83; *284, 286*. *See also* Chinese rebellion
Reglement ter beteugeling van pracht en praal See Measures to restrain display of pomp and circumstance
Relief for the treasury of the company (*Liberale gift*)   194
remittances   9, 18, 181
residence permits   60, 123, 166; penalty for not having: 120–21, 213; purchase of: 133–34, 165, 211; required: 67, 165. *See also* poll tax
retour ship *See jiaban chuan*
rixdollar   74, 158, 185; salaries in: 92, 151, 153; value of: 163, 169n
Roman law   11, 16
ronggeng (female dancer)   158; *291*

sailing season   8, 222
Sanhexing Wu (junk)   188
sawmill   194, 209
schepenbank See board of aldermen
schools   xiv, 38, 91–93, 178–79, 187
schrijver See clerk
second king *See* director general
secretary of the Kong Koan (*secretaris*; *zhugejiao*)   27, 35; establishment of: 151–53, 231; function of: 16, 39, 210; and *Kai Ba Lidai Shiji*: 36; lists of: 44–45; *279–80, 292*
secretary of the *weeskamer* (*meisegan zhu*)   91–92, 97; *291*
shahbandar (harbormaster)   89, 134n, 140, 141n, 156; tax farm for: 142, 181, 198; role of: 210; *291–92*

SUBJECT INDEX

Shangshu 72
-she See honorifics
sheriff *See temenggong*
ships 8, 10, 39, 52n, 54, 238; at Batavia: 11, 207–209, 226, 240; Chinese: 8–9, 60, 220, 227–28; European: 8, 10, 52n, 56, 58, 196; management of: 186, 187, 193, 210 shipbuilding: 64, 165n, 218; tolls for: 143
shuangbing 78; *292. See also* board of aldermen; *schepenen*
Shunyuan Wu (junk) 182
sick and disabled 91–92, 186, 214
sirih (betel) 69
slavery 80, 110, 189; acquisition of: 11, 18, 91, 111; background of: 10–11; burial certificates for: 97; girls: 19, 212, 214, 237; manumission of: 10, 19, 218; runaway: 144–45n, 190, 194; for sex: 212, 214; treatment of: 19, 237
smuggling 188, 213, 215
social services 22–24. *See also boedelmeester;* hospital; *weeskamer*
soldaat (soldier) 44, 66, 120, 165, 168, 243n; functions of: 71, 121, 142, 210; *290. See also dashi*
soldiers Balinese: 71, 82, 103, 113, 153, 154n; Bugis: 82, 103, 113, 153; Chinese: 154–55, 183–84; 57–58, 153; Dutch: 71, 82–83, 102–103, 111, 113, 125, 127–30, 151, 164, 184, 191
soldiers, Dutch 164, 188, 194, 197; in Banten: 153–54; against British: 170, 184; in Chinese rebellion and massacre: 125, 127–30; in Makassar: 71, 113; in Erberfeld rebellion: 102–103; in India: 103–104, 151; in Mataram: 82–84, 137; in police actions: 111, 191, 194
southern precincts *See zuider voorstad*
Spring and Autumn Classic 30
Stadhouder (Stadtholder) 51n, 146n
stadhuis (town hall) *See bicara*
States General 112, 158; and VOC: 3, 34, 51
stuiver (unit of currency) 198n; value of: 65n, 167n, 215n, 239n; *290*
sugarcane 3, 11–12, 62, 65n, 132, 240
supreme director *See opperbewindhebber*
susuhunan 52, 72, 81, 82, 218, 231; *292*

tael 208. *See also liang*
Tang da See captain (*jiada*)
Tang dynasty 72, 231

taxes and tax farms 8, 22, 38, 80, 112, 150, arrack: 142, 214; auction of: 22, 37, 78–79, 142–43, 156, 194, 197, 211; business: 215; Chinese control of: 22, 37; Chinese theater: 22, 92, 168–69; cock fighting: 80n, 142; evasion of: 207; fear of lost: 223, 226; fish ponds: 79, 142; funerals: 21, 74n, 92, 215; gambling: 69n, 79, 142, 160, 168–69, 214; on immigrants: 215; in China: 227; inland pass: 215; Javanese exempt from: 218, 238; lanterns and candles: 80, 142, 215; liquor: 79; lumber: 214; marriage: 19, 22, 215; milling: 143; numbers of: 22, 89–90, 142, 158; obligations: 145n, 170; opium: 141n, 143, 156; *peranakan*: 222; poll tax (*hoofdgeld*): 15, 22, 67n, 70n, 79, 120, 142, 152, 165, 170, 197–98, 211, 213–15, 225, 238; remittance: 186; rice (*midui*): 79–80, 90, 142; *ronggeng*, 158; sales: 79, 214; *shahbandar* and shipping: 89–90, 142–43, 181, 186–87, 214–15; slaughterhouse: 22, 79, 142; sugar: 143, 214; system: 16, 22, 37; textiles: 194; theater: 158, 214; tobacco: 89, 142; *warong*: 215; weigh-house: 69n, 143, 214; *290, 291*
temenggong 64, 182, 210, 214; inland (*baljuw*): 64; outer (*landdrost*): 64, 74. *See also baljuw; landdrost*
temple *See klenteng;* individual temples
Teylers Museum 62n
Tijdschrift voor Neêrland's Indië 28, 42
trade prohibitions 10; Chinese (*haijin*): 5, 68, 219–21, 226–27; Dutch: 210; lifted: 224, 226
treaties 75n, 82n, 86n
Treaty of Nanjing 28
Twabakong (*Dabogong*) 158n, **167**, 208

Uitkijk (watchtower) 75n, 207n
undertakers (*tugong*) 36, 44–45, 74, 144; 281–82
United (Dutch) East India Company (Verenigde Oost-Indische Compagnie; VOC) 21, 34, 40, 67, 110; archives: 17, 29, 32, 38, 48, 64n; in Asia: 3–5, 77, 82, 148, 170; commercial networks of: 7; criticism of: 31–32; decline of: 14; and English rivals: 170, 188; running of: 8, 10, 17, 34, 50, 51n; wharf: 187; *290*

vaandrig (ensign)   66n, 78, 244
't Vliegend Hert (ship)   180n
Verenigde Oost-Indische Compagnie *See* United (Dutch) East India Company)
vice king *See* director general

waag See weigh-house
wang See king
warden   67, 190
watch tower *See Uitkijk*
watergate   143, 150, 159. *See also* Canal
watermill   65, 171, 218
wayang (Chinese opera)   22, 92n, 157–58
weddings   16, 19, 22, **162**, 163
weeskamer (*meisegan*; orphans chamber)   142; function of: 38, 91, 93, 186; funding of: 91, 97, 163, 232n; secretaries of the: 91–92, 97, 159; *291*
weigh-house (*waag*)   16, 207, establishment of: 68–69, 71; taxes: 22, 143, 214
weights and measures   69, 71, 212. *See also li*
wen (unit of currency)   163, 169n
West India Company   66n
wijkmeester (quartermaster)   67, 161n, 177
windmill   64, 206, 218

wives   69, 73, 96, 111, 145; Dutch: 18, 23, 217, 232; indigenous: 10, 18–20, 68, 148, 192, 234–25
women   20, 96, 212, 217, 232; in marketplace: 18, 238; rulers: 72–73, 243–44. *See also* wives
wooden horse   135, 136n, 150–51

Xiamen University Press   25, 26, 30n
xiandali (holy men)   110; *285*
Xu Yunqiao edition   x, 30, 47, 82n, preface to: 48, 238n; commentary from: 82n; sources of: 42, 44
xueshi (witnesses)   214
Xunmintang Congshu   47

Yang Bodong manuscript   42, 44, 150, 152, 179n
yin and *yang*   37, 72–73
Yun'an Yiwen   238n

zamorin (lord of the sea)   104n
zee fiscaal See fiscaal   74
zhima ([*Compagnies*] *dienaar*)   210
zuider voorstad (southern precincts)   141n, 142

Printed in the United States
By Bookmasters